THE MISSOURI COMPROMISE

AND ITS AFTERMATH

THE MISSOURI COMPROMISE AND ITS AFTERMATH

Slavery & the Meaning of America

ROBERT PIERCE FORBES

The University of North Carolina Press
Chapel Hill

This book was published with the assistance of
the Fred W. Morrison Fund for Southern Studies of
the University of North Carolina Press.

Library of Congress Cataloging-in-Publication Data
Forbes, Robert Pierce.
The Missouri Compromise and its aftermath: slavery
and the meaning of America/by Robert Pierce Forbes.
p. cm.   Includes bibliographical references and index.
ISBN 978-0-8078-3105-2 (cloth: alk. paper)
ISBN 978-0-8078-6183-7 (pbk.: alk. paper)
1. Missouri compromise. 2. Slavery—Political aspects—
United States—History—18th century. 3. Slavery—
Political aspects—United States—History—
19th century. 4. United States—Politics and
government—1815–1861. I. Title.
E373.F67   2007   973.5'4—dc22   2006035002

To my parents

CONTENTS

THE MISSOURI COMPROMISE

AND ITS AFTERMATH

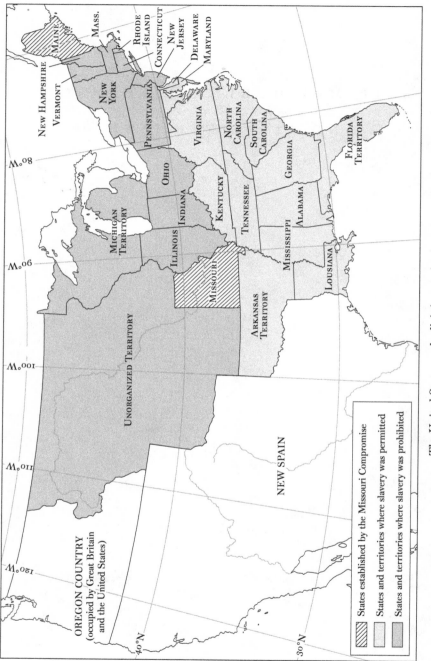

The United States and adjoining territories, 1821

Legend:
- States established by the Missouri Compromise
- States and territories where slavery was permitted
- States and territories where slavery was prohibited

INTRODUCTION

WHAT EFFECT DID slavery have upon the development of institutions in the United States? For much of our history, slavery has been regarded as an anomaly, a jarring distraction from more edifying and more central themes. The topics of slavery and race are "tangents to my subject, being American, but not democratic," wrote Alexis de Tocqueville, America's most famous critic, "and my main business has been to describe democracy."[1] Until recently, most commentators have been willing to follow Tocqueville and set these questions aside as tangential to the discussion of American institutions. Those who view the subjects of slavery and race as central to the American experience, on the other hand, have sometimes intimated that American democracy itself is, in some occult fashion, contaminated by racism in its very essence. Common to most studies of the subject is a mood of almost implacable destiny and inevitability. "Conceivably there was and is a way out" of the "vicious cycle" of racism for "the white man," Winthrop D. Jordan mournfully concluded his magnum opus, *White over Black*, but "there was little in his historical experience to indicate that he would succeed."[2] For a few short years after the Revolution, acknowledged Lerone Bennett Jr., it had seemed realistic to hope that the tide of liberty and equality might extend its reach to Americans of African descent as well as to whites. "Then the roof caved in. When did this happen? No man can say. . . . Caste lines hardened; racial hostility increased." Like James Joyce's Haines, most scholars of the subject seem resigned to the conclusion that "it seems history is to blame."[3]

There is a note of complacency in such declarations, it seems to me, even when uttered in tones of deep moral indignation. The historicist assumption underlying them—that history develops along impersonal, inexorable, and perhaps ultimately unknowable paths—is itself of recent creation, and its emergence in an American context roughly coincided with the first appearance of formal defenses of perpetual slavery.

This study is, in part, an attempt to answer the question of when, and more important how, "the roof caved in": how the United States moved from its post-Revolutionary consensus concerning the evil of slavery and sanguine expectations of its rapid demise to the Jacksonian-era rejection of abolitionism and acquiescence in the institution as ineradicable and not incompatible with the principles of the Union.

For generations, the impact of slavery has been written out of American history—indeed, with a few fleeting exceptions, such has been the rule throughout the nation's existence. Because the institution of slavery had such towering economic and social effects, and constituted, throughout the antebellum era, far and away the nation's largest store of capital beside land, this act of negation was no mean feat.[4] That it succeeded as long as it did is potent testimony to the power of narratives to shape understanding and even perception. As Einstein said, "It is the theory which decides what can be observed."[5] Both unconsciously and, as I shall strive to demonstrate, deliberately, Americans constructed narratives or "theories" of their nation in which slavery, the decisive economic and political force in their society, constituted no more than an epiphenomenon that could legitimately be relegated to a footnote, or dispensed with altogether.[6]

Evidently, a narrative that negates all traces of a matter as massive as slavery must inevitably distort the rest of the story as well. From the meaning of freedom to the understanding of human nature, to the perception of God's Providence, all elements of Americans' understanding of their great national experiment were warped and reshaped to conform to the demands of a version of the tale in which the enslavement and dehumanization of millions of their fellow creatures could be deemed compatible with the values of the republic. Moreover, given America's reputation in the international community as a vanguard of progress and change, as well as the nation's unprecedented growth and prosperity in the years before the Civil War, it was inevitable that America's radical reinterpretation of its own founding principles would be influential globally. It is vitally important, therefore, to understand the nature and the causes of this momentous change.

As a key to understanding the meaning of slavery in America, the Missouri controversy of 1819–21 is probably our most valuable text. The heat of sectional rhetoric during the Missouri debates reached a level never exceeded, and rarely matched, until the secession crisis of 1860. Moreover, nearly all the arguments for and against slavery in America were advanced at this time (with revealing exceptions, as we shall see). The Missouri

Compromise is said to have settled the slavery question for a generation; its repeal, in 1854, triggered the final stage of the sectional crisis, prompted the establishment of the Republican Party, and impelled the return to politics of Abraham Lincoln. It merits a heading in every American history textbook.

Yet traditional interpretations of the episode have at once overdramatized the episode and underemphasized its importance. Historians, inevitably struck by Jefferson's memorable image of a "fire-bell in the night," have tended to present the Missouri crisis as a full-dress debate over slavery that sprang up out of nowhere, and then submerged just as rapidly.[7] Few studies link the incident either to contemporary events in other fields—the Panic of 1819, the Adams-Onís Treaty on Florida, or the Supreme Court decision in *McCulloch v. Maryland*, for example—or to later sectional crises. Curiously, this remarkable two-year-long episode of fervor over slavery, in many ways an early political dress rehearsal of the Civil War, has been treated virtually as an epiphenomenon.

Even more peculiarly, while historians agree that the Missouri Compromise was a decisive event in the nation's history, there is substantial disagreement on what it in fact decided. Historians of the early national and Jacksonian periods, between the 1780s and the 1840s, generally view the outcome of the conflict as a signal defeat for antislavery forces and a victory for the slave South. Scholars of the sectional crisis of the 1850s and the Civil War, on the other hand, regard the Compromise as the cornerstone of antislavery nationalism and the chief bulwark against the growth of the "peculiar institution."

So basic a disagreement among historians about the meaning of such an important historical event is evidence, I would argue, of a fundamental discontinuity in the interpretation of American history—a crack in the master narrative, so to speak.

The larger, conceptual obstacle to grasping the significance of the Missouri episode stems from the historical effects of the contest itself. The line of demarcation between slave and free states established by the first Missouri Compromise came to seem such a fundamental, almost natural, fact of American political and social life that it grew difficult to recall how bitterly its institution had been contested and what a profound departure from earlier policy on slavery it had seemed to represent. In later years, supporters of the Compromise naturally encouraged the perception of the geographical division as immutable and eternal—even though its architects had originally promoted it as an imperfect but unavoidable expedient to salvage the Union. Ironically, by midcentury, opponents of slavery defended the Compromise line as a "sacred compact" while Southerners clamored for its repeal. Few Americans possessed the historical perspective to recognize that advocates of restriction had initially regarded the Missouri controversy outcome as a crushing defeat, while slaveowners had rated it a signal victory.[8] Moreover, the narrative power of the Jacksonian mythos has so overshadowed the span between 1815 and 1828 that the complex period denominated the "Era of Good Feelings" has often been regarded merely as a prelude to the "Age of Jackson," and sometimes virtually subsumed in it altogether. Thus the period's momentous debates over public policy have received short shrift from historians when they have not been overlooked entirely.

This is no accident, nor is it a recent development. Virtually from the moment of taking office—indeed, for several years prior—strategists of what was to become the Jacksonian, and later the Democratic, Party sought to wrest control not merely of the reins of government but of America's master narrative, and to redefine their alliance, which was essentially a breakaway faction of the single ruling party, into the anointed standard-bearer of orthodoxy. This great undertaking, which could almost be described as an ideological coup d'état, had largely been completed by 1844, and it has shaped interpretations of the 1820s ever since.[9]

Before the Missouri debates, few Americans understood how deeply intertwined the destiny of the nation was with the problem of slavery, and most discussions of the subject unfolded with no particular sense of urgency. Most Americans believed that they had effectively solved the problem of slavery when Congress voted to outlaw the African slave trade as of January 1, 1808. Received wisdom—borne out by gruesome experience in the sugar plantations of the West Indies—held that cutting off the supply of slaves was tantamount to ending slavery, since the brutal conditions under which slaves labored inevitably meant that they would soon die out. Moreover, the post-Revolutionary fervor for liberty had resulted in many thousands of manumissions in the South, while in New England and the middle states, slavery was virtually extinct already, well ahead of the date that would have been anticipated from the simple operation of the region's gradual emancipation laws. To be sure, some statesmen had cautioned that closing the trade might not be fully tantamount to ending slavery; but taking that step *had* proved sufficient to remove it from the consciousness of the majority of Americans who did not have direct contact with the institution. Afterward, because of the crisis sparked by the debates themselves, public figures would tread cautiously around the issue, having seen its potential to shatter the Union.

Moreover, the controversy unfolded at one of the rare moments in American life when the system of political parties was in flux, depriving those who wished to thwart the open discussion of slavery of one of their most effective tools. Thus it was that the intense two-year period of political crisis over Missouri constituted a unique tutorial on the impact of slavery on American society. The issue received a full and candid discussion on the floor of Congress and in state houses, town halls, churches, and auditoriums throughout the nation, uninhibited, at least at first, by an understanding of the explosive danger of such discussion that the episode would bequeath. Never again, while the Missouri Compromise was in force, would Americans grapple so openly with the meaning of slavery for their nation; and when the subject roared back to the forefront of national affairs after the repeal of the Compromise, Americans understood it as the prelude to war.

The Missouri debates ripped the façade of national consensus from American public life. The controversy exposed the hold that slavery had acquired over the process of national decision making, and revealed the powerful if unfocused antipathy toward the institution that existed in the northern states. Rather than a "fire-bell in the night," the Missouri controversy can perhaps best be understood as a flash of lightning that illuminated the realities of sectional power in the United States and ignited a fire that smoldered for a generation.

That fire was kept in check by the compromise of 1820, which admitted Missouri to the Union as a slave state, but set a limit of 36°30'—the latitude of Missouri's southern border—as the northern limit of future slave states to be carved from the Louisiana Territory. When this check to slavery's growth was repudiated, by the Kansas-Nebraska Act of 1854 and the *Dred Scott* decision of 1857, the smoldering embers burst into flame.

While the breadth of the movement to restrict slavery was greater than that to extend it, the conviction of the supporters of slavery expansion was undoubtedly more intense. This intensity had virtually nothing to do with ideology and very little to do with racial attitudes; at base, it was about security, property, and power. While antislavery Americans were advocating for abstract ideals, slaveholders defended their immediate and personal interests. There was nothing abstract or theoretical about their struggle. Upper Southerners' capital was overwhelmingly invested in slaves, who were worth far more than the land they tended. In 1819, nearly a third of the nation's 1.5 million slaves lived in Virginia, whose exhausted fields could provide productive labor for only a fraction of that number. At the same time, the states and territories that would come to constitute the "black belt" of the Cotton Kingdom were as yet only sparsely inhabited.[10]

The future prosperity, as well as safety, of Virginia slaveholders lay in selling their "surplus" slaves to the virgin cotton lands of the Southwest; thus a bar to the expansion of slavery, or "diffusion," as they preferred to call it, meant a decisive check to their fortunes, as well as to the future riches of those among them who chose to resettle in the fertile cotton lands of the trans-Mississippi West.

Southern advocates of slavery expansion thus had the advantages of unity and the passion that derives from protecting one's property and livelihood. What they did not have, as yet, was a well-articulated philosophy of proslavery—a plausible appeal to principles beyond raw self-interest. The interminable deliberations over Missouri statehood afforded defenders of slavery unparalleled opportunities to craft and hone such arguments, and to discard those that proved, in the crucible of debate, to have little plausibility beyond the Mason-Dixon Line. In a very real sense, the Missouri debates were the cradle of proslavery ideology.

At the same time, the opponents of slavery expansion found themselves caught in a dangerous dilemma. Many Americans believed in the almost mystical destiny of the American nation to redeem mankind by its example from the global thrall of despotism. And yet, they discovered that the invocation of the national ideals of liberty and equality had actually become threatening to the survival of the Union. For politicians to proclaim the nation's liberating destiny, and still more to advocate measures to implement it at home, was implicitly to offer a damning insult to slaveholders and thereby to imperil sectional concord.

In this constrained and threatening state of affairs, the talents of James Monroe came to the fore. One of the most surprising discoveries of my research is the leading role taken by this unheralded chief executive in navigating the waters of sectional discord with skill and tact. He stretched the powers of the presidency to achieve the unlikely passage of the first Missouri Compromise, employing flattery, cajolery, patronage, and punishment. Like his predecessor Madison, Monroe undertook many of his most important initiatives in secrecy; unlike Madison's achievements, Monroe's remained secret, until now.

In fact, the Missouri crisis reignited generation-old fears among some slaveholders that the entire project of a strong national government posed a deadly threat to slavery. Coming on the heels of the Supreme Court's ruling in *McCulloch v. Maryland*, which gave wide latitude to federal power, former anti-Federalists and younger converts to the doctrine of strict construction now adamantly opposed any undertakings by the general government not explicitly stipulated by the Constitution—and even balked at some functions, such as instituting a national tariff, that the document expressly authorizes.

The Missouri controversy marked the end of the old Jeffersonian alliance created to fight the centralizing and repressive tendencies of the Federalists. With the collapse of the Federalist Party after the War of 1812, it was no longer possible to argue that American liberty was endangered by northeastern "monocrats," and the first Republican Party lost its raison d'être. The uneasy coalition between lordly southern planters and northern yeomen farmers, mechanics, and artisans quickly fell apart without the specter of Federalism to unify it. Pennsylvania represented a telling case in point. Despite its Quaker heritage and proverbial hatred of slavery, the state had been "the faithful and steady and almost unpaid ally of the slave States," in the words of New York senator Rufus King. During the Missouri controversy, however, both leaders and rank-and-file Pennsylvanians took a leading role in opposing the admission of new slave states. In other states as well, northern Republicans—many of them former trusted allies of southern Republican Party chieftains—took the lead in the movement to restrict slavery. Clear-eyed southerners duly noted this alarming development. Thus, if for northerners the Missouri crisis had exposed the extent of slavery's stranglehold upon the South, for southerners it had revealed the shallowness of their northern Republican brethren's loyalty to them absent a credible Federalist danger. Without the pressure of a mutual outside threat, their northern Republican friends would desert them without a qualm when their interests diverged over slavery—despite the fact, these southerners reasoned, that the question was for them one of survival, not philanthropy.

Political leaders in both sections digested these new realities and responded in different ways. As the historian George Dangerfield has argued, one reaction was the retreat into sectionalism: "In a sense, the Tallmadge Amendment . . . summoned the South into being."[11] A significant minority of southern leaders concluded from the experiences of 1819–20 that the United States—as a nation, and also, one might say, as an idea—posed a fundamental threat to the institution of slavery, and hence to southern society. To these men, typified by Virginia's Spencer Roane and John Randolph and North Carolina's Nathaniel Macon, the role of the southern statesman was to curb the power of the federal government and to render it harmless to the South's "domestic institution," even if this made the national state impotent to undertake measures essential to "promote the general welfare." "If Congress can make canals," asserted Macon, "they can with more propriety emancipate."[12]

Pragmatic northern politicians recognized this state of affairs as well, and sought to counter the danger it posed both to their own political fortunes and to the Union by resuscitating the Republican Party—which meant, in practice, reviving the moribund threat of Federalism. Gathering force over the subsequent decade, the alarm sounded by Missouri put an end to the ill-fated Era of Good Feelings and prompted a return to the kind of heated party conflict that could justify and reinforce strict, hierarchical party allegiance and discipline. Thus, in addition to signaling the final collapse of the First Party System, the Missouri crisis also marked the genesis of the second, launched through the recapitulation of traditional Jeffersonian themes and the invention of an ersatz Federalist plot to hijack the White House and undermine the sanctity of slave property and the safety of slaveholders. The mutual goal of slaveholders to defend slavery from national attack and of Democratic leaders to mobilize slaveholders as a political bloc, in other words, constituted the most important reason for the creation of the Second Party System.[13]

If the first Missouri Compromise of 1820 promised a limit to slavery expansion, the second, passed a year later, contained the seeds of civil war. The leaders of Missouri, angered by Congress's assertion of a right to legislate regarding its internal affairs, threw down the gauntlet at its constitutional convention by incorporating a ban on the entry of blacks and mulattoes into the state. If blacks were citizens, then such a bar was a clear violation of the rights and privileges clause of the federal Constitution.

Astonishingly, given the pariah status of blacks throughout the nation, including the North, Congress soon found itself at a moment of crisis and deadlock if anything worse than the previous year's stalemate over slavery expansion. Although few congressmen were able to formulate the idea clearly, somehow many of them understood that if the Constitution was interpreted to exclude a particular class of persons, it would ultimately prove worthless. After several heroic, failed attempts, Henry Clay finally steered the Congress to a compromise deliberately framed to equivocate on the central question by declaring that the contentious clause of the Missouri constitution should not be interpreted as violating the rights of any citizen. No legislative language retains its equivocality, however; and the door was opened to Chief Justice Taney's ruling thirty-six years later in *Dred Scot v. Sandford* that blacks could not be citizens—thus nullifying, in the eyes of many Americans, the universal reach of the Constitution, and hence the utility of the charter itself. In the same decision, Taney and the Court held the first Missouri Compromise to be an unconstitutional abridgement of slaveholders' property rights. From the standpoint of a broad range of Americans, from Thomas Hart Benton to Abraham Lincoln, this two-fisted blast from the Supreme Court constituted an abrogation of the basic purpose of the American republic.

The massive southern resistance to slavery restriction and its rapid mutation into a full-fledged sectionalism illustrate how narrow the parameters of national politics had become as a result of the influence of slavery. Even strongly nationalist southern politicians such as Henry Clay were forced to adopt a stance in defense of the institution strident enough to alienate a crucial segment of the northern electorate, thus foreclosing his hopes of occupying the White House. It is clear in retrospect that such domestic initiatives as Clay's American System or the policies of hemispheric cooperation projected by the Panama Congress had no chance of adoption due to slaveholder opposition—indeed, the administration of John Quincy Adams was probably doomed from the start because of the unwavering antagonism of slaveholders and their allies.

The study of the Missouri crisis, therefore, demonstrates that the shadow cast by slavery extended far beyond those issues directly linked to the institution. The black hole of slavery drew everything near it within its gravitational field, even when it remained invisible itself. Moreover, the paradox of what Adam Smith called "slavery in a free government" engendered habits of evasive and dishonest public discourse, of hostility to far-reaching legislative responses to national problems, and even of antagonism to basic components of national sovereignty, which continue to haunt our civic life almost a century and a half after emancipation.[14] The United States did put an end to slavery, and the significance of this achievement should never be gainsaid. But the supporting structures of the institution, so pervasive throughout the society, were never uprooted—indeed, they were never fully addressed or even acknowledged.

———— ∽∞∞∽ ————

BECAUSE THE PRESENT STUDY departs sharply from the traditional narrative of the period, and many of the arguments are unfamiliar and often complex, a road map of sorts of the book is in order.

Chapter 1, "Monroe Takes Charge," presents the status quo ante in Missouri, detailing the ambitious nationalist goals of the Monroe administration as it came to power in the wake of the War of 1812, and delineating the narrow political window available to Monroe to accomplish them. Implicit in Monroe's sweeping plans for the economic and moral advancement of the nation was the need to remove the negative influences of slavery—and blacks—through a policy of federally backed colonization.

Chapters 2 and 3 portray in detail the politics of the two Missouri Compromises that brought the national legislature to a crisis and stalemate during two successive congresses. The first phase of the conflict played out on the floor of Congress itself, where the members, unprepared for Representative James Tallmadge's explosive amendment, debated the question with a candor and directness never to be duplicated. Thereafter, the center of activity moved offstage. As shown in chapter 2, "Missouri," even as northern public opinion crystallized in nearly unanimous support for restricting slavery, various strands of opposition—evidently coordinated through Monroe's White House—quietly began to gather strength. A proposal to link the admission of Maine to the acceptance of slavery in Missouri, instead of weakening northern resolve, generated fresh outrage; and, at the height of the furor, a New York congressman with close ties to Monroe floated a breathtaking proposal to end slavery entirely.

Chapter 3, "Compromise," reveals the multifaceted campaign waged by Monroe and his most trusted allies to secure a compromise that would permit the expansion of slavery in principle, while prohibiting it in practice from the rest of the Louisiana Territory excepting Arkansas. Employing all the considerable powers of the presidency—and all the levers of influence of the Republican Party—Monroe quietly built a majority for compromise while simultaneously assuring skittish slaveholders that he would give no quarter. He then secured their acquiescence in precisely the result he had promised to prevent by convincing them that his capitulation had saved the nation from a Federalist-abolitionist takeover.

The Monroe administration's campaign to consolidate support for the compromise laid the groundwork for a new national paradigm that distinguished "America" from "the South." This effort was thrown into disarray, however, when Missouri lawmakers submitted a constitution that barred free blacks, sparking an unlikely full-dress congressional debate over the question of black citizenship. Henry Clay defused this second crisis with a deliberately ambiguous second compromise that implied that Africans and their descendants were not U.S. citizens—a conclusion that, for some, pointed the way to the solution of America's painful contradiction of freedom and slavery, and for others undermined the very foundation of American republicanism.

Chapter 4, "Silence," sketches the beginning of a new, sectional political order whose architect—and intended chief beneficiary—was the New York Republican leader, Martin Van Buren, who sought to harness the South's fear of abolition as a political engine that could ultimately secure for him the White House. Van Buren's efforts to scuttle the nationalist Monrovian program were only partially successful, however, both because of the president's skillful political counterattack and also because of New Yorkers' distaste for Van Buren's proslavery machinations. The abortive Denmark Vesey rebellion in Charleston, tied by the authorities to the Missouri debates, chilled the national debate over slavery and initiated the first flowering of formal defenses of slavery. In the short term, Monroe's program of sectional reconciliation appeared fruitful.

Chapter 5, "Discord," surveys the deceptive tranquillity of the national political scene after the Missouri settlement, and reveals the seething sectionalism beneath the surface. It notes the profound spiritual cost—and extreme difficulty—of defending slavery in a free republic. In the wake of the Denmark Vesey plot, slaveholders mounted a variety of strategies to support an institution they regarded as under siege—the biblical defense, strict construction, and states' rights, which proved most effective, but increasingly radicalized southern leaders against virtually all forms of federal activity, including internal improvements and the imposition of tariffs. Van Buren's embrace of these extreme positions, as manager of the presidential campaign of the debilitated William Crawford, lent them credibility and emboldened proslavery ideologues to pose increasingly uncompromising demands on the national polity.

Chapter 6, "Beneficence," describes the high-water mark of progressive nationalism embodied by the John Quincy Adams presidency, and the ferocious struggle, coordinated by Martin Van Buren, to overthrow it. Lafayette's visit to America, organized by Monroe, temporarily defused political and sectional tensions and helped to insure Adams's peaceful accession; but southern leaders, fearful of the northern-western alliance of Adams and Clay, organized behind Van Buren to oppose the administration's every measure, including the very popular mission to the Panama Congress. The debate over Bolívar's meeting of the American states represented a new milestone in southern reaction against traditional American themes of liberty and equality, but even more significantly marked the birth of a new national narrative: one that viewed the progress of the white race, rather than the advance of freedom, as the guiding principle of American history.

Chapters 7 and 8 document the impact of Andrew Jackson in redefining America in ways that enabled slavery to remain central economically, while setting it apart from the American narrative. Chapter 7, "Democracy," explores Jackson's rise to the presidency and the implications of his power as a symbol of white racial power and destiny—the shift from God's Providence to Jacksonian Providence. On traditional republican grounds, many southern leaders sought to resist the military chieftain's bid for the White

House, but ultimately nearly all concluded that the threat to slavery's future posed by an Adams-Clay alliance and growing public discussion of slavery as a national issue left them no other option. While some South Carolina politicians sought to mobilize around the tariff as a more prudent test case than slavery on which to oppose federal power over state affairs, others, such as Robert J. Turnbull, frankly showcased slavery itself, asserting that any national discussion of the question threatened the state's existence and warranted withdrawal from the Union.

Despite his keen awareness of southern sensitivity to tariffs, Van Buren needlessly inflamed and alienated the southern gentry by orchestrating passage of a draconian tariff bill designed to harm Adams and help Jackson. In power, Jackson made forced removal of Native Americans a cornerstone of his administration's policy, deliberately dividing the electorate along the lines of attitude toward race. Indian removal provided the template for treatment of free blacks, inspiring antiblack mobs in Cincinnati, Philadelphia, and elsewhere. The escalating callousness of white Americans prompted the black activist David Walker to write, in his *Appeal*, the most powerful indictment of slavery from a traditional Protestant Christian perspective, which warned of a new theological order in which race, not grace, counted most.

Chapter 8, "Force," describes the entente between Andrew Jackson and Daniel Webster and the normalization of the slavery issue it effected. Webster's endorsement of "the Union as it is" in his Second Reply to Hayne made it clear to southerners that defending the Union did not necessarily threaten slavery, while Jackson's forcible response to South Carolina's nullification threat signaled that a supporter of slavery could also defend the Union. In Virginia, the searching reappraisal of slavery provoked by Nat Turner's revolt ultimately failed and generated new, more comprehensive, and more flexible defenses of the institution, incorporating religion and race. Jackson's skillful triangulation of such issues as the tariff, internal improvements, and the Bank of the United States, orchestrated by Van Buren, largely silenced his strict-constructionist critics, while his forceful suppression of nullification found favor with nationalists. In the summer of 1833, the moral and political volatility of slavery seemed effectively contained in American politics. Though this brief period of tranquillity was soon shattered by West Indian emancipation, which launched a new phase of immediate abolitionism, the structure of the Second Party System was able to absorb this challenge and stigmatize abolitionists as fanatics and incendiaries. The Monrovian tripwire of the Missouri Compromise line ensured, however, that the admission of new states would inexorably reopen the wound of 1819–20 and prevent the nation from coming to a true accommodation with slavery.

As the epilogue, "Kansas," illustrates, nothing more clearly demonstrated the significance of the Missouri Compromise than its demise. Significantly, it was a northerner, Stephen A. Douglas—seeking personal advancement and the political support of the "compact South"—who engineered the destruction of the Compromise, at a moment when southerners themselves were not clamoring for it. The abrogation of this master compromise wiped the slate clean of over two decades of compromises, and paved the way for the establishment of the long-forestalled northern party. With the collapse of compromise, and the deployment of federal troops to Boston to enforce the Fugitive Slave Act, came a return to revolutionary time, and reconsideration of the fundamental meaning of the American nation. To Chief Justice Taney, author of the *Dred Scott* decision, the Union was an end in itself, to be preserved even at the cost of its founding ideals. In the hands of Abraham Lincoln, this new departure became a rededication, finding in the original Constitution and the existing laws the antidote to the disease of slavery.

VIEWED FROM THE vantage point of 1820, the four decades culminating in the Civil War constitute a profound tutorial on the meaning of America. The century that followed the war did much to obscure this history. I will attempt in the following pages to recover the components of what I believe is an important narrative, one that was purchased at too high a cost to disregard.

1

MONROE TAKES CHARGE

UNLIKE SO MANY inauguration mornings, March 4, 1817, was a beautiful day. A warm sun beamed down on the Capitol, still scorched and battered after its burning by the British in the recent war. The fair weather was fortunate, since the Speaker of the House, Henry Clay, piqued over not being offered the position of secretary of state, had precipitated a dispute over protocol between the House and Senate that made it impossible to hold the ceremony in the "Brick Capitol," the temporary frame building used as the seat of government. And so, for the first time, the event would be held outdoors. Attracted by the balmy weather and the celebratory atmosphere, a crowd of about 8,000—perhaps the largest that had yet assembled in the city—turned out to witness the swearing in of President James Monroe. The streets of the capital were thronged with coaches of every size and description, companies of artillery and infantry, and "a large cavalcade of citizens on horseback," and the sidewalks overflowed with "men women and children fiddles fifes and drums altogether present[ing] a scene picturesque and animating."[1]

In appearance, Monroe hearkened back to the Revolution, wearing the swallow-tail coat, knee breeches, and silk hose of the previous century. In content, as well, Monroe's words invoked an era when the nation was united in a single cause. The fifth president took office, as he acknowledged, under unusually auspicious circumstances. The nation had emerged almost miraculously from a war marked by ill-preparedness and discord with its sovereignty intact and its people more unified than ever before. The recently war-drained treasury now boasted a surplus of nearly $10 million, with the nation's credit fully restored and the federal debt on the way to repayment. With the defeat of Napoleon and the establishment of lasting peace in Europe, the old divisions between Federalists and Republicans, based for the most part on their partisans' identification with England or

France, had largely lost their relevance. Accordingly, much of Monroe's address consisted chiefly of a review of "the great causes which have contributed in a principal degree to produce the present happy condition of the United States," and a pledge to "persevere in the career in which we have advanced so far and in the path already traced."[2]

Those who chose to view the new president as conventional and uninventive found in his words substantial fodder for their belief. Yet, as we shall see, concealed in plain view within Monroe's unadorned phrases was a rationale for a sweeping expansion of federal power in the service of programs designed to promote national unity and prosperity, including a radical campaign to eliminate slavery and the African presence from American life.

AS USUAL, MONROE introduced his innovations with elaborate (and generally convincing) assertions that he was but dutifully following the time-tested paths of his predecessors. He would govern the nation, he avowed, by observing the "great causes" responsible for "the present happy condition of the United States." The key factors he identified were self-government, the expansion of the nation's territory by "fair and honorable treaty," and the varied and interconnected sections of the country's vast domain, of which he asserted hopefully "that there is not a part of our Union that is not particularly interested in preserving it." Monroe portrayed the republic as a complex but perfectly balanced machine, in which sections and interests complemented each other in a compelling real-world illustration of the principles of Madison's Tenth Federalist:

> Our fellow-citizens of the North engaged in navigation find great encouragement in being made the favored carriers of the vast productions of the other portions of the United States, while the inhabitants of these are amply recompensed, in their turn, by the nursery for seamen and naval force thus formed and reared up for the support of our common rights. Our manufactures find a generous encouragement by the policy which patronizes domestic industry, and the surplus of our produce a steady and profitable market by local wants in less-favored parts at home.[3]

"Such, then, being the highly favored condition of our country," Monroe continued earnestly, "it is the interest of every citizen" to identify and defend against any possible "dangers" that might "menace us." Monroe did not name these dangers openly. Instead, he returned to his theme of strengthening the causes of "our present happy state," indicating only by allusion the factors he viewed as threatening.

The first of these was ignorance. Again stressing the sovereignty of "the people" as the supreme cause of American happiness, Monroe questioned whether, "had the people of the United States been educated in different principles, had they been less intelligent, less independent, or less virtuous," the nation could have prospered. "When the people become ignorant and corrupt," Monroe warned, they become incapable of self-government; therefore, he urged, "let us by all wise and constitutional measures promote intelligence among the people as the best means of preserving our liberties."[4]

Monroe identified threats from abroad as another potential danger to American prosperity, and to counter these, he proposed extensive improvements to coastal defenses and frontier fortifications, as well as increased attention to the readiness of the army, navy, and militia. In notably convoluted syntax, perhaps designed to evade the electorate's republican wariness of a standing military, the president argued for a substantial peacetime buildup of the "science" and "implements of war" and of the nation's naval resources (stressing, of course, as republican principles dictated, the supremacy of the state-controlled citizen militia).[5] As it turned out, both the army and the navy were to play crucial roles in the Monrovian master plan for national development, while the militia was to have a bit part in the unraveling of the Monrovian system.

The third danger to the nation stemmed from its dramatic expansion and the potential weakening of the ties of unity such growth entailed. This was a danger that Monroe had witnessed at first hand. By pursuing a federal program of roads and canals, Monroe asserted, "we shall shorten distances, and . . . shall bind the Union more closely together."

A fourth danger concerned Monroe, one he chose not to mention in his address: the multiple dangers posed to the republic by slavery. Although he had lived all his life among slavery and was a slaveholder himself, in recent years he had come to view the institution not simply as wrong—many southerners acknowledged that slavery was wrong in the abstract—but as a serious obstacle to national development and as a threat to American unity as well as to the safety of its citizens. Rather than dwell on the danger, however, Monroe chose to conclude his speech with a flourish of unity and optimism. "Discord does not belong to our system," the new president exulted. "The American People . . . constitute one great family with a common interest." Monroe seemed to project a caretaker's role for his presidency. All that was required of the federal government domestically, Monroe suggested, was to protect the "essential principles and features" of the American system by "by preserving the virtue and enlightening the minds of the people"; in addition, "as a security against foreign dangers," it was essential "to adopt such arrangements as are indispensable to the support of our independence, our rights and liberties."[6]

A wary strict constructionist might observe that Monroe had given himself considerable latitude in these phrases. What did Monroe have in mind by "preserving virtue" and "enlightening minds"? And what "arrangements" might he feel necessary to supporting America's "independence, rights and liberties"? In fact, Monroe's goals for helping his country to "approach perfection" were far more sweeping than his conservative tone suggested.

The public response to Monroe's address, while positive, contained a hint of condescension. Editors and statesmen stressed the new president's virtue, but they also underscored the "home-spun" character of his address, presaging an "upright and unsophisticated" administration.[7] Unlike his illustrious predecessors of the "Virginia dynasty," Monroe was no titan of the new republic. A loyal Jeffersonian, he was regarded as capable but stolid, reliable but unimaginative. The classic judgment of Monroe issued from the pen of William Wirt in his widely read *Letters of a British Spy*: "Nature has given him a mind neither rapid nor rich, and therefore he cannot shine on a subject which is entirely new to him."[8] He seemed, in Churchill's phrase, a humble man with much to be humble about.

It would be easy to exaggerate Monroe's simplicity, however. Born into a family of lesser tobacco gentry in Westmoreland County, within four miles of the birthplace of Washington, and settling as an adult in the Virginia Piedmont not far from Jefferson and Madison, Monroe actually had broader experience with the world beyond Virginia than any of them.

Monroe's own education, while not as extensive as Jefferson's or Madison's, was solid and practical, grounded in the society-building principles of the Scottish Enlightenment he imbibed at the Presbyterian parson Archibald Campbell's "little school for future statesmen" in Westmoreland County, which had educated Washington and Madison, and where Monroe was a schoolmate of John Marshall. The Revolution interrupted Monroe's formal studies at William and Mary after one year, but provided him, as it did so many of his generation, with a wealth of experience in blood, sweat, and tears worth more than any college.[9] From then on, he remained in public service without a break until the end of his presidency, serving as an elected official in both the legislative and executive branches of government, as a diplomat, and as a cabinet secretary, including the crucial posts of State and War. In addition, he had been a founding member of the Republican Party, one of Jefferson's most trusted and zealous lieutenants. Monroe was not merely present at the creation of the new republic, he was an integral part of it, and understood its workings at many levels—state, local, federal, territorial—intimately and at first hand.

For students of government in the era of the founding, the supreme authority was the Baron de Montesquieu's *Spirit of the Laws*.[10] Montesquieu asserted forcefully, on the basis of ancient and modern precedents, that the larger the territory of a republican state, the more precarious its freedom and the more likely its collapse. Monroe fully recognized the dangers of an extended republic stressed by Montesquieu; he knew them personally, not in the abstract. However, Monroe believed that the strains of distance could be offset by improved communication. A national transportation network of roads and canals would serve to connect the far-flung corners of the nation into a union "so compacted and bound together that nothing could break it."[11] America's natural waterways, with a little aid from the federal government, would enable the United States to expand westward and still retain the coherence and unity of a small republic.

The nation had doubled in size since the Revolution as a result of the Northwest Ordinance, which Monroe had helped to draft, and the Louisiana Purchase, which he had helped to negotiate.[12] Alone among the chief executives of his generation, Monroe had traveled extensively in the west; so he knew the land, its potential, and its people from direct experience. To Monroe, as to his mentor Jefferson, the western territories represented the future of the nation. But Monroe's vision of the West was at once more tempered and more practical. He regarded the land with the eye of the surveyor and the statesman rather than the speculative philosopher. The nearly 600 million acres of public lands represented an unparalleled source of national wealth—of homesteads, agricultural and mineral resources, and prospective federal revenues—as well as a dangerous threat to sectional harmony. The new territories, once admitted as states, spelled the end of the political dominance of the eastern seaboard, engendering schemes of secession among dispossessed New Englanders. As a member of the Continental Congress, Monroe had himself helped to thwart the earliest disunionist movement of the new nation, during the Jay-Gardoquí negotiations of 1785–86, when eastern Federalists had sought to bargain away American navigation rights to the Mississippi and thereby to detach the western settlers from the nation. For their part, the sheer distance of the western settlers from political and population centers in the East threatened the bonds of union. As Calhoun had said, "Those who understand the human heart best, know how powerfully distance tends to break the sympathies of our nature."[13]

Like Jefferson, Monroe had served as America's envoy to France, arriving in the thick of the Revolution with all the fervor of a Jeffersonian true believer—and had learned at first hand, and at great personal cost, the brutality and suspicion of a revolutionary regime. Monroe had also served in England, where he acquired a more balanced and realistic opinion of the English than Jefferson's reflexive disdain.[14] And unlike his mentors, who never ventured beyond the confines of the Old Dominion after their presidencies, Monroe traveled throughout the country, and had little patience with the intolerant brand of Virginia particularism, which typified the views of his neighbors and marred Jefferson's later years.[15] Married to a New Yorker with both Dutch and New England ancestry,[16] maintaining friendships and family ties throughout the North, Monroe viewed Americans from other sections realistically, not as caricatures. Where many Revolutionary-era southerners grew increasingly parochial and sectionalist as the nineteenth century unfolded, Monroe's nationalism deepened and matured, to the point that his fellow Virginia planters came to regard him with deep distrust.

Monroe viewed the American situation at the time of his election as an unprecedented opportunity to unite the country, and he intended to make the most of it. After a long and only partially successful diplomatic career, he had been well prepared for the role of conciliator. Having worked closely with Washington, Jefferson and Madison, he understood the nature and uses of presidential power and the delicacy of exercising it in a republic whose citizens remained excessively sensitive, even phobic, about its abuse. Above all, his diplomatic experiences had taught him the power of listening, a talent that, then as now, was both less acknowledged and less practiced than a gift for talking, which Monroe did not possess to any great degree.

In his dress and demeanor, Monroe self-consciously hearkened back to the era of the Revolution, recognizing that new nations more than any others need a bulwark of tradition. Like Washington a generation earlier, Monroe favored old-fashioned tricornered hats and breeches with silver buckles below the knees. But Monroe's purpose in invoking the Revolutionary era was to draw on its legacies of patriotism, civic virtue, and radical innovation, as well as the authority of tradition. Before the end of his presidency, he would tap into potent wellsprings of Revolutionary sentiment. He would need them.

Monroe also adopted from Washington a simple but effective technique for consolidating his administration's authority while gaining a first-person picture of national conditions: a presidential tour or "progress" that would take him throughout the states of the Union, giving thousands of Americans the chance to see the head of government in person, and enabling many thousands more to share in the excitement of the trip through newspaper accounts. By making the tour, the first such since Washington's, Monroe intended both to generate pride and interest in the relatively small and inconsequential federal government, and to reap the benefits personally in the form of increased stature and visibility.

Monroe had an exceptionally good understanding of the power of such "progresses." Not only had he witnessed Washington's famous tour of 1791; he had helped to orchestrate, two years later, the triumphant passage of the volatile representative of revolutionary France, Citizen Genêt, from South Carolina to the federal capital of Philadelphia. Monroe had learned at first hand the techniques of generating a momentum of popular excitement which for a moment had appeared capable of challenging Washington himself, before Genêt's effrontery sank his fortunes and nearly sandbagged his American friends, Monroe among them.[17] The power of political pageantry was great, Monroe learned; but so was the value of discretion.

Monroe incorporated all of these lessons in his trip around the nation. The stated purpose of his tour was to view the country's military installations, since, then as now, the watchword of national defense functioned as the most acceptable basis for schemes for strengthening the hand of the federal government. The nation's unpreparedness in the recent war with Britain, and the president's oft-stated concern for military preparedness, lent plausibility to the mission's official rationale.

In fact, Monroe intended to make his tour a public theater of political reconciliation. New England Federalists had strenuously opposed the recent War of 1812, and most Republicans still regarded them as tainted if not treasonous, and not fit for reintegration into national political life. Personally convinced of the loyalty of the vast majority of Federalists, Monroe intended his visits to provide them the opportunity to demonstrate their support for his Republican administration, and thereby to quell the extreme anti-Federalism in his own party, which he considered a threat to national recovery.

Monroe could not have accomplished this goal of his "Presidential Jubilee" more successfully. Tapping into a powerful reserve of pent-up patriotic emotion, Monroe was everywhere greeted with effusive outpourings of bipartisan applause. It was an arch-Federalist newspaper, Boston's *Columbian*

Centinel, which conferred on Monroe's administration its signature moniker, the "Era of Good Feelings."[18] Indeed, Federalists responded if anything more enthusiastically to the new president than did his own party's leaders—in part because his deliberate muting of themes of partisan conflict carried with it the threat of rendering the Republican Party obsolete.

Throughout his presidency, James Monroe was forced to walk a delicate tightrope. Although deeply committed to the goal of national unity, Monroe saw keenly how narrowly circumscribed were his options for action. While such federal programs as a rechartered national bank, moderate protective tariffs, and "internal improvement"—roads, canals, and other public works designed to open markets and extend commerce—enjoyed wide popularity with the public at large, they encountered bitter opposition from the conservative faction of die-hard southern Old Republicans who saw the expansion of congressional authority in these areas both as a threat to slavery in itself, and as a deadly precedent offering a green light to large-scale federal intervention in state affairs. If the Constitution empowered Congress to build roads and canals, warned one, it could "with more propriety" be invoked to "free all the slaves in the U.S."[19] It was these same Old Republicans—Virginians like John Randolph, Spencer Roane, and John Taylor of Caroline, many of them his Albemarle County neighbors, who had urged Monroe to stand for the Republican nomination for President in 1808 against Jefferson's hand-picked successor, James Madison, in order to punish him for his deviations from the orthodox Jeffersonian credo.[20] Monroe was at least partially receptive to the rebels because of his resentment of what he saw as high-handed treatment by Secretary of State Madison in rejecting the treaty he had negotiated with the British in 1806 without even submitting it to the Senate for a vote. At the next-to-last minute, Monroe had sensibly concluded to spurn the overtures of the disgruntled backbenchers and adopted a stance of dutiful support for the heir apparent and the regular system of succession. He had waited his turn, and his patience had been rewarded with the presidential nomination by the caucus of Republican congressmen.

Much had changed in the political atmosphere between the time that Monroe had been promoted as the Old Republicans' stalking horse and his actually assuming the presidency. Most important, the party conflict, which had threatened to dismember the Union, was over. Monroe was pained by the continued existence of malicious partisan rhetoric in political life and felt it threatened the integrity of the nation far more seriously than the activities of any political group. Specifically, he believed that the extreme hatred of zealous Republicans for many present and former Federalists was preventing national reconciliation and deferring the era of progress and prosperity that he saw as the next stage in America's destiny. His tour gave the Federalists "the opportunity . . . of making a strong exertion, to restore themselves to the confidence and ground which they had formerly held, in the affections of their brethern [sic], in other quarters."[21] But Monroe's purpose in restoring the Federalists to the good graces of their countrymen was not intended solely, or even principally, for their benefit (as his failure to appoint even a half-dozen of their number to federal office strongly indicated). Rather, Monroe wanted to leaven American political discourse with the Federalists' ideas and conservatism. These would be useful both in their own right and as a counterbalance to an ultrademocratic political culture that was becoming so constricted as to leave little room for governing. In 1816, for instance, the electorate revolted when Congress voted itself its first raise since the founding of the government in 1789, tossing out of office all but fifteen of the eighty-one members who backed the pay hike. As the Philadelphia editor Mathew Carey observed, Americans had mistakenly applied "to a free elective government, deriving all its powers and authorities from the voice of the people, maxims, and apprehensions, and precautions, calculated for the meridian of monarchy; [and] directed all their efforts, and all their views, towards guarding against oppression from the federal government."[22] This tendency had begun when Federalists had controlled the government under Adams; it had gained currency among Federalists when the Jeffersonians took power; and during the recent war with Britain it had nearly cost the nation its independence. Monroe was determined to prevent it from happening again, and he was willing to open political life—though not political office—to the ideological heirs of Hamilton to do it. If that meant facing the distrust among his own party stalwarts, for whom hatred of Federalists was an article of faith, so be it. Monroe completely accepted the Jeffersonian axiom that the "big-R" Republican Party was merely a means to the end of a "small-r" republic without parties—and truly believed it in a way that Jefferson and Madison could not.[23] Monroe's agenda for preserving the virtue and enlightening the minds of his countrymen, then, strayed far from Republican orthodoxy.

If the pageantry and symbolism of Monroe's progress showcased the grateful return of the prodigal Federalists to the political fold, the substance had at least as much to do with relations with his fellow Republicans. Although Monroe preached "amalgamation," he scrupulously refrained from awarding jobs to all but a tiny handful of Federalists. In part, this was due to his conviction that his party could not yield on any important matters to the Federalists, and that reconciliation should be accomplished "only by a union of parties on republican principles."[24] Equally important, however, Monroe felt the need to protect his flank from stalwarts of his own party skeptical of his aims and distrustful of his means. To most Americans, including many of the rank-and-file Republican party leaders Monroe met and conferred with on his tour, the Republican Party was a temporary expedient resorted to in order to quell the danger to the nation of Federalist ultraism. To the emerging class of professional party politicians, however, the party was an end as well as a means, a guarantor of status and sustenance as well as the repository of political truth. In the eyes of these men, Monroe was a threat, or even a traitor, and his avowed policy, the "amalgamation of parties," anathema.

The American public had shown itself ready for a new departure in the wake of the nation's deliverance after the War of 1812, embracing a rechartered Bank of the United States and, in many parts of the country, agitating for Congress to apply the $6 million bonus paid to the government by the bank as a down payment on an extensive federally sponsored transportation network of roads and canals. Like John C. Calhoun, the visionary young congressman from South Carolina, Monroe viewed the best hope for national integration in an expanded domestic commerce, "an active intercourse between the extremes and throughout every portion of our Union," made possible by a massive, federally sponsored transportation infrastructure.[25] After initially chartering an important national highway, the Cumberland Road, Monroe's predecessor had discovered new constitutional scruples against such measures, and vetoed Calhoun's popular Bonus Bill on the last day of his term. Madison's unexpected veto stunned Monroe and forced him to revise his inaugural address, and dealt a blow to his plans for domestic policy, in which internal improvements played a key role. A strict constructionist of the Constitution by training and politically conservative by necessity, Monroe was not going to reverse Madison's precedent lightly—even if Monroe found scant constitutional justification for it.[26]

Monroe had little political room to maneuver, and he knew it. Historians judge the Era of Good Feelings to have been fleeting, if not imaginary; but it was an opening, though a narrow one, and Monroe was determined to make the most of it. He was quite willing to forge alliances with those who could help his agenda, from evangelical Christians to state political bosses, whether or not their ultimate goals diverged from his. To implement his innovative policies while preserving, and even enhancing, his reputation for strict construction, Monroe appointed to his cabinet strong-willed individuals who could be counted on to push forcefully the programs they believed in. The department heads would be associated with the policies, and the president's fingerprints would be invisible. The drawback to this plan, of course, was that Monroe would gain little credit for his administration's successes; but that was a sacrifice he had no qualms about making.

Monroe's most important cabinet appointment was John Quincy Adams as secretary of state. The choice not only signaled the new president's essential agreement with the overarching nationalism of the intense, intellectual New Englander, it strongly suggested Adams as Monroe's choice as successor—since the holder of the key cabinet position had already come to be recognized as the presumptive heir to the presidency. Monroe paid a steep political price for the appointment, both in the alienation it produced in the haughty Henry Clay, who felt that by rights the post should have been his, and in the distrust it generated among orthodox Republicans and particularist southerners.[27] Nominally one of their own, Monroe felt he had the latitude to weather the suspicion of the Old Republicans, but the Northeast had to be placated after seeing yet another Virginia planter elevated to the presidency, since sons of the Old Dominion had now held the post for seven terms out of eight.

Political necessity also dictated the choice of vice president. For the third time in the republic's short history, a president from Virginia was linked to a vice president from New York. The Empire State was not only the most populous, but also the most politically powerful state in the confederation; its leaders, along with Virginia's, had forged the Republican Party, and the state's most powerful political faction, the "Bucktails," under the leadership of Martin Van Buren, was well on its way to institutionalizing permanent partisan competition as an accepted part of public life—something new under the sun.[28] The most popular political figure in New York was Governor Daniel D. Tompkins, who had led the state through the trials of the War of 1812 and, as one of his last official acts, secured passage of a law outlawing slavery as of July 4, 1827. Tompkins considered his claim to the presidency superior to Monroe's, and believed that his northern identity alone excluded him from the top job.[29] Republican congressmen, meeting in caucus to select the nominees, offered the second slot to the New Yorker, who somewhat grudgingly accepted.

Monroe wanted a westerner and a champion of internal improvement for the post of secretary of war. After Clay and former Kentucky governor Isaac Shelby rejected the position, Monroe offered it to John C. Calhoun, champion of the Bonus Bill. Clearly, despite the constitutional caveats in his inaugural address, this appointment signaled Monroe's continued support for internal improvements, and his intent to advance them as a measure for defense. Monroe took seriously the military threat to the country, but, more important, he recognized the powerful patriotic leverage that the military rationale offered. Monroe's selection harnessed the energy and ambition of the young former War Hawk to the department's great potential, as a bulwark of national security and a wellspring of patronage, to reshape the nation's infrastructure.

For his attorney general, Monroe turned to William Wirt, the Virginia lawyer and litterateur who had offered a disparaging evaluation of Monroe's intellect years earlier. Wirt was astonished to receive the president's request, but proved a highly capable choice. Having devoted twelve years to a biography of Patrick Henry, Virginia's avatar of resistance to tyranny (which Henry defined broadly enough to include the federal constitution), Wirt nonetheless proved an able champion of Monrovian federal expansion, arguing before the Supreme Court in the government's behalf such crucial cases as *McCulloch v. Maryland.*

The most disappointing cabinet choice was William Crawford at Treasury, a holdover from Madison's administration. Crawford was an able administrator and a hard worker, and as a congressman he had acted as a champion for nationalizing measures such as the Second Bank of the United States and a protective tariff. But his intense ambition for the presidency led him to set himself up as the standard-bearer of the "radicals," or orthodox Jeffersonian supporters of small government. Crawford transformed the Treasury Department into a nucleus of patronage and power and engaged in vigorous interagency guerrilla warfare against all potential rivals for the presidency. Since Calhoun and Adams fit this description, Crawford relentlessly attacked the South Carolinian's management of the War Department and mobilized his congressional supporters to slash its budget, while making it a "*point d'honneur*" to oppose any measure backed by the New Englander.[30]

Although his was not technically a cabinet position, Postmaster General Return J. Meigs II, who stayed on from Madison's administration, proved to be another key figure in Monroe's plans for national development. Without a reliable mail delivery system, the extensive settlement of the back country contemplated by the president would be impossible. Meigs presided over a spectacular expansion of the postal system, adding in six years more than 1,800 new post offices to the 2,600 or so that had been created over the previous fifteen, and nearly doubling the mileage of designated post roads.[31] The son and namesake of the legendary Cherokee agent who had instituted the policy of exchanging Indians' eastern possessions for western federal lands, Meigs attended Yale and earned a law degree in Connecticut before moving to frontier Ohio, where he became a postmaster, a judge, and the state's first supreme court chief justice. After stints in Louisiana (first as commandant of U.S. troops in the St. Charles district and later as a justice on that state's supreme court) and Michigan Territory, Meigs returned to Ohio and entered its fractious political life, serving as governor and commander in chief of the militia during the War of 1812.[32]

In addition to his political and military connections in four states, Meigs had valuable family ties throughout the close-knit and influential Meigs clan. His only child, Mary Sophia, was married to a Virginia congressman, John G. Jackson. Return's uncle, Josiah Meigs, a former president of Franklin College (now the University of Georgia) was commissioner of the U.S. Land Office, in charge of surveying the vast expanse of the public domain. Josiah's son Henry was a congressman from New York City with ties to Van Buren's Bucktails, who was married to a first cousin of Stephen F. Austin of Texas. Henry's daughter Clara was married to John Forsyth, the former Georgia congressman and future secretary of state, currently minister to Spain. For Meigs, family and personal allegiances trumped sectional or partisan identity; he was a valuable ally for Monroe.

In the Navy Department Monroe retained Benjamin W. Crowninshield, a capable Salem merchant and politician, but he proved a disappointment, failing to provide independent judgment in cabinet sessions. The final break came, however, in September 1818, when Crowninshield bungled arrangements for one of Monroe's naval inspection tours on the southern leg of his national "progress," and the president rebuked him in terms the secretary considered offensive (a rare display of temper that underscored the importance Monroe accorded to his tour). Shortly thereafter, Crowninshield resigned. It took Monroe almost four months to find a replacement—a period during which Madison suggested that the cabinet position be eliminated in favor of a Board of Navy Commissioners.[33] Monroe rejected this idea, because a large and strong navy, under reliable leadership, was essential to his plans for the nation's future.

On its face, then, his choice of Smith Thompson, a New York jurist and conventional politician with no significant naval experience, would seem strange. On closer examination, however, it reveals much about Monroe's methods and goals. First, Thompson was a close associate of New York's leading political manager, Martin Van Buren—so close that Van Buren had named his youngest son after him. And second, Thompson was a founding vice president of the American Bible Society, who swiftly requisitioned 3,500 Bibles to provide a copy to every officer and enlisted man in the Navy.[34] A strong supporter of the American Colonization Society as well, Thompson offered a link to the "benevolent empire" of elite evangelical philanthropic organizations whose support and assistance Monroe considered integral to his vision of national development.

The evidence suggests that the eradication of slavery was part and parcel of that vision. This goal was crucial not so much for the sake of the slaves themselves but chiefly because of the threat that slavery would do serious harm to the nation. Like other Virginians of his generation, Monroe was educated in the fundamental danger of slavery to the safety and liberty of a free republic, as stressed by Montesquieu and the Scottish philosophers. The institution, Montesquieu argued, "is neither useful to the master nor to the slave; not to the slave, because he can do nothing through a motive of virtue; nor to the master, because by having an unlimited authority over his slaves he insensibly accustoms himself to the want of all moral virtues, and thence becomes fierce, hasty, severe, choleric, voluptuous, and cruel."[35] In the abstract, then, in the eyes of authorities Monroe took very seriously, American slavery represented a jarring contradiction to the basic principles of liberty and equality on which the country was based. More concretely, slavery aggravated all the dangers of which Monroe had warned in his inaugural address. It fed on and fostered ignorance and corruption, which rendered citizens "incapable of self-government." It undermined domestic security by creating an enemy nation within the bowels of the state, a ready ally of potential enemies (as the country's experience in the Revolution and the War of 1812 had amply demonstrated).

Most significantly, slavery constituted a ready basis for sectional conflict, one that would only be exacerbated, not lessened, by improved communications and increased contact between the far-flung regions. Morality aside, the asymmetries that slavery generated ensured continued strife and the prospect of violence. To anyone not blinded by its power and profitability, slavery constituted a clear threat to the republic.

Here again, Monroe's attitude was shaped not only by Enlightenment theory but also by concrete experience. In 1800, while Monroe served as governor of Virginia, an enslaved Richmond blacksmith named Gabriel organized a large-scale slave insurrection against the seat of Virginia's government that involved seizing Monroe himself as a hostage. Only a freak rainstorm thwarted the plot, which had been followed by the grisly round of executions, transportations, and floggings typical in such cases. Significantly, Gabriel and his confederates seemed to anticipate that Monroe, given the stridency of the Republicans' rhetoric of liberty in the presidential election then in full sway, would be sympathetic to their cause. It seems likely that the Richmond slave conspirators' interpretation of the meaning of the three recent revolutions—French, Haitian, and Jeffersonian—caused the earnest Republican governor of Virginia to reexamine his understanding of the place of slavery in the American nation.[36]

Shaken by the scale of judicial bloodshed in the wake of the plot, the Virginia legislature instructed Governor Monroe to request the Jefferson administration to explore the feasibility of having rebellious slaves deported to Sierra Leone, the West African settlement for freed slaves established by British abolitionists. Jefferson instructed his minister in London, Rufus King, to make inquiries. The colony's managers forcefully rejected the suggestion, explaining that the beleaguered colony could barely support itself, let alone admit insurrectionary Virginia blacks. The proposal foundered and all records of the legislature's actions were sealed.

Monroe never gave up on the idea of Africa, however, not simply as a destination for intractable rebels but also as a homeland for free blacks and emancipated slaves. Among Andrew Jackson, Daniel Webster, Bushrod Washington, Francis Scott Key, and chair Henry Clay, the president-elect was the most powerful participant in the founding meeting of the American Colonization Society at Washington's Davis Hotel in December 1816. And while the village that would become the headquarters of Liberia's ruling True Whig Party was Clay-Ashland, named after the most ardent congressional supporter of colonization and his Kentucky plantation, it is noteworthy that the first settlement and capital city of Liberia bears the name of the Monroe family estate and the president's birthplace, Monrovia.

The colonization movement is generally regarded today as a morally compromised, impractical scheme, "futile and useless at best," and at worst, a cynical tool for the smoother functioning of slavery.[37] The rest of this chapter will address the questions of the morality and motive of the colonization project; we will return later to the issue of its feasibility.

The modern view of the American Colonization Society as a support for slavery is strongly influenced by the critique launched by William Lloyd Garrison in 1830, which became a cornerstone of the movement for immediate abolition. For the period before 1830, however, this perspective is inadequate. As an organized national movement for opponents of slavery, the ACS was, before the 1830s, the only game in town—as is demonstrated by the fact that nearly all of the future (white) leaders of all branches of the abolitionist cause came from the colonizationist ranks.[38] More fundamentally, white Americans gave almost unanimous assent to the basic principle underpinning the colonizationist cause: that the two races could never coexist in the United States on the basis of social and political equality. This principle served as an axiom that few Americans even conceived as open to question.

This was certainly true of James Monroe, for whose overall plan for national renewal colonization was a sine qua non. While the colonization movement was partly motivated by philanthropy toward blacks, its larger purpose was to make the American republic safe for whites. The underlying reason behind the desire for an exclusively white republic was not simply racism, although that was a significant component, and one probably inextricable from other, more admirable motivations. Nor was the ACS's aim to rid the nation of free blacks chiefly a matter of upper-class fears of a dangerous and unassimilable proletariat, even if this was a motive of some of its founders.[39]

There were two principal reasons why white Americans found it so difficult to imagine a nation shared with blacks. First, they simply had no model available to them of a successful multicultural republic. The classical sources from which they drew their precedents viewed ethnic and geographical uniformity as essential attributes of a successful state, and regarded any deviation from that norm as both evidence and cause of decline.[40] The modern philosophers to whom the Americans accorded authority made this point at least as stridently. According to Edmund Burke, national prejudices should be cherished as a defense against threatening incursions of fleetingly fashionable practices, "and the longer they have lasted and the more generally they have prevailed, the more we cherish them."[41] Montesquieu, who so forthrightly championed human equality, strongly believed that "men ought to remain where they are."[42] Other thinkers admired by educated Americans, from Vattel to Heineccius, candidly stressed the integrity even of nations regarded as barbarous, vindicating their rights in dealings with civilized states and asserting their inhabitants' equal capacity with Europeans for virtue or viciousness—but always in the context of their separate station in the world. Even Jefferson, whose denigration of the capacities of Africans probably exceeded most of his contemporaries, believed in blacks' capacity for self-governance, as Garry Wills has shown, but only as a homogeneous society. Discussing Jefferson's plan for the emancipation and removal of Virginia's slaves, Wills argues that "Jefferson felt that a certain homogeneity was necessary in any society of men contracting with each other on the basis of mutual affection. This is as apparent in his treatment of Indian society as in his effort to keep the bonds close in Virginia by limiting the number of white immigrants." Because of "deep rooted prejudices entertained by the whites" and "ten thousand recollections, by the blacks, of the injuries they have sustained," Jefferson believed, the two races could never live in peace. While Jefferson never denied blacks' right to equality or self-government, he insisted on their "right to self-rule *as a people*," not as individuals within the American body politic. "His deportation scheme was meant to assure for blacks the same right Americans were asserting," Wills explains. "But the blacks had first to have a *separate* station, for that to become an *equal* one."[43]

The second fundamental challenge that black equality posed for white Americans stemmed from the unintended consequences of the nation's founding documents, the Declaration of Independence and the Constitution, and the surprising expectations that they generated. We tend today to overlook the astonishing radicalism of these two charters taken in tandem: the first pronouncing in unequivocal terms the principle of universal human equality, the second securing full equality under the law for all free citizens. To the framers, myopically focused on the rather specific set of oppressions imposed on them by the Crown (and more generally, by the complex and arbitrary network of privileges and disabilities inherent in any ancient, aristocratic system of rule) it seemed appropriate, noble, and perhaps tactically necessary to assert a sweeping claim of universal principles as an underpinning for their revolutionary actions—little imagining, probably, the implications of such principles when taken to their logical conclusions. Discovering themselves "free" and "equal," but anchorless, in a society in which the traditional markers of identity such as class, wealth, religious affiliation, and hereditary privilege had at least no formal standing, many white Americans felt an almost desperate need for some other signifier of difference and distinction to fill the breach.

For their part, black Americans widely embraced the sweeping, universal statements of liberty in the nation's charter documents, choosing to see them as yardsticks against which to measure their society's shortcomings, rather than as the self-serving and hypocritical rationales of a cynical white elite. This made sense not only philosophically and ideologically, but also tactically, on the principle of Saul Alinsky's Fourth Rule for Radicals: "Make the enemy live up to their own book of rules."[44] Similarly, the rising generation of blacks freed under the North's gradual emancipation laws determined to press the boundaries of prejudice and law to extract the greatest measure of freedom and civic responsibility possible from their society. According to law, the children of enslaved mothers were to achieve full emancipation on reaching the age of majority (twenty-five for males). This meant that in the years between 1805 and 1829—twenty-five years from the passage of the first gradual emancipation law, by Pennsylvania, in 1780, and from the last, by New Jersey, in 1804—a generation of African American males came of age with the expectation of a measure of real freedom, including such rights of citizenship as an education, the vote, and the freedom to make a living. It is hardly coincidental that these years coincided with the rise of laws to restrict black citizenship in the North, of extralegal white action against blacks, and of colonization.[45]

Thus the tortured question of "whiteness" took on almost agonizing dimensions, as Scott Malcomson has shown, with "whites" locked in an inextricable embrace with "blacks": the former believing the latter's elimination to be essential to the fulfillment of America's destiny, while being negatively dependent on them for their own self-definition.[46] The deep contradictions at the heart of the colonization movement, unrecognized or at least unexplored by the colonizationist themselves, set the stage for convulsive reaction when, about a decade later, these contradictions would be probed relentlessly by the Garrisonian abolitionists.

Yet even as they could see no future for them in the United States, supporters of colonization were quite sanguine about the prospects for "repatriated" American blacks in their "own" country. The *African Repository*, organ of the American Colonization Society, is striking in its apparent Afrocentrism, seizing on evidence of that continent's cultural achievements with the fervor of a Garveyite or a modern black nationalist.[47] Furthermore, there is no gainsaying the commitment of the many missionaries who ignored the threat of malaria and other diseases and undertook the establishment and administration of the colonies at Sherbro and Cape Mesurado, well understanding the strong likelihood that the appointment was a rendezvous with death.

Of course, colonization was ultimately a means to an end: an American republic without blacks. Without a doubt, most whites felt, slavery represented a threat to Americans' morals and character. It also seemed uneconomical as well, both to northerners weaned on clichés of Yankee orderliness and prosperity versus southern indebtedness and squalor, and to planters of the tobacco-exhausted Upper South who faced the expenses and dangers of surplus chattel labor (and lacked the windfall profits of their cotton-state compatriots).[48] No manager of an aging nuclear power plant could be more acutely aware of the danger posed by the unstable energy source on which his wealth depended.

Nonetheless, even though most whites considered slavery dangerous, they could not conceive of emancipation without removal. "If the question were submitted, whether there should be either immediate or gradual emancipation of all the slaves in the United States, without their removal or colonization," Henry Clay said, "painful as it is to express the opinion, I have no doubt that it would be unwise to emancipate them."[49] Emancipation would have to be part of a package deal. And the emancipation and removal of black Americans would cost more—on a scale of millions—than anything the nation had undertaken before, the Revolution included. It would require a massive expansion of the scale and dynamism of federal power involving every branch of government and nearly every executive department, including a huge peacetime expansion of the navy. It would entail not merely the purchase and transportation of more than a million people, but also the reshaping of the actual landscape of the country. With few illusions about its difficulty, James Monroe assumed the office of the presidency prepared to take on the challenge.

2

MISSOURI

ON JANUARY 27, 1819, Indiana senator Waller Taylor responded to a request from the Connecticut theologian and geographer Jedidiah Morse for information about the western territories for an updated edition of his *Geography*. The growth of the West, Taylor reported, proceeded apace: "Instead of twenty-two counties in Indiana, there are twenty nine, if not thirty. . . . The people of the Missouri Territory have petitioned to be admitted into the Union . . . , and if there is time enough to act upon the subject, no doubt but their wishes will be granted, as they have the number of people required."[1] Neither Taylor nor Morse, nor, perhaps, anyone in the country, had any inkling that the Missouri Territory's orderly progress toward statehood would soon be interrupted, and that the debate over the terms over Missouri's admission to the Union, and by extension, the future of slavery in the unsettled American continent, would throw the nation into its greatest political crisis between the Revolution and the Civil War.

THE PERIOD IMMEDIATELY following the Napoleonic Wars witnessed a tentative rebirth of the international campaign against the slave trade and an increased concern with slavery at home. A particularly affecting and well-publicized tragedy in Washington, D.C., in which a woman attempted suicide rather than be sold away from her child, chanced to bring a free black family from Delaware who had been kidnapped and were about to be sent into slavery to the attention of the Washington public, including John Randolph, Francis Scott Key, C. T. Torrey, J. B. Lear, and Elias B. Caldwell. Randolph denounced the domestic slave trade on the floor of Congress and called for a federal investigation. (A committee was formed and a report submitted, but never printed.) Torrey, Key, Caldwell and Lear secured the release of the Delaware family, and shortly thereafter became active in the establishment of the Colonization Society.[2] In 1817, just before resigning to assume the vice presidency, New York's governor Daniel D. Tompkins persuaded his state's legislature to accelerate the end of slavery to July 4, 1827.[3]

At the same time, however, slavery continued to expand. The 1820 census showed a slave population of 1,538,038, an increase of approximately 30 percent over the 1810 figure. Although slavery was decreasing rapidly in most northern states, there were still over 19,000 slaves above the Mason-Dixon Line—more than 10,000 of them in New York.[4] The slave trade, illegal since 1808, continued to be both profitable and extensive, and involvement in it posed no insurmountable bar to acceptance in society, even in New England.[5]

Such facts invited bitter and sarcastic British condemnations of American cruelty and hypocrisy. Particularly telling—because universally read in polite circles on both sides of the Atlantic—were a pair of reviews of works on America that appeared in the *Edinburgh Review* in June and December 1818.[6] Although American critics reviled these reviews as unalloyed calumnies of American character and institutions, they in fact broke with the standard, often laughable hostility of the British reviewers and explicitly called for an end to the "unsparing detraction and bitter sneering" typical of British accounts of the United States. The articles presented a largely accurate and positive picture of the young nation, finding much for Britain to admire and even to imitate in American society: the astonishing economy of its government, its high standard of literacy and cultivation, its religious toleration, its remarkable rate of progress and growth of population. Their accurate information and sympathetic tone made these particular articles impossible simply to ignore. Moreover, they criticized America by American standards.

By such standards, the greatest threat to American character was slavery—an assertion affirmed by no less an authority than Thomas Jefferson, in his *Notes on Virginia*, quoted by a British travel writer and cited by the *Edinburgh Review*. "'There must doubtless' (says Mr Jefferson), 'be an unhappy influence on the manners of the people, produced by the existence of slavery among us. The whole commerce between master and slaves is a perpetual exercise of the most boisterous passions; the most unremitting despotism on the one part, and degrading submissions on the other. . . . The man must be a prodigy who can retain his morals and manners undepraved by such circumstances.'" The one great "blot upon" the Americans' "national character," the December reviewer asserted, with Jefferson's imprimatur, was slavery—"an evil which counterbalances all the excisemen, licensers, and tax-gatherers of England." In part this judgment represented honest indignation; in addition, however, it demonstrated an extreme sensitivity and a prickly defensiveness concerning American pretensions to moral superiority, as revealed in a histrionic passage: "If nations rank according to their wisdom and their virtue, what right has the American, a scourger and murderer of slaves, to compare himself with the least and lowest of the European nations? . . . Let the world judge which is the most liable to censure—We who, in the midst of our rottenness, have torn off the manacles of slaves all over the world;—or they who, with their idle purity, have remained mute and careless, while groans echoed and whips clank'd round the very walls of their spotless Congress."[7]

Unsurprisingly, this single excerpt from an eighteen-page review soon reverberated from one end of the United States to the other. The reviewer's hyperbole—particularly his premature celebration of Britain's tearing "off the manacles of slaves all over the world"—made an easy target for American respondents. Turning with relish to the traditional American theme of Britain's ancestral guilt in saddling the colonies with slavery, the American critics also painted a vivid picture of the mother country's continuing involvement in the villainous institution, copiously illustrated with quotations from Pitt, Wilberforce, and Clarkson. Evidently writing with a sense of self-mistrust, rather than overconfidence, the Edinburgh reviewer fatally overstated his case.

Hyperbole or no, however, the British critic's indictment struck a nerve. Targeting the American sense of moral superiority (and in particular, superiority over Britain) with a well-aimed attack on America's national honor, and using the author of the Declaration of Independence as his weapon, the author offered a challenge as well as a critique: "Every American who loves his country, should dedicate his whole life and every faculty of his soul, to efface this foul stain from its character." While Americans may have resented being "cited, officiously and triumphantly, before the world, by a British literary tribunal on the Areopagus of Edinburgh," neither patriotic Virginia Republicans nor anglophilic New England Federalists could any longer avoid seeing slavery through a British lens.

On February 13, 1819, James Tallmadge, a maverick single-term Republican congressman from Poughkeepsie with family and personal ties to New York governor De Witt Clinton, introduced an amendment to the Missouri statehood bill providing "that the further introduction of slavery or involuntary servitude be prohibited . . . ; and that all children of slaves, born within the said state, after the admission thereof into the Union, shall be free at the age of twenty-five years."[8] Although Tallmadge's motives in proposing his amendment have long been a subject of speculation, his own explanation seems sufficiently plausible. Tallmadge was a devout Christian and a staunch republican who believed that the nation should never appear to endorse impiety or injustice by sanctioning the spread of slavery. In the previous session Tallmadge had opposed statehood for Illinois on account of its constitution's ineffectual antislavery provisions. During that debate, he had leveled the familiar charge at England that that nation "had committed the *original sin* of bringing slaves into our country." Some time afterward he received a reproving letter from an Englishman living in South Carolina, arguing that England had taken steps to atone for her "original sin" by passing laws to protect and improve the condition of her slaves, while America had done nothing for their relief and did not even account the killing of a slave as murder. "I felt the severity of the reproof," Tallmadge averred; "I felt for my country." An erudite, literate man, Tallmadge had likely read the *Edinburgh Review*'s uncannily similar condemnation. If he did, he took to heart its admonition to take action to remove the "foul stain" of slavery from America's character.

Tallmadge's measure sparked one of the most remarkable weeks of debate in the history of Congress. As Glover Moore remarks, "The speeches preserved in Gales and Seaton's *Annals of Congress* on this occasion are worthy of careful analysis since they covered almost every phase of the arguments which would be used by the North and South for many years to come."[9] In fact, these speeches represent probably the most candid discussion of slavery ever held in Congress. By the time the next session convened, in November, the Missouri issue had become thoroughly politicized throughout the country, and debate rapidly degenerated into "speeches for Buncombe," contributing a new term to American slang but little new to the discussion of slavery.[10] Thereafter, deeply shocked by the volcanic anger and potential for sectional division revealed by the Missouri debate, Congress would rarely discuss slavery without recourse to euphemism and circumlocution.

As was frequently the case in the early sessions of Congress, the discussions of Tallmadge's amendment on the first day, February 13, were never recorded, although they were evidently stormy.[11] Speaker of the House Henry Clay, later to earn his reputation as a compromiser on this very question, appears to have unguardedly opened the debate for the opposition as a kind of quarterback for the slaveholders. Asserting "the inviolability of this species of property," he then spoke of the contentedness and "convenience" of slaves in Kentucky; favorably compared the condition of the "black slaves" of the South with the "white slaves" of the North; and "asked gentlemen if they would *set their wives and daughters to brush their boots and their shoes, and subject them to the menial offices of the family?*" By the time he finished, Clay's "boldness" in the defense of the "peculiar institution" had shocked many northern members and unified the southern—while counteracting his colonizationist reputation as a potentially dangerous critic of slavery.[12]

When Congress reconvened on the following Monday, February 15, Tallmadge's friend and fellow New Yorker, John Taylor of Ballston Spa, eloquently framed the debate. After reflecting that the actions of the few inhabitants of Missouri would, in large measure, "decide the destiny of millions" who would one day inhabit the vast regions stretching out to the "Western ocean," Taylor isolated the two central questions around which not only the Missouri debate but much of the future of the slavery controversy would revolve:

> "First. Has Congress power to require of Missouri a Constitutional prohibition against the further introduction of slavery, as a condition of her admission into the Union?
> "Second. If the power exist, is it wise to exercise it?"[13]

Quoting the language of Section 3, Article 4, of the Constitution—"the Congress shall have power to dispose of and make all needful rules and regulations respecting the territory, or other property, belonging to the United States"—Taylor concluded that the answer to the first question was "yes," and he cited the antislavery clause of the Northwest Ordinance, slavery limitations on the admission of Illinois and Indiana, as well as conditions imposed upon Orleans Territory, to demonstrate his point. The sovereignty of Congress over territories, Taylor concluded, "is unlimited." Both natural law and the nature of the government's tenure over the territory supported this view. Congress had purchased Missouri for money and had the power to sell it; could it then be maintained that Congress had no right to remove slavery from it "nor [to] establish those civil regulations which naturally flow from self-evident truth? No, sir, it cannot; the practice of nations and the common sense of mankind have long since decided these questions."[14]

Regarding the second question, the propriety of restricting slavery, Taylor simply reminded his slaveholding opponents of their own often-repeated declarations on the subject. "How have they wept over the unfortunate policy that first introduced slaves into this country! How have they disclaimed the guilt and shame of that original sin, and thrown it back upon their ancestors!" Now it was time for southerners to back up their habitually repeated words with actions. "If we reject the amendment and suffer this evil, now easily eradicated, to strike its roots so deep in the soil that it can never be removed, shall we not furnish some apology for doubting our sincerity, when we deplore its existence. . . ?" To fail to take this step, Taylor continued, would be to invite comparison with the Scribes and Pharisees.

Taylor's astounding assertion that slavery could be "easily eradicated" showed the extent of northern inattention to the growth of the institution. Likewise, his plea that slaveholders demonstrate their "sincerity" in opposing slavery sounded anachronistic, and certainly appears so in retrospect. In 1790, there had been 657,000 slaves in the United States; by 1820 the number had risen to more than one and a half million.[15] Before the rise of cotton, it is true that many Upper South slaveholders had cause to regard slavery as an economic as well as a moral burden, but with the cultivation of this crop, and the return of the peace, the value of slave property catapulted, from an average of between $400 to $500 for a prime field hand in 1814, to $800 to $1,100 in 1819.[16] At the same time, the value of exhausted agricultural land in the Old South had plummeted, so that in states such as Maryland, North Carolina, and particularly Virginia, capital in human beings represented planters' most valuable asset by far. In the meantime, many southerners' misgivings about slavery had adjusted to the new economic realities. It is true that many southerners, including John Randolph of Roanoke, Maryland's William Pinkney, and, of course, Jefferson, had denounced the institution in terms much stronger than Taylor employed in his defense of the Tallmadge Amendment; but by 1820 Jefferson would not scruple to recommend "a woman who brings a child every two years" to a nephew as the most "profitable" form of stock on a plantation.[17]

If John Taylor misjudged contemporary southern attitudes, Timothy Fuller of Massachusetts (father of Margaret) unwittingly stepped over a much more dangerous line in his speech in support of the amendment. The chief requirement the Constitution imposed on new states, Fuller observed, was that they adopt a republican form of government. The Tallmadge Amendment "merely requires that slavery shall be prohibited in Missouri. Does this imply anything more," he asked, "than that its constitution shall be republican?" To demonstrate his point, Fuller invoked the language on equality of the Declaration of Independence. Instantly, several southern members angrily denounced his implicit challenge to the republican character of the slaveholding states, and pointed out warily "the probability that there might be slaves in the gallery listening to the debate." "Sir, it is my wish to allay, not to excite local animosities," Fuller responded; "but I shall never refrain from advancing such arguments in debate as my duty requires, nor do I believe that the reading of our Declaration of Independence or a discussion of republican principles on any occasion, can endanger the rights, or merit the disapprobation, of any portion of the Union."[18]

Fuller's assertion to the contrary, most slaveholders quickly recognized that perhaps nothing could endanger their "rights" to their slaves more fundamentally than discussion of the Declaration of Independence and "republican principles." Fuller's simple statement of what he took to be undisputed American verities underscored the conflict between the Declaration and the practice of slaveholding that many of the Revolutionary generation had recognized, but had not been required to reconcile. Now defenders of slavery had little choice but to decide between attempting to delimit the reach of the Declaration explicitly to exclude black Americans, or rejecting its authority altogether.

If necessary, many slaveholders were willing to do either, and before the Civil War most would have to do both. But for southerners either to reject the Declaration of Independence or to abandon its universal reach would exact a high moral, political, and psychological toll. Morally, reading blacks out of the Declaration implied a rejection of the Hutchesonian, Scottish Enlightenment tradition of universality that undergirded American ethics and politics, as suggested in chapter 1—a tradition that, if anything, had a stronger presence in the Presbyterian-educated South than in Congregationalist New England.

Politically, the consequences of repudiating the Declaration may have been graver still. Jefferson's great instrument constituted not only the nation's chief basis of legitimacy, but an important wellspring of nationalism, much celebrated and frequently reproduced as the Monrovian Era of Good Feelings dawned.[19] More particularly, the Declaration served as well as a principal source of legitimation (along with the stature of Washington) of Virginia's perennial hold on the presidency, hence an indispensable tether to the Union and a vital counterweight to southern sectional impulses. For all these reasons, the choice that slaveholders were now being forced to make with regard to the Jeffersonian doctrine of equality could not help but have significant psychological consequences, as we shall see.

Unexpectedly backed into a moral and political corner over slavery, some southern congressmen, such as Virginia's Edward Colston, reacted violently, charging Massachusetts's Fuller with "criminality for asserting the natural rights of these people." Thomas Cobb of Virginia, perhaps bearing in mind the violent Haitian revolution that had followed the first French measures against slavery, averred that the Union would be destroyed if the restrictionists prevailed, graphically and prophetically accusing Tallmadge of having "kindled a flame which all the waters of the ocean cannot put out, which seas of blood can only extinguish."[20]

Other southerners sought to evade the dilemma by focusing on the first question isolated by John Taylor as central to the Missouri dispute, Congress's constitutional powers over slavery in the territories and newly admitted states, rather than the second, the expediency of restriction, which inevitably implied a discussion of the expediency of slavery itself. "The first objection," insisted Philip P. Barbour, "which meets us at the very threshold of the discussion, is this, that we have no Constitutional right to enact the proposed provision."[21] The defense of the constitutional rights of Missouri—and by extension, of other states later to be admitted to the Union—against the encroachments of the "General Government" became the centerpiece of the southern stand against restriction. This emphasis on constitutional questions—what one might call the "indirect" defense of slavery—prompted increasingly extravagant and unqualified southern assertions of federal impotence and states' (and, later, territorial) rights and powers throughout the antebellum period.

The "direct" defense of slavery also comprised a facet of the southern argument from the very beginning, steadily gaining prominence until the Civil War. Since northerners had directly assailed the expediency of slavery during the Missouri debates, southern congressmen had no choice but to defend it; but their efforts on this occasion appeared crude and unprepared. Clay's tactless arguments have already been discussed; Philip P. Barbour's were scarcely more effective. Slaves in the southern states were regarded as property, conceded Barbour, "yet they were considered and treated as the most valuable, as the most favored property. . . . We felt for them those sympathies which bind one man to another, though that other may be our inferior." Barbour disingenuously implied that southern whites' attachment to their slaves would bar them from a slave-free Missouri, since these ties of sympathy would preclude their going without them: "Such were the feelings of the Southern people towards their slaves, that nothing scarcely but the necessity of the master, or the crime of the slave, would induce him to sell his slave. If the master emigrated, he would carry his slaves with him," Barbour declared gallantly—only allowing, almost as an afterthought, that "going into a wilderness, where much labor was necessary, [slaves] were, on that account, peculiarly necessary." In comparison with later defenses of slavery postulated on Africans' inferiority and need for white "wardship," it is noteworthy that this key early spokesman for southern sectional solidarity vitiated his argument by entangling it with the classic language of sympathy of the moral philosophers, who condemn slavery on the very basis of sympathy. Barbour further undermined the abstract proslavery cause by bringing up, unprompted, the danger of slave insurrection in the slave states, offering the almost Pentagonese locution that, in time of war, "there must be an immense subduction from the efficiency of the slaveholding section of our country; its actual efficiency would consist only, or nearly so, in the excess of the white beyond the black population." Finally, restriction of slavery would result in a loss to the U.S. treasury, since it would remove southerners from the market for public lands beyond the Mississippi, thus depressing their price—and at the same time unfairly subsidizing northern purchasers at the expense of the South.[22]

Such arguments made little headway with antislavery congressmen, and it is unlikely that thoughtful southerners expected them to. The case against restriction rested unambiguously on the southerners' interpretation of the Constitution. "We must do the south the justice to admit that in this struggle over constitutional questions it did not indulge in the verbal quibbling which became more and more the rule in such debates," Hermann von Holst observed. "It placed itself openly, and without any duplicity, on the broadest basis upon which it could take position. It denied to congress the least shadow of right to make the admission of a territory as a state of the Union dependent upon any conditions whatever. This view was not based upon certain clauses of the constitution, but on the nature of the Union—that is, on state sovereignty." Some southerners, Holst noted, did not shrink even at this early stage from carrying the argument to its logical conclusion, as when Pindall of Virginia—a Federalist!—described the Constitution as an "international compact."[23]

It is important to keep in mind the rhetorical and political function of this extreme assertion of constitutional limitations on slavery's restriction: to forestall the discussion of slavery per se. This does not necessarily imply that slaveholders personally disapproved of the institution, although many of them did—for practical reasons of economics and safety as well as on moral grounds. As we shall see, those southern leaders who most keenly felt slavery to be indefensible often took the most radical positions in defense of states' rights.[24] Whatever their personal opinions, however, slaveholding congressmen in 1819 did not wish to do battle with northerners on the abstract question of the expediency of slavery, because they did not possess effective arguments to defend it, and knew they did not.

Most northern congressmen seemed caught off guard by southern militancy. Some seemed bewildered by the new southern tone, with its abandonment of obligatory expressions of anguish over slavery, and sought rather frantically to rediscover common ground. Others, however, would have none of it. Arthur Livermore, of New Hampshire, took aim squarely at slavery itself, describing it as a "sin" and "the foulest reproach of nations." Livermore refused to be drawn into the legalistic web of constitutional interpretation spun by the southerners and returned to the high ground of right and wrong: "How long will the desire of wealth render us blind to the sin of holding both the bodies and souls of our fellow men in chains! But, sir, I am admonished of the Constitution, and told that we cannot emancipate slaves." Although Livermore argued that the extension of slavery was incompatible with the ends stated in the preamble to the Constitution, to form a more perfect union, establish justice, insure domestic tranquility, provide for the common defense, and secure the blessings of liberty, he seemed to concede the southern argument that the Constitution protected slavery, foreshadowing the bitter language of the Garrisonians: "In the present slaveholding States let slavery continue, for our boasted Constitution connives at it." As for the elaborate southern argument against infringing the constitutional rights of Missouri and other new states, however, Livermore scornfully rejected them. "To be received as a State into this Union, is a privilege which no country can claim as a right. It is a favor to be granted or not, as the United States may choose."[25]

The real issue, Livermore insisted in closing, was what kind of a nation the United States intended to be:

An opportunity is now presented, if not to diminish, at least to prevent, the growth of a sin which sits heavy on the souls of every one of us. By embracing this opportunity, we may retrieve the national character, and, in some degree, our own. But if we suffer it to pass unimproved, let us at least be consistent, and declare that our Constitution was made to impose slavery, and not to establish liberty. Let us no longer tell idle tales about the gradual abolition of slavery; away with colonization societies, if their design is only to rid us of free blacks and turbulent slaves; have done also with bible societies, whose views are extended to Africa and the East Indies, while they overlook the deplorable condition of their sable brethren within our own borders; make no more laws to prohibit the importation of slaves, for the world must see that the object of such laws is alone to prevent the glutting of a prodigious market for the flesh and blood of man, which we are about to establish in the West, and to enhance the price of sturdy wretches, reared like black cattle and horses for sale on our own plantations.

Thus by the end of the second day of debate, a simple vote of the Committee of the Whole of the House of Representatives on an unanticipated amendment to a routine bill had turned into nothing less than a referendum on the meaning of America. The Committee of the Whole agreed to the amendment by a vote of 79 to 67.[26]

When the House reconvened the next day to consider the amendments reported by the Committee of the Whole, the debate resumed, as the House reporter delicately put it, "with considerable spirit." John Scott, Missouri's nonvoting delegate, insisted that by imposing "this suspicious, shameful, unconstitutional inhibition" upon Missouri, the representatives "were signing, sealing, and delivering their own death warrant" and hastening the day "when the General Government might, in turn, undertake to dictate to them on questions of internal policy." Besides, Scott averred, even if Congress required Missourians to form a constitution prohibiting slavery, they would simply draft a new one allowing it after admission, so there could be no point in passing a restriction. "Why expose the imbecility of the General Government, to . . . induce the people to an act of chicanery . . . ?" Scott asked provocatively. He concluded with the solemn warning that he "considered this question big with the fate of Caesar and of Rome."[27] Virginia's impetuous Edward Colston took this tone of intimidation one level farther, accusing Livermore of "endeavoring to excite a servile war," and insisting that "he is no better than Arbuthnot or Ambrister, and deserves no better fate."[28]

Into this charged atmosphere, James Tallmadge, recently returned from burying a young son and seriously sick himself, entered the debate for the first time to defend his amendment. There is evidence to support Tallmadge's assertion that the vehemence of southern opposition shocked him.[29] Once the battle had been fairly joined, however, he appeared willing, and believed the North willing, to see it through.

If a dissolution of the Union must take place, let it be so! If civil war, which gentlemen so much threaten, must come, I can only say, let it come! . . . If blood is necessary to extinguish any fire which I have assisted to kindle, I can assure gentlemen, while I regret the necessity, I shall not forbear to contribute my mite. Sir, the violence to which gentlemen have resorted on this subject will not move my purpose, nor drive me from my place. I have the fortune and the honor to stand here as the representative of freemen, who possess intelligence to know their rights, who have the spirit to maintain them. . . . As their representative, I will proclaim their hatred to slavery in every shape. . . . Here will I hold my stand, until this floor, with the Constitution of my country which supports it, shall sink beneath me. If I am doomed to fall, I shall at least have the painful consolation to believe that I fall, as a fragment, in the ruins of my country.[30]

The few days of debate on the Tallmadge Amendment transformed the debate over slavery from a rather abstract moral and philosophical question into a stark physical reality and a bitter political battle—indeed, into a rhetorical civil war. At one point during the debate a chance occurrence hammered home the institution's ugly reality when a slave trader drove a coffle of fifteen male and female slaves past the Capitol, in plain view of the congressmen. Tallmadge cited this frightful spectacle as an almost providential "elucidation of [the] argument, of bettering the condition of slaves, by spreading them over the country."[31]

Echoing New Hampshire's Livermore, Tallmadge forcefully dismissed southern claims of slavery's expediency. "If this class of arguments is to prevail, it sets all morals at defiance, and we are called to legislate on the subject, as a matter of mere personal interest." But, Tallmadge continued, he would not "cast an imputation so ungracious" on his adversaries as to press the southern argument to its necessary conclusion: "the moral right of slavery." "How gladly would the 'legitimates of Europe chuckle,'" Tallmadge thundered, "to find an American Congress in debate on such a question!" Evoking the humiliating accusations of American hypocrisy and immorality in the British quarterlies, Tallmadge delivered his most telling thrust:

> Sir, on this subject the eyes of Europe are turned upon you. You boast of the freedom of your Constitution and your laws; you have claimed, in the Declaration of Independence, 'That all men are created equal . . .'; and yet you have slaves in your country. The enemies of your Government, and the legitimates of Europe, point to your inconsistencies, and blazon your supposed defects. If you allow slavery to pass into Territories where you have the lawful power to exclude it, you will justly take upon yourself all the charges of inconsistency; but, confine it to the original slaveholding States, where you found it at the formation of your Government, and you stand acquitted of all imputation.[32]

In effect, Tallmadge's argument implied that failure to approve his amendment would constitute an abrogation of the fundamental principles cited by the Declaration of Independence as the basis for the separation from Great Britain, hence demonstrating a contempt for "the Opinions of Mankind" and effectually revoking the nation's claims to legitimacy as a sovereign state established under the "Laws of Nature and of Nature's

God." Although few Americans, North or South, would ever be willing fully to accept this conclusion, it did signal the start of the search for new bases of national legitimacy.

Fleetingly, at the very close of his speech, Tallmadge touched on the political implications of the vote. The Constitution, he recognized, provided that slaves be counted on a three-fifths basis for the purpose of congressional representation. To extend this privilege, "granted as a compromise and a benefit to the Southern States which had borne part in the Revolution," to the many new states to be created, "would be unjust in its operations, unequal in its results, and a violation of [the Constitution's] original intentions." Even apart from slavery's moral effects, Tallmadge concluded, "its political consequences in the representation under this clause of the Constitution demonstrate the importance of the proposed amendment."[33]

Tallmadge's extreme delicacy in raising this crucial point about the future makeup of the national legislature could not conceal its importance. Whether or not expansion was an economic necessity for the continuation of slavery, as southerners increasingly claimed, it was unquestionably necessary for the continuation of southern influence in Congress—and southerners increasingly began to think of themselves as belonging to a politically distinct region as they saw their influence start to slip away. The allocation of House seats based on the 1790 census had been 57 northern, 49 southern. By 1810 the proportion had shifted to 107 for the North and 79 for the South; and after the census of 1820, the North would gain 17 seats to the South's 10, giving the northern states a 35-seat majority. As Holst observed, "In these figures it was written, clear as day, that the slave states would have to yield the mastery of affairs to the north soon and forever, if they could not find in some other place a counterpoise to the north's growing power in the house of representatives."[34] In practice, this meant that the slaveholding states had to maintain their control of the Senate by admitting at the very least a new slave state for each new free state enrolled in the Union.

This point would emerge more clearly later. At the moment, the immediate problem for slaveholders was the passage of the Tallmadge Amendment in the House, by margins of 87 to 76 for the first section, prohibiting the further introduction of slaves into Missouri, and 82 to 78 for the second, emancipating slaves currently resident there at age twenty-five.[35] The debate over slavery in Arkansas, begun the following day, demonstrated the shakiness of the small antislavery majority in the House.[36] John W. Taylor's measure to restrict slavery in a newly incorporated territory stood on more solid constitutional footing than Tallmadge's measures to bar the institution from Missouri, which had met most requirements for statehood. No congressman who voted for the Missouri restriction claimed that slavery would be any less noxious in Arkansas, or that its establishment there would be less damaging to the interests of the nation. Yet the Taylor Amendment failed on a vote of 88 to 88, with Speaker Henry Clay breaking the tie. "We know we felt yesterday on the Missouri bill you have the power," North Carolina's Felix Walker pleaded with northern members before the vote; "you are the majority; but do not bear us down on this question. I trust that gentlemen will exercise on this vote a spirit of conciliation, and give the southern states an inheritance among their brethren, by suffering such of us as are disposed to become citizens of the Arkansaw to take our slave property with us."[37] This "conciliatory" approach paid off. Ezekiel Whitman of Maine, one of the northern congressmen who backed the Tallmadge Amendment but opposed the restriction on Arkansas explained his reasoning: "We must go on as we have begun; admitting some States with, and some without any restriction." Acknowledging an implicit line of demarcation between slave and free states, Whitman pointed out that Arkansas rested on a latitude south of Kentucky: "In my opinion, to do justice to our Southern brethren, they ought to have permission to carry with them their slaves, even further north."[38]

The logic of Whitman's position escaped the editor of the *New-York Daily Advertiser*, however, who professed himself "astonished" that anyone living outside of the "boundaries of cruelty, injustice and oppression" could vote "in favour of this crying national sin of our country."[39] In the *Advertiser*'s opinion, the existence of slavery threatened a dire providential judgment against America as a whole, which could not be averted by drawing arbitrary lines on a map.

Yet John Taylor himself, after the defeat of his Arkansas provision, proposed a territorial line of demarcation as a further amendment to the Arkansas Territory bill stating "that neither slavery nor involuntary servitude shall hereafter be introduced into any part of the Territories of the United States, lying north of 36 degrees and 30 minutes of north latitude."[40] Arthur Livermore, the fervent antislavery New Hampshire representative, welcomed the plan as "made in the true spirit of compromise," although he urged a different line—presumably a more southerly one. Future President William Henry Harrison of Ohio accepted "the expediency of establishing some such line of discrimination," and proposed one parallel to Missouri's northern border (ominously, almost contiguous with the future line between Kansas and Nebraska). But Philip Barbour opposed the proposition as "partial and inexpedient," arguing that "if the rule was wrong at the 25th degree of latitude, it was equally so at the 40th," and that to draw such a line was "as impolitic as it was unjust." Kentucky's Richard Clough Anderson denounced the amendment as "no compromise—its friends asked everything and gave nothing." Thomas Cobb of Georgia agreed, and called the question "to put an end at once to a debate . . . disagreeable to one part of the House, however agreeable it might be to the other." The House voted down Taylor's amendment by a margin of 67 to 74.[41]

Ironically, Taylor's rejected line of 36°30' was the identical boundary that would later be proposed by Senator Jesse Thomas of Illinois and passed to end the first Missouri crisis. A proposal that appeared, when offered at the beginning of the controversy by the chief antislavery spokesman in the House, as a clear-cut northern victory, would be hailed by southerners a year later as a miraculous escape from the imminent threat of northern domination.

In the meantime, the Senate proceeded along normally, with little sense of the drama unfolding in the other chamber. On February 27, 1819, the Senate struck out the antislavery amendments to the Missouri statehood bill and sent it back to the House, which refused to accept the change on March 2. Two days later, the Fifteenth Congress adjourned, and the Missouri bill failed.

The violent southern reaction to the Tallmadge Amendment effectively killed—for contemporaries, at any rate—the myth of the antislavery South. "It was the terror discovered by the opposition that opened my eyes," Harrison Gray Otis later asserted; ". . . I awoke as from a trance."[42] The passage of a bill to make the slave trade a capital crime, although it earned its sponsor, Virginia congressman Charles Mercer, the title of "the American Wilberforce," did little on closer inspection to alter the impression of southern intractability concerning slavery. For one thing, the bill's strongest support came from Virginia—the state whose slaveholders, as has already been noted, had the greatest pecuniary interest in suppressing the slave trade. This point had been hammered home by northerners during the Tallmadge Amendment debate, stripping several layers off the Virginians' carefully maintained "veneer of self-respect" regarding their relationship toward slavery. For decades, "Virginians were able to portray themselves as leaders of a humanitarian movement, despite any ulterior motives they might possess."[43] After the Missouri debate, assertions of "humanitarian" motivations behind Virginia's opposition to the slave trade—even, it should be noted, when genuine—would be regarded skeptically outside the state's borders. For patrician Virginians accustomed to an unchallenged acceptance of their philanthropic leadership (including praise for their stand on the slave trade), such a change constituted a deep humiliation. Neither bills against the slave trade nor statistics of southern contributions to missions and Bible societies could efface the impression that the South's extreme response to restriction had created. Henceforth, southern professions of hostility toward slavery, even when genuine, would be intended primarily for internal southern consumption—both because of the perceived need to present a "solid front" of support for the institution to the outside world and because in any event the rest of the country was not buying the idea.

Such skepticism reinforced the conviction of many southerners that the chief spur to the debate over Missouri was sectional political advantage, not concern over the welfare of the slaves. One of the principal southern arguments against restriction involved the assertion that spreading the slaves over a larger area would, in Jefferson's words, "increase the happiness of those [slaves] existing, and . . . dilute the evil everywhere and facilitate the means of getting finally rid of it";[44] had this not, after all, been the means by which slavery was extinguished in the North? Restrictionists compared this argument to proposing to fight the plague by extending it to more people. They asserted that extending the range of slavery would raise the market price of slaves, thereby increasing demand, while the spread to more fertile regions would lead to a rapid growth in the numbers of slaves according to fixed Malthusian laws of population. In fact, southerners were well aware of these principles, and several of their chief spokesmen conceded their validity.[45] Nonetheless, southern congressmen considered it essential to spread slaves across a wider area, for three reasons. First, representatives from the Upper South believed, perhaps not unreasonably, that their states could not profitably sustain large slave surpluses. Related to this concern was the fear of serious slave insurrections, a threat that was felt likely to grow as an expanding slave population faced a declining standard of living without the "safety valve" of out-of-state sale to enforce discipline and relieve overcrowding. (Nothing better illustrates the narrow outlook of many slaveholders than their argument that restrictionists would be to blame if slaves should "perish of hunger and want" in the depleted states of the Upper South!)[46] Finally, it seems unreasonable to discount the possibility of a lingering real humanitarian concern contained within the disclosure of ethical weakness: Virginians and other Upper South slaveholders may have believed that their slaves would have a better chance for emancipation if owned by someone else or removed to a jurisdiction where slavery was less entrenched.

In the previous chapter we saw how a well-established antislavery position, bolstered by the authority of moral philosophy and the Scottish common-sense tradition, had begun to erode under the pressure of slavery's vaulting profitability. Americans showed little desire to lance the boil of the slavery issue, while demonstrating a remarkable talent for equivocation. Illinois's de facto retention of slavery under coercive laws regarding indentured servitude may stand as a case in point, as may, perhaps, the entire colonization experiment.

But Tallmadge brought the question of the expansion of slavery in the territories to a head. Without his amendment, the polite evasion of the issue might have continued virtually indefinitely, with slavery gaining ground gradually enough to fail to provoke alarm.[47] Three days of tumultuous debate in Congress laid bare the contradiction at the heart of American democracy. "The paradox—the very complicated and difficult paradox—that slavery could have a legal existence in a land of free men was now . . . fully open to inspection," George Dangerfield observed, adding: "It would be too much to say that the country as a whole was willing to inspect it; the country as a whole was willing only to be surprised by it."[48]

Dangerfield's finely nuanced observation is correct, but the seed of self-doubt had been planted. The conduct of Virginia, in particular, shook Americans' complacency over slavery. No state had contributed more to the ideas of the Revolution; no state's leaders had more eloquently presented the thesis of freedom. Now, Virginians, with much the same ardor and determination they had shown then, defended its antithesis.[49] Just as the *Edinburgh Review*'s most telling attacks on slavery had consisted of quotations from Thomas Jefferson, thoughtful Americans recognized that a rejection by Virginians of the doctrine of antislavery called into question the validity of the American experiment. Yet, as we shall see, this crisis of national identity also opened the door to a still more sophisticated form of equivocation: the drawing of a sharp dichotomy between America and the South.

The Missouri controversy of 1819 was not the first time that slavery had come under shrill attack in Congress. However, as Don E. Fehrenbacher has noted, "The principal antislavery voices in national politics during the first decades of the nineteenth century were certain Northern Federalists—men no doubt motivated in part by moral imperatives but also fully aware that they were probing a weak spot in the armor of the enemy."[50] Thus southerners had been able largely to discount these earlier attacks on slavery as politically and sectionally motivated.

Such rationalization proved impossible during the Missouri debate. This time, Republican congressmen from traditional southern allies, the middle Atlantic states of New York and Pennsylvania, took the lead in restricting slavery. Even the Republican representative from Delaware, a slaveholding state that considered itself "northern," backed restriction (although Delaware's three Federalist congressmen opposed it). The message of this development was clear to southern leaders: in the absence of partisan conflict, where northern politicians had need of southern support, the South had no real allies in its defense of slavery. For many slaveholders, no subsequent developments or allegiances could ever efface this fundamental recognition.

Not surprisingly, other important developments related to slavery in the Fifteenth Congress were largely overlooked by the public—and by future historians. In particular, an "Act in addition to the acts prohibiting the Slave Trade," passed on the final day of the session, gave sweeping power to the president to employ the navy to suppress the slave trade, to seize slave ships, and to appoint agents in Africa to receive receptive Africans, in addition to establishing substantial bounties for each African rescued. On the day following passage of the bill, President Monroe welcomed a delegation from the American Colonization Society to the Executive Mansion. The meeting likely covered implementation of the new bill, and the opportunities for expanding support for colonization during Monroe's pending trip through the South.

The following Saturday, the Supreme Court issued a ruling with profound implications for colonization and for other potential federal undertakings. The *McCulloch v. Maryland* decision upheld the constitutionality of the Second Bank of the United States, and by extension authorized other sweeping, large-scale federal programs intended to implement broad constitutional objectives, such as internal improvement, resettlement, or even compensated emancipation. This was the kind of expansion of federal power, emanating from a familiar source—the Marshall Court—to which southern Old Republicans were sensitively attuned, and they lost no time in denouncing it. The threat posed by the Tallmadge Amendment took somewhat longer to register.

In the early stages of the Missouri controversy, few outside of Congress had any inkling of its significance. Indeed, even the senators did not at first recognize what had happened.[51] The rest of the country, unsurprisingly, took still longer to catch on. The *Charleston Courier* first reported the Tallmadge Amendment on February 24, without editorial comment. The principal New England Federalist paper, Boston's *Columbian Centinel*, barely touched on the issue during the spring and summer of 1819, giving more space to the Seminole War and the national bank. The organ of New York's Bucktail faction, the *Albany Argus*, also maintained a studied silence on the restriction, focusing instead on state and local politics. Thomas Ritchie's

Richmond Enquirer, the semi-official voice of Jeffersonian republicanism, denounced the Tallmadge Amendment, describing the Missouri debate as a "struggle of Eastern prejudice against southern principles,"[52] but many of his readers regarded the question more complacently. According to Harry Ammons, "Even the Virginia state leaders, ever hypersensitive to measures either impairing Southern interests or infringing on the rights of the states, gave little heed to the [Missouri] subject. . . . As late as December 1819, Spencer Roane, the most powerful Virginia defender of States' Rights, still gave priority to the bank issue, which was a matter of 'principle,' whereas the Missouri question was but a 'particular measure.'"[53]

One notable exception to this general lack of fervor over Missouri was the *New-York Daily Advertiser*, edited by antislavery Federalist Theodore Dwight. Determined to mobilize northern public opinion to push for slavery restriction, the *Advertiser* weighed in early in the controversy with exclusive reports provided by one or more prorestrictionist congressmen.[54] Almost alone among northern editors, Dwight grasped the full political impact of the Missouri question from the outset. A veteran of sectional battles since the 1780s, and more recently the secretary of the notorious Hartford Convention, Dwight saw the Missouri controversy as a critical danger to the antislavery North—and at the same time as an opportunity to recover lost political, and moral, ground. According to Dwight's *Advertiser*, no issue had ever come before Congress "*in which the states where slavery does not exist . . . have so vital an interest.*" The survival of the North depended on the future of the West: "if . . . the SIN OF SLAVERY be fastened . . . upon that boundless region which the United States possesses beyond the Mississippi, THE DEATH-WARRANT OF THE POLITICAL STANDING AND INFLUENCE OF THE FREE STATES WILL IRREVOCABLY BE SEALED."[55]

At about the same time, New York senator Rufus King, a framer of the Constitution who, as the Federalist presidential nominee in 1816, was in some measure the standard-bearer of the party, wrote to his brother William, a member of the Massachusetts Senate from Maine. "I think it wd. be well," King suggested, "to instruct yr Senators, to vote agt. the admission of slavery in any New State west of the Mississippi, admitted into the Union—!"[56] In other northern states, the impact of the Missouri issue was beginning to make itself felt as well. Ephraim Bateman, a Republican congressman from New Jersey, informed his constituents: "As the decision in the case of Missouri will probably be a decision for the whole range of country west of the Mississippi, I cannot but consider it as a question of the greatest magnitude to the interest of humanity that was ever debated in the Congress of the United States." Bateman implicitly called for popular agitation, advising that "as the subject will no doubt come up again at the next session, it is desirable that the public sentiment respecting it, should in the mean time be freely expressed."[57] On July 20, the *Cleveland Register* reprinted an article from Charleston about the horrible torture and murder of a slave, remarking: "And yet these are the 'rights' that the citizens of Missouri so clamorously contend for, and which they disclaim against congress for unjustly depriving them of[.] Such is the infatuation and avarice of man; but, we believe, there is not a disinterested individual (and we might add, many that are interested) that does not sincerely deplore the existence of slavery in the U. States, and wish, if practicable, its speedy termination."[58] Such sentiments were not limited to northern publications. Hezekiah Niles, a Baltimore publisher whose *Weekly Register* commanded a larger readership than any other national journal, authored an important six-part series titled "Mitigation of Slavery" that appeared between May and August. It commenced with the proposition "That slavery must, at some future day, be abolished in the United States. There is no man who believes that GOD is just, or affects a veneration for our republican institutions, that can bear the assurance to his own mind, that this blot, or curse, is to remain as long as our country endures." Niles asserted that while there was room for debate as to whether Congress had the *authority* to restrict the expansion of slavery, he saw no room for doubt about the *justice* of such a step.[59]

Meanwhile, the Philadelphia editor Robert Walsh published a closely-argued, 505-page tract titled *An Appeal from the Judgments of Great Britain respecting the United States of America.*[60] This work, a massive response to the criticisms of American institutions leveled by the British reviewers, included a point-by-point rebuttal of the attacks on slavery in the *Edinburgh Review,* which won for it the warm approval of numerous southerners—including Thomas Jefferson, whose personal integrity and consistency the British journals had directly called into question.[61] In frequently quoted passages, Walsh offered the definitive exposition of the theme that England bore responsibility for the introduction and perpetuation of American slavery, adding a devastating indictment of Britain's continuing engagement in the brutal institution. He also elaborated one of the earliest polemics comparing the conditions of American slaves with those of British manufacturing laborers, later a staple of proslavery rhetoric. Many slaveholding admirers of Walsh's "*vindicia Americana*" overlooked his final, crucial point, however: "While a really practicable plan of abolition remains undiscovered . . . ; and while the general conduct of the Americans is *such only as necessarily results from their situation*, they are not to be arraigned for this institution." Walsh's defense of American slavery rested on the assumption that no measures would be taken to exacerbate it. If the nation permitted the expansion of slavery into territories where it had not previously existed rather than restricting it and placing it on a course of extinction, America would assume the guilt which it did not currently bear and would merit the condemnation of the world.[62] Read carefully—which it rarely was—Walsh's *Appeal* contained one of the most powerful arguments offered for slavery restriction.

Throughout the North, those congressmen who had opposed the Tallmadge Amendment increasingly found their vote a political liability. In New Hampshire, a Republican party leader irritably informed Senator John Fabyan Parrott, who had voted against the Tallmadge Amendment as a representative, that the party ticket would run well, "but for the *slave vote*."[63] Some northern congressmen, such as Senators Otis of Massachusetts and Daggett of Connecticut publicly repudiated their votes against restriction (although privately continuing to harbor doubts), while others, such as Massachusetts Federalist congressman Henry Shaw, offered well-publicized defenses to their constituents.[64] While nationally circulated newspapers kept the controversy simmering over the spring and summer by printing the speeches delivered on the issue the previous winter, contradictory and often disturbing reports emanated from Missouri about conduct of the slavery debate. Although the *St. Louis Enquirer* asserted that "no *citizen*" in St. Louis would "support" the contention that Missourians were "divided in their opinion" that Congress had no right to restrict slavery, the paper acknowledged that there might be "many" who opposed slavery "in principle." Indeed, it appears that many Missourians signed petitions against the institution.[65] A German traveler who visited St. Louis on July 27 wrote that "everywhere much is being written now concerning the possibility of getting rid of slavery as an acknowledged evil in the entire compass of the free states, so that people in general actually entertain the hope of seeing even the southern states soon freed from this plague." Perhaps because of the strength of the challenge, proslavery Missourians felt it necessary to mount a public relations offensive, employing the authority of "a very able and ingenius [*sic*] article" from a Pennsylvania newspaper that came perilously close to an open defense of slavery, arguing "(1) that 'the holding of slaves is defencible by the law of nature;' (2) that 'slavery is so by the law of God;' (3) that 'slavery is so by the municipal laws of the great majority of the civilized nations, ancient and modern;' (4) that 'slaves are property;' (5) that 'negroes have no right to object to negro slavery;'

(6) that 'Congress has not the *right* to prohibit slavery in the Missouri territory;' (7) that 'under present circumstances it is not *expedient* to prohibit it.'" The author of the article claimed to be "no friend to slavery"—simultaneously demonstrating the ubiquity, and the frequent meaninglessness, of antislavery pronouncements.[66]

The historian of Missouri's struggle for statehood has offered a convincing picture of the territory's residents' attitude toward slavery:

> As a general proposition it may be stated that throughout the territory slavery as an institution was deprecated and was regarded as a great evil, even as a curse. This attitude of the inhabitants of Missouri towards the institution did not, as one might logically conclude, carry with it a desire for either emancipation or restriction. It was a position that was reflected in many of the speeches of even the Southern members of Congress, who at the same time strove hard to prevent restrictions being placed on slavery. They were willing, in most cases, to waive the moral issue since the ark of the Constitution was deemed strong enough to repel any attack along this line. History and law favored slavery; these combined with the political and economic strength of that institution were so powerful as to overcome the moral opposition to it.[67]

Slaveholding Missourians were not willing to trust the defense of their property exclusively to "history and law," however; at least some of them determined to apply violence and intimidation as well. One night in mid-July, a mob of slaveholders beat and whipped one Humphrey Smith, an immigrant from New Jersey who had publicly announced his intention to oppose slavery. According to the Illinois *Spectator*, "The mob declared their intention 'to kill, or drive out of the country,' any man who should open his mouth against slavery." Proslavery settlers successfully employed fear and brutality to enforce the appearance of a "*unanimity* of sentiment" in the territory.[68] The threat of physical violence must be taken into account in any evaluation of Missouri antislavery sentiment—or, for that matter, of antislavery sentiment throughout the South.

About the time that reports of proslavery atrocities in Missouri began appearing in the northern papers, a number of opponents of slavery, many of them patrician eastern Federalists, embarked on a major campaign to unite the North against the expansion of slavery in the coming session of Congress. On August 30, Elias Boudinot, the aging former president of the Continental Congress, chaired an antislavery meeting in Burlington, New Jersey, that laid the groundwork for further action. Boudinot also drafted a circular letter to other "persons of respectability & importance" in the Northeast stressing the moral urgency of slavery restriction.[69]

During the relative calm between congressional sessions, President Monroe traveled throughout the South on the second phase of his national tour. Newspaper accounts of his visits to various towns and cities paint a portrait of a carefully orchestrated campaign with distinctly emphasized themes—central among these, national unity and support for the American Colonization Society. Among the toasts delivered at a dinner for Monroe in Athens, Georgia, were these: "The Colonization Society.—Planned by the wisest heads and purest hearts. May it eventuate in the happiness of millions." "The Slave Trade.—The Scourge of Africa; the disgrace of humanity. May it cease for ever, and may the voice of peace, of christianity, and of civilization, be heard on the savage shores."[70]

One stop on the president's itinerary, Tennessee's Brainerd Cherokee Mission School, impressed him enough to extend his stay there for an additional day. The Cherokee youths' educational attainments "much pleased" and impressed Monroe, and he warmly congratulated the tribe's venerable Indian agent, Return J. Meigs, the legendary soldier, statesman and diplomat (also the father of Monroe's postmaster general). The school's rustic log cabin dormitories struck the president as "not good enough," however, and he instructed the Brainerd missionaries to construct "good two-story house[s], with brick or stone chimneys, glass windows, &c . . . at the public expense"—a striking apparent departure from his much-touted strict constructionism.[71]

The campaign for restriction heated up as the opening session of the Sixteenth Congress drew near. By October, Elias Boudinot's circulars, the *New-York Advertiser*'s editorials, and Rufus King's quiet but intense lobbying had begun to bear fruit. Although Republicans had taken the lead during the Missouri debates of the previous winter, it appeared that, outside of Congress, Federalists more quickly grasped the issues at stake for the North and generally took the lead in organizing public sentiment around the country, although they were careful to involve prominent Republicans in every antislavery event. On October 29, citizens of Trenton assembled to pass resolutions opposing the extension of slavery in a meeting chaired by Jesse Upson, Republican vice president of the Legislative Council, at which William Griffith, a former Federalist judge who was one of President Adams's "midnight appointments" (and Boudinot's former law student), served as secretary. A speech at this meeting by Joseph Hopkinson, another prominent Federalist lawyer, "rivetted the attention of every auditor."[72] The meeting appointed a committee made up of both Republicans and Federalists to implement the resolutions it adopted. A series of bipartisan county meetings followed.[73]

At this point the center of activity shifted to New York, where organizers held a planning meeting on November 6 to prepare for a major public demonstration ten days later. On November 13, Theodore Dwight's *New-York Daily Advertiser* employed block capitals to alert its readers to the importance of the issue: "THIS QUESTION INVOLVES NOT ONLY THE FUTURE CHARACTER OF OUR NATION, BUT THE FUTURE WEIGHT AND INFLUENCE OF THE FREE STATES. IF NOW LOST—IT IS LOST FOREVER."[74] The advance work paid off. More than 2,000 New Yorkers assembled in the City Hotel to adopt resolutions against the expansion of slavery and, reminiscent of the Revolution, to form Committees of Correspondence with other states. The meeting also called on Rufus King to publish the substance of his speeches in the previous session of the Senate in favor of restriction. These became the principal organizing tool for rallying northerners against the expansion of slavery and southern influence.[75]

By this time, not only southerners but also northerners who relied on the South for their livelihood or political fortunes began to grow alarmed. The *Franklin Gazette* of Philadelphia, an ultra Republican paper with ties to the state's extensive manufacturing interests, reported the New York proceedings "with profound regret. . . . The worthy men, who are at the bottom of them, know not what mischief may result from them. The creation of geographical parties in our country, is one of the least of the evils we apprehend from a further agitation of this question, in the spirit in which it has commenced."[76]

Within days, the *Gazette* had a Philadelphia rally to report, chaired by Jared Ingersoll and with Robert Ralston as secretary. The following week witnessed meetings in West Chester and Lancaster—which named James Buchanan, the future prosouthern president, to the Committee of Correspondence.

Massachusetts, the cradle of New England sectionalism and recent hotbed of antisouthern agitation, came late to the cause of restriction. The cause of this apparently surprising tardiness is not hard to deduce. State Federalist leaders, chastened by national outrage at their near-treasonous resistance to the War of 1812 and loath to make the same mistake again, bent over backward to avoid the appearance of disloyalty or sectional prejudice. On November 8, Rufus King dined in Boston with Massachusetts leaders Daniel Webster, William Tudor, Jeremiah Mason, and Judge Joseph Story and lamented "the total indifference which reigned" there on the Missouri question, "the most important one that had been discussed since the adoption of the constitution." The seed King planted began to take root. Tudor "conversed with a few of our leading people and got them slowly to assent to an effort to excite public opinion; engaged some young men to write; if we had a town meeting Webster agreed to speak." Shortly thereafter, the growing momentum for restriction "produced a meeting of several gentlemen" to organize a mass meeting for December 3.[77] Within a short time, the Boston establishment seemed firmly on board the restrictionist bandwagon, and even a crusty conservative such as Harrison Gray Otis felt exhilarated to be campaigning, for a change, on what looked like the winning side of history: "I feel as if I had been working hard again for my old friends and old principles. . . . I have the satisfaction of feeling well upon the occasion, & that is about as much of a reward as any federalist in our Country is entitled to expect."[78]

As the first session of the Sixteenth Congress approached, antislavery activity in the northern states continued unabated. On December 2—the day before mass meetings on the Missouri question in Boston and Hartford—the *Richmond Enquirer* reported on the publication of Rufus King's "Observations on the Exclusion of Slavery from the State of Missouri" and the *New York Evening Post*'s views concerning the essay. "This spirit is likely to spread over the Eastern States," the *Enquirer* mournfully predicted: "Public meetings will be held and legislative resolutions will probably be passed. But in the slave-holding states, not one meeting, not one resolution."[79] Mass meetings continued and northern state legislatures addressed the issue. On December 16, asserting that "upon this topic there is but one opinion in Pennsylvania," the state legislature unanimously adopted a resolution instructing its senators and representatives "to vote against the admission of any territory as a state into the Union," unless the territory adopted the language of the Tallmadge Amendment. Defenders of Missouri's unrestricted admission "propose[d] to spread the crimes and cruelties of slavery from the banks of the Mississippi to the shores of the Pacific," the preamble to the Pennsylvania resolution stated. "When a measure of this character is seriously advocated in the republican congress of America, in the nineteenth century, the several states are invoked . . . to protest against its adoption, to refuse to covenant with crime, and to limit the range of an evil that already hangs on awful boding over so large a portion of the Union." No other state could enter such a protest "with greater propriety" than Pennsylvania, the lawmakers asserted, noting that "this commonwealth has as sacredly respected the rights of other states as it has been careful of its own."[80]

Lawmakers in both the North and the South well understood the meaning of this remark. Protests against slavery from New England might irritate slaveholders, but could not alarm; Pennsylvania was different. Notwithstanding her Quaker heritage and a long tradition of opposition to slavery, including the first gradual emancipation act of any legislative body, the state had deep economic and political ties to the South.[81] Her representatives had backed the three-fifths clause and the fugitive slave act, and had guaranteed the right of slaveholders to sojourn with their slaves. In the opinion of Rufus King, "Up to this hour [Pennsylvania] has been the faithful and steady and almost unpaid ally of the slave States and with her help and our divisions, they have ruled the nation."[82] The state's unsettled political situation, including the complete breakdown of party regularity, facilitated a vote in which old allegiances played no role, and it suggested to southerners the ominous conclusion that, absent the discipline of strong national political leadership with southern direction, even the publics of the middle states would overwhelmingly support antislavery measures.

In confirmation of this proposition, the South faced more unsettling desertions over the next several weeks, as the legislatures of New York, New Jersey, and Delaware, with no recorded dissent, instructed their congressional representatives to bar the entry of any further slave states. "Whatever may be the public feeling *south* of the Potomac," intoned Isaac Hill, stalwart Republican editor of the *New Hampshire Patriot*, "there is but one sentiment *north* of the Chesapeake on this subject—and that is, if the evil which already exists cannot be prevented, at least that slavery shall not be permitted to spread beyond its present confines."[83] Never had the North appeared so unified, nor the South so destitute of allies.

It would have been folly to imagine that this great upsurge of antislavery sentiment could advance unchallenged. By late autumn, astute observers in the middle Atlantic region had begun to detect a quiet effort to squelch the restriction movement. The Missouri agitation "seems to have run like a flaming fire thro our middle states," Elias Boudinot reported to his nephew on November 27, "and causes great anxiety. It is whispered about by the knowing ones, that there is a wheel within a wheel and that there is some bargaining taking place between the East & Southern Interests. I know not how this is," Boudinot continued, "but this I can pretty clearly guess at, that if it should take place there is an End to the happiness of the united States."[84]

Boudinot's warning of "bargaining" over Missouri at this early stage in the controversy is intriguing and deserves to be credited, although details are lacking. What is clear is that a coordinated antirestrictionist response had begun to take shape. In November, a series of articles by "An American" in the *National Intelligencer*, often viewed as the Monroe administration's mouthpiece, staked out what was clearly intended to represent the Virginian position on slavery. Although entitled "To the Edinburgh Reviewers," the essays were intended, of course, to influence the reviewers' American readers. The author began with the standard assertion that the British were in no position to criticize slavery as "the great curse of America," since they had introduced it into the colonies. Americans had been the first to oppose the inhuman slave trade. Moreover, he argued, the presence in the middle states of abolition societies and in the South of colonization societies proved that "the evil which you . . . denounce is not viewed with indifference here."[85]

Having addressed the points of the British reviewers to his satisfaction, "An American" proceeded to address American colonizationists in a long and extraordinary footnote, entreating them to "examine attentively . . . the history of all the humane schemes that have been projected, from the era of Peter the Hermit down to Mr. Wilberforce and the present day," and ask whether they had not almost always either failed, created new mischiefs, or increased the evil they were intended to relieve. Colonizationists should consider whether "the distinction which they are perpetually bringing into view, between the slave-holding states and the other states, is not calculated to weaken the bond of union among them, and . . . to impair the very source of our national strength and prosperity." They should further consider whether the exclusion of Missouri from an equality of rights with the other states might not be imputable to the "puritanical" spirit that "such societies are calculated to cherish and promote." With almost palpable anger, the writer came to his central point, denouncing "the ecclesiastical members of these societies, who, instead of confining themselves to their ministerial functions at home, go about seeking, by their activity and zeal in public missions and agencies, a crown of worldly glory," and suggesting that these ministers should stick to their formal religious duties, rather than embroiling themselves in "secular concerns." Rhetorically the writer asked, "What has been, *invariably*, the condition of mankind when they have had the direction of affairs? . . . My advice to them, offered in all humility, is, 'touch not, taste not, handle not.'"[86]

In the second article, the author dispensed entirely with platitudes about southern benevolent societies and opposition to the slave trade, flatly asserting that it was currently beyond "the power of human wisdom, to devise a plan for the gradual abolition of slavery which does not require for its completion a degree of virtue, philosophy, and moderation, among both whites and blacks, which it would be folly to anticipate. . . . There is, indeed, no plan that can be devised, which will not bring, even upon those intended to be relieved, incalculable suffering." This was strong language, embracing southern amelioration schemes as well as northern interference and taking a far more "advanced position," to use the emerging jargon of proslavery rhetoric, than the vast majority of southern political leaders did. Momentarily the author appeared to retreat to a more orthodox, long-range gradualist antislavery position: "The question, therefore, must be referred to time." But for "An American," the appeal "to time" only confirmed a sweeping, comprehensive denial of the human capacity for change:

> There are moral as well as physical evils in this world, which no human agency can remove. You cannot wash the Ethiop white, nor can you impart to him the active intelligence of homo sapiens Europæus; and, in defiance of all the benevolent Societies of Europe and America, Africa will continue for ever to be what it has been for nearly six thousand years—the residence of slavery and barbarism. Asia has been, through all past time, and will always continue to be, a vast theatre of despotism, ignorance, and superstition. The Arab of the desert now, is the Arab of the desert of the most ancient days to which our histories ascend. And whatever the speculations of agents and missionaries may suggest, the red man will for ever be a savage, if left to himself, and utterly stupid and worthless, when brought within the limits, and subjected to the restraints, of civilized society.[87]

It would be hard to find a more comprehensive repudiation of the spirit of the age—a spirit fired, in large part, by the American Revolution and inseparable, until now, from American self-understanding.

A number of features of the argument are particularly interesting. The first is the author's shrewd rhetorical device of linking the scriptural metaphor of the Ethiop's skin to the assertion, couched in quasi-scientific taxonomic jargon ("homo sapiens Europæus") of European intellectual superiority. Intriguingly, the author cannot unilaterally dismiss *Africans* from historical consideration; to do so he must reject the entire Enlightenment doctrine of environmentalism and additionally condemn all non-Europeans—including Jefferson's admired Native Americans—to unchanging misery and stasis. Indeed, his assertion of the immutability of slavery entails, in addition to a willful historical amnesia about Africa, a virtual repudiation of human progress; a rejection of "all humane schemes that have ever been projected." As a finishing touch—a further radical deviation from standard Virginia doctrine—"An American" includes the abolition of the slave trade in the list of failed "humane schemes"; it is now being conducted "with circumstances of more aggravated cruelty, with a more terrible devastation of human life, than were ever known before the period of Mr. Wilberforce's humane interposition." This may have been true, and it had been suggested by others, but as an argument against *slavery*, not against abolition of the trade. "Mr. W. may weep, and Humanity will weep with him," the author concluded, subtly and provocatively changing the subject to bloody slave revolts, "but he must weep still more when he casts his eyes on the island of Barbadoes, and recollects the awful catastrophe of St. Domingo."[88] One might conceivably expect such dyspeptic and mean-spirited reflections from a high Tory, Filmerian restoration divine—but not from an enlightened Jeffersonian Republican.

Articles appearing under the pen-name "PHOCION" and widely circulated in the Pennsylvania and Upper South press recommended the letters of "An American" to the eastern public, and hinted at possible southern retaliation for antislavery activity.[89] "The consequences of the spirit manifested by the northern states, in intermeddling with what they ought to know, cannot be remedied . . . begin to manifest themselves in the southward. Already the southern states begin to regard the question of *manufactures* in the manner suggested by their local interests!"[90] Ultimately, indeed, a southern attack on tariffs and other measures to protect manufactures was to be one of the "consequences" of northern antislavery mobilization; but other opportunities emerged as well. The problem southern leaders faced in the Sixteenth Congress was straightforward: how to secure the handful of northern votes in the House of Representatives necessary to overturn the Tallmadge Amendment. One of the most promising places to look for votes came from an unlikely source: the northeasternmost corner of the Union.

While the Missouri issue heated up over the summer and fall of 1819, lawmakers in Massachusetts's District of Maine met in Portland to draw up a state constitution. For decades, and particularly since the War of 1812, the district's largely Republican population had chafed under the yoke of Federalist Massachusetts; after a prolonged legislative dispute, the state had given its consent for Maine's separation, provided that Congress pass a bill admitting it as a state before March 4, 1820.[91] William King, Rufus's Republican brother, served as president of the constitutional convention. Delegate John Holmes, like King, an ex-Federalist-turned-Republican and one of Maine's seven congressmen in the Massachusetts delegation, pushed hard for an inclusive constitutional convention in which "not only every part of the District, but every class of society," had representation. He extended this democratic principle to the question of suffrage in the new state, eloquently opposing a proposal to exclude blacks from the vote: "I know of no difference between the rights of the negro and the rights of the white man; God Almighty has made none; our [Massachusetts] declaration of rights has made none. That declares that 'all men (without regard to color) are born equally free and independent.'"[92]

Holmes's lofty principles were soon to be tested. At the beginning of the first session of the Sixteenth Congress, Holmes duly notified the House that Maine had completed all of the requirements necessary to be admitted as a state, and a bill for its admission was placed on the calendar. It was postponed, postponed again, and postponed yet again, for a variety of vague technical reasons.[93] At last, on December 21, a bill for the admission of Maine to the Union was presented to the House. On the same day, the Maine Republican organ, the *Argus*, guardedly came out in favor of admitting Missouri with slavery, endorsing the "diffusion argument" that slaves would be happier and better treated if spread over a greater area.[94] This may have been a signal of events to come. Within a week, Mark L. Hill, one of Maine's congressmen, wrote to William King urgently summoning him to Washington: Maine statehood was in deep trouble.[95]

Two days later, when Holmes reported a bill for the admission of Maine to the Committee of the Whole, Henry Clay announced that "he was not yet prepared for this question." Although he was not opposed to Maine's admission, "he wished to know the extent of the principles which gentlemen meant to defend" in attaching conditions to new states. He reminded his colleague that Kentucky's admission to the Union had been delayed for a year and a half, "until Vermont was ready," the two states coming in together. He intended, in other words, to hold Maine's admission hostage to the admission of Missouri.[96]

Representative Holmes professed surprise and outrage at this move. Maine had struggled for twenty years to gain its independence from Massachusetts; the terms of its separation agreement required that Congress admit Maine by March 3, 1820, or "the whole proceeding which had taken place was void, and the question would be referred back to Massachusetts. . . . Will anyone say we ought not to be admitted into the Union?" Holmes demanded. "We are answered, yes; and that, unless we will agree to admit Missouri into the Union unconditionally, we ought not be admitted! I hope the doctrine did not extend quite as far as that. [Mr. CLAY here said, in an undertone, yes it did.]"

The questions of Maine and Missouri were "wholly unconnected," Holmes protested; and if he were not personally opposed to the proposed slavery restriction on Missouri (a rather disingenuously inserted "if"), "I should forfeit the chance of Maine rather than forfeit my opinion."[97]

By tying the admission of Maine to that of Missouri, antirestrictionist leaders adopted a high-stakes strategy. In embracing a policy frankly based on political blackmail rather than principle, they risked alienating even those northern congressmen opposed to slavery restriction. The admission of Alabama as a state on December 14 decreased the danger somewhat, as it added two southern votes to bolster the antirestrictionist majority in the Senate; but the move seemed certain to stiffen the resolve of an already adamant House.

It was a risk antirestrictionists were willing to take. To understand why, we must consider the makeup of the antirestriction coalition. Traditionally, historians have searched for the motives of the advocates of restriction, rather than for those of their antirestrictionist opponents. In this, they are following the lead of Republican contemporaries and two generations of Compromise supporters, whose version of events Glover Moore accepted without challenge and handed down as historical fact. Unquestionably, purely political considerations played a role in the actions of some restrictionists, particularly Federalists who saw in the Missouri issue a chance to recoup their faded fortunes, just as tradition has it. As we have seen, however, northern Republicans took the lead in the restriction movement, with the solid backing of their constituents, and often under considerable pressure from them. Those who opposed restriction had the harder case to make. Once we recognize the serious political difficulty of their position, we are in a much better position to investigate the dynamics of the Missouri Controversy, and the question of how antirestrictionists mobilized the political forces necessary to defeat the Tallmadge Amendment takes center stage.

Such a reconsideration must begin with the role of James Monroe. As his biographer, Harry Ammon, notes,

Historians have usually portrayed Monroe as an ineffective and indecisive figure during the Missouri crisis, in which he shrank from assuming the leadership needed to save the nation from impending disaster. . . . However, within the limitations imposed upon the executive in the early nineteenth century both by tradition and Republican theory, there was little that he could do. Indeed, open pressure on his part would have set up a cry of executive interference and driven many moderates to adopt extreme positions in order to prove their independence. In order to exert an effective influence the President had to remain behind the scenes, allowing others to function as his spokesmen and permitting them to affirm his support, whenever such endorsement could serve a useful purpose. As deeply concerned as he was during the Missouri debates, Monroe kept his activities on behalf of a compromise deeply veiled.[98]

More than "tradition and Republican theory" constrained Monroe to keep his role in the Missouri negotiations out of sight; personal political necessity dictated it. The hysteria shown by southern congressmen during the initial Tallmadge Amendment debate alerted Monroe and his political associates that they were vulnerable to attack from the South because of their broadly national stance; they could hardly allow themselves to appear flexible in the defense of slavery. Virginia posed a particular problem for the president. His ties to the dominant Richmond Junto had never been strong, and his rise in popularity among Federalists and nationalists in New England and the West had proportionately diminished his standing among states' rights leaders in Virginia. Old Republicans such as Spencer Roane and John Taylor of Caroline had already nearly given up on Monroe because of his support for the Bank of the United States, and Richmond Junto leader Thomas Ritchie had ominously invoked the Kentucky and Virginia Resolves of 1798 as "the law and the prophets" concerning the bank question.[99] Monroe's support of Marshall's decision in *McCulloch v. Maryland* appeared to these extreme states' rights men as a serious affront to liberty, virtually as political apostasy and an endorsement of Federal despotism. Had the Virginia Old Republicans suspected Monroe's ardent support for internal improvements, to say nothing of his designs against slavery, their outrage would have been volcanic.

In this atmosphere, the Missouri question seems to have appeared to Monroe as an opportunity, albeit a dangerous one, to recoup some stature in his home state. After angrily observing the president's frequent steps toward "consolidation," Old Republicans viewed with satisfaction and some surprise the way in which Monroe's son-in-law and erstwhile campaign manager George Hay led the charge against restriction in Virginia, evidently with the president's blessing and even assistance. "Mr. Hay is writing for us as you will see in the *Enquirer*; and it is wonderful that he should, after acquiescing in the ground taken by the Supreme Court," noted Spencer Roane. "That acquiescence worked to an estoppel (as the lawyers say) to his objecting to the measure in question."[100]

The apparent author of the plan to tie Missouri to Maine was James Barbour of Virginia, Monroe's closest collaborator in the Senate, and the strategy initially had the president's blessing. This, too, represented the kind of standing up to the "Eastern people" that Monroe's wary followers expected and demanded. At the same time, the unflappable chief executive remained confident that a solution to the crisis would be forthcoming. As early as January 8, the president informed his secretary of state, John Quincy Adams, of his conviction that a compromise would be found; a few days later, in a letter to Hay, he spelled out the essential features of the plan to propose a geographic dividing line between free and slave states. "This statement, which was made a month before the compromise was introduced in the Senate, indicates the close contact between the President and congressional leaders, for no hint of such a solution had appeared in the press."[101]

Monroe's reputation as an unimaginative, hands-off administrator and a rigid strict constructionist, combined with the descent of the Republican Party into faction and intrigue during his second term, has lent credence to the view of Monroe as a mediocre leader. A recent historian has asserted that "Monroe possessed but few carrots and proved reluctant to use them, as in the case of patronage."[102] Glover Moore dismissed evidence of Monroe's employment of presidential patronage to press for acceptance of a compromise on Missouri with the rather contemptuous assertion that "the President was too undecided in his own mind about Missouri to bring pressure to bear on anybody else." Such assertions are chiefly valuable, as we shall see, as evidence of Monroe's success in concealing his fingerprints.[103]

On the question of opposing slavery restriction, the Virginians brooked no compromise and apparently assumed that Monroe felt the same way. This prickly southern position convinced the administration that it would be safer to pressure northerners, even at the expense of alienating them. Presumably Monroe felt that he could rely on Republican party discipline in the North to enforce a policy that he sincerely believed to be in the nation's best interest, and to swallow a concession to the South in exchange for that region's acquiescence in policies crucial to northern interests on finance, tariffs, and federally funded internal improvements.

This assumption proved a serious miscalculation. Northern opposition to slavery extension continued to mount, and even the most doctrinaire northern Republicans were furious at what they viewed as indefensible southern extremism. Isaac Hill's *New Hampshire Patriot* published an anguished letter by a Republican congressman from New Hampshire shocked by southern insistence on permitting the expansion of slavery: "On such a question, one would think there could be no difference of opinion. To me indeed it was something new to hear slavery justified and defended." Archly noting that some northern representatives, "from constitutional scruples, or from other motives," were willing to admit Missouri without a restriction on slavery, the congressman expressed satisfaction that New Hampshire's

House delegation, at least, would be united on the question.[104] On Christmas Eve, Hill himself put the issue in even starker terms (employing language nearly identical, it should be noted, to the admonition to Americans in the *Edinburgh Review*): "The step which shall be taken by the present Congress will mark an era in the history of *Slavery in the United States*—it will determine whether as a nation, we will tolerate an evil which *can* be remedied, or whether we will wipe away the foulest stain on our national character."[105]

Even perennially popular northern congressmen such as New Hampshire's John F. Parrott, Pennsylvania's Henry Baldwin, and New Jersey's former governor and Revolutionary War general Joseph Bloomfield, sustained withering criticism from their constituents for their prosouthern stance.[106] Still more significantly, hostility to slavery remained undiminished in Maine, the southerners' chief target, in defiance of the threat posed to the statehood movement. Writing on New Year's Day of his meeting with Monroe, James Barbour, and other eminent politicos, John Holmes breezily advised William King that "Governor Barbour and several others thought it would be best that the *Mother* should have *twins this time.*"[107] Holmes was quickly able to convert his colleague Mark Hill to the cause of Missouri's unrestricted admission, probably by convincing him that his constituents would hold him responsible if Maine's decade-long bid for statehood failed. Conversations with other members of the Maine delegation soon apprised Hill, to his chagrin, that Maine's citizens considered the move to extend slavery an outrage and that he and Holmes were alone in supporting it.[108]

Squeezed between his pro-Missouri stance and an angry antislavery firestorm at home, Hill wrote somewhat desperately on January 3 to King (who had failed to heed Hill's call to come to Washington) to ask whether he and Holmes were "to be mobbed, blackguarded and villified on their return" for choosing the "positive good" of statehood for Maine rather than "quarrel[ing] about doubtful rights," "or will our constituents come out and support us in this trying dilemma?" Above all, Hill instructed, King should not try to take any action regarding the Missouri linkage in the convention (which was scheduled to reconvene to ratify the constitution), "but do it through the medium of a committee." On the sixth Hill wrote again, urging King to pressure Maine members to vote en bloc against restriction. Among the delegation, only Joshua Cushman was "willing (as it appears) to act prudently, and Mr. Holmes has no difficulty." Otherwise, however, the delegation looked shaky. "Our members must be *written* to and instructed to act together, or the whole thing will have the go by at last, and the thought of it is enough to make one feel desperate." Numbers of Maine congressmen were "fanning the flame" against slavery, Hill reported, "and [they] plainly declare that Maine ought to be sacrificed, rather than flinch from the restriction on Missouri."[109]

Hill was even more isolated than he thought; he was mistaken in his reliance on Cushman. The Kennebec congressman evidently concluded that acting "prudently" in this instance meant denouncing slavery and campaigning against John Holmes for one of Maine's new senate seats. In a circular Cushman distributed privately (but which the Republican Portland *Argus* obtained and printed), he charged that Maine Republican leaders were in collusion with the South and called for northern sectional unity.[110]

Nor was William King entirely willing to serve as a loyal lieutenant to southern interests. In late January, at a meeting in Boston of the Maine delegation to the General Court of Massachusetts, King coauthored the legislators' instructions to their representatives in Congress, urging them "to disentangle our question from the Missouri one." If this proved impossible, they should insist on a provision prohibiting slavery in Maine. "You will in this way represent truely [*sic*] the opinions of an immense majority of the people in our District as well as the best interests of the country."[111]

While this directive preserved a certain artful ambiguity (it did not explicitly reject Maine's statehood with the Missouri linkage, but merely called for an essentially symbolic antislavery clause), it was widely perceived as a repudiation of Holmes's stand.[112] At the same time, Holmes came under withering attack in the northern press and on the floor of Congress. On February 2, Daniel Cook, the fierce new antislavery representative from Illinois, recalled his former admiration for Holmes's services to the nation during the War of 1812, but feared he was

presuming upon the character he then acquired. . . . Yet, sir, I will not say to him, as the Poet said to his once loved mistress, that

> "When I lov'd you, I can't but allow,
> I had many an exquisite minute,
> But the contempt that I feel for you now,
> Has far more luxury in it."

No, sir, it might seem too severe.[113]

On the day of Cook's attack, Barbour reported to Monroe that the southern side had a majority of just one vote on the question of tying the admission of Maine to that of Missouri with slavery. "How far that vote may be relied on in all the conjunctions that may occur, I know not," Monroe cautioned. Northern anger at Maine's being used as a political hostage to slavery threatened to cost antirestrictionists their lock on the Senate, even with the accession of the two new members from Alabama. Monroe thus instructed Barbour to back down and drop the policy of linkage. "This course will put the Southern members on high ground. . . . To give effect to this suggestion you ought to have immediately a meeting of the Southern members and act promptly."[114]

Barbour may have wanted to follow Monroe's instructions, but he did not drop the Maine-Missouri tie. The southerners were in no mood to make concessions. It appeared that Barbour's hardball tactics had deeply alienated the North, and stiffened the position of the South, while failing to shake any pro-Missouri votes loose from Maine. In the meantime, while the debate in Congress intensified nearly to civil war, the Monroe administration and its allies scrambled to marshal every scrap of leverage at their disposal—through politics, patronage, intimidation, appeals to interest and to idealism—to wring sufficient northern votes from the House to pass a compromise measure.

In the midst of the furor, Representative Henry Meigs of New York offered a preamble and resolution breathtaking in its scope:

Whereas slavery in the United States is an evil of great and increasing magnitude; one which merits the greatest efforts of this nation to remedy: Therefore,

Resolved, That a committee be appointed to inquire into the expediency of devoting the public lands as a fund for the purpose of—

1st. Employing a naval force competent to the annihilation of the slave trade.

2d. The emancipation of the slaves in the United States; and

3d. Colonizing them in such way as shall be conducive to their comfort and happiness in Africa, their mother country.[115]

The proposal, quickly tabled, has been almost completely overlooked by historians. It was not overlooked by slaveholders, however. Meigs's resolution offered them a vision at once tantalizing and terrifying, which shaped the South's approach to federal power for more than a generation.

3

∾∾∾

COMPROMISE

ACCORDING TO THE traditional narrative of American political history, the Monroe administration marked the period of the breakdown of Republican Party unity and discipline following the disappearance of the Federalist threat. And yet the winter of 1819–20 witnessed a strange development: the forceful reassertion of Republican Party discipline on both a state and national level. Since popular support in the northern states for the restriction of slavery remained high, northern politicians had strong incentives to oppose the admission of any new states with slavery. Yet Republican leaders had numerous tools at their disposal to ensure compliance with party policy—and it became increasingly evident that the party demanded statehood for Missouri with no slavery restriction.

Less clear were the party's motivations for opposing restriction. While most southerners (and some northerners) rejected congressional limitations on slavery in new states altogether, other Republicans were privately willing to accept slavery in Missouri in exchange for a more general bar to the institution in the western territories—to allow the expansion of slavery in the West in principle, in other words, while excluding it in practice. To carry their point, these antislavery pragmatists, led by James Monroe, had to conceal their objective from uncompromising restrictionists and anti-restrictionists alike, and to work closely with the latter without revealing their ultimate purpose. They accomplished this goal so successfully that only a few contemporaries discovered or suspected their double game, and historians have thus far overlooked their handiwork completely. As this and the subsequent chapter will show, however, Monroe decisively severed his alliances to key antirestrictionists, including Martin Van Buren, immediately after successfully achieving the compromise, and crafted other significant roadblocks to impede the future spread of slavery.

For the present, however, the key objective was to peel off enough northern votes in the House of Representatives to defeat the Tallmadge Amendment. A close reading of state-by-state developments related to the controversy illuminates the multifaceted components of a coordinated and centrally directed campaign that sufficiently undermined northern unity to enable narrow passage of the compromise bill to admit Missouri as a slave state.

Although historians consider the Maine-Missouri linkage the South's principal leverage against the North, antirestrictionists never intended to rely on pressure on Maine alone to secure the votes they needed to defeat the Tallmadge Amendment. Instead, they probed for weaknesses in every northern state's delegation. As it happened, each state had its Achilles' heel.

Although Pennsylvania and New Jersey had first picked up Tallmadge's anti-Missouri banner, both states had long and close southern ties. The near-unanimity of votes in both states' legislatures against extending slavery masked considerable private willingness to cooperate with the South. Specific circumstances in each state encouraged that cooperation. New Jersey's senior senator, James J. Wilson, suffered from a drinking problem so severe that he had virtually ceased to function by 1819; he cast no vote at all on the Tallmadge Amendment, and the following year resigned under pressure from the New Jersey General Assembly. Wilson's replacement, Samuel Southard, harbored antirestrictionist sentiments that may not have been known to most of the legislators who installed him. A close associate of Secretary of War Calhoun, a key supporter of the compromise, Southard played a role in the passage of the final Missouri settlement and may have influenced his father Henry, a member of the House, to vote for it as well.[1]

In Pennsylvania, Republican Party unity had collapsed. For a time the rival factions competed for the antislavery mantle.[2] Ultimately, however, political disorganization worked against the antislavery majority's ability to assert its will. Numerically small but politically and economically important interests such as merchants, manufacturers, and financiers wielded disproportionate influence under the state's unsettled political conditions, and key figures in all three of these groups eventually decided to back Missouri's admission with slavery under the compromise worked out by Republican leaders in Washington. In Pennsylvania as in New Jersey, Calhoun had important allies. The Calhoun-connected faction that eventually emerged triumphant in Pennsylvania politics, George Mifflin Dallas's "Family Party," quietly but rapidly reasserted the state's prosouthern tilt, confirming Philip S. Klein's observation: "Conservatively inclined professional politicians have ever succeeded in supplanting real demagogues or sincere popular leaders as champions of the masses of Pennsylvania. Upon every occasion when vested rights and properties interests have been threatened by a popular upheaval, political leaders have hastened to plant themselves under the popular banner but after their election put the brakes on radical government."[3]

Equally important, Monroe had a valuable ally and confidant in Philadelphia: Nicholas Biddle, then a young lawyer, politician, and litterateur whom the president had recently appointed to the board of the Bank of the United States. In Biddle, Monroe had an astute observer of the Pennsylvania political scene and a loyal appointee with impeccable connections.[4] Biddle's reports to the president proved invaluable in helping him to maneuver effectively in the volatile Pennsylvania political environment.[5]

Another of Monroe's Bank of the United States initiatives may have helped settle the Missouri crisis.[6] In 1819, Monroe and Treasury Secretary William Crawford pressured the bank's directors to remove its inefficient president, William Jones, replacing him with South Carolina's Langdon Cheves.[7] Although Jones, a Pennsylvanian outspoken in his antislavery views, had been willing to step down without controversy as the bank's president, he had expected to stay on as a director; he expressed his outrage in a letter to Pennsylvania senator Jonathan Roberts at the "intriguing" engaged in at the stockholders' meeting by the "friends of Cheves," who sought to remove Jones by spreading erroneous rumors about his "*supposed declining health.*"[8]

At about the same time as these maneuvers in Baltimore, on November 6, Vice President Daniel D. Tompkins arrived in Philadelphia to solicit Cheves for a loan of $75,000 from the Bank of the United States. Tompkins faced severe financial straits after the auditor of New York, citing possible defalcation, refused to pay him the amount authorized by the New York State legislature to reimburse him for purchases he claimed to have made for the defense of the state while he served as governor and commander in chief of the militia during the chaotic days of the War of 1812. Tompkins offered his property and businesses in Staten Island as collateral, although, perhaps recognizing that they would be unlikely, at a time of severe economic depression, to be worth so much, he promised to secure the loan in six months' time with his own note, endorsed by Gilbert L. Thompson, his son-in-law and son of Navy Secretary Smith Thompson.[9] Cheves, one of South Carolina's strongest nationalists and a virulent foe of slavery restriction, must have been gratified to have Tompkins in his debt. Although politically wounded by the defalcation charge and saddled with a deepening drinking problem, the vice president remained one of the most popular political figures in New York. As governor, his most celebrated accomplishment had been securing the passage of the state's emancipation act, so that, despite his ties to the Virginia establishment, his antislavery credentials were unimpeachable. Moreover, his brother Caleb had provided one of the votes for the Tallmadge Amendment in the House of Representatives. Conceivably the vice president might be able to prevail on his elder brother, an unremarkable jurist and Bucktail loyalist, to change his mind when the vote came up again.

On November 8, Tompkins set out from Philadelphia for Washington, his praises trumpeted along the route by the antirestrictionist *Franklin Gazette* and the *Trenton True American*.[10] Although his financial problems and the bottle had kept him from presiding over the Senate for most of the previous session, this term he was deeply engaged. On January 24 he reported to his wife: "I have been tremendously occupied in the Senate where the debate on the question of restricting slavery in Missouri has been debated for 12 days past with great animation and at great length and in the meantime have had much business in the public office."[11] A week later, however, Tompkins left Washington for Albany to stand for governor against De Witt Clinton, having decided, to the dismay of Bucktail leaders, that only by being elected by the people of New York could he recoup his damaged reputation.[12] Tompkins's return route from Washington took him through Baltimore, Philadelphia, Trenton (where the New Jersey legislature was in session and he intended to "spend half a day"), and New York City. Such an itinerary would have given Tompkins an opportunity to brief Republicans, currently holding caucuses, on developing strategy and the "party line" on Missouri, although specific evidence of such briefings is lacking.[13]

Tompkins would have had to employ great discretion in such discussions, since most New Yorkers, like other northerners, advocated restriction—a position reflected in the legislature's unanimous vote on January 17 to instruct the state's congressmen to vote against the admission of any new slave states.[14] "Is it true that [Tompkins] was against any restriction in regard to slavery in Missouri?" a Clintonian leader in Albany anxiously queried Congressman Solomon Van Rensselaer. "It is very important that we should be able to fix that charge upon him if it be true—let me know as soon as possible."[15] Since the strongly prorestrictionist Federalists held the balance of power in a close race between Clintonian and Bucktail Republicans, it was indeed essential to Tompkins's chances that he not be identified with the southern position. In the event, Tompkins could not overcome a lingering suspicion that he had played a role in engineering the compromise, an impression that may have cost him the election; he does, however, appear to have been sufficiently discreet to have left no paper trail.

Anyone familiar with the years of bitter conflict between Massachusetts and the Virginia-led federal government might have expected the New England Federalist bastion to emerge as a hotbed of antirestrictionist activity. It did not. Massachusetts was led in 1819 by John Brooks, a moderate Federalist who "came to personify the nonpartisan 'Era of Good Feelings'" in the state. Governor Brooks, a distinguished Revolutionary War hero, welcomed Monroe on his visit to Boston, appointed Republicans as well as Federalists to office, and refused to act as a Federalist leader; it was said of Brooks that his "very name seemed to disarm party spirit with talismanic power."[16] It would seem natural that the easy-going Massachusetts governor would wish to assist the administration on the Missouri problem — especially since the president had just awarded his brother the post of consul at Manchester, England.[17]

An exchange in the Senate in January pointed toward other difficulties Massachusetts faced in attempting to take the lead on restriction. The memory of Massachusetts Federalists' flirtation with treason and disunion was still fresh in the minds of partisan Republicans, and "Hartford Convention" remained the Republican rallying cry wherever the Federalists mounted electoral campaigns. In arguing against the linkage of Maine and Missouri, Harrison Gray Otis, a guiding spirit of the Hartford Convention, unwisely raised the issue of the valorous conduct of Maine's citizens during the War of 1812. The acid-tongued William Smith, Republican of South Carolina, wondered "why such stress had been laid on the military prowess of the people of Maine. He could not distinguish between the particular sections of Massachusetts. He knew she was highly distinguished for valorous achievements in the course of the Revolutionary war; but he fancied her fame stopped there. If she had achieved any thing during the late war, she had been most egregiously slandered."

Wounded, Otis nonetheless blundered on. He had not, he averred, intended "to set up the military prowess of Massachusetts" as an argument against linking Maine and Missouri. Most Mainers had remained "attached, and strongly attached," to the Union, and had "furnished many soldiers for the army during the late war." Otis was in agony, but it was too late to stop: "Without going further into the subject, which he hoped the gentleman's courtesy and comity would not force him to do on this occasion, he would venture to affirm that no State in the Union, taking Maine and Massachusetts together, had more men in readiness from the beginning to the end of the war. . . . As much Massachusetts blood was spilt, in the late war, as of any other State in the Union."

Smith replied with cutting irony that "he had no intention to raise the honorable gentleman's feelings, but was very glad to be informed on the subject from authority so satisfactory on this point as that of the honorable gentleman."[18]

This species of humiliation quickly convinced Otis and other Hartford Convention Federalists to soft-pedal the Missouri question to the point of inaudibility. Indeed, it was not until Daniel Webster's reply to Robert Hayne in 1830 that a Massachusetts statesman would again attempt to do battle with a South Carolinian on the subject of the patriotism of Massachusetts;[19] for now, in what became an almost Pavlovian response of ex–Hartford Convention Federalists to criticism, Otis withdrew from the controversy to draft a lengthy pamphlet in defense of that hopelessly lost cause.[20] Although Otis continued to oppose Missouri's admission in the Senate, he wrote to Federalist associates in Boston to keep quiet on the issue and "let the Democracy *lead*. . . . Let them be irretrievably committed on the slave question before the fears on this subject become merged in their fears of federalism which are always likely to predominate."[21]

The gun-shy Essex Junto needed little guidance to display caution. Rufus King's close associate, the aging Federalist stalwart Christopher Gore, tried for some weeks to have King's speeches on Missouri printed in the *Columbian Centinel*, Boston's chief Federalist paper. Finally its editor told Gore "that some Friends to the good Cause had thought to postpone for the present any Discussion of the Subject . . . on which the people of Massachusetts have no Doubts to be removed, nor Errors to be corrected." Other Federalists, Gore informed King, also counseled caution:

> Mr. [John] Lowell had travelled to Washington and there met many Virginians & Carolinians . . . who inveighed most bitterly against the Attempt to annex Conditions to the admission of Missouri. He came home impressed with Fears & Doubts and communicated these to the Printers. Letters from Washington, it is said, urged most vehemently a total Silence on the Subject. [Josiah] Quincy, who was one of the Boston Memorialists [of December 3], cooled off entirely & hesitated on the Propriety of doing anything. . . . Everything must give way to the Production of a right Understanding relative to the Hartford Convention, and to the Establishment of the fair Fame of its members, which would be interfered with, if this Disposition against Slavery was expressed too loudly.

In Gore's view, this policy of caution "ha[d] its origin and Motive in an Attempt to conciliate all, who have the Disposal of Office & Distinction," and its consequence would be "the Degradation of the State and the entire Destruction of its influence."[22]

⬤⬤⬤

OTIS PROVED ASTUTE IN his prediction that the "fear of federalism" might secure Missouri's admission.[23] That the Missouri controversy would strengthen Federalists at the expense of Republicans had been clear at least since December, as the "Letter from Washington" published in the *New Hampshire Patriot* on the 28th (discussed in chapter 2) had disclosed. But it was not until January that opponents of restriction first charged publicly that the entire movement was a Federalist plot to place Rufus King and De Witt Clinton in the White House.

On its face, the charge had little plausibility. Republicans had initiated the controversy and carried the debate in the Fifteenth Congress. Republicans controlled most of the state legislatures that had voted for restriction. Initially, almost as many Federalists as Republicans voted against restriction, and in slaveholding Delaware, Federalists had opposed restriction while Republicans had supported it. It is true that Federalists took the lead in organizing many of the public meetings against slavery extension in the fall and winter of 1819–20, but the attendance of such meetings and the makeup of the Committees of Correspondence they engendered were always scrupulously bipartisan.

It is not clear when the charge of Federalist-Clintonian instigation was first raised or who first proposed it. In January 1820, Representative Thomas Cobb of Georgia remarked in a letter that he had been "laughed at" the year before "for suggesting that Clinton originated this [Missouri] question—Everyone *now* thinks the same."[24] The accuracy of Cobb's analysis aside, the chronology he offers of the acceptance of the theory—by southern Republicans, at least—is highly significant.

One can trace its development as a tactic in the shifting stances of Jonathan Roberts, a staunch Pennsylvania Republican senator who had played a crucial role in securing his state's support for Monroe in the previous election. In the Fifteenth Congress, Roberts had voted with the South to strike out the first section of the Tallmadge Amendment, but in the following session he quickly assumed a leading role in the drive for restriction. By the time the first Missouri Compromise came to a vote, however, Roberts had become an ally and strategist of the antirestrictionists. According to Glover

Moore, Roberts was "driven into the arms of the compromisers by the fear of a Federalist revival."[25] This is not exactly what happened.

In early January, after southerners had forced the linkage of the Maine and Missouri statehood bills, Roberts, a Quaker, wrote his brother Matthew that "the most diligent reflection has made it my consciencious [sic] duty to insist on the restriction against slavery in the new state by the exertion of every faculty of my mind. I anticipate an opportunity for claiming my full share in the deliberations upon it."[26]

Roberts had important political motivations for his stance as well. On January 1, a constituent, Robert Frazer, informed Roberts that to punish him for his failure to back Governor Findlay's reelection, the governor's partisans were spreading the rumor that Roberts was "inimical to the restriction ag$_{st.}$ slavery in the Missouri-bill." "I have been taking some pains to shew . . . otherwise," Frazer assured Roberts, trusting that his "meddling" would "not be disapproved."[27] Shortly after receiving this letter, Roberts offered an antislavery proviso to the amendment admitting Missouri to the Union, delivering a major speech that placed the effort to restrict the spread of slavery alongside the declaration of American independence and the promulgation of the Northwest Ordinance in a providential sequence of great undertakings progressing toward the "fulfillment of the great end for which [God] created man—happiness." In the cadences of Deuteronomy and the Declaration of Independence, Roberts reviewed the sacred history of the nation's founding and her ongoing reaffirmations of her commitment to liberty. The preamble to Maine's constitution began with the declaration that "all men are born free and equal," Roberts noted. "Here is a substantial pledge to the good old faith." To Maine, Congress might say, "Come, sister, take your place in our constellation: the lustre of your countenance will brighten the American galaxy. But do not urge us to admit Missouri, under a pretence of congeniality—with the visage of a savage, deformed with the hideous cicatrices of barbaric pride—with her features marred as if the finger of Lucifer had been drawn across them."[28]

A few days later Roberts still basked in the glow of celebrity. "I am confident I made a strong and impressive speech. So far it has stood the test of controversy. My conclusions have been denied tho' my arguments have not been refuted." He professed not to be intimidated by "a most furious sally" on him made by William Pinkney, one of the Senate's most formidable debaters, revealing remarkable egotism but also a hint of apprehension in his evaluation of their relative skills: "He is nothing more than a vain cox comb & if I do not cut into him I am much deceived in my own strength &

his weakness. This task is imposed upon me & by the way I do not dread it. I know I shall task him severely but I will take care to handle the rod discretly. I have had occasion to state pretty distinctly that I would retort upon him to his friends. They have tryd to soften me by representing him to be a rough tempered man. My reply was he has made it my duty to soften it a little."[29]

As the debates wore on, Roberts grew increasingly astounded at southern audacity. "Thee can have no idea of the doctrines preached by the men of the south," he wrote his brother. In the weeks before Rufus King returned to the Capitol, Roberts appeared to view himself as the North's champion in single combat against the celebrated Pinkney—a circumstance that, while gratifying to his ego, clearly carried with it a high personal cost. "I am prepared to review [Pinkney's] heresies with temper & reason & may do so to day or tomorrow. His rudeness makes it difficult to avoid harsh retort. It is generally looked for from me & by many demanded of me." A former War Hawk who had launched his congressional career with Clay and Calhoun in the battle against northern sectionalism, Roberts found the prospect of battling southern extremism in coalition with Federalists deeply troubling, particularly as his former colleagues subjected him to unrelenting pressure to change his position: "I see no alternative but to become as much opposed to doctrines of the south as I have been to those of the East. It is not to imagine the art & finesse that have [been] used to betray me from my ground. I am viewed as the principal obstacle that at present thwarts the southern ambition & cupidity in the Senate. [Rhode Island senator] Burrill and me [sic] are certainly those who they look upon as presenting to them most difficulty. I however am the greatest sinner because so they say I have broken the bonds of brotherhood with them."

By this time, opponents of restriction had hit upon the strategy of denouncing the Missouri controversy as a plot to put Rufus King or De Witt Clinton in the White House, and they tried to persuade Roberts of it. "It is they say a scheme of ambition & wonder how I can countenance it. No doubt there is much of ambition in New York as well as in Virginia," Roberts mused, perhaps beginning to waver; but in the next sentence he seemed to regain his resolve: "I detest as much the doctrine now preached by [the] south as ever I did those of the East. I cannot consent ever not to do right with the east nor to [do] wrong with the South." In 1820 the old categories of Federalist and Republican no longer held sway. "We have arrived at a new era," Roberts observed. Still, he could not ignore the dangerously exposed position in which his chosen role in the "new era" put him: "I am in a conspicuous place, under the devolution of arduous duty. I hope

I shall not betray my trust nor be found wanting in industry & zeal. The rest must be left to heaven."[30]

Roberts took the floor again "with unfeigned reluctance" several days later. "I have listened," he said, "with equal surprise and regret, to hear gentlemen, with whom in this place I have long been gratified to act and think, deny or explain away what I deem to be the sound and fundamental principles of political truth." Striving to counter unprecedented northern unity on Missouri, James Barbour had eulogized those brave statesmen "who, in doing what they believe to be right, breast the storm of public opinion at home." Roberts bristled at the Virginian's characterization of "the supple politicians, who yield so obsequiously to every breeze of public opinion," declaring that he was "glad to learn" of the Pennsylvania legislature's unanimous resolution against slavery. "Having no doubt of my duty before, I still hail with gladness this strengthening evidence of their concurrence."[31]

Perhaps sensing the pressure Roberts must be enduring, William Jones wrote him a long letter on the Missouri question. "I know there are many enlightened advocates of the proposed restriction on the people of the Missouri territory who regret the present agitation of the question, but why I am unable to discover." Pointedly, Jones described Pennsylvania as "the great state whose preponderating but conciliatory influence had acquired for it nothing more than the humble office of a makeweight between the contending rivals for power who have alternately occupied the scales." In Jones's view, if the free states had either to yield on the principle of restriction of slavery, "upon which the security and happiness of unborn millions, and the rights of the free states depend," or face disunion, then "the period is not remote when every other great principle and interest that may conflict with the views of the dominant section must also yield to that influence, or dismemberment which had been abhorred as the greatest of political evils, will lose all its terror." Jones concluded the letter by apologizing for setting forth his restrictionist views to Roberts at length, since "after the discussion which the subject has received with you it will be sending coals to New Castle[.]"[32]

Despite Jones's assurance of his senator's steadfastness, other, more powerful influences were at work on Roberts. Although a recognized leader in the drive to restrict slavery, he was frequently consulted by key antirestrictionists, including the president. Roberts wrote to William Jones after one such interview assuring him of Monroe's continued regard for him despite his removal as a director of the Bank of the United States; shortly afterward Roberts was able to offer Jones a consulship as recompense.[33] The antirestrictionists' assiduous cultivation of the Pennsylvanian appears to have paid off. By early February, Roberts was purveying the assertion that "the election of Mr. King to the Presidency either by a direct vote or by selection of Congress, is now not an event the least improbable." If his friend Jones was willing to be surprised by this information (as well he might), he stubbornly refused to regard it as cause for alarm.[34]

When the measure to unite the Maine and Missouri bills came before the Senate on February 16, Roberts voted against it—along with every other northern senator except Edwards and Thomas of Illinois and Indiana's Taylor. The linkage passed by a vote of 23 to 21. "The non slave states if they were [true?] have one state of majority counting Delaware," Roberts informed his brother. "We ought to have four votes of a majority but such is the fatuity of man on the restriction they have an immense majority [*sic*— one vote?] against us." Fueled by his conversations with antirestrictionists, however, Roberts's fear of Rufus King, who he described as "strong but imprudent," continued to grow, as did his receptivity to Pinkney, the "vain cox comb" whom he had earlier promised to "cut into" and "task . . . severely." In Pinkney's response to King, Roberts reported that the South Carolinian "retracted almost all the heresies of his first speech" and, more important, "strongly bepraised" Roberts "for my discretion & intelligence & called me his friend." Now Pinkney was ready "to meet me on ground of fair compromise. He and I stand prominent in two sections ready to baffle the factions."

The rest of Roberts's letter belied this pose of statesmanship and confidence, however, displaying the turbulence of his mind in its shifts of position almost from sentence to sentence:

Keep the question open and King will very probably be the next President. Every consideration points to compromise. It is the genius of our government. On the restriction the Senate majority is immovable. The house it is expected will be as fixed the other way. Happily King cannot rally his own party. I never did see a man so heckled as he has been since his speech. . . . I hope we shall thro' the protection of a kind providence pass this shoal unhurt. We have some knaves & some madmen but the [greater] number are honest. Clay Lowndes Pinckney [*sic*; i.e., Pinkney] and others see & feel our danger and are disposed to act like reasonable men. Virginia is the spoild child of the Union. . . . There is a feeling to the south I had now to learn existed there. After all it is well to have been called back to first principles. Men should often be tested by them. The southern patriots on whom we judged of southern opinion are gone & a new generation with new habits of thought have grown up. I met [British educator] Josiah Lancaster on the street to day. He said he had come up to see we did no mischief. He concurred with me that the agitation now awakened on the subject of slavery would be useful. The whole community will be taught [to] reflect upon it & nothing can resist the force of truth. Dislike of slavery must gain ground.

In the meantime, however, Roberts had decided to cast his lot with the administration on what he termed, with unintended irony, "the compromising question"—Jesse Thomas's proposal to divide the Louisiana Territory into slave and free sections. While he recognized that his stance would hurt him politically at home, he had decided to adopt Senator Barbour's model of the courageous northern politician: "My object is to do what is right & take the consequences." Roberts then revealed that Thomas, whose vote had provided the "huge majority" against the North on the vote to link Maine and Missouri, had "made me his confidant from the first." Sounding unconvinced himself, he attempted to explain the motives that impelled the Illinois senator to propose the Louisiana split: "His purpose is honorable tho' I have some doubts if he has acted wisely. It was not for me to advise[;] he thought the confidence of the southerners was necessary. Perhaps it was for they are a stiffnecked race. There was so much scruple to the North too that there was no possibility of getting restriction even with his vote."[35]

If Roberts found the compromise difficult to swallow, less malleable politicians from both North and South remained adamant in their opposition. Most northerners considered the prohibition of slavery in the territory above the line 36°30' as a meaningless ruse, while many southerners regarded it as a dangerous abandonment of principle. Roberts found himself shocked by the extremism of anticompromise southern congressmen, whose violence threatened to drive northern Republicans into the Federalist camp. In the midst of the chaos, however, he found time to reassure himself with some self-congratulatory reflection:

I am pretty confident my notions of life and respectability have undergone no change for the worse since I started in life. There is some diminution of prejudices I hope. I feel my early habits as strong as ever & really feel as if [I] had obtained something I have aspired to in character. I wish to improve a little on that of my father not that I desire to be a better man but to practice his virtues avoiding his foibles. I believe I am here entirely esteemed as an honest man & am allowed some share of ability without becoming any mans rival or enemy. My wish is to return from [my] station with an approving conscience to habits of industry & temperance. I would rather work [for] myself than for the public & I would not wish to be without work.[36]

In his next letter Roberts's conversion appeared complete. "Really the Ultra federalists look to this question to regain power. This is well understood. I have seen it from the first." In an intriguing detail, Roberts reported that the nation's most powerful Federalist remained on the fence: "[Chief Justice John] Marshall whom Randolph calls the Archimedes of Logic is embarrassed how to act & he keeps a large mass in suspense." Roberts's precise account of the attitudes of congressmen and the maneuvering of restrictionist lobbyists such as Daniel Webster and Joseph Hopkinson contrasted sharply with his vague and implausible scenario of a grand Federalist conspiracy, which he tacitly admitted was not playing well among northern members: "It is believed De witt [sic] Clinton & King are in concert. The latter is to be Pres^t & the former secretary of state with right of succession after four years—such is the crisis & the catastrophe is to be averted only by a speedy settlement of the question. This the republicans all feel but whether the public danger will bring them together is yet problematical."

In the meantime, Roberts's pivotal position continued to bring him much respectful attention, even though he recognized its cause. "Penn^a is the great bone of contention," he wrote. "She is the toast of the day[.] Her wooers are all sinister [i.e., have hidden motives]. Yesterday John Randolph came out of his way to speak to me. It has been long since he has done it before. I cannot flatter him nor put up with his arrogance and so we seldom see each other & seldomer salute each other. He has been for some time flattering Penn^a always however [illegible] every thing in Virginia on grounds of high performance. The other side too court us. R King has even [quietly?] made such approaches to me." While flattered by the attention he received, Roberts felt the perils of his position intensely, as did other members of the Pennsylvania delegation. "Lowrie [Pennsylvania's junior senator] & I have had very delicate ground to tread," Roberts observed, conceding that "it has been difficult to avoid compromisement."[37]

----⊗≫⊗----

MANY OTHER NORTHERN politicians besides Roberts came under various forms of pressure to support a compromise—in particular, the fear of being tarred with Federalism. As Roberts implied, his senatorial colleague Walter

Lowrie received the unremitting attention of antirestrictionists, including Pennsylvania House member Henry Baldwin, who provided him with a detailed memorandum on constitutional aspects of the Missouri question—a sort of "crib sheet" for the controversy.[38] Baldwin, a single-minded advocate for the Pennsylvania manufacturing interests, to whom he was "deeply and dependently in debt," labored strenuously to bring Lowrie over to the antirestrictionist camp, a position made difficult by the fact that Lowrie had asserted in the Senate that "if the alternative be . . . dissolution of the Union, or the extension of slavery over this whole western country, I for one will choose the former."[39] As a pious evangelical, Lowrie found himself particularly vulnerable to the standard Jeffersonian insinuations of "canting hypocrisy," Federalist propensities, and rank ignorance of the ways of the world—the last of which may well have had some foundation in fact. Other openly devout restrictionist congressmen faced similar pressures. We have seen how Mark Hill of Maine anticipated no trouble convincing Representative Joshua Cushman, an ordained Congregationalist religious teacher, to "act prudently" and change his vote on Missouri; in the event, to his colleagues' surprise, he stood firm.

New Hampshire senator David Morril, a Presbyterian pastor, did not. Newspaper editor and Republican leader Isaac Hill had backed away from his earlier ringing denunciations of slavery extension and now held that the real purpose of the Missouri controversy was "to effect sinister and party purposes." He had Morril's mail monitored and spread reports of the "mischief" he was "industriously and constantly plotting," noting to Senator Parrott that Morril's "correspondence . . . is more with federalists than with republicans—and federalists too of the most inveterate class, 'orthodox' clergymen, etc."[40] Although Morril had delivered a speech in favor of restriction that "occupie[d] eight closely printed columns of the National Intelligencer" in February 1820, he ultimately voted for a compromise—in apparent defiance of the instruction of the New Hampshire legislature, but in accordance with the wishes of Hill's Concord Republican machine.[41] Representations of the Missouri question as a "Federal measure," as well as "the influence of the Palace, which after all is heavier than the [State] Capitol, have produced a considerable change here," explained New Hampshire congressman William Plumer Jr. to his father.[42]

The most critical target of pro-Missouri lobbying, however, was Maine's William King. Whether he was aware of it or not, King represented the key to the antirestrictionists' strategy. Because he was Maine's preeminent political figure, his opinion could be expected to carry significant weight both with the Maine delegation and in justifying a vote for compromise to constituents back home. More important, if King could be convinced to join the antirestrictionists, his adherence would implicitly validate the charges currently circulating that his brother Rufus was the real instigator of the Missouri agitation. With William's endorsement, the 36°30' compromise had a good chance of securing enough northern support for passage; without such an endorsement, bipartisan northern unity against any extension of slavery seemed likely to hold.

As late as the end of January, King gave little indication of signing on to such a scheme. In his letters to Rufus he maintained a staunch line against the efforts of the antirestrictionists. "In the attempt to associate the admission of Maine and Missouri together," William wrote his half brother, "the motive is so apparent, that it has excited general disgust in this State." Maine's citizens desired statehood, but only "on terms honorable & correct . . . they will not, I am sure, consent to bargain their way along let the consequence be what it may." John Holmes was the only member of the Maine delegation intending to vote with the South, William informed his brother; "it is hardly fair to judge his motives, altho' opinions are expressed freely on the subject." As late as February 6, William still appeared highly critical of Holmes's machinations: "Mr. Holmes' course is generally complained of here, and I am inclined to think his constituents will not be disposed to overlook his present conduct."[43]

Within days, however, King began to see things differently. Mark Hill wrote to inform him on February 9 of a meeting Hill and several other northern Republicans had had with the president. Hill gave the impression (an impression Monroe frequently conveyed) that his visitors had done most of the talking and the president most of the listening; Hill informed King that he and his fellow northerners had "induced the President to *think*, and advise his southern friends to be cautious."[44] It seems that Hill believed, and convinced King, that he had secured a pledge from Monroe to disconnect the Maine bill from Missouri. In fact, as is discussed in chapter 2 above, although he had decided the week before that this would be a politically expedient step, Monroe had retreated from the plan after Barbour found the Virginians explosively opposed to it.[45] Monroe's promise alone, however, and the impression that their forcefulness had extracted it, proved sufficient to win over Hill and other northern Republicans to support his measures.

In the meantime, supporters of slavery sustained barrage after barrage of attacks on the floor of Congress. Some of these hit home. On February 11, Rufus King, now haunting southern nightmares as the future president, again took the floor of the Senate, and delivered a speech so stinging that, reported John Quincy Adams, "slave-holders . . . gnawed their lips and clenched their fists as they heard him."[46] This time King attacked the morality of slavery directly, not simply the injustice of slavery-inflated southern political power, asserting that all laws and compacts supporting slavery were "absolutely void, because contrary to the law of nature, which is the law of God." According to David Brion Davis, "no statesman or political leader in the world had publicly made such a radical declaration of slavery's illegality."[47] Without a doubt, the former Federalist standard-bearer was living up to his growing reputation as a radical crusader against southern slavery. The next day, Pennsylvania's Baldwin fired off letters to state political leaders informing them that slavery restriction was purely designed to augment Federalist power: "Genl William King of the province of Maine in a letter which I saw yesterday says this is the object and such an opinion from him has great weight. He is the brother of Rufus King."[48]

For his own part, William King remained ambivalent about the prudence of branding the Missouri question a northern conspiracy to agitate the slavery issue. On the one hand, as soon as he decided to embrace the Republican leadership's line on Missouri, he quickly took charge of the rather desperate effort to bring the rest of Maine Republicans in line. "The gentlemen who contemplated a new party, the North against the South, will in this State I am sure be much disappointed," King affirmed in a letter to Holmes, adding that "we are now taking measures to have all the Republican papers in Maine give such a direction to this business as will destroy their hopes here." On the other hand, King urged Holmes not to stress the charge that the restriction movement was a Federalist plot, as this would irrevocably turn Maine Federalists against him.[49]

King's views faced opposition within the Maine Republican camp. Joseph F. Wingate, a Maine member of the Massachusetts legislature, conceded that King might be right that a charge of Federalist conspiracy would cost some support. However, he felt "that we should gain more by uniting, in this way, the scattered forces of the Republicans, than we should lose by an open & independent course toward the opposition." Moreover, since many Republicans had publicly committed themselves to restriction, they "would rejoice at finding a satisfactory apology for abandoning their present ground—by making it a party argument of Federalists this apology is certainly furnished them." For their part, ex-Federalists-turned-Republicans, seeking an opportunity to separate themselves from their "former associations," would "not desert us for any trifling imaginary cause." Unconverted Federalists need not be pandered to, since they "will not suffer an opportunity to pass however tender [*sic*] we may treat them, of doing us all the harm in their power. . . . Another election will see them in full opposition to the State administration—at least if it is the kind of administration *we ought to have* in Maine."[50]

Wingate's letter illustrated the strong political incentives to employ the charge of Federalist conspiracy, while at the same time offering a veiled warning to ex-Federalists—such as William King and John Holmes—to avoid any conduct that might call their loyalty to Republicanism into question.

The conversion of William King represented an important step toward one of the antirestrictionists' key objectives: neutralizing Rufus King as antislavery standard-bearer. The circumstances of King's reelection to the Senate had already placed him in a delicate position. He owed his unanimous selection by the New York legislature to the ringing endorsement of Bucktail leader Van Buren, who, as King well realized, had taken a serious political risk by backing a Federalist—"one of the most difficult political chores the Red Fox ever undertook."[51] After all, Van Buren's political power rested on the two pillars of resistance to Federalism and his alliance with southern leaders, in particular Thomas Ritchie's Richmond Junto—perhaps the most militant opponents of restriction in the country.

Van Buren had staked his political career on his ability to compel his Bucktail faction's acquiescence in King's nomination, but he had done so with a keen appreciation of the potential rewards. When, in late 1819, Van Buren decided to back King, he dismissed as groundless the rumors that King's ambition lay behind his antislavery efforts: "The Missouri question conceals *so far as he is concerned* no plot & we shall give it a true direction" (emphasis in the original).[52] It is not clear in context precisely what Van Buren meant by giving the question "a true direction" (nor what kind of "plot" he felt the Missouri question *did* conceal). Most immediately, Van Buren expected that King would sway enough Federalist votes in the coming gubernatorial election to the yet-undetermined Bucktail candidate to oust De Witt Clinton. Van Buren also sought to win King's gratitude and enlist his strong sense of loyalty. "The part taken by Mr. Van Buren has indeed been most liberal, and as I conceive at the risk of impairing his high standing and influence among his political friends," King wrote to his son John, a Van Buren confidant; "do not fail therefore to inform him that I can never be insensible of his generosity & that no occasion can arrive, that I shall not be ready to prove to him the personal respect & esteem with which he has inspired me."[53] For New York's arch-Republican to place the nation's most influential Federalist in such a position clearly seemed to justify the political risk Van Buren had run.

Van Buren believed that he had reaped another advantage in placing King in his debt. King's sons, John and Charles, disciples of the Bucktail leader and phobic anti-Clintonians, not only served as persuasive and often effective lobbyists with their father for Van Buren's policies, but also operated as conduits of information to the Red Fox—spies might not be too strong a word—from the heart of the restrictionist camp. It is clear from their letters among each other that John and Charles King shared all information of importance from their father with their political mentor, a fact that the elder King must have been aware of. Perhaps spurred by paternal ties as well as political gratitude to Van Buren, King seemed to ignore the evidence of his sons' and Van Buren's hostility to slavery restriction in Missouri, discussing sensitive points of strategy and information with them.[54] The alternative—that King deliberately provided information to his sons that he knew would be transmitted to Van Buren and passed on to the anti-restrictionist leadership—is an intriguing possibility, but one that cannot as yet be demonstrated.

It should be remembered that at this stage Van Buren's interest in national affairs related chiefly to the control of New York State—a larger prize, in terms of patronage, than the federal government itself. The Bucktail leader stalked his erstwhile chief De Witt Clinton as obsessively as Melville's Ahab pursued the white whale, and Van Buren intended to use King's high reputation as a weapon to unseat his nemesis from the governor's mansion. Despite Van Buren's valiant efforts to convince Daniel Tompkins not to run, the vice president had decided to seek the governorship and duly received the Bucktail nomination. King would probably have been willing to overlook Tompkins's drinking problems and fiscal irregularities in order to demonstrate his "respect & esteem" for Van Buren, but he could not close his eyes to the evidence of the candidate's efforts to defeat restriction. Responding to his son John's direct request to endorse Tompkins, King replied that "I certainly cannot, and do not, object to your taking such part between Mr. C. and his political opponents as you deem proper . . ." While he acknowledged an "aversion" to Clinton and "much of good will, as well as an obligation toward" the Bucktails, however, King had grave misgivings concerning Tompkins's stance on the expansion of slavery, "which, whether regarded solely in reference to its great and essential merits and importance, or as respects the strength of my convictions concerning it, . . . I cannot possibly disregard." He continued plainly:

It has been, and still is, asserted that the V.P. entertains doubts respecting the power, and even concerning the policy of restraining this unnatural and dangerous mischief. There are some truths so plain and incontestable, that no language or definition can make them more so; and when we find men in doubt respecting the same, we are wholly at a loss to understand them. I will not enlarge upon this point. I hope it is not true that the V.P. has any scruples respecting measures without which our Constitution is worthless and defenceless, and our liberties in the most imminent danger. . . . Obliged as I feel myself to the V.P., solicitous as I am that he should attain his object in opposition to Mr. Clinton, if he seek by any understanding with others, or by deliberate purpose to give the influence of N. York, or to co-operate with the slave States, or in opposition to the free States, in order to extend slavery into new regions, [although] I will take no step to promote the purpose or wishes of his opponent, [I] should find it utterly impossible without degrading my fixed opinions of public and private Duty to do what it might otherwise be decorous and my inclination to do.[55]

By implication, King's qualms about Tompkins were really misgivings about Van Buren, since the debilitated vice president ran under the Bucktail banner and effectively served as the proxy of its chief. Accordingly, it was Van Buren and not Tompkins who responded, firing off a letter informing King that he had spoken to the vice president and that King was mistaken in his suspicions. In oddly formal language mirroring John Taylor's initial formulation of the Missouri question, Van Buren quoted Tompkins as stating "that he did not think that the restriction was unconstitutional, nor had he ever questioned its expediency." He continued in a patronizing vein likely to have infuriated the venerable Federalist: "At some future day I will give you my ideas upon the question of the expediency of making this a party question. I am persuaded that notwithstanding the people of this state have felt a strong interest in the question, the excitement which exists in regard to it, or which is likely to arise from it, is not so great as you suppose."[56] Beyond Van Buren's casual dismissal of the moral argument involved in the Missouri controversy, his hypocrisy in admonishing King for making it a "party question," while his Bucktails were actively and knowingly promoting the falsehood that the agitation concealed a Federalist plot, is little short of breathtaking.

In the meantime, John King also wrote to Tompkins and asked him for a letter to respond to "rumours misrepresenting your opinion, upon this subject, being afloat at Washington, as well as here."[57] He sent Tompkins's response to his father the next day, in which the vice president dutifully pronounced the shibboleth: "My opinion is that by the Constitution Congress have the discretion of requiring as a preliminary condition of the admission of a State, not composed of territory not originally in the U.S., that slavery be prohibited in such new State & that it is expedient & just to require that condition to be performed in relation to Missouri and all other territory acquired therewith."[58]

"I am . . . gratified to find that these insinuations respecting [Tompkins] are without foundation," Rufus King replied to his son, "which indeed, had I received no authoritative contradiction of them, I should have inferred from the silence that has lately prevailed respecting them." King still could not bring himself to endorse Tompkins for governor, however. He suggested obliquely that he did not believe the assurances he had received, but understood what had prompted John to procure them: "You must pause for a moment and weigh the difference between youth and age: the one is confident and adventurous, the other cautious and hesitating: the object of the one is to acquire, of the other to preserve reputation—both are right; I therefore do not discourage you, nor disapprove of your views; and I hope that you will make due allowance for mine."[59] King's refusal to back Tompkins probably cost him the gubernatorial election and constituted a setback to Van Buren's New York plans.

As we have seen, Martin Van Buren himself privately refuted the charge that King intended to use the Missouri controversy for personal political gain, a judgment confirmed by modern scholars.[60] Ironically, however, the charges that De Witt Clinton planned to use Missouri as a means to achieve political power were true—even though he had nothing to do with instigating the crisis. Rather, Clinton regarded the slavery issue through the tunnel vision of his vaunting ambition, much as he had the War of 1812, as an opportunity to be exploited to unite the North behind him.

Effectively, this was impossible. For many reasons, Clinton was not capable of constructing a genuine antislavery coalition. In the first place, his antislavery bona fides were suspect. As John W. Taylor, the Tallmadge Amendment's chief backer, observed, "It was not until the Missouri Question became a major political issue—in the sense that an ambitious party leader might extract some solid profit from it—that De Witt Clinton had decided to give his endorsement to the antislavery cause."[61] Moreover, his reputation for "political tergiversations, intrigues, caballing, and insatiable ambitions," in Rufus King's description, ensured that respectable and prudent politicians steered clear of Clinton.[62] The malcontent and disaffected, on the other hand, did occasionally rally to his standard.

A case in point is William Duane, editor of the *Philadelphia Aurora*. A talented journalist who had authored the preamble and resolutions against the extension of slavery passed by the Pennsylvania legislature in 1819, Duane turned up in mid-January at the office of Senator Richard M. Johnson with offers to run guns on commission to South American revolutionaries or to serve as the government's agent to Venezuela. Johnson conveyed the proposals to Secretary of State John Q. Adams, who took them up with the president. As Adams reported, Monroe regarded "the project of furnishing ten thousand stands of arms to Venezuela for the sake of making a profitable job to Duane" to be "disgusting: and that it was to be secretly done made it worse." Monroe would never consider sending him "as an Agent to South America," since "he had no confidence in him, and believed him to be as unprincipled a fellow as lived." To commission "a man such as Duane" as a public agent "would give a general disgust to the people of this country who would universally consider it as buying off his opposition"; and in Monroe's view, "he was not worth buying."

To this stinging response, Adams entered his own judgment on Duane: "[He] has been nearly twenty-five years editor of the *Aurora*, the most slanderous newspaper in the United States. But as his industry is indefatigable, and as he writes with facility, his editorial articles are interesting, and he has often had much influence, especially in the State of Pennsylvania. He is now poor, and growing old, and his present proposal is substantially to sell his silence. The President offers nothing for it but his contempt."[63]

Thus humiliatingly rebuffed, Duane retaliated by redoubling his advocacy of slavery restriction and throwing his paper behind a Clinton bid for the White House, urging every "sincere opponent" of slavery, "whatever may be his *party*," to reject that "miserable drone . . . *James Monroe*" and "vote the *anti-slavery electoral ticket* for president and vice president of the United States."[64]

The rather pathetic episode with Duane speaks volumes about the president's handling of the controversy. It substantiates the impression that his administration engaged in exchanging offices and emoluments for cooperation. More important, however, it demonstrates Monroe's complete self-command. He would take every measure necessary to secure Missouri's unrestricted admission, but no unnecessary ones. He would not be blackmailed. While Adams indulged in visions of prospects "dark and unpropitious abroad" and "far more gloomy and threatening" at home; of "stormy and violent" episodes in an "appalling" future, Monroe complaisantly remarked that "as to the Missouri question, he apprehended no danger from that. He believed a compromise would be found and agreed to, which would be satisfactory to all parties."[65]

Monroe's gift in dealing with congressmen, at a time when the predominant ideology regarded involvement by the executive in legislative affairs as high-handed interference and an abuse of privilege, was to make them feel like high-level players in a secret plan to save the nation—which may have been in large part true. There was great exhilaration for these ordinary men—in some cases *very* ordinary—in feeling that they were transcending the parochial interests of their states and region and even ignoring their own political futures for the sake of preserving the Union. By backing a compromise plan that would at once close much of the nation's territory to slavery and thwart a conspiracy of evil men, they would gain no glory—on the contrary, they would be vilified and reviled—but, like Harvey Birch of James Fenimore Cooper's *The Spy* (1821), they would secretly merit the gratitude of their country, and of their president, who would also, somewhat more tangibly than Cooper's Washington, reward their selflessness and courage with appropriate tokens of appreciation: appointment as a customs collector, a postmaster, a circuit judge, a western land office clerk. Monroe soothingly assured northern Republican compromisers that they stood with him, for the Union, against the extremists of the South and the Federalists of the North. Shaw Livermore has well captured the attitude of these northern doughfaces:

> As southern leaders became more implacable, freely threatening disruption of the party and even the nation, northern Republican leaders became increasingly apprehensive. Thus the 36°30' provision, which appeared to resolve for the moment fears about the intra-party balance of power, was welcomed. These leaders could not, however, publicly express their relief, because the compromise proposals as a whole were not widely acceptable in the North. Those who dreaded the splintering of their party and a possible Federalist renaissance were compelled to find a plausible reason for supporting the compromise. Were not Federalists responsible for their woes? . . . It was not difficult, nor necessarily hypocritical, for them to enshroud votes for compromise in the noisy charges of Federalist perfidy and baseness. Warmth of feeling mercifully softened exaggeration.[66]

With respect to charges of Clintonian plotting, Republicans had less recourse to exaggeration. Opponents of restriction searching for a hidden Clintonian hand behind the crisis quickly found confirming evidence in the actions of men like Duane, which lent credence to charges such as those of Mason of Massachusetts "that the bringing up this question is altogether an intrigue of De Witt Clinton's to get over the State of Pennsylvania."[67] Thus the involvement of the "Magnus Apollo" in the Missouri affair, far from uniting antislavery forces, rather lent plausibility to the conspiracy theories with which antirestrictionists frightened wavering politicians.

Although he had substantial evidence that the Monroe administration was using patronage and removals to effect its policies in New York, Clinton's gross lack of finesse led him to mishandle this potentially explosive information. Clinton's associates had discovered that the administration, through Navy Secretary Smith Thompson, a close Van Buren associate, had employed the Brooklyn Navy Yard as a patronage trough to secure allies through lucrative government jobs.[68] Of more moment was a letter from Van Buren to Henry Meigs, an antirestrictionist New York congressman and the nephew of the postmaster general, recommending the removal of certain "Rascally Post Masters" for purely political reasons. Instead of carefully collecting evidence and deftly employing it to maximum political effect, Clinton announced at the outset of the investigation his intention "to lay before the Legislature at their request evidence of the interference of the General Govt. in our Elections," and then imperiously demanded, or had members of Congress demand, that administration officials turn over incriminating documents.[69] At the conclusion of his search the governor melodramatically deposited his discoveries before the legislature in a large green baize bag. The effect of Clinton's imperiousness and theatricality was to focus the public's attention on himself, and distract it utterly from the unprecedented Bucktail–White House collaboration that was the ostensible subject of his investigation. Because his self-centeredness made him incapable of recognizing that the administration's activities in New York had much broader objectives than unseating him, Clinton squandered the opportunity to expose possibly wide-scale White House intervention in the politics of a northern state to promote the admission of Missouri with slavery.

Unlike the previous session, when the floor of the House of Representatives had served as the true stage of the controversy, the ceaseless speechifying of the Sixteenth Congress afforded a kind of long-running Washington sideshow to the session's real action over Missouri, which took place in back rooms, saloons, boarding houses, and executive department offices. Nevertheless, the narrow margin between restrictionist and antirestrictionist forces demanded that every representative remain in his seat through every tedious disquisition against the possibility that a surprise vote might be called. "My life here is a constant scene of monotony," New Hampshire senator Parrott complained to his wife.[70] Still, some members considered the debate itself worthwhile. "I presume the good people of the North by this time begin to think we have been long enough upon this question,"

Representative Henry Waggaman Edwards acknowledged to a fellow Connecticut Republican political leader.

> Perhaps if I was not here I should think so too, but as it is my impressions are far otherwise. . . . When I came here I was disposed to consider it as a question originating in party or sinister views. We have been so much in the habit of considering all questions as being of this nature, and being influenced in our feelings respecting them by these considerations, that we hardly had an idea of any thing else. This subject whether on account of its intrinsic importance, or on account of the present weakness of party feelings, as they respect the general government, has risen far above all feelings of this kind, and the only feelings, which are discoverable, are those which spring from the subject itself, except perhaps in some few instances.[71]

Nonetheless, as the weeks dragged on, and the oratorical titans such as Clay, Barbour, Sergeant, and Lowndes had long since weighed in, the debate grew increasingly stale and the speeches perfunctory and designed for home-district consumption.

While the debate on the floor rumbled along, Monroe and his adjutants struggled to assemble and hold together a majority in Congress for a compromise while putting out dangerous fires in Richmond. The two tasks nearly proved mutually exclusive. On January 30, 1820, Abner Lacock, a retired Pennsylvania senator born in Virginia, penned a thoughtful letter to the president warning of "the demolition of the fairest fabric of human invention, & the last hope of freedom on earth," and urging his support of the amendment that Senator Jesse Thomas planned to introduce a few days later: "Let the slave holding states accept Missouri Arkansaw, & the Floridas, & give an equivalent to the others in the west. Can there be anything either unjust or dishonourable in such a compromise[?]"[72] Four days later, Monroe wrote to his lieutenant, Senate majority leader James Barbour, recommending the quick admission of Maine without entanglement with Missouri and the adoption of the Thomas Amendment with its 36°30' provision.

On February 6, Barbour injudiciously revealed to a Virginia legislator that he and the president planned to back a compromise excluding slavery from much of the Louisiana Purchase. When Monroe's plan became known to the Virginia legislature, it triggered "a state of fervid excitement" and "indignant feeling" among the members. "Mr. Monroe must . . . make up his mind to retain his Southern friends or *exchange* them for those of the North," Henry St. George Tucker wrote to Barbour. "He cannot keep both."[73]

On this note of anger and betrayal, the caucus adjourned, taking no action on choosing presidential electors and resolving not to renominate Monroe without his pledge that he would veto any compromise. Barbour, too, came under heavy fire at Richmond—enough so that he believed his political life to be in danger.[74] Monroe clearly had to abandon his preferred strategy of northern conciliation. Instead, he scrambled to provide an explanation—more accurately, perhaps, a pretext—to the Virginia diehards for his apparently unaccountable behavior. A largely illegible memorandum Monroe drew up at this time, clearly written in haste and under the pressure of emotion, appears to be the draft of such an explanation. The most coherent passages of the memo included these lines:

> In this no bargain has been made, nor any obligation entered into. It was a mere understanding between those who wished to save the union—No It is unfortunate that it should be made public. . . .
>
> The idea was that if the whole arrangement, to this effect, could be secured, that it would be better to adopt it, than break the union
>
> Neither did Mr. Barbour, nor any other person alluded to, favor this, but to save the union, believing it to be in imminent danger.

Rare are the episodes in which Monroe so plainly lost his cool. It was at this point, in direct response to the extreme reaction of the Richmond caucus, that Monroe apparently found himself forced to accept, and even amplify, the claim that northern extremists stood poised on the brink of capturing the government, and to explain his misguided overtures of compromise as a panicked response in the face of this danger.

In short order, the policy of moderate accommodation vanished from the political landscape. On the floor of the Senate, Jesse Thomas retracted his proposal for a compromise along the line of 36°30', and Monroe abandoned his suggestion that Barbour decouple Maine from Missouri.[75] Instead, Barbour wrote to Virginians that the principle of "Yield nothing" would henceforth be his "law"; and Monroe informed his Virginia campaign manager, Dr. Charles Everett, in a much-circulated letter that he would oppose restriction "even to the hazard of the Union."[76] Monroe's son-in-law George Hay went to work on a refutation of Rufus King for Thomas Ritchie's *Enquirer*, and even John Marshall, the embodiment of evil to Virginia strict constructionists, lobbied hard for the president. "I for the first time in my life engaged in a discussion of politics with the C. Justice," Ritchie reported to Barbour. "'I hope (says he [Marshall]) the caucus will be over before the Missouri (Question) is decided.' He added that he was afraid of Monroe's re-election; that the non-slaveholding States might determine to place no man in the chair who would object to the restriction."[77]

Having sufficiently mollified the Virginians, or terrified them with the specter of a Clinton presidency, Monroe's lieutenants now aggressively prosecuted the second part of the president's new Missouri strategy: frightening northerners into taking the disunion threat seriously. A principal target of this effort was John Quincy Adams, the administration's most influential northern member. Almost daily, prominent, strongly nationalist southerners filled Adams with alarming visions of separation. On February 13, while the two men walked home from the Capitol, Henry Clay told Adams that "it was a shocking thing to think of, but he had not a doubt that within five years from this time the Union would be divided into three distinct confederacies."[78] Nine days later, John C. Calhoun painted a picture even more intolerable to this self-conscious son of one of the principal architects of American independence: In case of a separation, the South would be forced "to form an alliance, offensive and defensive, with Great Britain"—in other words, as Calhoun conceded, to return "to the colonial state."[79] Whether or not Calhoun really meant it, no argument could have been more effective in inducing Adams to set aside his deep objections to slavery in favor of a Union-saving compromise.

If these southerners were bluffing in their threats of disunion, they certainly mounted a convincing act. "You can hardly conceive of the rage & fury which prevail[s] here on this subject," Plumer, of New Hampshire, wrote to his father. "It was seriously proposed by the leading men on the other side, Lowndes, Clay, Barbour, & others, if we succeeded, that they would merely pass the appropriation bills, & then adjourn, to consult their constituents whether they should ever come back again! A dissolution of the Union was spoken of as certain, & hardly to be regretted." At one point, Clay announced his readiness to return to Kentucky to raise troops, and Barbour went around to free-state senators proposing a constitutional convention to agree on terms of dissolution of the Union.[80] "I for one was not much moved by these threats," Plumer asserted, "yet to tell the truth there was some danger."[81]

Indeed, danger there was, for if Lowndes, Clay, and Barbour were bluffing about secession, Randolph and the Richmond delegates were not. "You can have no possible idea of the excitement that prevails here," Representative John Tyler wrote his brother-in-law (echoing Plumer). "Men talk of a dissolution of the Union with perfect nonchalance and indifference."

Dropping the third person, Tyler endorsed a militant posture: "For myself, I cannot and will not yield one inch of the ground."[82]

It was at this critical moment that Representative Henry Meigs of New York, a consistent opponent of the Tallmadge Amendment, introduced his resolution calling for a comprehensive approach to ending American slavery, including the "annihilation of the slave trade," full-scale compensated emancipation, and the transportation of the freed slaves to Africa. As if to underscore the inevitability of the colonization scheme, a federally sponsored expedition consisting of the USS *Cyane* and the ship *Elizabeth* sailed for the west coast of Africa about the time that Meigs gave his speech, to capture slavers and to establish a colony of freed American blacks, as per the legislation passed at the end of the previous Congress to give the president power to act against the slave trade. As we have seen in chapter 2, the goals of Meigs's resolution had substantial support in Monroe's administration, and the president had been putting various pieces of the program into place since the start of his term. Given the timing of the resolution, however, it is hard to avoid the impression that Meigs intended it at least in part as a warning to southerners and a preview of the kind of antislavery designs that would inundate the Seventeenth and future Congresses—and that a northern president would not hesitate to approve. Nor was it lost on knowledgeable observers that Meigs's own father, Josiah, was the commissioner of the U.S. Land Office, the man with the greatest knowledge in the country about the extent and value of the public domain. From this moment forward, then, the South was put on notice that the nation had at its disposal, in the public lands, a powerful tool for the destruction of slavery, and influential individuals with the determination and the expertise to employ it.

It appears that in February Monroe decided to enlist the support of Thomas Jefferson on the question to serve as a trump card for loyal Republicans in Virginia and elsewhere. Hugh Nelson, a Virginia congressman who tendered "unquestioned support" to Monroe, spelled out the administration's position on Missouri to Jefferson and obtained his support for a compromise.[83] Jefferson needed no prompting to regard the movement for slavery restriction to be a Federalist plot. His support, although he detested the idea of "the coincidence of a marked principle, moral and political, with geographical lines,"[84] may have been helpful in bringing Virginia Republicans to accept the 36°30' division; it later proved crucial to holding onto northern votes when the Missouri issue reopened in the following session, as we will see.

By the end of February 1820, the atmosphere in Congress reached a nadir. The extremism of the southerners, given no check by Barbour and other administration allies, had attained a level that disgusted even John Holmes, and struck fear into other northern recruits to nonrestriction that their conversions would be in vain. "We are fast approaching a crisis here— the folly of the Southern men I fear will give the ultra federalists a triumph," Jonathan Roberts wrote his brother on the twenty-fifth.[85] Sectional coalitions on other issues, notably the tariff, collapsed. A lobbyist for the manufacturers' association reported that Pennsylvania congressman Henry Baldwin was "in a very uncomfortable state of mind; and . . . nothing can be done to calm or conciliate him" because, he believed, the manufacturers had destroyed their hopes with the southern members "by their zeal on the slave subject."[86] On the twenty-ninth, Holmes, serving on a House-Senate conference committee on the admission of Maine, wrote William King that "the south have made offers of a compromise which the north & even Maine reject."[87] On that same day, the House once again agreed to an amendment to restrict slavery in Missouri by a vote of 94 to 86. Storrs of New York then introduced an amendment to bar slavery in the territories west of the Mississippi above 36°30', described in the *Annals of Congress* as "the amendment commonly called the compromise," which faced fierce opposition from the South—Cobb of Georgia speaking "at considerable length, and very warmly, against all restriction whatsoever, as tending to universal emancipation." Concerned that the March 4 deadline to admit Maine before it reverted back to Massachusetts might expire before a bill could clear the conference committee, Storrs withdrew his motion, and the Missouri bill, with the slavery restriction attached, passed by a narrowing margin of 93 to 84. Among the congressmen present was Kentucky's David Walker, who, though desperately ill, insisted on being carried to the House chamber on a stretcher to cast his vote against restriction. He died at eight o'clock the next morning.[88]

At the morning's session on March 1, at the request of the dying Walker, the House departed from its usual rule of adjourning in memory of a departed member and resumed battle over the Missouri bill. The incensed John Randolph spoke against the measure for "more than three hours," after which the House called the question again: yeas 91, nays 82—a loss of two restrictionist votes, but no gain for the South.[89]

The next day, March 2, saw the Senate as a model of harmony and cooperation. Senator Barbour proposed once again to strip the ban on Missouri slavery from the House bill. Since the subject "had been so fully discussed, and so often passed upon," he felt it unnecessary to discuss the vote or even to call the roll. Rufus King declared himself "perfectly ready to concur" in

Barbour's proposal; but Outerbridge Horsey, of Delaware, "having been necessarily absent" when the question had been previously voted on, requested an opportunity to record his vote. The amendment passed by a vote of 27 to 15. Senator Thomas then reintroduced his amendment to bar slavery north of 36°30'; this passed without a roll call being requested. William Allen Trimble, the young war hero from Ohio, then proposed a more comprehensive restriction, barring slavery entirely from the Louisiana territory "except the State of Louisiana, the territory included in the proposed State of Missouri, and the Arkansas Territory." This more sweeping restriction, which Trimble believed "contained principles on which" the House would be sure to pass the bill, was rejected by a vote of 30 to 12, after which Thomas's amendment was adopted—even though a careful examination of the map would have showed that the territory remaining open to slavery under Trimble's and Thomas's proposals was identical! The Missouri bill now passed the Senate, its title amended by adding the language, "and to prohibit slavery in certain territories," and the managers of the conference committee sent it back to the House, where the struggle continued.[90]

After a three-hour debate on whether to print the report of the House-Senate conference committee, the restrictionist dike began to crack. Charles Kinsey, a New Jersey paper manufacturer with a strong interest in a protective tariff, announced his change of heart. While restrictionists had "treated the idea of a disunion with ridicule," to Kinsey it appeared "in all the horrid, gloomy features of reality." If "we reject the olive branch now offered," Kinsey counseled, "the most disastrous consequences will follow." The southerners had conceded nine-tenths of the Louisiana Territory; "can we wish to deprive them of the remainder?" However his constituents might view his change of heart, Kinsey was confident that "my God, my conscience, and my country, will approve the act."[91]

James Stevens of Connecticut followed suit, reminding his colleagues that "you hold your seats by the tenure of compromise. The Constitution is a creature of compromise; it originated in a compromise; and has existed ever since by a perpetual extension and exercise of that principle; and must continue to do so, as long as it lasts." Although he was not in accord "entirely in sentiment with the proposed compromise," and still hoped that better could be achieved through "a free communication," Stevens would vote for the bill as it now stood.[92]

In addition to Kinsey and Stevens, Samuel Eddy of Rhode Island changed his vote; and New York's Walter Case and Caleb Tompkins and Connecticut's Henry Waggaman Edwards managed to be absent from the floor at the crucial moment. The amendment to drop the restriction of slavery from Missouri passed by 90 to 87.

At this point, John W. Taylor, in a gesture paralleling Trimble's in the Senate, moved to strike out the words "thirty-six degrees thirty minutes north latitude" and replace them with language excluding slavery "from all the territory west of the Mississippi, except Louisiana, Missouri, and Arkansas"—precisely the area open to it under the 36°30' clause. Taylor's meaningless amendment was overridden, and the original restriction passed by an overwhelming margin of 134 to 42. The Senate's amendment to add the words "and to prohibit slavery in certain Territories" was accepted without a roll call vote. "And so, all the amendments being concurred in, the bill was passed by the two Houses."[93]

THE PREDOMINANT MOOD among northern restrictionists after the Missouri vote appeared to be one of sullen demoralization. "I consider myself & associates as conquered," Rufus King wrote his son John after the vote. "The slave States, with their free corps, have subdued us." King dismissed the 36°30' restriction as "a mere tub to the whale."[94] Most southerners, on the other hand—even those who had decried the Compromise as an abject surrender of their rights—tended to view the vote as a major victory. Charles Pinckney of South Carolina, one of the most unyielding antirestrictionists, crowed: "We have carried the question to admit Missouri and all Louisiana [south of 36°30'] free of the restriction of slavery. . . . It is considered here by the slave-holding states as a great triumph."[95]

Not all southerners hailed the "triumph," however, nor did all northerners mourn the defeat. John Randolph, whose attempt to have the Missouri vote reconsidered had been foiled by a somewhat underhanded parliamentary maneuver of Speaker Clay, bitterly sneered that he had always known that the northern representatives who voted for the Compromise "would give way. They were scared at their own dough faces—yes, they were scared at their own dough faces!—We had *them*, and if we had wanted *three* more, we could have had them: yes, and if *these had failed, we could have three more of these men, whose conscience, and morality, and religion, extend to 'thirty-six degrees and thirty minutes north latitude.'*"[96]

This hardly seems the statement of a victorious supporter of slavery. Indeed, Randolph was never more sincere than in his frequent professions of hatred for the institution. It is apt that the wracked, erratic, half-mad Virginian should have coined the peculiar epithet, "doe face," that became, in a curious mutation, "doughface," the universal term of contempt for such "Northern men with Southern principles," or rather, as Randolph implied, with no principles at all.[97] As we will see, Randolph's own complicated principles, so often misinterpreted when not simply discounted as the ramblings of a disordered intellect, offer a key to the Virginian encounter with slavery and to the real tragedy of the Compromise.

In striking contrast, tidings of the Missouri vote brought "great Joy" to the originator of the restriction amendment and its principal backer. From former representative James Tallmadge, John W. Taylor received fervent congratulations: "You have in this business a monument to your fame. Accept the thanks of a sincere friend for your perseverance—Talents—& devotion to the cause of your nation—& of suffering human nature." For his part, as he wrote his wife, Taylor also felt satisfaction: "We have gained all that was possible, if not all that was desired. . . . an ample recompense for all the time and labour it has cost us."[98]

Moreover, the struggle to admit Missouri was hardly finished. The principal task for opponents of restriction was consolidating their position. They had prevailed by just three votes, and even if, as I think it should be, Randolph's assertion that six more northern votes waited in the wings if needed is taken seriously, this still amounted to a tenuous margin.[99] By every indication, most "doughfaces" could expect stiff reelection challenges; the Seventeenth Congress would undoubtedly be still more unfriendly to slavery expansion.

News from Missouri inflamed the antislavery North and guaranteed that the issue would not fade away. Residents of St. Louis gratuitously celebrated their state's victory over restriction by displaying a huge illumination "representing a slave in great spirits, rejoicing at the permission granted by Congress to bring slaves into so fine a country as Missouri."[100] In an eastern counterpoint to the St. Louis illumination, Federalists in Connecticut burned in effigy James Lanman, their doughface senator, for his Missouri vote.[101] Newspapers throughout the North published "black lists" of the names of northern congressmen who voted for the Compromise,[102] and some Republican caucuses regretfully withdrew their backing from dutiful doughfaces. "Last week Bernard Smith the member from Jersey who changed his vote on the Missouri question, call'd upon me," New York doughface Henry Meigs reported. "He was in a melancholy mood in consequence of the proceedings of a Republican Caucus which has dropp'd him, Bloomfield & Kinsey on ac[coun]t of their Missouri votes. Mr. S is not one of those who can be content with the 'mens sibi conscia recti' alone; and altho' he is somewhat 'Rusticus' he is not extremely 'abnormus sapiens' or other*wise*."[103] Connecticut Republican doughface congressmen faced similar difficulties. Neither Samuel Foot nor James Stevens received renomination, though they did gain recompense: Stevens obtained the postmastership of Stamford and later a judgeship, while Foot received endorsement for a seat on the state legislature and later won renomination to Congress at a caucus where party leaders "distinctly and particularly urged" his self-sacrificing vote on Missouri "as a reason why he should be supported."[104] Chastened by his doughface experience, however, Foot became a loyal sponsor of pronorthern measures, later gaining a measure of fame for introducing the resolution to restrict land sales that provoked the celebrated Webster-Hayne debates. Of the Connecticut doughfaces, only Henry W. Edwards managed to secure renomination to the Seventeenth Congress, since he convinced the Republican caucus and constituents that he had not missed the crucial House vote on Missouri intentionally, but had only left his desk to get a bite to eat.[105]

In nominally "slave-state" Delaware, the three Federalists who voted for the Compromise faced opposition from the public for their stance, while the lone Republican, who voted against it, encountered opposition from his party. In June, with the backing of Federalist antirestrictionist Louis McLane, the Monroe administration removed the antislavery Wilmington postmaster, Joseph Bringhurst, replacing him with Nicholas Williamson, who promptly threw himself into an ultimately unsuccessful movement to win Republican endorsement for McLane.[106] In the following election, Willard Hall, the Republican who had voted for restriction and against the Compromise, lost, probably on account of his antitariff views; but voters replaced him with a landslide for Caesar A. Rodney, an even stronger abolitionist who had led the public campaign in Delaware opposing slavery's extension.[107]

New York had provided four doughfaces: two, Henry Meigs and Henry Storrs, voted for the Compromise while two others, Caleb Tompkins and Walter Case, absented themselves. None of the four won reelection to the Seventeenth Congress, and only Storrs—a Federalist—resumed a political career of more than local significance.[108]. The most significant victim in New York of the Missouri question, however, was the vice president, Daniel D. Tompkins. Suspicions over his role in the controversy probably resulted in the slender margin by which he lost the April gubernatorial election to De Witt Clinton.[109] To New Yorkers who voted against him, the belief in Tompkins's involvement was based on circumstantial information only; the active Clintonian "truth squad" produced no damning revelations. If knowledge of the vice president's solicitation of a $75,000 loan from President Cheves of the U.S. Bank had come to light, the vote against Tompkins would likely have been many thousands greater.

Tompkins's failure may also have dealt a setback to the career of Jonathan Roberts. The Pennsylvanian recognized that his surprising emergence as a doughface meant that his career in the Senate was at an end. As he confided to his brother, "Thee thinks it probable I may be re-elected. I cannot say I think it even possible."[110] His southern friends had dangled an enticing alternative before him, however. If Tompkins won the election in New York, it would leave a vacancy in the vice presidency. "Some of the southern and Western men look toward me as the man they would prefer from Penn[a] & it is Penna they wish most to conciliate," Roberts reported. Although he could enumerate the drawbacks the position would entail (the modest "four thousand doll[ar]s" salary "would not render" the post "easy to me"), the senator could at least take joy in the fact that, as the offer showed, "For the moment I am beloved and confided in."[111] Unfortunately for Roberts, no vacancy opened up; and as he had predicted, the Pennsylvania legislature declined to reelect him to the Senate.

Curiously, although Daniel D. Tompkins lost the election for governor of New York to De Witt Clinton, Tompkins did succeed Clinton in another important post a few weeks later. On June 5, 1820, the Grand Lodge of New York elected Tompkins as "Sovereign Grand Commander of the Supreme Council of the Thirty-Third Degree for the Northern Masonic Jurisdiction of the United States of America." The historian of New York Freemasonry is ambiguous about how or why this transfer of power took place, stating that Clinton's replacement "appears to have been brought about by the machinations of opponents envious of his success in the political field. These had stirred up strife within the Fraternity which was beginning to assume a serious character."[112]

However it was engineered, Tompkins's accession as Grand Master of New York carried with it important powers of persuasion, which he invoked in his inaugural address, stressing that "mutual respect and esteem" should be the rule between members. "But above all," he continued, "we should scrupulously examine and guard ourselves against the indulgence of sectarian or political feelings with in these sacred walls."[113] Given the bitterness of Tompkins's recent campaign for governor, as well as the turbulence of his short tenure as grand master, it seems highly probable that Tompkins attempted to employ the office for political ends, perhaps both in support of the Missouri Compromise and to promote his policies in the New York constitutional convention of 1821, which he chaired—and where he once again did battle with Rufus King.[114]

The history of the Masonic fraternity offers a largely unseen counterpoint to the rhythm of public events during this period, one that can be evaluated only with difficulty, if at all. Nonetheless, the significance of Masonic ties during the Missouri controversy should not be underestimated. Henry Clay, chief architect of the second Missouri Compromise, was "active and influential in the order," and Henry Meigs, who had proposed a sweeping program of slave emancipation and colonization, festooned his letters to his father with brilliant watercolor sketches on Masonic themes.[115]

The works of Dorothy Ann Lipson on Connecticut and Randolph Roth on Vermont have discussed the growth and influence of the Masonic Order in those states and hinted at the potential political clout the Craft could command.[116] Of Freemasonry in Pennsylvania, Philip S. Klein has written, "If ever a fraternity could claim a monopoly of men of talents and character, the Masonic Order in Pennsylvania could claim it during the early 1820s. It is impossible to pick up the history of a Pennsylvania lodge and scan the list of members without arriving at the conclusion that their selection represented the most outstanding men of the community." Clearly, then, Pennsylvania Freemasonry included many of the combatants on both sides of the restriction question, and any effort to enlist the ties of brotherhood on either side would have deeply compromised the unity of the Order. As Klein observes, the Pennsylvania lodges engaged in no formal political activity during the 1820s, and political letters before the Antimasonic controversy make no reference to Masonry. The same is true of Masonry in New York. Yet the Order simultaneously underwent tremendous upheavals in both states, involving resistance and even secession by rural lodges sparked by "dictatorial" policies imposed by the Grand Lodges in Philadelphia and Albany, precisely at the period of the Missouri controversy and the accession of Tompkins as sovereign grand commander.[117] The schism in Freemasonry that occurred at this time had not fully healed by the end of the decade, and its lingering effects may be seen in the hostility toward the Order demonstrated by ex-Masons during the scandal surrounding the death of the Masonic turncoat William Morgan that sparked the creation of the Antimasonic Party—itself a forerunner of the abolitionist movement of the 1830s. In the chapters that follow, I will further explore this lineage; with regard to the role of Masonry in the Missouri affair I can do no more here than to raise possibilities of connections, rather than offer conclusions.[118]

John C. Calhoun took the most active role of Monroe's cabinet officials in seeking to forge sectional harmony between congressional sessions. The most brilliant and charismatic member of the administration, as well as the most expansively nationalist, Calhoun was an ideal choice to send on a fence-mending trip to New England and the middle states. Ostensibly on an inspection tour of northern military facilities, Calhoun also used the trip to charm restrictionist leaders such as Webster—and also, unsurprisingly, to promote his own political fortunes as well. For the most part, his visit was a triumph, although the New York leg proved wearisome as Tammany and Clintonian factions competed to exploit his presence for political gain.[119]

As important as Calhoun's overtures to northeasterners were, however, he dedicated as much effort to keeping the South in line, working as hard to calm southern fears of northern extremism as he had earlier tried, in such conversations as the one with Secretary Adams described above, to frighten northerners about the intentions of the South. In earnest letters to southern leaders Calhoun repeatedly stressed that the greatest danger to the Union came not from northern fanaticism, but rather from misguided southern militancy based on misunderstanding of the North. To Alabama's Charles Tait, Calhoun insisted that the number of individuals in the North who, "for private objects," wished to split the Union, was "very small, and the few there are, are to be found almost wholly in New York, and the mid[d]le States. . . . We to the South ought not to assent easily to the belief [*sic*], that there is a conspiracy either against our property, or just weight in the Union," he warned Tait. "A belief of the former might, and probably would, lead to the most disasterous [*sic*] consequence. Nothing would lead more directly to disunion with all of its horrows [*sic*]. That of the latter, would coöperate, as it appears to me, directly with the scheme of the few designing men in the North, who think they see their interest in exciting a struggle between the two portions of our country. If we, from such a belief, systematically oppose the North, they must from necessity resort to a similar opposition to us."[120] In view of the Carolinian's future career, Calhoun's argument is certainly remarkable.

No one worked harder to consolidate the antirestrictionist position than Thomas Jefferson. With regard to the Missouri question, he had entered the political arena late, but he made up for lost time. Jefferson's famous description of the crisis as a "fire bell in the night. . . . the knell of the Union," came in an April letter to Maine's John Holmes, returning from Congress to anger and vilification at home for his part as the arch-doughface of the Missouri capitulation. It could be argued that nothing less than an endorsement from the author of the Declaration of Independence himself could have salvaged Holmes's political career in Maine. Fortunately for him, he had exactly that. "I regret," Jefferson wrote, that I am now to die in the belief, that the useless sacrifice of themselves by the generation of 1776, to acquire self-government and happiness to their country, is to be thrown away by the unwise and unworthy passions of their sons, and that my only consolation is to be, that I live not to weep over it. If they would but dispassionately weigh the blessings they will throw away, against an abstract principle more likely to be effected by union than by scission, they would pause before they would perpetrate this act of suicide on themselves, and of treason against the hopes of the world. To yourself, as the faithful advocate of the Union, I tender the offering of my high esteem and respect.[121]

Armed with this powerful document by the founder of their party, with its forecast of doom for the infant nation, Holmes secured election as one of Maine's first senators from the new state's chastened Republican legislature.

But Jefferson reserved his tone of fatalism for northerners and anticompromise southerners. Three weeks after his letter to Holmes, Jefferson wrote enthusiastically about America's future prospects in a letter to Monroe, welcoming the Senate's apparent failure to ratify Spain's treaty with the U.S. as a convenient prelude to the annexation of Florida and Texas, the latter of which "will be the richest state in our Union, without any exception. Its southern part will make more sugar than we can consume, and the Red river, on its north, is the most luxuriant country on earth." Foreshadowing a century of filibustering and imperialist tactics, Jefferson argued that "[Texas], the Floridas and possibly Cuba, will join us on the acknowledgment of their independence, a measure to which their new government will probably accede voluntarily." Jefferson's emphasis on the new state's suitability for growing sugar, the most labor-intensive of cash crops, as well as his interest in acquiring Cuba, implicitly sanctioned a greatly expanded role for slavery in the United States, one that would almost certainly have involved an augmentation of illegal importation of Africans (a practice for which Texas was already a major American entrepôt). Jefferson could hardly have been unaware of the great "Sugar Revolution" currently under way in Cuba, spurring an almost unlimited demand for slave labor and accounting for the greater part of the illegal slave trade. He concluded his letter to Monroe with a jauntily pan-American salutation: "God bless you and preserve you *muchos años*."[122]

Nothing in Jefferson's boldly activist letter to Monroe reveals any trace of pessimism for the nation's prospects. Nor did he display deep concern when he briefed Lafayette on the controversy in December: "With us things are going on well. The boisterous sea of liberty indeed is never without a wave, and that from Missouri is now rolling toward us, but we shall ride over it as we have over all others."[123] To Albert Gallatin, however, Jefferson wrote on the very same day, "At home things are not well. . . . Nothing has ever presented so threatening an aspect as what is called the Missouri question." Gallatin, a pronounced Republican opponent of slavery then serving as U.S. minister to France, still counted as a pivotal figure in his home state of Pennsylvania. Jefferson sought to convince him that the Missouri question had nothing to do with morality but merely represented Federalism's newest tactic to divide the states. Ultimately, Jefferson warned his old colleague, "the whole will depend on Pennsylvania. While she and Virginia hold together, the Atlantic States can never separate. Unfortunately in the present case she has become more fanaticized than any other State. However useful where you are, I wish you were with them. You might turn the scale there, which would turn it for the whole."[124]

Also on the same day, Jefferson penned a letter to his old friend David Baillie Warden, an Irish Presbyterian encyclopedist and dedicated opponent of slavery and racism who had translated the abbé Grégoire's *Enquiry Concerning the Intellectual and Moral Faculties, and Literature of Negroes*, which had contained a stern condemnation of Jefferson's racial views.[125] The Missouri controversy, Jefferson assured Warden, is "a question having just enough of the semblance of morality to throw dust into the eyes of the people, & to fanaticicse them; while with the knowing ones it is simply a question of power. . . . Real morality is on the other side," Jefferson insisted, for "the spreading [slaves] over a larger surface adds to their happiness and renders their future emancipation more practicable."[126]

With southerners, Jefferson adopted yet another tone, a more troubled one reminiscent of that of the author of the *Notes on Virginia*. To Joseph C. Cabell, the Virginia canal builder, Jefferson prayed that the example of De Witt Clinton's "gigantic efforts" would inspire Virginia's legislature "to look to the reputation and safety of their own country, to rescue it from the degradation of becoming the Barbary of the Union, and of falling into the ranks of our own negroes."[127] Commiserating with South Carolina's Charles Pinckney, one of the House's most militant antirestrictionists, Jefferson snarled that "the leaders of federalism. . . . are wasting Jeremiads on the miseries of slavery, as if we were advocates for it. Sincerity in their declamations should direct their efforts to the true point of difficulty, and unite their counsels with ours in devising some reasonable and practicable plan of getting rid of it."[128]

Jefferson's letter vividly demonstrates how little room to maneuver the

Missouri crisis had left southerners who considered themselves opponents of slavery. By this time, southern doctrine had adopted the position that northerners had no business interfering in the discussion of slavery, not even to "unite their counsels" on plans to put an end to it. The unified voice of the South, including Jefferson's, opposed the geographical restriction of slavery beyond the Mississippi. This left only colonization as an approved means of confronting slavery where northerners and southerners could meet; and slaveholders, such as the *Richmond Enquirer*'s "American," had begun to denounce even this most modest of approaches. What did Jefferson regard as "the true point of difficulty" and what kind of "reasonable and practicable plan" did Jefferson have in mind? The impression is inescapable that southerners were running out of alternatives to becoming "advocates" for slavery. The next chapter of the controversy deprived them of much of the little room they still had left.

———— ✺ ————

SOUTHERNERS REPEATEDLY insisted during the Missouri debate that the purpose of restrictionists was to unite the North and divide the Union—or at least that would be its outcome. In fact, however, it has been argued that the Missouri affair called the South into being. Why did it not do the same for the North?

Some northerners indeed hoped it would. Certain New York Clintonians in particular sounded a note of sectionalism as strident as the most chauvinist Virginian.[129] In truth, however, the sectional compromise along the line of 36°30' offered a much simpler and less jarring dichotomy: that of "America" in contradistinction to "the South," or, just as often, "Virginia."

This transformation required a major shift in perspective, as David Brion Davis has observed, for Virginia not only had epitomized Revolutionary values, but also had taken the lead in opposing slavery in the early years of the republic. "Yet Virginia's early leadership made it all the easier to sectionalize the national burden of inconsistency. For Virginia, as critics discovered at the time of the Missouri debates, had never been sincere. She had eagerly welcomed the importation of slaves, so the argument ran, until further numbers posed the threat of declining slave prices and possible insurrection. . . . The Missouri debates revealed Virginia's true colors. Henceforth, the contradiction between Revolutionary and secular time, which had seemed to lead to irreversible declension, could be conceived as a contradiction between two cultures—or as a contradiction in American space."[130]

This conceptual firewall between the South and the nation solved a host of problems. It soothed the consciences of northerners with the thought that slavery was not their concern, thus squelching the impulse to interfere in the institution equally effectively for the South's friends as for its bitter enemies. A lifelong hater of southern institutions such as Josiah Quincy could wish, like Jonah at Nineveh, that settlers beyond the Mississippi be allowed to sink through their sins, and not be "rescued" by restriction, just as easily as his Massachusetts colleague Henry Shaw could urge nonintervention with regard to slavery in order to preserve "harmony and good will."[131]

The South as such defined itself and was defined by its involvement with slavery; "America," although including the South for political and other purposes, need not be preoccupied by the existence of slavery, now cordoned off (conceptually if not in reality) into a discrete region, leaving the nation, the whole, untainted by whatever ill effects the institution might inflict on the society that condoned it. One no longer needed to worry, as Arthur Livermore had, whether the Constitution had really been "made to impose slavery, and not to establish liberty."[132]

The new principle of sectional laissez-faire created a strange dynamic whereby traditional expressions of nationalism came to seem threatening to the Union and the constitution, while an insistence on only the most minimal definition of national unity and repudiation of the idea of mutual responsibility became the paradigm of patriotism.[133]

But to the extent that isolating the slavery issue to the South soothed the consciences of northerners and eased the immediate political pressures on slaveholders, it placed the burden of "irreversible declension" on that section alone. It is ironic that Henry Shaw opposed the Tallmadge Amendment on the grounds that it would have "created a distinction between slave-holding and non-slave-holding states; a distinction that loses none of its mischievous qualities from the ability to trace it on the *map of our country*."[134] This was, of course, precisely what the Missouri Compromise line of 36°30' did, as Thomas Jefferson mournfully observed to John Holmes: "A geographical line, coinciding with a marked principle, moral and political, once conceived and held up to the angry passions of men, will never be obliterated; and every new irritation will mark it deeper and deeper."[135] Educated southerners had been schooled in the same values as their northern counterparts; they did not care to be written off to morality as a cost of doing business in a slave-based society by "men whose conscience, and religion, and morality, extend to the line of thirty-six degrees and thirty minutes north latitude," in John Randolph's words—to be psychologically as well as geographically "damned up in a land of slaves by the Eastern people," as Judge Roane put it.[136] Nor were Anglophilic southern would-be aristocrats insensible to the growing hostility to slavery displayed in English letters, society, and religion. Western slaveholding politicians such as Clay and Benton, even if personally opposed to slavery, sought in their political efforts only to create a workable arrangement whereby slaveowners could employ their stock, make money, and be left alone. Consistently, from 1820 to the Civil War, slaveowners in the Old South refused to allow America simply to leave them alone.

Throughout the spring and summer of 1820, disturbing reports emanating from Missouri strongly indicated that the issue of its admission would not be laid to rest. To begin with, if it is true, as Glover Moore suggests, that many northerners mistakenly believed that Missourians might elect a majority of antislavery delegates to their constitutional convention, the rout of the antislavery ticket must have come as a bitter shock.[137] Not content with beating antislavery advocates at the polls, Isaac Henry, Thomas Hart Benton's coeditor at the proslavery *St. Louis Enquirer*, physically assaulted the editor of the rival antislavery *Gazette*, one week after the vote.[138]

Reports of such violence were received as mere sideshows, however, compared to the content of the Missouri constitution itself. Its provisions prohibiting the legislature from passing any future emancipation act and directing the enactment of laws excluding free blacks from the future state did not merely outrage restrictionists but represented an egregious insult to northern backers of the first Compromise and a deep embarrassment to moderate southerners. Such distinguished figures as Robert G. Harper, William Gaston, and Langdon Cheves all privately considered the articles incompatible with the U.S. Constitution.[139] The extreme provisions also provided a telling picture of Missouri proslavery populism. According to one observer in the House, both John Scott, Missouri's delegate to Congress, and David Barton, president of the convention, opposed them. In the face of public opinion, however, both lawmakers quickly endorsed the measures.[140]

In effect, the framers of Missouri's constitution ratcheted up the demands that slavery made on both the American political system and traditional American ideals. Missouri's new, entrepreneurial slaveholders rejected the genteel contradiction that most other southerners lived by and confronted the anomaly of America's revolutionary heritage head on. It seems that the territory's slaveholders were willing that Missouri go it alone as an independent republic if the Congress chose not to admit it into the union without conditions; thus moderates in Congress and the administration had no leverage with which to induce territorial leaders to compromise. The Missourians had no incentive to play by the elaborate rules of circumlocution that had been worked out in the previous Congress whereby antirestrictionists had sought to contain the debate to the constitutionality of slavery restriction rather than its expediency. For whatever reason, Missourians sought to force the debate over slavery per se that most southerners, Virginians in particular, dreaded.[141]

Some slavery advocates, especially South Carolinians, were willing to go a long way in the defense of slavery; lawmakers from districts with large black majorities often showed little interest in keeping alive abstract principles of blacks' natural liberty or equality. But many southerners persisted in attempting to keep the debate focused on John W. Taylor's original question of slavery's constitutionality, even at the price of abandoning all rational argument. Their strategy was the audacious one of declaring that Missouri *already was a state*, even in the absence of any congressional action to admit it.[142] On its face, this seems to be a preposterous argument, and even prosouthern historians have been at a loss to justify it. Glover Moore, citing Arthur Schlesinger Sr., argues that "it is axiomatic that those who advocate state rights are often guilty of inconsistencies, and this was certainly the case in 1819–1821."[143] However true this may be as a general principle, these states' rights antirestrictionists demonstrated unflinching consistency in pursuing their fundamental goal: rendering moot a direct defense of slavery by asserting constitutional objections. Linn Banks, the speaker of the Virginia legislature, had reported to Senator Barbour the legislature's consensus on state sovereignty: "After the admission of a new State into the Union the inhabitants thereof have an undeniable right as a free, sovereign and independent people to frame their own constitution or system of government, so that *that* constitution . . . is not repugnant to, or in conflict with, the Federal Constitution."[144] In this case, if Missouri were already a state, then its constitution and laws would be sovereign and not subject to congressional discussion.

The first practical application of this constitutional theory came shortly after the opening of the second session of the Sixteenth Congress. After an acrimonious debate and many inconclusive ballots, the House had finally selected a Speaker: John Taylor of New York—the floor leader of the fight for the Tallmadge Amendment in the previous congress.

Almost immediately after Taylor's election, southern anticompromisers forced the House into two days of debate over the seemingly trivial question of whether the words "State of" should precede "Missouri" in the record of the House. Much of the violent debate was directed at Speaker Taylor, probably in an attempt by southerners to wear him down. Even if it did not accomplish this, it may have had the effect of making him gun-shy.

This semantic showdown served merely as dress rehearsal for the explosive scene to come. First, however, antislavery leaders in the House took up the offensive Missouri constitution as new grounds for rejecting the territory's bid for statehood. Curiously paralleling the Virginians' unwillingness to debate slavery head-on, however, the restrictionists chose to focus not on the constitution's provisions restricting the legislature's power of emancipation, but instead to attack the clause restricting the immigration of free blacks and mulattoes as a violation of Article IV, Section 2, of the federal constitution: "The citizens of each state shall be entitled to all privileges and immunities of citizens in the several states."

At first glance, this seems like a strange tactical decision. The provision to bar the state legislature from terminating slavery without the permission of slaveholders—which would have the effect, as all understood, of prohibiting emancipation altogether—was entirely unprecedented in a state constitution. Certainly this cruel provision garnered the lion's share of the unfavorable reviews of the Missouri convention's handiwork. By contrast, the constitutions of several northern states limited suffrage to whites, and several had passed laws limiting the rights of blacks to travel or reside in them. On its face, then, the citizenship provision seems like the far more difficult case for northerners to make.

In practical terms, however, Missouri's constitutional call for legislation excluding blacks represented the only potential ground to bar the territory from the Union, even if it opened a host of problematic questions about northern treatment of the same group. Although Missouri's constitutional provision against emancipation was draconian, it was not unconstitutional. On the other hand, if free blacks were U.S. citizens, then Missouri's constitution clearly violated the privileges and immunities clause of the federal constitution, and Missouri could not be admitted until it amended or repealed the offending article. Even if Missouri's residents proved willing to make such a change, it would certainly cause a delay of several months, by which time the Sixteenth Congress would have adjourned, giving way to the more antislavery Seventeenth Congress, which would have a better chance of excluding a slaveholding Missouri altogether.

Perhaps surprisingly, few legislators, even in the South, had formally disputed the citizenship of free blacks. At least 5,000 blacks had fought on the American side during the Revolution, fulfilling that traditional test of qualification by military service. Blacks had been barred from the navy in 1798 by a War Department interpretation of the Militia Law of 1792; but, less famously, that regulation had been revoked a few years later, when it was found effectively impossible to supply the needs of the service without seamen of color.[145] The impressments of American sailors, blacks among them, had been a principal cause and rallying cry of the War of 1812, with Representative John C. Calhoun thundering on the floor of the House against Britain's inexcusable injustice to "our citizens." At the crucial final battle of the war, no less a figure than Andrew Jackson entreated the free blacks of New Orleans to come to the aid of their country and join the city's militia, fulsomely apologizing for past injustices and promising (untruthfully, as it turned out) proper recognition of their rights in the future.

Even the most responsible badge of citizenship, the ballot, was not beyond the reach of all southern free blacks. Those who met the property qualifications in Tennessee and North Carolina not only could vote, but did—as opposed to blacks in Pennsylvania, who, with few exceptions, refrained from exercising their legal right to the franchise in the face of overwhelming unofficial white disapproval. Indeed, a former South Carolina state legislator related to a Connecticut congressman during the Missouri debates that a proposed South Carolina law barring blacks from the state, similar to Missouri's provision, had been rejected as in violation of the federal constitution.[146] In short, the critical distinction with regard to citizenship was between slave and free, not between black and white, and states could and routinely did impose restrictions of various kinds without infringing on the right of citizenship.

However logically, historically, and constitutionally sound the focus on the citizenship rights of free blacks might be, in terms of practical politics it constituted slippery ground to defend. Beyond the awkward problem of the hypocrisy of northern legislatures in the discriminatory treatment of their own free black citizens, the decision shifted the debate from slavery, where restrictionists held the high ground, to the largely uncharted region of race, where popular prejudice held sway. It was one thing for a northern congressman to face the slings and arrows of the South to oppose the insidious encroachment of the slave power on American liberties, and quite another to bring the government to a standstill to protect the untrammeled right to free movement of a despised and degraded caste.

From another perspective, however, the restrictionists had lighted on precisely the key issue in contention. Given the nation's history and founding principles, supporters of slavery could never successfully defend the institution in the abstract; the excuse for its existence in the United States would ultimately have to be grounded on the fitness of Africans for enslavement—on the African exception to the American affirmation that "all men are created equal." In this as in so many of the key sectional struggles that were to come, the question of free blacks, not of slaves, proved to be the principal battleground. In retrospect, it is surprising that many northerners were willing to take such strong stands on questions of free blacks' rights in a variety of important future confrontations, from Samuel Hoar's 1844 mission to South Carolina to defense of personal liberty laws and opposition to the Fugitive Slave Act of 1850, not to mention the *Amistad* incident of 1839–41 (in which Chief Justice Taney acquiesced in a decision in favor of African rights in direct opposition to his infamous decision in the *Dred Scott* case sixteen years later). Nonetheless, the liberty of black Americans seemed a slender reed indeed on which to rest the hope of a limit to slavery.[147]

In the meantime, the mood in the capital grew somber, as room for a compromise diminished and the consequences of failure loomed ominously. Although the combatants largely abandoned the theatrics of the previous session, the atmosphere was, if anything, more grave. In this setting, Clay searched for a workable formula to achieve Missouri's statehood. On February 2, 1821, he assembled a committee of thirteen—"a number suggested by that of the original states of the union"—that reported a resolution to the House eight days later authorizing the admission of Missouri on the condition "that the said state shall never pass any law preventing any description of persons from coming to or settling in the said state, who are now or may hereafter become citizens of any of the states of this union," and requiring Missouri's legislature to enact a public proclamation of assent to this condition.[148]

The language of this resolution proved unsatisfactory to members on both sides of the question. Connecticut representative Gideon Tomlinson, a member of the select committee, observed that the legislature of Missouri would be required "to stipulate" that it would "never pass a law which their constitution makes it their duty to pass"—a power that the Missouri legislature could not possess and that Congress could not grant.[149]

Following a notably vitriolic debate, the House proceeded to a series of razor-close votes in which the Clay committee's resolution was rejected by the committee of the whole, the rejection overturned by the House, and finally, on the vote for a third reading, the resolution defeated by a vote of 80 to 83, with John Randolph and two like-minded southerners notably voting with most northerners in the majority.[150]

To Randolph's annoyance, Clay reintroduced the bill the following day, ostensibly in order to enable members who had unavoidably been absent an opportunity to vote.[151] When the debate was renewed, Charles Pinckney

of South Carolina, a signer of the Constitution, offered a sweeping sum-
mary of the slaveholders' argument in favor of Missouri. Its constitution,
he asserted, was the most perfect of any state, building on the wisdom of its
predecessors and avoiding the flaws that marred them. With regard to the
one defect its opponents charged it with, the unconstitutionality of its bar
against blacks and mulattoes, Pinckney found it "infinitely more probable
that other reasons of a much more serious nature" were "at the bottom of
this unexpected and inexcusable opposition."[152]

Dramatically, Pinckney asserted that he himself had authored the article
of the Constitution that guaranteed that "the citizens of each State shall be
entitled to all the privileges and immunities in every State"; thus "I must
know, or perfectly recollect, what I meant by it. In answer, I say, that, at the
time I drew that constitution, I perfectly knew that there did not then exist
in the Union such a thing as a black or colored citizen; nor could I then
have conceived it possible such a thing ever could have existed in it; nor,
notwithstanding all that is said on the subject, do I now believe one does
exist in it." The "only true question," Pinckney insisted, was "what is a
citizen of the United States?" Using logic similar to Philip Barbour's in the
first Missouri debate, Pinckney then set out the qualification of a citizen,
starting from the understanding of his home state. In South Carolina, all
whites born in the state, or "adopted according to law," were citizens. Were
women and unpropertied white men citizens? Yes; although "their privileges vary according to their sex and situation. Females are wholly excluded
from a right to vote, or to office, and are confined to their proper sphere."
Otherwise, all whites in South Carolina were equal—"except clergymen,
who, on account of their office, are excluded from the Legislature." Pinckney did not feel it necessary to note the unequal property qualifications that
gave greater electoral privileges to slaveholders than to nonslaveholders;
nor did he bring up the state's notoriously undemocratic provisions regarding districting, taxation, and representation. After reviewing the rights of
such white citizens in South Carolina, Pinckney turned to the condition of
"the *black* or colored man, such as he is in the Eastern or Northern States,"
questioning whether "for the comparatively few rights of such a being as he
is . . . gentlemen can be serious in refusing the admission of Missouri, and
risking the consequences." Blacks in the eastern states were treated with
contempt, denied service in the militia or on juries, prohibited from marry-
ing whites, and even refused residence for more than two months "under
penalty of whipping." Pinckney clinched his argument with an example
that, like Philip Barbour's argument in the previous Congress about the
danger that slaves posed of foreign invasion, seemed to prove the opposite

of what he wished to demonstrate. "The only solitary privilege" granted to blacks, "on pressing occasions, when votes are wanted," is the franchise! "These degraded beings are frequently, in a most improper state, dragged to the polls, with tickets in their hands which they cannot read, compelled by men under whose influence they are obliged to act, to disgrace, in the most shameful manner, the highest privilege our Republic boasts."[153] Thus, while Pinckney attempted to prove that blacks were a degraded class *because* of laws and customs disqualifying them from civic rights such as the franchise, he laid bare the real ground of his objection by arguing that the franchise itself was degraded by being exercised by blacks.

Pinckney then launched into a remarkable tour de force of quasi-historical exegesis, relying on the same uniquely flexible principles of logic. Citing no evidence or authority, he asserted that Africa, alone of all quarters of the world, remained "completely unaltered from the creation until the present moment," and the African "still as savage as ever . . . as unchanged as the lion or the tiger which roams in the same forests with himself." Why should the African alone, though "always in the neighborhood," and within the reach of civilization, have "continued the barbarous and cannibal race they were from the beginning? The reason is plain," Pinckney affirmed, "from the only data given us to judge from. They certainly must have been created with less intellectual powers than the whites, and were most probably intended to serve them, and be the instruments of their cultivation." He chose not to explain what "data" provided the basis for this conclusion, or how it was "given." Nonetheless, "some of the most able philosophers in both continents, among whom may be named Mr. Hume and Mr. Jefferson, have invariably expressed the same sentiments." The fact that "the most enlightened nations of Europe"—England, Spain(!), France, and Holland—chose to enslave Africans to labor in their American colonies, rather than Asians or native Indians, proved Africa's degradation. So did the fact that the Romans, like the Greeks, enslaved only whites: "It does not appear that they even condescended to make [Africans] their slaves."[154] Thus the presumptive inferiority of Africans explained why they were both peculiarly fitted for enslavement and peculiarly unfitted for enslavement.

Ultimately, Pinckney came to his strongest case: economics. The most pressing reason to seek compromise, and to strengthen the bond of union, stemmed from the importance of revenues and trade. The "distressed situation of commerce everywhere, and particularly in the Northern and Eastern States," was manifest from the deluge of petitions and memorials flooding the Congress. The chief cause of the distress was the collapse of the market for eastern wheat, a result of the postwar expansion of agricultural production in Europe. The northern and middle states "must become more dependent now than ever on the Southern and Western States, as well for the employment of their shipping as by the furnishing them with exports; for almost the whole employment their shipping now receives is from them, and almost all their trade is by the import and re-export of the Southern and Western products." Pinckney produced the hard figures that made his case: total exports from the South and West totaled more than $34 million, while those of the North and East tallied less than $17 million—of which the greater part consisted of the reshipment of southern commodities. "In this state of things it is almost superfluous to ask if it is not of much greater consequence to the Northern and Eastern States to preserve an Union from which they derive such very important benefits, than to risk it to give to a few free negroes and mulattoes the right to settle in Missouri contrary to the declared unanimous wish of the people of that State?"[155] After Pinckney's speech, the House voted once again on the question of ordering the resolution to be engrossed for a third reading, and once again rejected the motion—this time by a vote of 82 to 88.

When the House and Senate met the following day, on February 14, for the count of the electoral votes for president and vice president a startling drama unfolded regarding Missouri's status. The southern-controlled Senate considered Missouri already admitted to the Union simply by virtue of having fulfilled the conditions required to apply for statehood. The House did not. A joint committee failed to adopt a procedure agreeable to both houses, settling on reading two sets of votes—one counting Missouri and one not. When New Hampshire's Livermore objected to Missouri's votes being counted, the Senate withdrew as a body, whereupon Virginia's John Floyd called "in a violent & frantic manner" for Missouri's votes to be accepted and John Randolph seconded his motion "in a speech of extreme severity & violence." Henry Clay then took the floor and convinced the House to lay the resolution on the table and ask the Senate to return, scoring points with northerners for his "great force & dignity [and] liberality." The Senate returned and the counting resumed, but the two irascible Virginians were not to be so easily placated. As New Hampshire representative William Plumer described the scene,

The President of the Senate [John Gaillard of South Carolina] then proceeded to make proclamation of the election of Mr Monroe & Tompkins, when he was interrupted by Floyd & Randolph, who enquired whether the votes of Missouri had been counted—Mr Gaillard . . . was confused and distressed by this interruption, & neither knew which way to look or what to do—He however at length said that he could answer no questions, & had nothing to do but declare the election—This he began again to do, when he was again interrupted by Floyd, who, in the most violent manner, with menacing gestures, & in a tone of defiance & rage, exceeding any thing I ever saw, attempted to prevent the vote being declared—Randolph also interfered, but they were both called to order from all quarters of the House & Senate—& directed by the Speaker [Henry Clay], who displayed great firmness & presence of mind on this trying occasion . . . to take their seats— Floyd appealed from the decision, but was again ordered down by the Speaker—Gaillard then made his proclamation—When he closed, Randolph renewed his question midst cries of order,—The Speaker ordered him to sit down—but he continued speaking—when a motion was made by one of the Senators to retire, which was put by their President, & that dignified body retired in some haste, & with little order, from the House,—glad, I believe, to get out of a place where they were treated with so little ceremony or respect.[156]

The riveting display of these southerners must be interpreted as an act of pure principle, since Missouri's electoral votes, counted or not, would have had no practical effect whatsoever in an election in which Monroe received every vote but one. But precisely what principle was at stake? It is plainly inaccurate to describe the Virginians' stance here as motivated by their belief in "state rights," since the issue was whether Missouri already constituted a state, not what its rights would be if it were one. Moreover, despite similarities to the Kansas doctrine later propounded by Stephen A. Douglas, it seems most unlikely that John Randolph, arch-aristocrat and staunch opponent of Virginia electoral and constitutional reform, would consciously advocate a doctrine of "popular sovereignty" implicitly much more radical than the Illinois Democrat's.

It is significant that Randolph and Floyd should have been the two congressmen who asserted Missouri's statehood most stridently, almost fanatically. These congressmen had also been among the most ferocious in their opposition to the ban on slavery north of 36°30' of the first Missouri Compromise. Moreover, both had demonstrated a strong antipathy toward slavery throughout their careers that went beyond mere words: Randolph had introduced many measures against the slave trade and had worked to forestall the introduction of slavery in Indiana, as well as arranging to have his own slaves freed at his death; Floyd would later confide to his diary that he would "not rest until slavery is abolished in Virginia," and quietly helped to coordinate the emancipation efforts of 1831–32.[157] There is a strong underlying consistency to the positions of Randolph and Floyd, but it is not a constitutional one; rather, their position flows logically out of a refusal to countenance official sanction of slavery combined with a deep-seated fear of the consequences of tampering with it.

Historians, and most contemporaries, generally have explained the extreme position adopted by Floyd and Randolph as stemming from a devotion to "state rights" and to southern prerogatives. Modern historians in particular have been singularly willing to accept these values as irreducible principles, almost as "subjects of ultimate concern," in Paul Tillich's usage, and have been uninterested in subjecting them to serious analysis. This is understandable; most of what is essential in the Virginians' position is implicit and unstated in their public utterances, particularly those made for a national audience. Nor have historians shown much curiosity in trying to square such positions with Randolph's oft-cited and frequently displayed hatred of slavery, writing the conflict off either to Randolph's legendary eccentricity, or to a supposedly pervasive and unremarkable Virginian characteristic of hypocrisy with regard to the peculiar institution. More important, historians have largely accepted without reflection the idea of a unitary, slavery-supporting South. Glover Moore is hardly alone in the reflex that brings him to describe a poem condemning slavery as an attack on the *South*—thus granting to southern secessionists without a struggle the principle they labored for forty years to achieve.[158] The "strict constructionism" of Randolph and Floyd has a very different character, in my opinion: it represents an extreme effort to forestall the need for an open defense of slavery by asserting the unconstitutionality of Congress's discussing the issue at all.

On February 21, Representative William Brown of Kentucky submitted a resolution repealing the eighth section of the Missouri statehood act—the provision barring slavery above the latitude of 36°30'. The prohibition had represented the southern concession in the Compromise; the northern concession, the admission of Missouri, had not happened. Brown had delayed his resolution at the request of Pennsylvania's Henry Baldwin, he said; and he had kept it from his fellow Kentuckian, Henry Clay. Having concluded that kindness, persuasive arguments, and solid reasoning were in vain, Brown "acknowledge[d]" that he knew "of no course left more likely to avoid greater evils, than a mild, but unvarying system of retaliation."[159]

Whether or not Brown had in fact adopted his drastic course independently of Clay, it set an appropriately menacing backdrop for the former Speaker's final exercise of parliamentary legerdemain. The following day—appropriately, Washington's birthday—Clay moved to appoint an unprecedented joint committee of the House and Senate "to consider and report to the Senate and the House whether it be expedient or not to make provision for the admission of Missouri." The resolution passed by a vote of 101 to 55. The composition of the committee included leading antirestrictionists, wavering restrictionists, and diehard anticompromisers such as Randolph and King, whose presence, even in dissent, would be necessary to lend credibility to the committee's proceedings.[160]

The new wording that Clay's committee arrived at three days later—undoubtedly drafted by Clay himself—represented a landmark in deliberately obfuscatory legislative language. It said that the clause of the Missouri constitution calling for laws to prohibit free blacks from entering the state "shall never be construed to authorize the passage of any law . . . by which any citizen, of either of the states in this Union, shall be excluded from the enjoyment of any of the privileges and immunities to which such citizen is entitled under the constitution of the United States."[161] What this was supposed to mean, no one could say, since its purpose was to be sufficiently obscure to permit widely differing—even contradictory—interpretations. To southerners, it served to legitimate the Missouri constitution. To northerners, on the other hand, Clay's compromise meant in essence that Missouri's constitution should not be interpreted to say what it plainly said. The only explanation for its passage was that legislators had concluded, partly out of apprehension for the Union but to a not insignificant degree out of exhaustion, that the issue had to be disposed of; and Clay's fuzzy language gave them a marginally sufficient pretext for doing so.

After the submission of the Clay committee's report to Congress, once again Monroe turned to Nicholas Biddle, his Philadelphia ally, to pull out all the stops for its passage. Biddle's influence helped to succeed in turning three House votes—those Samuel Moore, Thomas J. Rogers and Daniel Udree—and it may also have swayed Walter Lowrie in the Senate.[162] On February 26, 1821, the House voted to remove the restriction on Missouri's admission, and the legislative controversy was ended.

———— ❦ ————

IN MISSOURI AND THE REST of the South, there was jubilation in response to the news that the crisis was over. Reaction to the settlement in the North varied. The *Philadelphia National Gazette*, a paper that had been founded expressly to oppose Missouri, spoke for many on both sides when it wrote that "the mere exit of this question can distress no one who has the least appetite for variety in topics either of legislation or newspaper composition. It had produced satiety and fatigue even in those who felt most deeply the importance . . . of preventing the extension of negro-bondage beyond the Mississippi."[163] The *Repertory* of Massachusetts, another restrictionist paper, found the firmness of "members from this part of the country" on Missouri "gratifying" but argued that in any event the yielding of principle in this case was not "of any great practical consequence."[164] The *Exeter Northern Republican* strongly disagreed. "It was hardly to be expected that the majority . . . would have capitulated on terms like these," the paper related in shock. "A child might penetrate the flimsiness of the evasion, on which [Clay's compromise] resolution is grounded. When the very basis of all the arguments of all the defenders of that infamous constitution was the assumption, that a free black is not a citizen, was it manly or decorous, by simply inserting the word citizen in the resolution, to leave it to the sovereign will and pleasure of Missouri herself to decide, whether she will retain or expunge the obnoxious article? Let her declare that a free black, is not a citizen, and she and her constitution are thus beyond the reach of [America's] control."[165]

The *Northern Republican* proved more prescient than the *Repertory*. Supporters of the Compromise argued that the vagueness of its language should not be held against it, since it served the greater purpose of enabling a vote that they believed had helped to preserve the Union. Yet it proved impossible, despite Henry Clay's best efforts to achieve a definitive ambiguity, that a clause that had borne the weight of such a momentous controversy should not be invested with genuine meaning. Ultimately, the only logical way to square the language of Clay's compromise with the privileges-and-immunities clause of the Constitution, which decrees that "the citizens of each state shall be entitled to all privileges and immunities of the citizens in the several states," was to conclude that blacks were not citizens. This questionable language, drafted out of political expedience by an exhausted committee in order to eke out a bare majority for a controversial vote, came to serve, for the North as well as the South,[166] as an important precedent in the direction of stripping blacks of their citizenship, and ultimately (as the *Dred Scott* decision would show) of the presumption of freedom as well—thus at once rendering slavery more racial and racism more national. It is ironic that the second Missouri Compromise should have provided the earliest and most significant (if unacknowledged) precedent for Chief Justice Taney's assertion that blacks "had no rights which the white man was bound to respect," a basic foundation for his ruling that the essential feature of the first Compromise, the 36°30' slavery restriction, was unconstitutional.

This would be one of the two great legacies of the Missouri controversy. The second would be the recognition, now general throughout the Union, that the issue of slavery could not be discussed publicly without exposing unbreachable fissures in the Union, and thus, to preserve the Union, nothing should be said about slavery at all. "Much more might be said on these heads and ought to be said hereafter," counseled the *Philadelphia National Gazette* (a strongly prorestriction journal); "for the present . . . the best rule . . . may be found in the old ghostly discharge—*requiescat in pace.*"[167]

4

SILENCE

"'AFTER A STORM comes a calm.'" Looking back from the vantage point of 1868, Horace Greeley sought to describe the national mood in the aftermath of the Missouri controversy. "From 1821 to 1835 . . . the Northern people—busy, usually prosperous, and pretty steadily increasing in numbers, wealth, and power—very generally ignored the subject of Slavery. The convictions of that portion of them who may be said to have had any were not materially changed; but what use in parading a conviction which can have no other effect than that of annoying your proud and powerful neighbor?"[1]

Intriguingly, opponents of Missouri's admission seemed not to bear a grudge against the man who rallied the awakened South to resist the Tallmadge Amendment. "The conduct of Mr Clay on this occasion has been extremely honorable to himself & useful to the country," acknowledged a diehard restrictionist after the crisis of the electoral vote count.[2] Clay reciprocated by praising "the assiduity, impartiality, ability, and promptitude" with which the Speaker of the House, John W. Taylor, "administered the duties of the Chair"; Clay's motion for a vote of thanks to Taylor passed on voice vote with only one audible dissent.[3]

To be sure, some southerners remained convinced that some northerners continued to pose a grave danger to national tranquillity. "Whether the question excited is dead, or only sleepeth, I do not know," Thomas Jefferson remarked warily to William Eustis, Madison's northern former secretary of war. "I see only that it has given resurrection to the Hartford convention men. They have had the address, by playing on the honest feelings of our former friends, to seduce them from their kindred spirits, and to borrow their weight into the federal scale. Desperate of regaining power under political distinctions, they have adroitly wriggled into its seat under the auspices of morality, and are again in the ascendancy from which their sins had hurled them."[4]

Although his assessment of Federalist strength was extravagant, Jefferson's suspicions were not entirely without foundation. A few northerners, among them former Federalists, did intend to exploit the divisions engendered by the Missouri controversy for political ends. Robert Walsh, deeply angered that his friendly admonitions to the South against the expansion of slavery had been rejected, abandoned for a time his efforts to promote intersectional harmony and openly embraced the concept of "Northernness." In 1822, envisioning a political alliance of New Englanders and western emigrants of New England stock behind a northern presidential candidate (preferably Adams), Walsh called for the uprising of what he termed "the Universal Yankee Nation" (surely one of the great oxymorons of American history).[5] Likewise, unrepentant Clintonians such as Charles G. Haines continued to issue northern calls to arms.

But if sectional tensions persisted, they represented the exception, not the rule, in the years immediately following the controversy. Even before the final settlement, the nation's most influential journal, the *North American Review*, downplayed the threat of sectionalism. "For ourselves, we are inclined to think that there will be no permanent new division of parties at present," the journal argued. "The Missouri question, which came as near forming such a new division as could have been done . . . , failed even in the moment of its own decision, to produce a perfect geographical organization." Not "a single subsequent vote, on any disconnected topic, was affected by a reference to the Missouri question," the *Review* maintained—technically true, perhaps, although the tariff, bankruptcy, and auction reform laws had all failed largely because of southern anger over Missouri. The article concluded:

> We doubt . . . whether any party, purely and unanimously *geographical*, can subsist among us. The old party divisions were nourished and kept up, by having, not state against state, nor section against section, but town against town, aye, family against family, and the son against the father. . . . This makes hatred keen, deep, and precious. . . . So long, therefore, as the question of slavery produces unanimity among our Southern and Western brethren, (and there was not a single defection among them in the last session . . .), we think there is no danger of its becoming the ground of a permanent party division.[6]

In part, the exhaustion of its leaders precluded the creation of a northern party. Federalists in particular reeled from the dual setback of the defeat of restriction and the gratuitous political attacks their party had sustained in the controversy. Even before the final vote, a "general apathy" had begun "to pervade the federal party."[7] John Sergeant, the Federalists' dynamic and eloquent House leader, professed himself "heartily tired" of the Missouri question and longed to leave Congress as soon as it was settled.[8] Constitutional changes and electoral losses at home compounded the Federalists' distress, leaving many feeling alienated and virtually disenfranchised. Roger S. Baldwin confessed to his fiancée in 1820 that Election Day "was to me a very tedious & unpleasant day. . . . Indeed I felt as if the occasion required mourning, rather than rejoicing, especially when I looked into the Senate chamber and saw those seats which were once filled by the most eminent men in Connecticut, now occupied by some of the most worthless and depraved."[9] As Greeley's recollection suggested, the antislavery activism of many former Federalists lay dormant for more than a decade.

Clintonians, too, found themselves thwarted in their efforts to unite the North. The New York governor's second "presidential campaign" attracted no following whatsoever. Although Clinton had narrowly won reelection to the Albany statehouse in a campaign that owed much to anti-Missouri sentiment, Van Buren's Bucktail candidates, having adequately avoided contamination with the issue, won a sufficient majority in the legislature to control the powerful Council of Appointment, which proceeded to purge the state rolls of the governor's allies, leaving him little more than a figurehead in the executive seat. Having grasped the levers of state power, the Bucktails quickly moved to consolidate their control by redrawing the state constitution in a convention headed by Daniel D. Tompkins.[10] The convention, with Tompkins's vigorous support, voted down a proposal by James Tallmadge to accelerate the end of slavery in New York.[11]

For their part, most Republicans wanted as little to do with the slavery issue as possible. The unpopularity of the doughface stance had compelled most northern Republican state caucuses to drop those congressmen who had voted against restriction; but privately, antirestrictionist leaders sought to reward those Republicans who had backed the sub rosa party line and punish those who had not. Pennsylvania's doughfaces returned to Philadelphia after the final Missouri vote to a heroes' welcome from the elitist "Family Party" faction of the state Republican party and a testimonial dinner attended by U.S. Bank attorney George M. Dallas and principals Langdon Cheves and Nicholas Biddle, along with prominent Philadelphia politicians. "My Republican friends in my district are well satisfied with my vote and my efforts to settle this odious and distracting question," one of the fêted doughfaces, Thomas J. Rogers, reported to John C. Calhoun. "After I explained to them the motives which governed me, and the danger to this Union by keeping it open until the next session of Congress, they were highly pleased, and consider that those who were instrumental in settling the question, deserve credit for the stand they made." Rogers regretted that more Pennsylvania Republicans had not been willing to vote for restriction. "However," he added tersely, "we had enough." The Pennsylvania congressman assured Calhoun that he would "not be backward" in exposing "the true motives" of some of the Pennsylvania delegation who had wanted to keep the Missouri question open until the following session, and he felt sure that many others had already changed their minds: "Depend upon it, if the question were now to be decided, there would be more of the delegation with Dr. Moore and myself."[12]

Samuel Moore, more sensitive than Rogers to the political implications of their eleventh-hour change of heart on Missouri, sternly counseled more discretion: "There is no danger, and I have never believed there would be, if our personal and political friends will not incite any disapprobation by offering improper apologies for our conduct which I think needs no apology, and attempting to defend it on principles which we never adopted and can not approve," Moore insisted. "I never had any confidence in the discretion of our Philad[a] democrats at least those who take the lead, & do not find it much increased," he added pointedly. "Their meaning was no doubt very friendly to us, but I never felt our reputation on the subject of our Missouri vote in any danger until I found they had made a dinner on the occasion and proposed toasts to be published abroad through the Country, without knowing what had been our difficulties nor on what principles we had been able to over[come] them." The fact that Moore and other Pennsylvania representatives had personal interests in tariff-sensitive manufacturing industries (Moore himself owned a woolens factory) might easily raise the implication that his support for Missouri had been offered to the South as a quid pro quo—a conclusion that, in the case of his colleague Henry Baldwin, seemed inescapable. Lavish celebrations sponsored by the powerful Bank of the United States gave off a comparable odor of impropriety. Although Moore felt no qualms about his vote, he recognized the impossibility of an open public discussion of his motivations. He strongly agreed with Rogers's suggestion that "we had better not write any thing on the subject."[13]

THERE IS REASON TO believe that Moore and at least some of the other northern "doughfaces" genuinely believed that their votes had struck a blow against slavery—although ironically, as Samuel Moore suggested, they could not disclose this motive publicly. Indeed, the nation probably emerged from the turmoil of the Missouri contest with the institution of slavery facing greater impediments than before. In spite of Rufus King's lament that "we are beaten, and beaten utterly," bolstered by South Carolinian Charles Pinckney's claiming the Missouri vote as "a great triumph" for the slaveholding states, the reality was more complicated, and suggested an alternative interpretation of some southern intentions.

It seems likely that Monroe explained the implications of his policy in private discussions with key northern politicians. This could help to explain the late vote changes of congressmen such as New Hampshire's David Morril and Pennsylvania's Moore, as well as Moore's anger at Pennsylvania Republicans' "improper apologies for our conduct which . . . needs no apology, and attempt[s] to defend it on principles which we never adopted and can not approve." It would explain Monroe's refusal to contest Spain's title to Texas—a concession that denied a huge field to slavery, and one that many southerners considered a betrayal. It would also shed light on perhaps the greatest mystery of the Missouri affair—Speaker Taylor's consistent support of Clay's policies and committee assignments and complete unwillingness to employ his parliamentary powers to do anything, however minor, to block the second Compromise. It will be recalled that Taylor, champion of the Tallmadge Amendment and the author of the Arkansas slavery restriction amendment, also first proposed a line of demarcation between slave and free territory. It seems plausible, then, that Taylor deliberately cooperated with the Monroe administration on Missouri, feeling that he was in no way thereby compromising his antislavery principles.

Beyond the exhaustion of the combatants, then, it appears that one of the causes of the relative tranquillity over the slavery issue in the early 1820s was the administration's success in convincing at least some of the most influential antislavery leaders that their concerns had been satisfactorily addressed. If this premise is correct, a thorough reevaluation of the Monroe administration's policy on slavery, as well as its politics, is clearly demanded.

There is important corroborating evidence of Taylor's cooperation with Monroe that helps to elucidate Monroe's policy on slavery and sectionalism and the opposition to it. On November 29, 1821, just before the start of the Seventeenth Congress, Taylor met with John Quincy Adams to solicit the administration's support for his reelection as Speaker. At the meeting, Taylor made Adams "an explicit offer of confidential intercourse during the ensuing session," and Adams spelled out the president's goals for the remainder of the term.[14] On the following day, New York representative

John D. Dickinson called on the secretary to inform him that Taylor did not have the support of his own state's delegation. Adams informed Dickinson that, although he had never before attempted to influence the choice of a Speaker, he believed Taylor "would be friendly" to the administration, and "from various important political considerations" he "wished Mr. Taylor might be re-elected."[15]

It is not clear whether Dickinson intended to undermine Taylor's position with Adams; he claimed to share the secretary's view that the Speaker ought to be reelected.[16] Yet Dickinson's visit may have had an ulterior motive. The Troy congressman, a close associate of the Van Rensselaer family, was a messmate at Strother's Hotel of Martin Van Buren, who had arrived earlier that month to begin his term as Senator.[17] It was probably from Van Buren that Dickinson learned of the strong opposition to Taylor within the New York delegation—indeed, Van Buren was the organizer of that opposition. Van Buren's anger at Taylor appears to have stemmed from his refusal to back Tompkins in the late gubernatorial election.[18] Jabez D. Hammond, the New York politician and historian, later wrote: "I can by no means excuse [Van Buren] for depriving his own state . . . of the influence which a speaker would have had in the house of representatives of the Union, merely because the New-York candidate had declined to vote for the man whom Mr. Van Buren believed ought to be chosen governor, when at the same time he and that candidate cordially concurred in the support of the same measures and the same men in the national government."[19] Although Hammond expressed a commonly held view, it is far from clear that Taylor and Van Buren "concurred in the same measures." As we have seen, support for Tompkins carried significant national implications in relation to the Missouri question, and Taylor, like Rufus King, would have been in a position to know about Tompkins's antirestrictionist role. Moreover, as competition for the 1824 presidential election heated up, fissures had appeared in the unified political front the administration had presented over Missouri, and the Speaker, with his power to appoint committees, would inevitably be in the center of the forthcoming political battles.

In this area, Taylor had already made enemies. In particular, Calhoun blamed him for appointments damaging to the War Department, and other cabinet members bore grudges on the same score. To Adams, Taylor explained that he had made these unfriendly committee appointments only because of his ignorance of the representatives' true views. Although Monroe recognized that his influence would be necessary to reelect Taylor, he decided against personal involvement, probably out of unwillingness to alienate Calhoun, the Speaker's chief opponent.

Calhoun, meanwhile, eager to enlist Van Buren's political assistance on this and other issues, had been the first person to call on the freshman senator on his arrival at Strother's Hotel.[20] It proved to be only the first of many times that Calhoun would be outmaneuvered by the man who would become his political nemesis.

Van Buren was only too happy to assist Calhoun in removing Taylor. Unfortunately, the secretary of war had given less thought to who would replace the Speaker; typically, Calhoun thought only one move ahead, while Van Buren had mapped out an entire game. Navy Secretary Smith Thompson, acting as Van Buren's surrogate, had caucused with the majority of the New York delegation and settled on Caesar Rodney as their nominee to replace Taylor, with Louis McLane as the second choice.[21] The logic of these selections is revealing as an insight into Van Buren's political strategy and principles. Rodney, an outspoken opponent of slavery, would smooth the feathers of northerners irked by Taylor's removal, while as a member from a middle state he would theoretically have wide national appeal—or at least be unobjectionable to both sections. Unfortunately, although Rodney was sufficiently "uncontroversial," he was also regarded as "mediocre. . . . a self-serving nonentity," and was able to garner hardly more than half the requisite votes.[22] McLane had no antislavery bona fides—quite the contrary, he had championed the southern cause in the Missouri debates. This would help him with the South, while, like Rodney, he was from Delaware and thus still nominally a northerner. He was attractive, intelligent, well regarded, and a messmate and confidant of Van Buren. He was also, however, a Federalist—and thus effectively ineligible for the post.[23]

The election of Rodney would have been politically popular with New Yorkers, and perhaps beneficial to the state, and McLane's election would at least have been neutral. But with both of them out of the running, and a third border-state candidate, Samuel Smith of Maryland, less popular than either, Van Buren had to abandon his preferred strategy of filling the Speaker's chair with a congressman from "neutral ground" and back an unambiguously southern candidate, the militant Virginia partisan Philip P. Barbour, who could, with New York's votes, obtain the Speakership. In the words of his biographer, John Niven, "Van Buren could no longer conceal the responsibility of sacrificing the pretensions of his own state to his concept of party loyalty."[24]

This is, to say the least, a curiously phrased observation. For Van Buren to sacrifice the "pretensions" of his state sounds somehow noble and high minded—far better than sacrificing its legitimate interests to the South for political gain. Ambiguous, too, if technically accurate, is Niven's choice of words in describing Van Buren's "concept of party loyalty"—a concept broad enough to award precedence to a Delaware Federalist and a states' rights Virginia sectionalist for the Speakership over a lifelong Republican from his own state. Not without reason did Adams warn Calhoun of "the mischief of bringing into the Government of the Union the squabbling of New York State politics."[25]

In retrospect, Van Buren's endorsement of Philip Barbour for the Speakership appears to have marked a turning point in the development of American parties. In his seminal 1966 article, "The Missouri Crisis, Slavery, and the Politics of Jacksonianism," Richard H. Brown argued that "the central fact in American political history to 1860" was the South's domination of national politics. "In Jackson's day the chief agent of Southern power was a Northern man with Southern principles, Martin Van Buren of New York."

In Brown's view, Van Buren arrived in Washington in 1821 intent on "return of the speakership to the slave states," and with the plan already formulated to cement a coalition between his Albany Regency and the Old Republican Richmond Junto, wherewith to govern the nation according to pure Jeffersonian principles. As Brown saw it, "Van Buren believed implicitly in the whole system of republican polity as Thomas Jefferson had staked it out. Committed to the principle of the least possible government, the Republican party was the defender of that republican liberty which was the whole political concern of the disinterested agrarian constituency for which, through life, Van Buren saw himself as a spokesman, and which constituted the majority of Americans. That majority was strongest where it was purest, least subject to the corrupting power of money. That was in the South."[26]

Brown's analysis of the linkage between northern and southern Old Republicans in the creation of the Jacksonian party is a masterful reinterpretation that contributes more to the study of the antebellum period in seventeen pages than virtually any full-scale monograph of the last half century. Obviously, however, Brown's broad picture needs to be fleshed out, and certain details require revision. While it seems clear that Van Buren recognized, at this early date, the dangers of an alignment of North versus South and the usefulness—to the Republican Party and to himself—of close coalitions between New York and the slave states, and while he had cultivated a relationship with *Richmond Enquirer* editor Thomas Ritchie for some years,[27] his early efforts to steer the Speakership either to Rodney or McLane of Delaware appear to show that he did not intend at the outset to throw his lot in with the Virginia Old Republicans, as a matter of principle, as it were, but rather found himself pushed into the alliance as a matter of political expediency.

There is an alternative possibility: that Van Buren intended from the start to throw the Speakership to Barbour and cement his alliance with the Radicals, but, recognizing that the New York delegation would not endorse the Virginian except as a last resort, he put up Rodney and McLane with the knowledge that they could not be elected. This, however, would be an extreme view of Van Buren's capacity for intrigue.

Moreover, there is no evidence to suggest that Van Buren possessed deeply held personal convictions of any kind concerning slavery. In New York as in western Europe, the Dutch proved the most stubbornly resistant to embracing antislavery views,[28] and, indeed, Van Buren's own family had owned slaves. Like his political mentor, Andrew Jackson, Van Buren believed that the value of the Union far transcended "visionary" notions about equality and freedom that might endanger sectional harmony. On the other hand, Van Buren had no particular disposition in favor of slavery. His links to slavery's defenders were tactical, not ideological—purely a matter of realpolitik. Like Stephen A. Douglas in a later era, it could truly be said of Van Buren that he "didn't care" one way or the other about the institution. Tactically as well as philosophically, he believed that it was best left to the states to determine their own policies, and during the 1819–21 period he deferred to the antislavery preferences of New Yorkers to the greatest extent compatible with his ambitions for national leadership and his belief in federal noninterference in the affairs of the states.[29]

This required walking a tightrope: In 1820, Van Buren agreed to let his name be listed as a member of a committee on the Missouri issue, but did not in fact attend the meeting and refused to endorse the resolutions it adopted; in the New York constitutional convention of 1821, he opposed a constitutional bar against granting the vote to free blacks, but endorsed a high property qualification that virtually secured the same end.[30] Once he had linked his political destiny to the Virginians in the Speakership election, however, he dropped any pose of "non-committalism" and adopted without reserve or hesitation what he took to be the tenets of Old Republican orthodoxy on slavery—although subtly shading them toward his own ends.

Within days of his election as Speaker of the House, Barbour's actions had exceeded the administration's gloomiest expectations. "Calhoun and [Navy Secretary Smith] Thompson were joking about the new Speaker and his committees, which they thought as ill chosen and as ill sorted as they could have been if drawn by lot," reported Adams, who sarcastically "told them they had truly done themselves good service by changing the Speaker."[31] Many of the new chairmen were known or soon to be revealed as partisans of William Crawford, the treasury secretary and the presidential candidate of the so-called Radical wing of Congress, extreme states' rightists who opposed Monroe's moderate nationalism on grounds of constitutional and fiscal conservatism. Before long, Barbour too came out openly as a Crawford supporter.[32] His appointments were hardly made "by lot"; they were deliberately designed both to undermine and embarrass Adams and Calhoun, Crawford's competitors for the 1824 election, and to weaken Monroe and scuttle his nationalist initiatives. Calhoun in particular had reason to rue his opposition to Taylor (as Adams repeatedly reminded him). To head the crucial House Committee on Military Affairs, which oversaw the War Department, Barbour chose "Madison's penny-pinching Secretary of War, William Eustis," who mulishly battled Calhoun for every dollar he sought.[33]

Behind the Barbour election, and behind the harassment inflicted by Barbour's committee appointments, lay the maneuverings of Van Buren—undertaken partly to assist Crawford, whose election bid Van Buren supported, but mostly to advance his own interests and sabotage Monroe's nationalist program. If Calhoun had not yet grasped this fact, the president had, and he was prepared to take steps to fight back.

An ideal opportunity presented itself to do so early in the term. On December 26, Albany congressman Solomon Van Rensselaer, wrote to his cousin Stephen, the patroon, about the attentions he was receiving from the president and the secretary of war. Van Rensselaer, a prominent Clintonian Federalist with a heroic war record, had recently been displaced in favor of a Van Buren spoilsman by the Bucktail-controlled Council of Appointment from his position as New York's adjutant-general, a largely ceremonial but remunerative post, which he had held for decades. The people of Albany had overwhelmingly reelected him to Congress as a sign of their confidence in him and as a rebuke to the Bucktails. Van Rensselaer received an appointment to the House Committee on the Military, over whose chairman, William Eustis, he claimed to possess great influence: "[Eustis] is amiable, weak and honest, [and] he is particularly friendly to me," Van Rensselaer reported to a relative. "He is easily managed, has no opinion of his own. The Committee will go with me, and as that is well known I receive every attention." Indeed, Calhoun had spent the morning with Van Rensselaer to seek his assistance in funding for West Point, and had asked him to dinner, "which I declined as I was engaged at the Presidents—*out of alphabetical order*."[34] Van Rensselaer's private engagement with Monroe is of deep interest, for reasons that will become clear shortly.

Although Calhoun wanted to employ Van Rensselaer's influence over Eustis to counteract the Radicals' policy of retrenchment of his department, the New Yorker did not plan to remain in the House much longer. Before he left Albany, Van Rensselaer had learned that the city's postmaster was deep in arrears. He lost little time in capitalizing on this information. Somehow, he managed to obtain the endorsement of twenty-two of the twenty-six other members of the New York delegation without Van Buren or his confederates learning a thing. For good measure, he garnered support from six other states' delegations as well. "Van Buren is very civil, he and all the Bucktails have been to see me," Van Rensselaer reported. "I am upon good terms with them all. . . . Van Buren . . . spoke at the table in handsome terms of me. He knows nothing of the object I have in view."[35]

It appears that the congressman had skills for political intrigue not much inferior to those of Van Buren himself, and perhaps, at this period at least, a better nose for the political atmosphere of the Congress than the newcomer from Kinderhook. Although Van Buren had been able to enforce party discipline among the New York delegation on the ouster of Taylor, it had come at a high political cost, and it had not resulted in any great enhancement in southern respect for the New York members, who were "detested by the very men they voted with on the subject of the Speaker," according to General Van Rensselaer—a viewpoint that echoed the contemptuous epithet of "doe face" applied by John Randolph of Roanoke. Thus these representatives were open to the overtures of a patriotic New York soldier whose "ambition" it had "ever been . . . to promote the prosperity, and maintain the honor of the State."[36] Besides Calhoun and the members of the New York delegation, Van Rensselaer had other allies in Washington as well; Return J. Meigs Jr., the postmaster general, was his "decided friend," and had no reason to wish Van Buren well after the public embarrassment he had caused him over the removals of the "Rascally Post Masters" the year before.[37] Finally, Van Rensselaer had the attentive ear of the president. The Albany congressman had been Clinton's chief point man in his attack on improper presidential influence in New York affairs and a central figure in the campaign to restrict slavery in Missouri.[38] An alliance with Van Rensselaer, scion of one of New York's most powerful families, would thus help Monroe to reestablish equable relations with Clinton and his followers, bestow a mantle of legitimacy on the Missouri settlement in the heartland of restrictionist sentiment, and send a message to Van Buren and his surrogates in the administration, Tompkins and Smith Thompson, that if they continued to employ the U.S. government in service of "the squabbling of New York State politics" now that the Missouri emergency was over, they could expect the president to respond in kind. Monroe's symbolism in placing a Clintonian Federalist in the chief government post in Albany, the nerve center of Van Buren's influence, could not be misinterpreted by astute observers—nor could the practical advantage of controlling the Albany mails. Monroe had fired a decisive preemptive strike in a contest that Van Buren had waged up to now as an undeclared guerrilla war.

With the characteristic discretion that misled historians and contemporaries alike, the president gave no hint of his involvement in the Albany postmastership affair when he raised it with Adams a week after his private dinner with Van Rensselaer. "The President told me that a very unpleasant affair had occurred yesterday, and had not yet terminated," Adams recorded in his diary on January 4. Deadpan, Monroe recounted to his secretary of state the version of the incident that would be transmitted to posterity:

The Postmaster at Albany, Solomon Southwick, was to be removed by the Postmaster-General for delinquency in his accounts. A recommendation of General Van Rensselaer to be his successor had been signed by twenty-two of the members of the New York delegation, and all of the political parties. The Postmaster-General came to him yesterday and told him of these circumstances, adding that his mind was made up to appoint General Van Rensselaer, unless the President had an objection, but he would wish to consult the Secretary of the Navy.

He accordingly saw Mr. Thompson, who objected in the strongest manner. But he informed Vice-President Tompkins and the New York Senator, Van Buren, of it, and they had been exasperated to such a degree that Tompkins broke out into the most violent language against the President himself, and in presence of a person who he must have known would report all he said to him. And thus the matter now stands. Mr. Thompson came in while the President was relating to me these circumstances, upon which he changed the subject of conversation.[39]

The reckless response of the ailing vice president vividly displayed the degree to which the reputed master manipulators of the Albany Regency had been outflanked and outfoxed by the unprepossessing chief executive. Tompkins fired off a letter to his brother-in-law, Jonathan Thompson, revealing the dire news. "It will surprise you to know that *sixteen* of our representatives have recommended Mr. Van Rensselaer," Tompkins expostulated. "'Whip me such republicans!'" Tompkins asked Thompson to tell Van Buren's Albany associates of what had occurred and to inform Van Buren of their wishes, noting with chagrin that "it would be advisable that they should send it part of the way by private conveyance or *mail* their communication this side of Albany." Such would be the undignified arrangements necessary to conduct basic communications among the Regency under a Van Rensselaer postmastership.[40]

Although equally as "exasperated" as Tompkins, Van Buren maintained his composure and refused to condemn the President publicly, which he recognized would be fatal. Instead, he fought for time, dragooning Tompkins and Rufus King to cosign a request to Meigs to delay the appointment for two weeks. The postmaster general gave them the weekend.[41] At a cabinet meeting on Saturday, Monroe called on Meigs, who said he intended to go through with the appointment unless the president objected. Meigs rehearsed Van Rensselaer's patriotic services and congressional endorsements. The appointee would clearly be popular with "the people of Albany," since they had just reelected him to Congress. Finally, Meigs averred, "no other candidate had been presented to his consideration." Navy Secretary Thompson, who had evidently learned the outcome of a crisis meeting of New York Bucktail representatives (most of whom Van Buren pressured to rescind their backing of Van Rensselaer), indiscreetly asked the postmaster general whether the name of John Lansing Jr., former chancellor of New York State, had not been presented to him—the candidate on whom Van Buren had hurriedly settled because of his presumed friendship with Monroe. No, Meigs said, adding "that Mr. Lansing was nearly seventy years of age." The postmaster general asserted that a delay would jeopardize the public trust, and that the deputy postmaster could not serve, being a member of Southwick's family and under his control.

After Meigs left, Monroe stated that "he thought it very questionable whether he ought to interfere in the case at all." After "a warm discussion," which a somewhat naive Adams seemed to think genuinely related to the merits of the case, the president dissolved the meeting without making a decision, asking Thompson to stay behind; the details of that conversation have not been preserved. Afterward, Calhoun, who had hardly spoken during the meeting, told Adams that he agreed with his view that the postmaster general had acted correctly. "Why did he not say so while the discussion was going on at the President's?" Adams wondered irritably.[42]

Later that day, Monroe received a letter from Van Buren enclosing the petition of eleven New York representatives, seven of whom had earlier endorsed Van Rensselaer, urging him to postpone the Albany postmaster appointment. Monroe responded on January 7 with the unimpeachable, gilt-edged strict-constructionist dogma that historians have dutifully ascribed to his presidency:

By the law, establishing the Post Office department, the appointment of all the officers employed in it, under the Post Master General, is exclusively vested in him, without reference to the President. Had it been intended that the President should control the appointments in detail, or take any agency in them, the provisions of the law, and the powers granted by it, would have been different. Such also according to my experience and information on the subject, has been the uniform practice of the executive. For these reasons I deem it improper to interfere.[43]

If he had had a sense of humor, this response might have evoked a guffaw from De Witt Clinton, who had assiduously documented removals and replacements of postmasters, directed by Van Buren and sanctioned by the executive, in his ineffectual "green bag message" of the previous session.[44] To have the president turn the tables on his manipulative adversary, Van Buren, must have afforded Clinton rare pleasure—the more so because of its unexpected source.[45]

A few months later, Monroe took another step to distance himself from the antirestrictionist coalition he had worked so hard to create, but which he now considered dangerous and importunate. Earlier, in deference to the wishes of Maine governor William King and Senators Holmes and Hill, Monroe had appointed Ashur Ware, editor of the staunchly doughface *Eastern Argus* of Maine, to a district judgeship, instead of his preferred candidate, General Henry Dearborn. In May, when an opening came up for the position of minister to Portugal, Monroe decided to offer it to Dearborn, explaining to Secretary Adams "with a good deal of feeling that he meant that those gentlemen [Holmes, Hill and King] should be sensible that he was not entirely in their hands." Although Adams did not object to the appointment of Dearborn, it was "certainly not a nomination" that Adams "should have suggested," and represented the kind of game-playing that he could not abide. "What a whimsical play of political machinery it is! Because a District Judge in Maine is indecently crowded upon the President by the Maine Senators, he takes his revenge by mortifying them in the appointment of a Minister to Portugal."[46] Adams's scruples notwithstanding, Monroe's appointment of Dearborn did what it was meant to do: it sent a powerful statement of the president's independence from an influential camp of Crawford supporters and allies of Van Buren.

VAN BUREN, FOR HIS PART, proved unaccountably inept in his first months as a senator. In his handling of the affair of the Albany postmastership, he had clearly alienated a sizable number of the New York congressional delegation and had angered many Republicans at home.[47] In turning immediately to Federalist Rufus King to cosign his letter to the postmaster general against the Van Rensselaer appointment, Van Buren undermined his ostensible chief objection to the nominee—that is, his Federalism. As Ammon observed, Van Rensselaer's political ties "scarcely seemed to justify the intensity of Van Buren's protest . . . , for he, too, had once been a Clintonian and had no hesitation about associating with Federalists."[48] At the same time, King's involvement in the affair canceled out a good deal of his personal debt to Van Buren, while also eroding King's credibility as a Federalist leader. The whole episode represented a profligate squandering of Van Buren's political capital.

In part, the political damage Van Buren inflicted on himself reflected the natural imbalance produced by his transition from Albany to Washington—not a wider world politically, perhaps (since Albany politics far outstripped the national capital's in complexity, as contemporaries freely acknowledged), but a new one; and after all, Van Buren was trying to manage both worlds simultaneously. More important, however, Van Buren's missteps underscored the sheer difficulty of the task he had taken on: to rebuild a coalition between a northern state political organization with a constituency deeply committed to restricting the expansion of slavery and a southern political faction as deeply opposed to such restriction, devoted to state sovereignty, and distrustful of northern intentions, including Van Buren's.

The president's policy of "amalgamation" of parties and sections—the "Monroe heresy," as Van Buren came to call it—made the Red Fox's goal much more difficult. With the assistance of Henry Clay, a founding member of the American Colonization Society whom Van Rensselaer could describe as "a sagacious counselor and statesman," Monroe had engineered an "amicable agreement between the North and South" that had the tacit support of New England Federalists, southern nationalists, northern Republicans, and even New York Clintonians.[49] If this incongruous array of political organizations seems too disparate to have cohered into a durable coalition, it should be remembered that Monroe's intention was not to create a new party, but to dissolve parties altogether:

We have undoubtedly reached a new epoch in our political career, which has been formed by the destruction of the federal party . . . by the general peace, and the entire absence of all cause, as to public measures, for great political excitement, and, in truth, by the real prosperity of the Union. In such a state of things it might have been presumed that the movement would have been tranquil, marked by a common effort to promote the public good in every line to which the powers of the general government extended. It is my fixed opinion that this will be the result after some short interval. . . . Surely our government may get on and prosper without the existence of parties. I have always considered their existence as the curse of the country. . . . Besides, how keep them alive, and in action?[50]

To Martin Van Buren, born after the close of the Revolution and raised in the fervid atmosphere of New York politics, Monroe's antiparty view seemed almost a sin against nature. Van Buren's ideal political system consisted of "two great parties arrayed against each other in a fair and open contest"; the inevitable consequence of an absence of parties, he believed, would not be tranquillity and a general devotion to the common good, but the unseemly power struggle of "personal factions," precisely as occurred in 1820–24,[51] as well as a renewal of sectional antagonisms held in check only by the imposition of strict party discipline. Ultimately, Van Buren measured the worth of statesmen by one key criterion: their adherence to party regularity.[52] "There has been no period in our history . . . to which the sincere friend of free institutions can turn with more unalloyed satisfaction, than to that embraced by the administrations of Jefferson and Madison," Van Buren later wrote. "Jefferson and Madison were brought forward by caucus nominations; they, throughout, recognized and adhered to the political party that elected them; and they left it united and powerful."[53] By this standard, Monroe fell short. According to Robert V. Remini, "It is quite probable that the President's failure to act as party chieftain, far more than his Federalist appointments, is the true reason for Van Buren's intense dislike of him. Monroe had a clear responsibility to the party by the very fact that he was President of the United States[!], a responsibility he could not—indeed, dared not—disregard. But he did disregard it. . . . Monroe's sole accomplishment, Van Buren said, was to destroy the party that had given him office."[54]

While it is possible to find Monroe's belief in the withering away of parties naive, as did Madison,[55] it is another thing to find it venal. It strongly appears that politics represented to Van Buren an irreducible value in itself: an end, not a means. With due deference to his biographers, Donald Cole, Robert V. Remini, and John Niven, it is difficult to avoid the conclusion from a dispassionate evaluation of Van Buren's political actions that the search for deeper, underlying principles is ultimately chimerical. Most significantly, as Niven acknowledges, Van Buren took no interest in, and had virtually no knowledge of, the wider culture of which he was a part. In a world of public figures steeped in the narratives of history and literature, Van Buren's ignorance was striking. "His knowledge of books outside of his profession," wrote James A. Hamilton, a close acquaintance, "was more limited than that of any other public man I ever knew."[56] The impression is strong that Van Buren's real motivation for engaging in politics was the love of a game which he played better than practically anyone else in the nation's history, in no small part because he possessed no larger vision to cloud his view of his political interest.

On one subject, however, as his defenders rightly observe, Van Buren cannot be charged with "non-committalism": after the Missouri settlement, he never wavered in his commitment to oppose all efforts "to disturb the domestic peace of the States in which slavery had long and fixedly existed, by interference with the subject within their borders."[57] Van Buren quickly established himself as the most dependable, if not the most unguarded, northern defender of southern prerogatives regarding slavery.

Van Buren's attitude toward party regularity offers the key to his position on slavery. In the presidential election of 1824, Van Buren backed Treasury Secretary William Crawford, even though the Georgian was less popular among New Yorkers than either of his initial major competitors, Adams and Calhoun. This position engendered widespread opposition both at home and across the North.[58] Closer to home, Van Buren's high-stakes southern strategy took a toll on his popularity. In July 1823, Azariah Flagg, a loyal Van Buren lieutenant, found "widespread and vociferous opposition to Van Buren from the voting public" in Tammany-dominated New York City, which had rolled up huge Bucktail majorities in recent elections. "What has caused such a change? I answer that a very general belief has gone abroad (whether true or false is not for me to say) that [Van Buren] has offered to barter this state for the purpose of furthering his own views."[59]

The exasperated tone of Flagg's report testifies to the depth of the anger at Van Buren's policies even among the most loyal Bucktails. Tired of southern domination of the federal government, most anti-Clintonians also believed that the election of Adams, Clinton's natural rival in the North, would effectively put an end to the influence of the "Magnus Apollo." Despite the North's advantage in population and congressional representation, Van Buren had early rejected the strategy of governing by attempting to bring the dozens of squabbling northern factions into line, preferring instead to rely on establishing ties to what Jabez D. Hammond called "the great,—the compact South."[60] Although Van Buren extravagantly admired southern leaders as "a race of great and good men," his attraction for the South was at base strategic, not aesthetic or ideological, and it derived from the region's "compactness"—the fact that its citizens could be organized to vote as a bloc if mobilized around the issue that moved them most: slavery.

In its internal dynamics, southern politics exhibited no greater discipline than northern—indeed, in many sections of the region, electoral activity remained disorganized and idiosyncratic, at least in comparison with the North, throughout the antebellum period and beyond. In the South's relations with the rest of the nation, however, the slavery issue supplied the place of party regularity and enforced regional political unity far more effectively than whips, caucuses, the spoils system, or the ward organization ever did in the North.[61] Van Buren, with his virtually exclusive devotion to politics, his conviction that slavery "had been so deeply planted as to forbid the hope of seeing it eradicated except thro' Providential means," and his fundamental belief that the institution presented no serious obstacle to "the advance of liberty . . . and the growth and maintenance of free institutions,"[62] quickly grasped the enormous benefit a northern politician might derive from an alliance with the "compact" South, and entertained no qualms about exploiting the opportunity.

Van Buren's perennial problem, the one that was to sink him politically two decades later over the issue of Texas annexation, was the impossibility of winning the complete trust of his wary southern allies without fatally distancing himself from his northern base. Against this difficulty, party regularity offered the only defense. The deep unpopularity of his prosouthern policy dictated that Van Buren employ the levers of party discipline to limit the unmediated influence of the New York electorate as drastically as possible. At Van Buren's direction, the Bucktails defeated the constitutional plank for universal suffrage; sought to shift to the governor the power to appoint justices of the peace (a privilege traditionally vested in the localities); and defeated a bill that would have selected presidential electors by popular vote, rather than appointment by legislative caucus. Such efforts, naturally, were always clothed in the garb of Jeffersonian democracy as necessary measures to enable the Republicans to combat the people's enemy, the aristocracy. Although scholars such as Dixon Ryan Fox and his successors accepted these rationalizations at face value, and such modern biographers as Remini and Niven continue to lend them credence in principle, contemporaries dismissed them as little more than partisan posturing, as historian Alvin Kass has shown.[63] "Call a country town meeting an aristocracy!" Rufus King thundered when he heard Van Buren's rationale for centralizing justice of the peace appointments. "What then may it not be called!"[64] The conclusion is inescapable that Van Buren deliberately sought to restrict New Yorkers' suffrage in order to ease the way for a political strategy that employed as its cornerstone an unpopular coalition with overtly sectionalist elements of the South.

Van Buren's sinking popularity and antidemocratic measures offered an opening to his Republican rivals. Seeking to capitalize on Bucktail embarrassments, a group calling itself the People's Party under the leadership of Henry Wheaton and James Tallmadge formed to run on a platform of democratizing the political process in New York. Ironically, the party whose leaders were most closely identified with the movement to restrict slavery backed John C. Calhoun as its choice for president. Compounding the irony, when Calhoun's candidacy later collapsed, the People's faction shifted their support to John Quincy Adams, more or less with the approval of the South Carolinian. At the same time, William Crawford, the campaign's most explicit spokesman for the South, had the endorsement of arch–New England sectionalist Harrison Gray Otis—as well as of the young New Bedford newspaperman, William Lloyd Garrison. What all these unlikely coalitions demonstrated—besides the almost impenetrable complexity of antebellum political alignments—was the degree to which, with the slavery question at least provisionally settled, North-South political coalitions were able to flourish on issues of common concern.

Yet both of these movements seemed to cut against the grain of modern trends. The nation was poised for a leap of social and economic progress that appeared to render their concerns obsolete. The settlement of the slavery extension issue worked out by Monroe, Barbour, and Clay at once provided for the protection of the slave-based capital of current slaveholders by enlarging the western market for their surplus and guaranteeing slavery in Alabama and elsewhere south of the 36°30' line, while it ensured, through the Thomas restriction and treaty cessions, that the dominion of slavery within the American republic would be effectively curtailed, allowing for the evolutionary growth of antislavery politics and sentiment, and sustaining hopes that slavery would, in the not-too-distant future, die away. Congressman Charles Fenton Mercer's bill of 1820, declaring slave trading to be piracy and punishable by death, put teeth into the 1808 prohibition and reasserted the somewhat tattered southern commitment to antislavery—even while many slave states instituted new, draconian restrictions on their slaves to defeat further possible rebellions in the aftermath of Denmark Vesey's planned Charleston revolt. What is more, deep apprehensions stemming from the Vesey incident helped to enforce a policy of silence concerning slavery, which provided valuable "cover" for the compromise, inhibiting strident criticism by northern restrictionists and southern expansionists alike.

To a significant extent, efforts at sectional conciliation during the Monroe administration appeared successful, and most Americans did not care to inquire too much about the cost. As Vincent Harding has observed, "There was much about America in the 1820s that made it possible for white men and women, especially in the North, to live as if no river of struggle were slowly, steadily developing its black power beneath the rough surfaces of the new nation."[65]

5

DISCORD

"IT HAS . . . BEEN SAID that the Missouri Compromise put the question of slavery to sleep for many years," remarked George Dangerfield. "But this is not true. It never slept again."[1] In retrospect, the decade following the Missouri controversy appears to be one of quiet over slavery—especially in contrast to what followed in the 1830s, as Horace Greeley's recollection at the opening of the previous chapter suggested. In fact, however, Dangerfield is right: the issue of slavery remained at or near the boiling point throughout the 1820s, threatening to explode more than once. The reason it did not is that emancipationists and anti-emancipationists remained stalemated. Opponents of slavery remained unable to offer a practical plan for its termination, while its advocates failed to develop a plausible defense of the institution within the framework of the Union. Even in this period of relative calm, however, slavery tested the strength of federal ties and dictated the boundaries of federal action. As this chapter and the ones that follow will show, the issue of slavery derailed the burgeoning nationalism of the Monroe and Adams administrations and dictated that the nation adopt what Lee Benson has called "a philosophy of the *negative* liberal state."[2]

SUCH AN OUTCOME could hardly have been farther from the thoughts of President Monroe and his cabinet after their successful negotiation of the Missouri compromises. With the contentious issue of slavery removed from center stage, new vistas opened up that appeared to offer a glimpse of America's full potential. In November 1823, John Quincy Adams recorded his conviction that the Monroe administration would "hereafter . . . be looked back to as the golden age of this republic."[3]

Certainly, Adams had grounds for his belief. The Supreme Court had finally laid to rest lingering questions about the constitutionality of the Bank of the United States, now under the capable management of a talented director, ensuring the stability (if not the open-handedness) of American credit markets. Manufactures would soon recoup and expand under the protection of a judicious tariff. Temporary economic distress appeared to be giving way to brisk recovery, fueled by the rapid expansion of western markets. Federal retrenchment would soon be offset by the incalculable natural resource of the public lands, the sale of which, responsibly administered, could provide sufficient revenues to the federal government to finance a wide array of major undertakings on which northern and southern seaboard states could reasonably be expected to collaborate.[4] Indeed, the public lands might reasonably offer a solution to the vexing slavery problem itself, as former presidents Jefferson and Madison had privately suggested and Representative Henry Meigs had proposed on the floor of Congress in 1820, by employing proceeds from land office sales in purchasing slaves and resettling them in Haiti, Africa, or elsewhere, perhaps west of the Mississippi, although, like his father, Adams was skeptical of colonization schemes.[5] More important in Adams's view, with Monroe's signature on bills to repair the Cumberland Road and to provide for a general survey of roads and canals, the question of internal improvements at last appeared settled, presenting the opportunity for the nation finally to develop its unmatched resources and embrace its destiny for greatness.

Under the leadership of Secretary of War John C. Calhoun, the Army Corps of Engineers mapped and surveyed rivers, harbors, and trails in preparation for an unprecedented expansion of internal improvement based on his long-deferred congressional report of 1819, which had proposed a national road from Maine to Louisiana, an extensive canal system, and large-scale federal aid to regional transportation projects.[6] In part, Calhoun's vision was a product of ambition. He must have envied the adulation bestowed on De Witt Clinton, the national leader he most closely resembled in intellectual and political style, for his Promethean accomplishment in galvanizing New York's commerce with his Erie Canal—as much a triumph of Clinton's will as of modern engineering.[7] What Clinton had done for New York, Calhoun would do for all of America—receiving a proportionate measure of glory. More specifically, however, Calhoun looked to national development to safeguard the South's special interests. Whereas Adams's devotion to internal improvements stemmed from his sense of America's providential mandate, Calhoun sought to elide differences between the sections by channeling the nation's great resources into projects designed to "bind the Republic together with a perfect system of roads and canals," to "conquer space." Drawing on the principles of Adam Smith, Calhoun argued that "the more enlarged the sphere of commercial circulation, the more extended that of social intercourse; the more strongly we are bound together, the more inseparable are our destinies."[8]

Like fellow nationalist southerner James Barbour, Calhoun believed that personal, political, and business relationships between key northern and southern leaders could surmount most sectional difficulties. Calhoun proposed to embrace the concerns of the North's mercantile, commercial, and manufacturing interests as his own, with the assurance that his appreciative northern counterparts would return the favor. In particular, he moved quickly to establish alliances with former anti-Missouri leaders, including New York's James Tallmadge, and to recement his ties to eminent northern Federalists such as Jedidiah Morse.[9] When Yale geology professor Benjamin Silliman and his guests dined with Calhoun in Washington in May 1824, the "distinguished graduate of Yale College" impressed the company with his "extensive and detailed" plans for federal public works, which "included not only a ship-canal between Lakes Superior and Huron, by the Sault St. Mary, but even a cut across the neck of Cape Cod, thus uniting Buzzard's Bay with Massachusetts, or Cape Cod Bay, and saving a dangerous navigation across the Cape."[10] This was in keeping with views Calhoun had held since his Bonus Bill speech of 1817, when he dismissed "refined arguments on the Constitution" against Congress's right to fund such improvements, even projects within one state, arguing that the Constitution "was not intended as a thesis for the logician to exercise his ingenuity on. It ought to be construed with plain, good sense."[11]

Calhoun's vaunting national vision embodied what had until recently been the typical outlook of his state. South Carolinians had helped to draw the nation into the War of 1812 and had taken the lead in promoting national development afterward. In addition to Calhoun, South Carolinians such as William Lowndes, Langdon Cheves, and Joel R. Poinsett ranked among the most eminent and nationalist political figures in America, while jurist William Johnson occupied arguably the most strongly nationalist position on the Supreme Court. The state's representatives routinely voted for protective tariffs and espoused the view that economic development represented the best means of surmounting sectional tension. In the words of William Freehling, "The thought of disunion brought universal scorn."[12]

But nationalism in South Carolina came increasingly under fire after 1816—figuratively and literally. While War Secretary Calhoun battled Treasury Secretary Crawford's "Radical" faction in Washington, Radicals and Calhounites fought even more bitterly at home. Calhoun's South

Carolina opponents, clustered around Senator William Smith, combined an intransigent devotion to states' rights with deep personal antipathy for the state's nationally celebrated statesman. In 1821, George McDuffie, Calhoun's closest lieutenant and a vehement nationalist, entered into a fierce political controversy with a faction of South Carolina Crawfordites known as the "Trio." The dispute escalated into a pair of duels with the Trio's leader William Cumming that left McDuffie gravely wounded and permanently embittered.[13]

Other South Carolinians, including Dr. Thomas Cooper, Josiah Evans, Robert J. Turnbull, and David R. Williams, adopted a stance of aggressive antinationalism. In part this rising hostility to the Monrovian nationalist vision simply reflected the internal dynamics of South Carolina politics; in part it represented a localist reaction to perceived economic injury inflicted by the tariff and other national policies. Undoubtedly, some South Carolinians were genuinely motivated by the constitutional considerations that all proclaimed to be paramount. To a great degree, however, South Carolina's leaders adopted strict constructionism under the conviction that federal action implicitly threatened the existence of slavery—and while some conceded the institution to be in a measure antagonistic to the nation's republican ideals, more regarded it as indispensable to their society's existence.

<hr />

IN ORDER TO UNDERSTAND the extreme response of many southerners to even the most conservative measures to combat slavery, it must be recognized that Americans possessed no model from modern times of peaceful emancipation of a true slave society. As David Brion Davis has observed, "Emancipation decrees were never far removed from violence or the threat of violence."[14] When Georgia congressman Thomas W. Cobb had cried, during the Missouri debates, that Tallmadge's amendment to bar slavery from Missouri had "kindled a fire which all the waters of the ocean cannot put out, which seas of blood can only extinguish," he did not speak presciently out of a prophetic vision of the American Civil War sixty years later, but rather with the images of the whites slaughtered during the Haitian Revolution of barely twenty years before still vividly imprinted on his mind.

These fears were if anything more immediate in South Carolina, since Charlestonians had received a large number of refugees from St. Domingue and had listened to their horror stories at first hand. These shaken survivors reinforced the Carolinians' conviction that rumors of emancipation could trigger destructive slave revolts. Contributing to the discomfort of South Carolinians and other slaveholders was the knowledge that such revolts were fully justified according to principles southerners accepted—the same principles, indeed, enunciated in the Declaration of Independence. The French Revolution and its aftermath had profoundly chilled the ardor of most southerners for the rhetoric of liberty and equality. American slaveholders could not disagree with the Cuban official who had observed in 1794 that the Haitian revolutionaries were "less fearsome for their weapons than for their words and for the contagion of the spirit of sedition and anarchy which they seek to inspire."[15] After Haiti, the implicit contradiction between Americans' revolutionary rhetoric and slavery-sustained reality became explicit and recognizably dangerous: "The sight of a slave listening to a Fourth of July oration chilled the bravest Southerner."[16] As the power of American republican rhetoric to inspire oppressed peoples to revolution became progressively clearer as the century unfolded, southern Old Republicans adopted a language and outlook increasingly similar to those of the Old World despotisms they had formerly denounced and despised.

The congressional debate over the future of slavery in Missouri contributed substantially to slaveholders' unease. In 1820, South Carolina governor John Geddes informed the legislature that the "Missouri question . . . ha[d] given rise to the expression of opinions and doctrines . . . which tend[ed] not only to diminish" the value of slave property, "but also to threaten our safety." The legislature responded with acts outlawing emancipation, barring free blacks from the state, and increasing the penalties for introducing "incendiary" papers.[17]

The public nature of the Missouri controversy demonstrated the futility of this last provision, since every newspaper printing the official record of debates in Congress offered an extensive discussion of slavery's flaws. Perhaps the most comprehensive statements in opposition to the expansion of slavery were Rufus King's two speeches of 1819 and 1820. In the second speech, King asserted that "all laws and compacts" imposing slavery "upon any human being are absolutely void, because contrary to the law of nature, which is the law of God."[18] Aghast, the speaker of the Virginia House of Delegates concluded from King's language that the North "would sound the tocsin of freedom to every Negro of the South and we may have to see the tragical events of St. Domingo repeated in our own land."[19]

A free black carpenter from Charleston, Denmark Vesey, read the same meaning into King's remarks. The reports of Vesey's planned insurrection, perhaps the most extensive ever mounted in the United States, shook South Carolina society to its foundations. Like the Nat Turner revolt in Virginia nine years later, the event provoked some slaveholders to calculate the value of the peculiar institution.[20] But in South Carolina, unlike in Virginia, talk of emancipation never moved from the stage of reverent hope to political program—indeed, it never developed any political constituency at all. South Carolina had always had the highest ratio of slaves to whites of any of the states, and as of 1820 slaves outnumbered whites by almost 10 percent. Not only did white South Carolinians' security depend on an iron control of slavery, their political standing within the Union did as well, since slaves accounted for nearly half of the state's eleven electoral votes. With its slaves counted under the federal ratio, South Carolina tied for seventh place in congressional representation; without them, it would be ranked fourth from last, no higher than Vermont.[21] Once it was decided, as it was almost immediately, that slavery must be preserved, South Carolinians had no illusions about the severity of the measures necessary to defend it.

At the same time, slaveholders were extremely limited in the measures they could take while maintaining republican government and civil freedom for whites, let alone free blacks, and while remaining within the framework of the federal constitution. In the context of the moral spirit of the age, slavery clearly constituted a national issue with repercussions for all Americans (as Americans of all sections learned, for example, when confronted on the subject when traveling abroad). To many southerners, however, any discussion of the moral or political drawbacks of slavery could be equated with invoking "a Toussaint, or a Spartacus, or an African Tecumseh," as South Carolina's Whitemarsh B. Seabrook angrily asserted.[22] While almost all southern whites angrily denied the right of outsiders to meddle in their "domestic institutions," the demands of internal white southern solidarity, however, proved equally onerous. Whites, too, suffered "within the shadow of coercive proscription supposedly reserved for the control of blacks."[23]

Not only the institution of slavery but also the limited options that southerners not unreasonably believed were available to them to deal with it created a set of stresses that indelibly marked southern society. Nothing in the educational, religious, or political training of the southern gentry prepared them to be effective enforcers of a draconian slave code; and although necessity steeled them to the task, they undertook it with a certain knowledge of the spiritual and moral costs it entailed. This perhaps helps to explain why, as William R. Taylor and Larry Tise have documented,[24] so many of the programmatic defenders of slavery subsequently to emerge were nonsoutherners or newcomers to the South. Possessed of a strong incentive to justify their allegiance and to demonstrate their bona fides to the slave system, and ignorant of the complex contradictions concerning slavery inherent to a native southern upbringing, they turned to the task with a relish rarely seen among the native-born. An Englishman like Thomas Cooper could denounce "race mixing" out of an antipathy to blacks virtually incomprehensible to slave-raised, slave-nursed Carolinians; a post–Revolutionary War immigrant from British West Florida such as Robert J. Turnbull could entertain visions of "civil war" and the "dissolution of the compact" with few of the qualms of a native.[25] The introduction by outsiders of "advanced" defenses of the institution became a conspicuous feature of the slavery debate during the 1820s, as we shall see, and while southerners embraced these imported proslavery arguments, many did so reluctantly. In the immediate aftermath of the Denmark Vesey upheaval, however, such arguments were not yet available, and the only defenses of slavery at hand were conservative, even reactionary. Southerners employed them for want of better ones, but not willingly or comfortably; and the strain, often expressed in the form of hypersensitivity and belligerence, showed.

If the standard historical view of the Missouri controversy as an isolated flare-up of antislavery sentiment were correct, one would perhaps be entitled to regard the extreme reactions of South Carolina planter representatives and others primarily as evidence of slaveholders' "pathological" fears.[26] However, as William W. Freehling has concluded, these "impractical" and "absurd" early southern fears need to be taken seriously, and their potential reasonableness investigated more fully.[27] Southern spokesmen considered the nation's commitment to slavery to be dangerously insufficient to guarantee the continuance of an institution on which their way of life rested—indeed, they regarded the majority as actively hostile toward slavery. To these southerners, in contrast to the hindsight of historians, the agitation over Missouri seemed to have disclosed "a solid North and a divided South."[28]

———— ∞∞∞ ————

IF SLAVEHOLDERS FOUND themselves demoralized in the wake of the Missouri controversy and its dangerous aftermath, emancipationists were no less disheartened. It may have been true in fact that the terms of the geographic compromise left slavery seriously weakened and acutely circumscribed. But the Monroe administration's strategic decision to portray the outcome of the Missouri controversy as a southern victory succeeded too completely: in addition to providing indispensable political "cover" for what the settlement's architects actually regarded as its long-term antislavery consequences, it sowed confusion in the ranks of slavery's opponents. I have discussed in chapter 4 the stinging defeat the extension of slavery into Missouri inflicted on Federalists and Clintonians. Its impact was equally great on committed abolitionists. The decision left white emancipationists frustrated and demoralized, crushed blacks' hopes for peaceful change, and emboldened proslavery forces in Illinois, Indiana, and Ohio to attempt to establish slavery in the nominally free states of the Old Northwest. Additionally, America's failure to restrict slavery in Missouri probably helped to prod British abolitionists to adopt a policy of opposition to slavery itself, not simply to the slave trade—which in turn stoked southerners' sense of isolation and embattlement while it helped to channel new antagonisms over slavery into the old sectional ruts still left over from the Federalist era.[29]

Thus the outward appearance of calm over the slavery issue in the early 1820s must be viewed in the context of a perpetual high state of tension within the South itself, and between the South and the nation. In fact, the muted level of debate over slavery in the years following the Missouri controversy testifies not so much to its resolution, as to the delicacy of the issue, and indeed, to the fragility of the Union itself. It is undoubtedly true that most Americans had their eyes on other questions than slavery during these years—years of increasing prosperity and tremendous national expansion and enterprise. From the perspective of these Americans, one can understand how the period could appear to be the "golden age of the republic." More significantly for our purposes, however, of those Americans who did consider the slavery question paramount—defenders as well as opponents—many viewed the nation's prospects with alarm, if not despair.

Not all slaveholders in the early 1820s regarded the institution as seriously threatened. Indeed, even during the height of northern militancy over the admission of Missouri, southern newspapers pleaded with readers to demonstrate their resolve over the issue (largely to no avail), while southern congressmen made excuses for the apathy of their constituents.[30] A few southerners, on the other hand, regarded slavery as under siege and in imminent danger. It is not surprising that South Carolina, possessing the highest proportion of slaves to whites, containing the heaviest influence of Haitian planter refugees, and having been the site of the most dangerous recent slave conspiracy, took those fears most seriously. In order to gauge how realistic these fears may have been, it will be useful to review the main lines of defense open to anti-emancipationists, and to examine the limitations and pitfalls of each.

From the convening of the First Congress, strict construction of the Constitution had served as the first line of the defense of slavery, and it remained the preferred approach throughout most of the antebellum period. For reasons that will be discussed below, strict construction proved a problematical tool for the purpose (not least for those southerners, such as Calhoun, who had long promoted an expansive view of constitutional interpretation). The assertion of state sovereignty, distinct from strict construction although linked to it, proved stronger medicine. Reliance on federal protection also had a venerable history, and though it fell into disfavor around this period, it did witness a renaissance of sorts when coupled with the patronage of strong parties, particularly the Democrats.[31] Finally, a hardy perennial of proslavery thought, the religious defense, experienced a brief flowering in the period of the Missouri debates and their aftermath. It is to this strain of ideology that we shall turn first because it provides an instructive example of the difficulties Americans encountered in trying to square slavery with Christianity and morality.

As Eugene Genovese has noted, scriptural arguments in defense of slavery in British America date back to at least as early as the eighteenth century, but they "picked up considerable momentum" after the turn of the century in response to rising antislavery sentiment.[32] As with so many aspects of the slavery debate, the Missouri controversy marked a turning point in the development of the biblical defense of slavery. South Carolina senator William Smith's fiery invocation of *"Moses and the Prophets"* in support of the institution had shocked many observers of the Missouri debate. Smith's remarks, although echoed by a few others, stood as probably the most extreme post-Revolutionary statement of the Biblical case for slavery before 1823.[33] Although Smith's speech is cited by Edwin C. Holland in *A Refutation of the Calumnies Circulated against the Southern and Western States, Respecting the Institution and Existence of Slavery. . . .*, a pamphlet explicitly devoted to combating mounting religious attacks on slavery published in the aftermath of the Denmark Vesey plot, Holland handles Smith's religious defense with respectful circumspection, not introducing Smith's pertinent arguments until page 41, and devoting less than a paragraph to them.[34]

In the months immediately following the crushing of the Vesey plot, still-reeling South Carolinians turned to religious leaders Richard Furman, head of the South Carolina Baptist Convention, and Frederick Dalcho, an influential Episcopalian minister, to calm their nerves and soothe their consciences. Ostensibly, Furman's and Dalcho's tracts were written to promote the wresting of slave religion from black preachers and white northern itinerants into the hands of reliable, indigenous white southern ministers. In reality, the treatises were intended to restore the shaken morale of a battered and wavering planter class. Richard Furman's tortuous efforts to justify slavery by means of Scripture in his *Exposition of the Views of the Baptists Relative to the Coloured Population of the United States in a Communication to the Governor of South Carolina* testify clearly to the novelty of the project, while his deference to the authority of the "benevolent Wilberforce" and other "highly respectable" religious and political writers against slavery underscores the difficulty faced by relatively cultivated southern clergymen in attempting to defend the institution.[35] In fact, Furman's work is less a defense of slavery than an assertion of the place of religion in a slave society: "To pious minds it has given pain to hear men, respectable for intelligence and morals, sometimes say, that holding slaves is indeed indefensible, but that to us it is necessary, and must be supported," wrote Furman, who consequently turned his pious mind toward divining a defense for a practice he fully regarded as necessary.[36] Thus it is clear from the text that, far from a magisterial ex cathedra statement of eternal verities, the scriptural defense of slavery in Furman's *Exposition* is a reactive attempt to mount a viable challenge to the dominant, antislavery paradigm of biblical interpretation, and to protect Christianity from impious slaveholders' defensive critiques.

Frederick Dalcho, recognizing the inadequacy of Furman's effort, offered another attempt within the year. Dalcho devoted more than half of his pamphlet, *Practical Considerations, Founded on the Scriptures, Relative to the Slave Population of South-Carolina*, to tying modern Africans to Noah's curse of Canaan—interesting in itself, since the link is so often regarded as a given in later proslavery writing.[37] The exercise proved inordinately difficult, forcing Dalcho to invoke Arabic translations of the Bible, strained etymologies, and highly uncanonical authorities such as Abulfaragi and Procopius—after all of which he had only succeeded in identifying Canaanites with the peoples of the North African littoral, nations whom Dalcho uncomfortably concedes have not always been "slaves of slaves" but have produced great empires, including Egypt, the font of civilization and "for many years . . . a great and flourishing kingdom."[38] By identifying Egypt with the progeny of Canaan, moreover, Dalcho was opening another dubious line of reasoning for an ostensible proslavery tract, since a standard contemporary providential interpretation explained Egypt's present degraded estate as the judgment of Providence for that country's crime of enslaving the Israelites.[39] Dalcho's earnest effort thus demonstrated a key drawback of employing the Bible to justify black slavery: it ended by lending biblical dignity and historical importance to Africans while contributing little or nothing to claims of their special, much less exclusive, suitability for enslavement.

At the same time, the narrative force of the Exodus story—so recently and so powerfully employed by Denmark Vesey—tended to reduce the Bible's various endorsements of slavery to at best secondary importance.

Much of the rest of Dalcho's pamphlet underscored the "delicacy" of the question of the proper religious instruction of slaves, emphasizing the confusion and difficulty even experienced southern planters faced in approaching the problem. Even "they who are born and brought up in the midst of tens of thousands of Negroes [and] have so much at stake upon the issue . . . are greatly at a loss as to the proper means of instructing them," Dalcho observed. Since "patriotic, enlightened, judicious and pious" Carolinians could "form correct opinions on the existing order of things in their own State" as well as college-trained interlopers from the North, "it is not . . . to be wondered at that we claim the right of managing our affairs, according to our own discretion."[40] This is true; what is far more "to be wondered at" is that the Charleston defenses of slavery in the wake of the Vesey conspiracy give one a strong sense of a planter class in ideological disarray, with no clear consensus whatsoever of how to manage its affairs.

In fact, it is hardly accurate to describe Dalcho's tract as a defense of slavery at all. "We are ready to confess that, the present state of things, is not in accordance with all our feelings," he wrote ambivalently. "We deprecate the evil which attends it." Most remarkable, given South Carolina's reputation for maintaining a solid front against even what William Freehling has termed the "conditional termination" of slavery, is Dalcho's assertion that "if the non-slave-holding States will purchase our plantations and slaves, and sell the latter to Africa, under the patronage of the Colonization Society, or dispose of them in any manner which the general government may think proper to direct, I do not in my conscience believe, there would be many Planters in South-Carolina, who would hesitate one moment, to get rid of both, even at something below their value." It would be hard to pack more heresies against South Carolina dogma into a single sentence—compensated emancipation, colonization, the uncontested cession of authority (over slaves, no less!) to the "General Government." The next sentence clarifies the sense of dread that spawned such dire thoughts: "As to parting with them without an equivalent, [that] is out of the question. . . . We shall never choose beggary for ourselves and our families, *when it is left to our choice*" (Emphasis added).[41] Fearful that South Carolina might be stripped of its slaves by force—either of arms or of law—Dalcho was unwilling to shut the door to compensated emancipation, even at a discount. So soon after narrowly escaping what could have been the largest and best-organized slave insurrection in the United States, many formerly complacent Charlestonians had not yet concluded that their best hopes for security lay in unqualified and uncompromising support for perpetual slavery.

Noteworthy in Dalcho's treatise is his evident belief that the "general government" was not necessarily hostile to the interests of South Carolina. A perennial line of thought in the South regarded reliance on a strong federal government and union as the soundest bulwark of slavery. Supporters of this viewpoint stressed the need for a strong federal fugitive slave law, as provided for in the constitution; for federal military force to suppress possible slave insurrections, and, increasingly as the era wore on, the need for U.S. protection against foreign hostility. "Without the aid of the whole United States, we could not have kept slavery," diarist Mary Chesnut's father-in-law, James Chesnut Sr., would regularly intone. "I always knew that the world was against us. That was one reason why I was a Union man. I wanted all the power the United States gave me—to hold my own—&c&c."[42] Chesnut's reasoning was typical of conservative southern Unionists, who, in the circles of their northern acquaintances in the summer havens of Saratoga or Newport, rarely heard any expressions of opinion likely to shake their conviction that the North would unflinchingly stand by its slaveholding brethren through thick and thin. Such men could be found in both the Jacksonian and Whig parties in the South, although temperamentally more suited to the latter. More imaginative and better-informed southerners recognized, however, that this reliance on the Union to save slavery was outdated given the trend of the times, or soon would be.

The preferred defense of slavery by most southerners was to preclude on principle any discussion of the question at all. This position asserted that the sectional compromises concerning slavery that secured the adoption of the Constitution relating to slave representation, the return of fugitive slaves, and the regulation of the international and domestic slave trade positively enjoined any federal interference with slavery. The purpose of this argument, as we have seen, was to fence off discussion of the expedience of slavery and of emancipation by the seemingly neutral device of constitutional prohibition, and its advocates took the doctrine to remarkable lengths during the Missouri debate.

True proponents of strict construction (as opposed to those, such as Georgia governor George Troup, who employed its rhetoric on occasion when tactically useful) did not regard the principle as limited to slavery, but applied it to virtually every federal action not specifically enumerated in the Constitution. On its face, this would seem to suggest that the strict constructionist viewpoint represented the consistent and scrupulous position claimed by its adherents, founded purely on traditional Whig distrust of power and of unfettered government's tendency toward consolidation and corruption.

Strict constructionists of the early 1820s, particularly those who described themselves as "Old Republicans," habitually stressed their fidelity to Republican Party philosophy of the 1790s, when such policies were formulated. But as Norman K. Risjord has convincingly demonstrated, in the years following the War of 1812, Republicans virtually abandoned constitutional scruples against nationalist undertakings, and projects such as the Bank of the United States, internal improvements, and a protective tariff passed Congress with "almost no objection to any of the three in principle."[43] A small number of southerners, notably Nathaniel Macon of North Carolina and John Randolph of Roanoke, consistently attacked all three measures. Macon lamented that he seemed to be the only congressman who had voted against the first Bank of the United States who still found the second Bank of the United States constitutionally objectionable. Randolph trained his fire on the tariff, although he did not always base his objections to the tariff on constitutional grounds. While the tariff soon became the chief rallying cry for southern strict constructionists, it had the drawback of being among the congressional powers explicitly enumerated by the Constitution—indeed, the very first power listed.[44] Randolph appeared to recognize this problem in 1816, when he rested his opposition to the tariff not on constitutional principles but on economic grounds, declaring that it constituted "a tax on the nation at large for the benefit of the manufacturing interest," a tax that would fall on "poor men, and on slaveholders."[45]

Randolph's formulation, beyond its canny appeal to class hostility, underscores the underlying anti-emancipationist basis of strict construction. While we shall look more closely later at Randolph's conviction of the tariff's antisouthern bias, and at the larger issue of why southerners considered the tariff so dangerous, here it is enough to stress that once an element of sectionalism began to intrude into the strict-constructionist argument, it undermined its effectiveness as a political weapon against emancipation, since consistency, or at least equity, was necessary to secure crucial northern and western support. Ironically, as Risjord has pointed out, Old Republicanism lost its effectiveness and usefulness just at the moment of its greatest influence, because of its capitulation to sectionalism.[46]

As I have suggested, strict construction remained the preferred defense of slavery, since it allowed advocates to avoid discussing the merits of the issue at all. This feature of the argument was particularly important to some southern spokesmen, such as Virginia's Thomas Ritchie and William Rives, both of whom had scruples against slavery and acute sensitivity to the political pressures on their northern Republican allies. Increasingly after the Missouri debates, however, other southern leaders began to employ the strict-constructionist argument in ways virtually guaranteed to alienate even sympathetic northerners.

Nowhere was this breach more striking than in John Taylor of Caroline's rebuke of Pennsylvania senator Henry Baldwin, perhaps the South's most dedicated northern advocate during the Missouri controversy. Baldwin, it will be recalled, had bent over backward to placate the South in order to garner southern support for a protective tariff and other measures vital to the manufacturing interests Baldwin served. To Baldwin, it was bad enough that southern votes defeated his entire package of legislation; but Taylor went further and, in his polemic *Tyranny Unmasked*, cited Baldwin's 1821 report on the protection of manufactures as "containing doctrines" likely to lead to national consolidation and monarchy and "to terminate in a tyrannical government." In justice to Baldwin and the other members of his committee, Taylor graciously averred that he did not believe that they intended such an outcome; but this in no way lessened the danger of their doctrines.[47] Even if no one could wade through all 349 pages of Taylor's turgid and convoluted prose, it could not have been pleasant to Baldwin— particularly after his political sacrifices to the South—to be described as the author of an inevitable slide toward tyrannical government; nor could it have encouraged other northern politicians to stick their necks out for the cause of sectional harmony. Although couched in the sectionally neutral language of strict construction, Taylor's broadside helped to explode the possibility of intersectional cooperation, and appears almost designed to do so.

But the fundamental flaw of the strict-constructionist argument as a defense of slavery is that it did not, indeed could not, work. For one thing, the Supreme Court, final arbiter of the "law of the land," while consistently supporting a southern interpretation on most cases directly related to slavery, had ruled decisively in favor of a broad interpretation of the Constitution that implicitly conferred extensive powers to Congress to enact legislation indirectly threatening to slavery. More to the point, as R. Kent Newmyer has argued, many perceptive southerners, such as Henry St. George Tucker, recognized that "the real problem" in employing strict construction to restrain the expansion of national power was not the makeup of the Court but "the Constitution itself." Ultimately, John Taylor of Caroline reached the same conclusion, believing that abandoning the Articles of Confederation had been the South's "fatal mistake." Newmyer argues that "what these southern conservatives realized"—what historians have missed by focusing too much on the conservative motives of the framers of the Constitution and not enough on the document they framed—was that the Constitution of 1787 was a Trojan horse of radical social and economic transformation."[48] In direct response to events that unfolded in the wake of the Denmark Vesey affair, opponents of emancipation relied more and more heavily for protection on the principle of states' rights, in the process drastically modifying the doctrine of constitutional strict construction or, increasingly, abandoning it altogether.

⊷⊷⊷

ALTHOUGH THE TWO concepts are often invoked together, implying interchangeability, the doctrine of states' rights is not the same as strict construction. States' rights proved to be a far more reliable tool for the defense of slavery than constitutionalism, because the means required by a state to defend slavery within its borders often required trespassing on the Constitution in no uncertain terms. This was perhaps most clearly demonstrated by the controversy over the South Carolina Negro Seamen Acts that commenced in 1823.

The irreconcilable conflict between broad nationalism and slavery in the 1820s is encapsulated in the history of the South's Negro Seamen Acts. In December, 1822, the South Carolina legislature passed a law identified as "an act for the better regulation of free negroes and persons of color, and for other purposes," designed to restrict contact between local slaves and free black seamen, in order to prevent "the moral contagion of their pernicious principles and opinions."[49] The act required that black seamen serving on ships entering any South Carolina port be jailed until the ship's departure, and that the ship's captain pay the sailors' expenses; otherwise they were to be sold into slavery to recover costs. This law, passed in the immediate aftermath of the Denmark Vesey affair, represented a response to a genuine fear, not simply a vindictive measure against free blacks—although it was that as well. It is noteworthy that the act was aimed at black sailors, not passengers.[50] This distinction suggests that South Carolina officials intended to target rather narrowly what they perceived as a serious threat. The danger to a slave society posed by free black mariners—the most mobile, best-informed, and among the most prosperous groups in free black society—was real and immediate, as the experience in the Caribbean in the era of the Haitian revolution had demonstrated.[51] Antislavery literature had been carried into South Carolina by black seamen on at least one occasion, in 1809, and quite possibly on other occasions. The Charleston slave conspirators of 1822 had spoken of anticipated assistance from Haiti and Africa, and had employed a black seaman as a courier in an attempt to contact Haiti's president and enlist his nation's support. Moreover, Vesey himself had spent a considerable time at sea; it made sense to the South Carolina authorities that he had imbibed his dangerous ideas of freedom through these experiences.[52]

Despite its resolutely pacific official foreign policy, southerners viewed Haiti with intense suspicion and anxiety. Most South Carolinians regarded the republic as a source of an "infection" of freedom of which black seamen were likely to be "carriers." Viewed in this light, one can understand the logic of the South Carolinian assertion that the seamen act constituted the equivalent of a quarantine. There was some validity to the concern that black sailors could spread a contagion for liberty; but a few slaveholders recognized that an ordinary Fourth of July oration represented at least as great a threat.[53]

If the Negro Seamen Act constituted an understandable response to a real danger, it also posed a direct challenge to federal authority and to international and interstate commerce. Indeed, it would be hard to design a law with greater constitutional and diplomatic ramifications. By imprisoning citizens of other states, the South Carolina authorities would be violating the equal protection clause of the constitution. If the seamen were citizens of Great Britain, their detention would represent a violation of the Commercial Convention of 1815 which guaranteed free access of British and American seamen to each others' ports. In either case, the act could be regarded as an infringement of the Constitution's commerce clause. Thus the South Carolina Negro Seamen Act starkly illustrated how even the most essential police regulations for a slave regime inevitably produced momentous institutional confrontations that threatened the harmony of the federal union.

Perhaps even more significantly, the controversy over this piece of legislation demonstrated the inability of civil institutions themselves to contain the conflicts generated by slavery. The executive branch, the Congress, the Supreme Court, and even the state of South Carolina itself, all failed to impose their authority effectively in this matter, superseded by a private organization, the South Carolina Association, without any official standing whatsoever. This aspect of the episode has received little notice from historians; and yet, considering the deterioration of the rule of law that marked later antebellum U.S. society, as well as escalating southern hostility toward voluntary organizations, it seems particularly important.[54]

Almost immediately after the act's passage, the authorities began seizing and jailing free persons of color on vessels in Charleston harbor. British and American ship captains protested against the act to Supreme Court Justice William Johnson, sitting as judge of the Charleston Circuit Court. Johnson, nominated to the Supreme Court by Jefferson for his "good nerves in his political principles," with the hope that he would stand up to John Marshall, was a jurist of talent, courage, and remarkable independence—the first member of the Court to write a dissenting opinion.[55] Believing that the seamen act "had been passed hastily and without due consideration" in the aftermath of the Vesey hysteria, Johnson referred the captains' complaints to the state's courts and prevailed on the British consul and the American captains to be patient and rely on the sober second thoughts of the South Carolina judiciary. Unsurprisingly, however, the courts upheld the constitutionality of the act. Several masters then petitioned Congress for relief; equally unsurprisingly, Congress did nothing.

The official complaint of a foreign government, however, was harder to ignore. Four free black British subjects from a Nassau ship had been imprisoned in Charleston and their master secured their release only with difficulty. The British minister in Washington, Stratford Canning, protested this event to Secretary of State John Quincy Adams on February 15, 1823.

Adams took quick but quiet action, calling the problem to the attention of two South Carolina congressmen, Joel R. Poinsett and James Hamilton Jr., both of whom he believed to be reliable nationalists. Adams conveyed Canning's note to the congressmen and evidently urged them to suggest to the South Carolina authorities that the law simply not be enforced.[56]

Apparently, Adams's appeal bore fruit; within five weeks, black seamen "once more had a free run of Charleston."[57] Several factors, besides the merits of the request, probably contributed to this result. Free blacks composed up to a quarter of the total work force on merchant ships—the entire crew on some; so that strict enforcement of the act would have created an enormous disruption of the smooth running of Charleston port and, just as important, threatened private property. In fact, as Judge Johnson noted, one set of arrests left not "a single man on board the vessel to guard her in the captain's absence."[58] Clearly, this sort of circumstance could not be acceptable to the state's mercantile interests.

On June 17, Adams finally responded in writing to Stratford Canning's remonstrance, assuring the British minister that the United States had taken steps "for effecting the removal of the cause of complaint . . . , which it is not doubted have been successful, and will prevent the recurrence of it in future."[59] Adams's confidence probably derived from assurances from Johnson, who intervened personally with the South Carolina authorities.

At any rate, the judge later wrote that as soon as the "state officers" had called to their attention the "unconstitutionality, and injurious effects upon our commerce and foreign relations" of the law, they displayed "every disposition to let it sleep."[60]

This was not the end of the story, however. An influential group of South Carolinians was determined to keep this issue from going dormant. A month after Secretary Adams's message to Canning, a "cryptic notice" appeared in the *Charleston Courier* announcing a meeting of "The Association." Ten days later, on July 24, the newly formed South Carolina Association revealed itself. Among its officers it numbered many distinguished figures of the South Carolina planter aristocracy, including Keating Simons, Thomas Pinckney, Henry Deas, Joseph Manigault, Stephen Elliott and Robert J. Turnbull. Although ostensibly "not an association of individuals combining for party purposes or political influence," the early membership of the organization did tend noticeably toward Federalists (or ex-Federalists) and officers of the State Bank.[61] While the purpose of the South Carolina Association, according to "A Member," was merely to put an end to "the daily violation or evasion of the laws, made to regulate the conduct of our colored population," and "to aid the execution of the laws founded upon the *local and peculiar policy of South Carolina*, by giving to the Civil Magistrate, through its agents . . . information of their infringement," such an apparently modest aim hardly squared with the author's description of the society as "perhaps the most important association that ever has been, or ever can be formed, in the Southern States."[62] Though the language of public affairs in early nineteenth-century America is suffused with exorbitant superlatives, these were unlikely to be bestowed on an ordinary southern vigilante committee. The South Carolina Association was established specifically for the purpose of enforcing the Negro Seamen Law, with full awareness of the implications for interstate and international relations.[63] It appears that the author of this notice intended no exaggeration by his remarkable assertion of the organization's pivotal importance. Subsequent statements, as well as actions, of spokesmen for the South Carolina Association pointed to the members' conviction that the simple "execution of the laws" required to preserve slavery could not be accomplished while the state remained within the bonds of the Union.

———◦◦◦———

THE CHRONOLOGY OF EVENTS leading up to the formation of the South Carolina Association suggests that it may have been organized in response to the federal government's reply to Britain's protest of the Negro Seamen Act. Secretary of State Adams met with Congressmen Poinsett and Hamilton before the adjournment of Congress on March 3; enforcement of the act was suspended later that month. Within ten days of Adams's letter to Canning, however, the South Carolina Association made its appearance, and in less than two weeks arrests under the act resumed. On August 7, the association's lawyers appeared in court before Justice Johnson to defend the act's constitutionality.[64] Thus it appears that, while the state's most prominent anti-emancipationists might be willing to tolerate unofficial non-enforcement of the black code, Adams's formal assurance to Britain that the U.S. government had "effect[ed] the removal of the cause of complaint" crossed a line that these South Carolinians could not countenance.

In early August, the issue came dramatically to a head. The sheriff of Charleston removed Henry Elkison, a black British subject born in Jamaica, from the Liverpool ship *Homer* and placed him in jail. Elkison's lawyers immediately petitioned Justice Johnson for a writ of habeas corpus, and on August 7 Johnson listened to arguments before a packed chamber. Significantly, the state of South Carolina took no part in the proceeding, with Benjamin Faneuil Hunt and Isaac E. Holmes, attorneys representing the South Carolina Association, appearing in defense of the law.[65] Hunt argued that the seamen act was essential to South Carolina's self-preservation, while Holmes, going further, maintained that he would rather see the Union dissolved than South Carolina relinquish the power to restrict blacks' entry.[66]

Johnson's anger at Holmes's suggestion was palpable. "Everyone saw me lay down my pen, raise my eyes from my notes, and fix them on the speaker's face," the judge wrote. Yet Holmes proceeded, "in a style which bore evidence of preparation and study."[67] Johnson concluded that much more was at stake than the constitutionality of a single act; that the South Carolina Association had a portentous agenda, which it was pursuing from outside the bounds of the regular political process. Pressing the enforcement of the seamen act constituted "rather a private than a state act," he averred; neither the federal nor the state government had a hand in it. As to the constitutionality of the act itself, "it is not too much to say that it will not bear argument." This was as much as conceded by Holmes and Hunt, Johnson argued. "Neither of the gentlemen has attempted to prove that the power, therein assumed by the state, can be exercised without clashing with the general powers of the United States . . . and indeed, Mr. Holmes concluded his argument with the declaration, that if a dis[s]olution of the union must be the alternative he was ready to meet it." Likewise, Hunt had asserted that South Carolina remained as much a "sovereign state" as when she adopted the Constitution. This "candid exposé" of their constitutional grounds was superfluous, argued the justice, because the power assumed by the act lay self-evidently "with the powers of the general government," and tended "to embroil us with, if not separate us from, our sister states." "In short," Johnson argued, the act looked toward "a dissolution of the union, and implie[d] a direct attack upon the sovereignty of the United States."[68]

Johnson continued by observing the dangerous precedent, as well as the irrationality, of a law aimed at a class of persons based on the color of their skin. The acknowledged purpose of the law, Johnson noted, was to prohibit ships entering Charleston harbor from employing colored seamen, of any nationality. "But if this state can prohibit Great Britain from employing her colored subjects, (and she has them of all colors on the globe), . . . why not prohibit her from using those of Irish or Scotch nativity; if the color of his skin is to preclude the Lascar or the Sierra Leone seaman, why not the color of his eye or hair exclude from our ports the inhabitants of her other territories?" The law might equally be used to enslave Moroccan or Algerian seamen, "all colored," or the crew of a Massachusetts ship "composed of Nantucket Indians, known to be among the best seamen in our service. These might all become slaves under this act." Moreover, observed Johnson, if enforced, the act would provoke retaliation, "and the commerce of this city, feeble and sickly, comparatively, as it already is, might be fatally injured." All Charleston shipping might be barred from foreign or out-of-state ports, or the United States "involved in war and confusion"; such considerations demonstrated how drastically the act interfered with Congress's constitutionally delegated right to regulate commerce.[69]

Johnson then turned to the alleged "offense" of Elkison, the imprisoned crewman: "that of coming into this port . . . in the capacity of a seaman." Yet "the laws and treaties of the United States" guaranteed his right to enter the country, and his captain's right to bring him. Thus the South Carolina law constituted "in effect a repeal of the laws of the United States pro tanto, converting a right into a crime."[70]

Next, Johnson considered the key argument of the South Carolina Association, that of necessity. If each state were to be its own judge of "necessity," the nation would be returned to the condition of the "old confederation," and "the union becomes a mere rope of sand." Moreover, the judge disputed the necessity, or even the usefulness, of the law for its intended purpose of preventing "contamination" of slaves by free blacks. If the law was designed to keep free blacks from "holding communion with our slaves," it "pursues a course altogether inconsistent with its object," since "this method of disposing of offenders by detaining them here, presents the finest facilities in the world for introducing themselves lawfully into the very situation in which they would enjoy the best opportunities of pursuing their designs"—that is, by placing them in jail alongside of the most rebellious and dangerous members of the Charleston slave community.

Finally, in a paragraph revealing of both the status of blacks in the American naval service and public perceptions of them, the judge warned of the consequences of applying the provisions of the act to American warships. "Send your sheriff on board one of them, and would the spirited young men of the navy submit to have a man taken?" Johnson scoffed. "It would be a repetition of the affair of the Chesapeake. The public mind would revolt at the idea of such an attempt." The persuasiveness of Judge Johnson's claim, incidentally, was demonstrated the following December, when the South Carolina legislature exempted black sailors on American or foreign warships from the provisions of the act.[71]

Despite Judge Johnson's obvious fury with the Negro Seamen Act, and his evident concern for the rights of Elkison and others imprisoned under it, all of the foregoing discussion of the act's unconstitutionality was, as he conceded, only an obiter dictum, and he was powerless to order Elkison's release. Under the terms of the Judiciary Act of 1789, the jurisdiction of the U.S. District Court extended only to civil matters; thus Johnson was unauthorized to issue a writ of habeas corpus. Indeed, the judge concluded that the act had deliberately been drawn "so as to leave the objects of it remediless." Thus Johnson could only advise the petitioner to take his case to the state courts—where, the judge conceded, he would be unlikely to find relief.[72]

Johnson's decision provoked an uproar in Charleston. The city's newspapers kept up a steady stream of attacks on the judge for weeks, and Johnson wrote to his patron, Jefferson, that he had "received a warning to quit this city." Much of this vituperation stemmed directly from officers of the South Carolina Association, former Federalists of whom the ultra-republican Johnson ironically observed, "The very men who long since made such an outcry against self-created societies are now heading a most formidable one in this place. . . . They now pronounce the Negros the real Jacobins of this country, and in doing so shew what they meant when they honored us with the same epithet."[73]

The episode led to a breach not only between Justice Johnson and the slaveholders of Charleston, but also between Johnson and Jefferson; they exchanged no further letters. "The two Republicans had reached an impasse," observed Johnson's biographer. "To one the greatest danger lay in federal centralization, to the other, in state excesses and disunion."[74]

∽∾

ALTHOUGH THE TACTICS of the South Carolinians proved remarkably successful in the short run, federal assurances of noninterference with slavery, and even tacit acquiescence in the states' rights philosophy, ultimately proved unavailing in calming slaveholders' fears. This was because of a serious deficiency in the argument itself. No matter how practically effective it might be in foreclosing possible federal action against slavery, the states' rights position remained an essentially negative principle—one at loggerheads with progress, and increasingly at odds with the spirit of the age. Such conservatism might prove a problem even in the "despotic" European states whose desperate efforts to hold off change had become staple fare in American newspapers; in America itself, it seemed fatal.

This point must be stressed because it is central to the larger framework of my argument. According to Robert M. Cover, "No set of legal institutions or prescriptions exists apart from the narratives that locate it and give it meaning."[75] The larger narrative implicit in the Negro Seamen Act and other draconian statutes designed to safeguard slavery suggested a world under siege, struggling to exclude an "infection" of ideas about liberty. While this represented a familiar stance for some of the more conservative Federalists among southern opponents of emancipation, it was hardly congenial to such Republican champions of liberty as Attorney General Robert Y. Hayne, or Thomas Cooper, who espoused the "RIGHT OF FREE DISCUSSION, in its fullest extent; as applied to any and every question, opinion, tenet, or doctrine," and asserted that "all attempts at restraining knowledge, in the present day, are likely to be in vain."[76]

Presidential politics coincidentally helped to strengthen the perception of the states' rights position as antidemocratic. After a string of three authentically popular Republican candidates from the South, party insiders fixed upon a candidate genuinely unpopular with the public at large, William C. Crawford. In spite of his "political obscurantism," including support for a national bank and no clear position on a protective tariff, Crawford had successfully positioned himself as the champion of the states' rights party, and they stuck by him doggedly through thick and thin—even after a paralytic stroke rendered him manifestly incapable of governing if elected.[77] Political fixers North and South went to almost comic lengths to manipulate election laws and forestall reform in order to force Crawford on an unwilling electorate. Cooper, the former English radical and current proslavery South Carolinian, denounced "attempts to throw the election of a President exclusively into the hands of the people" as "a Consolidation measure," adding that "the election of a President . . . is a State affair, and ought to be managed by the States, and not by the people."[78] Ultimately, the Crawford partisans succeeded only in making their antidemocratic efforts the central issue in an otherwise almost issueless campaign; and Crawford ended up securing only the electoral votes of those states—Virginia and his home state of Georgia—that could be successfully "managed."

Anti-egalitarianism was not the only albatross around the neck of the states' rights cause. By resorting to threats of disunion, states' rights spokesmen nullified the effectiveness of the "Hartford Convention" charges against opponents that had served as the keystone of Republican rhetoric for nearly a decade, thus undermining Republican cohesion and breathing new life into New England nationalism. This was throwing away an enormous moral, political, and psychological advantage—one that Daniel Webster would later capitalize on in his famous debate with Hayne.

Still, the argument of state supremacy would have to do because, at this juncture, opponents of emancipation had no better one. Missing from the anti-emancipationist arsenal was a true "proslavery" argument—a defense of slavery as a positive good, and an elaborated theory of racial inequality on which to erect it.[79]

This point is crucial, and it is easily overlooked. Since the arguments mounted against emancipation by this time included, in embryo, virtually all of the elements that would come to be assembled as the proslavery argument in its mature form, it is easy for the modern reader, more or less unconsciously to make connections that contemporaries did not, and, as it were, to "fill in the blanks" in these early treatises to convert them into much more coherent and more unqualified statements than their authors in fact could create.[80] In particular, anti-emancipationists in the early 1820s uniformly failed to make the critical rhetorical turn that characterizes the most effective later proslavery literature, and that produced the most ruinous consequences: the argument that persons of African descent have no history, no role in human affairs, and occupy a position beneath the consideration of whites. This was a step defenders of slavery were profoundly uncomfortable in taking—indeed, it was a view adopted more frequently by *opponents* of slavery, such as John J. Flournoy, the eccentric denizen of Athens, Georgia.[81] Once taken, however, this interpretive move drastically recast the proslavery argument, and inexorably shaped historians' views of the entire earlier debate.

In their effort to freight the states' rights defense of slavery with overtones of liberty, and thus ameliorate its somber conservatism, anti-emancipationists invoked the Virginia and Kentucky Resolves of 1798 and 1799, drafted by Madison and Jefferson in response to the Federalist-sponsored Alien and Sedition Acts. According to these resolutions, each state had "an equal right to judge of itself" violations of the Constitution by the general government, as well as "the mode and measure of redress" by the states, declaring nullification of obnoxious laws to be a "rightful remedy."[82] Tying their cause to the "spirit of '98" and its tradition of resistance to improper federal authority—a tactic frequently employed by strict constructionists, most recently in the unsuccessful struggle against the charter of the Second Bank of the United States[83]—offered slaveholders a peculiarly appropriate solution to the ideological dilemma of formulating a "republican" defense of the peculiar institution. First, it tied the protection of slavery rhetorically to the high principles of freedom of speech, of the press, and of religion expounded by the Virginia and Kentucky Resolutions, cloaking it in an unimpeachably liberal Republican mantle.[84] Second, it mitigated the sectionalism inherent in a defense of slavery by recasting it in the terms employed when the South had championed endangered civil rights and the North had united to defend apparently repressive Federalist authority. At the same time, however, the impeccable Republican pedigree of the resolutions (Jefferson had acknowledged his connection to them in 1821) encouraged the party faithful from whatever section to embrace the states' rights argument, and at least hypothetically cast the dispute in national and not sectional terms.[85] Finally, and most ominously, recourse to the principles of '98 implicitly spelled out a course of resistance to federal interference: state "interposition" between obnoxious laws and the people, or "nullification" of the laws themselves. It is no surprise that the injunction to "uphold the 'spirit of '98'" became the principal admonition charged to politicians sent to Washington with an Old Republican imprimatur.[86]

Since before 1800, Nathaniel Macon, North Carolina's oracle of strict construction, had scented the danger to slavery inherent in the sedately millennial language of the preamble of the Constitution: "We, the people of the United States, in order to form a more perfect Union, establish justice, insure domestic tranquility, provide for the common defense, promote the general welfare, and secure the blessings of liberty to ourselves and our posterity do ordain and establish this Constitution." William Lloyd Garrison might call the instrument a "covenant with death," but to Macon, no less than to antislavery constitutionalists Lysander Spooner or Frederick Douglass, each clause of the preamble seemed incompatible with the continuation of the peculiar institution. Slavery stood in clear opposition to the "more perfect Union" for which the Constitution had been formed. It was hardly compatible with the desire to "establish justice." It manifestly threatened "domestic tranquility" and the "common defense"; it could hardly be seen as promoting the "general welfare" or as helping "to secure the blessings of liberty" to present and future generations.[87]

Macon tried for years to open the eyes of his younger colleague Bartlett Yancey to his conviction that any federal move to improve the nation's communications or transportation systems threatened the continued existence of slavery. "I must ask you to examine the constitution of the U.S.," Macon wrote Yancey in 1818, ". . . and then tell me whether if Congress can establish banks, make roads and canals, whether they cannot free all the Slaves in the U.S."[88]

Intriguingly, Macon believed that American reformers would ultimately press Congress to legislate an end to slavery—a dream rarely broached by even the most radical antislavery advocates, who were usually willing to concede that the Constitution placed such action out of bounds. Macon, to the contrary, regarded such a policy as implicit in the logic of the march of American progress and power: "We have abolition-colonizing bible and peace societies . . . and if the general government shall continue to stretch their powers, these societies will undoubtedly push them to try the question of emancipation." When Yancey demurred from Macon's unorthodox constitutional interpretation, the older man persisted: "Examine again, the constitution of the U.S. and you will perceive your error. If Congress can make canals they can with more propriety emancipate." He admonished his younger colleague not to let "love of improvement, or a thirst for glory" blind his "sober discretion and sound common sense," warning that his "error in this, will injure if not destroy our beloved mother N. Carolina and all the South country."[89] Ultimately Macon's appeals to Yancey proved unavailing, although the congressman's avid championing of "our Road"—a proposed national highway from Washington to New Orleans that would have passed through western North Carolina—was perhaps motivated less by a "love of glory" than by a fear of retribution at the polls had he opposed it.[90]

While Macon refrained from publicly tying his opposition to internal improvements to the defense of slavery, John Randolph had no such qualms. In a speech on the floor of the House of Representatives in 1824, Randolph made the remarkable argument against an act merely authorizing a national survey of transportation projects, that "if Congress possess the power to do what is proposed by this bill, they can not only enact a sedition law,—for there is precedent,—but they may emancipate every slave in the United States—and with stronger color of reason than they can exercise the power now contended for."[91]

Randolph's apparent non sequitur concerning the Sedition Act was strictly in keeping with the Old Republican policy of relating all efforts to defend slavery to the "spirit of '98." We must now consider more carefully why, in effect, Macon and Randolph seemed to believe that *any* federal initiatives beyond the explicit scope of the letter of the Constitution would inevitably culminate in a congressional effort to abolish slavery. Why, for instance, did so many southerners believe that increased federal outlays for internal improvements intrinsically threatened their region? Historians have frequently accepted states' rights leaders' strictures against internal improvements at face value, without examining their premises closely. As John C. Calhoun well knew, federal proposals for internal improvements had been designed with an eye toward winning southern support by showering the region with valuable projects.[92] Although increasingly, southern leaders adopted a stance of hostility toward internal improvements, many did so with reluctance and often at serious political cost. Southerners stood to benefit from improved transportation facilities at least as much as other Americans. Planters in the cotton belt, closely tied to the international market system, needed improved facilities for bringing their staples to ports on the Gulf and the Atlantic, particularly since the precipitous drop in cotton prices after 1819 demanded that producers cut costs wherever possible. Meanwhile, many southerners who had stayed behind during the "cotton rush" regarded the proposed national system of public works projects as offering the hope of reinvigorating their agriculturally worn-out communities. A resident of Bolivar, Tennessee, boasted in 1826 that his town ought soon to "attain considerable importance," since, "if the spirit of improvement . . . should continue to be a favorite subject with the nation as it now seems to be, a canal will be constructed connecting the Hatche and Tennessee rivers, and thus Bolivar will be situated on the great thoroughfare from East Tennessee and Upper Alabama to New Orleans."[93] During his campaign for the presidency in 1824, John C. Calhoun encouraged "free expression of the publick opinion on the great subject of the route of the National Road to New Orleans" as "very desirable" and calculated "to fix and consolidate the public sentiment" on his behalf.[94] Supporters of William Crawford in North Carolina who maintained their candidate's hard line against federal support for roads and canals faced political rebellion from the underdeveloped central part of the state, which bolted to Andrew Jackson, then thought by many to be a strong economic nationalist.[95]

Virginians in particular stood to benefit from federal outlays that might bolster the failing productivity and profitability of their swollen slave stocks. Indeed, the investments of the Adams administration were to have precisely this effect. "Virginia has, within a few years, entered largely into the spirit of internal improvements," observed the *National Intelligencer* in 1830, thus increasing the "demand for labor" and virtually doubling the rates for sale and hire of slaves.[96]

Under these circumstances, Virginia's Littleton Waller Tazewell found himself in a painful position after being sent to the Senate on an antitariff platform in 1824. Tazewell represented Norfolk, long one of the principal southern recipients of federal largesse in the form of naval and canal appropriations. In response to suspicions about his "soundness" on matters of strict construction, his biographer reported, "Tazewell's sensitivity to the extension of federal power in any form was more obvious in the early months of his senatorial career than ever before. When the matter of nationally supported internal improvements again arose, he reluctantly felt it necessary to take a position detrimental to the best interests of his own borough." As a senator, elected by the state legislature, Tazewell was answerable to the state's ruling political machine, the Richmond Junto, not to his Norfolk neighbors. Like many southern leaders, Tazewell's opposition to internal improvements did not stem from a belief that the South was not receiving its fair share of the benefits, but rather expressed itself in rejecting such benefits outright.[97]

Clearly, then, neither economic nor political reasons adequately explain why the Junto and other conservative southerners took such an adamant position against internal improvements. Nor is the cause of southern hostility toward the tariff self-evident. The traditional view that southerners deprecated the tariff because they did not want to pay it, while logical from the point of view of economic self-interest, does not square with the language of the antitariff men and, later, the nullifiers, who make it clear that, more than they resented the *expense* of the tariff, they feared the *revenues* it would generate, and the possible purposes to which these revenues might be put.[98]

William W. Freehling's magisterial *Prelude to Civil War* long ago provided needed clarification of Richard Hofstadter's well-known observation that "tariffs, not slavery, . . . first made the South militant," by demonstrating how inextricably interwoven the two issues were. More recently, Freehling has demonstrated the plausibility, from South Carolina planters' perspective, of what he and other historians traditionally dismissed as their "absurd" fears of gradual emancipation (or the "conditional termination" of slavery, as Freehling puts it), stressing in particular the attraction of colonization to a wide segment of Americans and the shaky commitment to slavery of the Upper South.[99] Unquestionably, this is a key component of the Lower South's unease, and helps to explain otherwise perplexing developments such as Deep South laws prohibiting the interstate slave trade—planters in these states feared that Virginia, Maryland, Kentucky, and other Upper South states would be ripe for emancipation and absorption into the northern economic and political orbit if their ability to "dump" their slave property southward were to continue unchecked.[100]

But none of these factors adequately explains the pervasive fear of the fruits of federal spending expressed in so much anti-emancipationist writing. Fundamentally, the sources of this fear were twofold. First was the persuasive power of money itself. When he took office in 1829, Andrew Jackson later observed, Congress had before it more than $100 million in proposed federal improvement projects—money that could and would be used to cement political loyalties and purchase political loyalty.[101] No one understood the influential power of these expenditures better than John C. Calhoun, who had deployed it himself as secretary of war, expertly juggling three possible routes of the Washington–New Orleans road in order to line up support from representatives of districts located along all three paths. After his conversion to sectionalism, his first-hand view made him extremely sensitive to the power of the federal purse to sway policy.[102]

The second reason for slaveholders' fear of federal revenues is at once the simplest and the most profound: they dreaded the disruption that change would bring to a closed system. The report of South Carolina's Nullification Convention rendered a stunning judgment on the inflexibility of its slave society when it denounced the application of the American system of protection and internal improvements to "the great Southern section of the Union" on the grounds that "local circumstances" rendered the region *"altogether incapable of change"* (emphasis added).[103] Nothing could better illustrate the brittleness of the slave system than this sweeping statement. Although this pronouncement came in 1832, considerably later than the period we are discussing, I believe it spells out the sense implicit in the words of Macon, Randolph, and the defenders of the Negro Seamen Act.

In the meantime, under the sustained pressure of the South Carolina Association, Charleston authorities continued to enforce the provisions of the seamen act in defiance of the protests of the federal government. By October 1823, according to the association, *"one-hundred and fifty-four* colored persons" had been imprisoned under the act. When the South Carolina legislature convened the following month, the association escalated its demands, presenting a memorial calling for laws "to prevent ANY FREE COLORED PERSON FROM ANY PART OF THE WORLD *ever entering again into the limits of the States of South Carolina*, by LAND OR BY WATER." Although the legislature passed most of provisions the association called for, it also took steps to reduce conflict with the United States and other governments by repealing the provision mandating the enslavement of black seamen who could not pay jail costs, and exempting free black sailors on American or foreign warships from imprisonment.[104]

In July 1824, after further requests from Adams to intervene in the case, Justice William Johnson wrote the secretary of state to express his frustration at his inability to halt the arrests. The judge was particularly infuriated, he told Adams, at being "obliged to look on and see the Constitution of the United States trampled on by a set of men who, I sincerely believe, are as much influenced by the pleasure of bringing its functionaries into contempt, by exposing their impotence, as by any other consideration whatever."[105] Although most modern commentators have tended to assume that Johnson's forceful reaction to the seamen act derived from his commitment to the nation's commerce and his conviction that the Constitution granted sweeping power to the federal government to regulate it, it seems likely from this letter, and his earlier one to Jefferson, that the justice's personal knowledge or belief in the South Carolina Association's intentions led him to pronounce dicta that one biographer describes as "unwise politically and injurious legally."[106]

In any event, the controversy ignited by the Negro Seamen Act continued to inflame opinion in Charleston and elsewhere.[107] In Washington, at a dinner at General Henry Dearborn's attended by John Quincy Adams, South Carolina senator Robert Y. Hayne "showed so much excitement & temper" on the subject "that it became painful and necessary to change the topic."[108] Southerners typically responded to challenges on the issue of slavery not with the kind of high-principled ardor in defense of their constitutional rights or with the hot-blooded indignation at perceived affronts to their honor that so many historians have described; rather, they reacted with the sort of anguished rage displayed by characters confronted with a guilty family secret in plays by Ibsen or O'Neill.[109]

For its part the federal government refused to force a challenge to South Carolina's assertion of sovereignty and the "higher law" of self-preservation —both out of sensitivity to the state's real danger from slave insurrections, which the Vesey revolt had irrefutably demonstrated, and because of the administration's recognition that the Union might well indeed break apart on this issue.[110] President Monroe remembered the threat to his reelection that even appearing to sanction efforts to limit slavery had posed; and despite his willingness to work with anti-Missouri northerners and his anger at Treasury Secretary Crawford's states' rights faction, he continued to bend over backward not to offend the South. Secretary of State Adams remained traumatized by the specter of southern alliance with Great Britain with which Calhoun had frightened him during the Missouri controversy; moreover, as a candidate for the presidency in a race against slaveholders, he was at pains to stress his sympathy with the South.[111] Indeed, neither as candidate nor as president did Adams take any action, or make any public pronouncement, that could be interpreted as intentionally hostile to slaveholders' interests. Thus it is not inaccurate to describe South Carolina's course as effectively nullifying the decision of a Supreme Court justice.

The dangerous conflict between a slave state and the general government, unfolding before the public in the pages of *Niles' Register* and other publications, convinced many Americans of the need for a more permanent solution to the problem. The legislatures of two states, Georgia and Ohio, presented very different approaches to the nation. The constitutional amendments these bodies drafted and circulated among the states, while important in their own right, also represent a crucial background to nullification and other later sectional developments.

The nuances of South Carolina's complex constitutional showdown with the administration with regard to free blacks were lost on lawmakers from Georgia. If the General Government believed that barring free blacks from a state was unconstitutional, Georgia legislators reasoned, then why not remedy the Constitution? Thus, in December, the Georgia legislature passed a resolution proposing a constitutional amendment to permit state governments to exclude blacks. This approach, while callous, had the virtue of simplicity; it would also have put to rest any lingering questions about the constitutionality of Missouri's prohibition against blacks and mulattoes, which had caused so much controversy in 1821.

The Ohio legislature, by contrast, adopted a proposal calling for the "general government" to pass a law mandating the emancipation and foreign colonization of all slaves born after its passage upon their reaching the age of twenty-one. Such a law should have "the consent of the slaveholding states," the resolution insisted; but, although it asserted that emancipation might be effected "without any violation of the national compact, or infringement of the rights of individuals," and provided for the removal of slaves only with their consent, the resolution said nothing about securing the consent of the slaves' owners. Rather, the Ohio lawmakers asserted that a system of emancipation "should be predicated upon the principle that the evil of slavery is a national one, and that the people and states of this Union ought mutually to participate in the duties and burthens of removing it."[112]

This language was perhaps meant to be conciliatory and understanding of the South's predicament. Instead, by emphasizing the national evil of slavery while dropping the obligatory platitudes concerning the necessity of those states burdened with this evil to resolve it as they saw fit, the clause served as a red flag to a bull. In the eyes of extreme anti-emancipationists, the Ohio legislature's description of slavery as a "national" problem implied the right of the federal government to take action to abolish it over the heads of the slaveholding states. Moreover, the statement that "the people and states" should share in the "burthens" of removing slavery could be interpreted as sanctioning a nationally administered assessment—such as the tariff—for the purpose, or paying for the project out of the proceeds of the nation's great common treasure, the public lands.

It is highly unlikely that the Ohioans intended any such meaning. Initially, indeed, southern legislatures offered no response to the measure; but after a series of threatening national political developments later in the year, including the collapse of Crawford's states' rights presidential campaign, the passage of an augmented tariff, and U.S. Attorney General Wirt's ruling that South Carolina's Negro Seamen Act was unconstitutional and void, dedicated anti-emancipationists mounted a campaign to convince the South that the Ohio resolution represented a blueprint for a concerted attack.

As the election of 1824 approached, sectional rhetoric grew more heated. In November, Thomas Cooper published a tract titled *Consolidation*, essentially a Crawford campaign document containing a fiery denunciation of internal improvements. In both structure and content, *Consolidation* followed the model of John Taylor of Caroline's thoughtful and learned 316-page exposition, *New Views of the Constitution of the United States*, published the year earlier, although Cooper jettisoned Taylor's judiciousness and magisterial length for a slash-and-burn partisan attack. Examined in the light of the anti-emancipationist concerns we have been considering, however, Cooper's pamphlet provides an extraordinarily revealing portrait of the rhetorical strategy of the states' rights movement.

Cooper's principal intention was to portray all of Crawford's rivals in the presidential campaign—Adams, Clay, Calhoun, and Jackson—as Federalists of the Hamilton stamp. How was this feat accomplished? Cooper found the evidence for their Federalism in their support for internal improvements. The general welfare clause provided the only constitutional basis for internal improvements, Cooper argued; Federalists such as Hamilton and Gouverneur Morris had interpreted the general welfare clause for the purpose of establishing a "national consolidated government"; ergo, those politicians who favored internal improvements ipso facto ranked themselves with "the Federal party."

We have seen in the concerns of Nathaniel Macon and John Randolph the fear that the general welfare clause of the Constitution might be turned against slavery. Cooper's *Consolidation* begins to spell out this fear and enlarge on it. "If congress have a right to pass any act which they may deem conducive to the general welfare," Cooper argued, "why . . . may they not legislate on the Missouri question?"[113] What appears to be an attack on aggressively nationalist politicians turns out to be, on closer inspection, a challenge to the preamble of the Constitution itself. Although he maintains the obligatory states' rights position that the Constitution, narrowly construed, is the true bulwark of liberty, he describes himself as an "Anti-Federalist," consciously adopting the name employed by opponents of ratification of the Constitution.[114] This impression is strengthened by the boldface heading that opens the pamphlet: "DECLARATION OF INDE-PENDENCE." Implicitly, then, Cooper is invoking a return to the political structure of the Confederation—just as Carolina nationalists such as George McDuffie charged.[115]

Shortly after the appearance of Cooper's pamphlet, South Carolina governor John Lyde Wilson echoed and amplified its extreme states' rights tone in a message to the legislature. Speaking on the conflict with the United States over the Negro Seamen Act, Wilson asserted South Carolina's right to exclude "persons . . . whose organization of mind, habits and associations, render them peculiarly calculated to disturb the peace and tranquility of the State" as directly analogous to its right to bar carriers of infectious disease.[116] A week later, on December 1, Wilson adopted a much more militant tone in an almost frenzied address in which he linked the British foreign minister (George Canning), the attorney general, and the Ohio legislature as conspirators in a common crusade against slavery. "The crisis seems to have arrived when we are called upon to protect ourselves," the governor asserted, calling for "a spirit of concert and of action among the slaveholding states, and a determined resistance to any violation of their local institutions." He charged that the British foreign ministry had beguiled the president and his attorney general, "by an argument drawn from the overwhelming powers of the general government," into adopting a position on black seamen not only "at war . . . with our interests, but destructive also of our national existence." The British, having introduced the danger of slavery into America, were now hypocritically embarking on a policy certain to trigger an explosion: "The evils of slavery have been visited upon us by the cupidity of those who are now the champions of universal emancipation." Wilson urged the legislature to preserve South Carolina's "sovereignty and independence," histrionically declaring that "there would be more glory in forming a rampart with our bodies . . . than to be the victims of a successful rebellion, or the slaves of a great consolidated government."[117]

Responding to the governor's sanguinary message, the Senate adopted an equally defiant set of resolutions, asserting the duty of the state to guard against slave insurrections as "paramount to all *laws*, all *treaties*, all *constitutions*," and pledging to "be ready to make common cause with the state of Georgia, and the other southern states similarly circumstanced in this respect."[118] The lower house, however, voted to table these aggressive resolutions, passing instead a more restrained resolve that bleakly informed the Ohio legislature "that the people of this state will adhere to a system, descended to them from their ancestors, and now inseparably connected with their social and political existence."[119] If a minority of South Carolina lawmakers were inclined to invoke scenes of a southern confederacy in a bloody final stand to defend slavery, then a clear majority considered their existence impossible without it.

<hr />

THREATS OF "CONCERT AND of action among the slave-holding states" thus beset President Monroe's effort to secure a union free from faction to hand over to a worthy successor. Under these circumstances, the president's success in containing southern apprehensions over internal improvements represented a substantial achievement. Monroe's biographer Harry Ammon suggests that the internal improvements question "remained almost the only issue not involved in the Presidential electioneering in progress," but this assessment fails to acknowledge the precarious balancing act Monroe performed to prevent the issue's flare-up.[120] Apparently acting on the advice of Calhoun, who understood the delicacy of the subject in the South, Monroe in May 1822 vetoed a bill calling for toll collection on the Cumberland Road, forwarding with his veto a disquisition on the constitutional issues involved in federal internal improvements—thereby ensuring his reputation with historians as a strict constructionist, while providing sufficient political cover for his expansive nationalism to permit his proposed legislation for an increased tariff, additional fortifications, and an appropriation for the repair of the Cumberland Road, to pass without significant opposition or even controversy.[121] Indeed, in 1823, even in the midst of a national election campaign in which constitutional construction constituted one of the most compelling issues, Nathaniel Macon conceded that his opinions had "become too old fashioned for the present time; they are out of fashion and called, the old school."[122]

In this context, it seems appropriate to address the supposed "failure of presidential leadership after 1808" so sternly reproved by James Sterling Young in his influential study of political culture in Washington during the Jeffersonian period. This presidential dereliction of duty, "an event of profound significance in the political history of the republic," a failure in "one of the fundamental tasks of government," which Young lays squarely at the door of Monroe perhaps above all, ensured a Congress "incapable" of "managing major social conflict" and led to a government unable "to provide security against the rupture of the Union itself"—a situation only remedied with Andrew Jackson's accession to the White House and the return of strong presidential leadership.[123] One of the few modern historians who has devoted his efforts to understanding the functioning of government during the "neglected period" before the accession of Old Hickory, Young has unfortunately fallen into the standard trap of viewing the period through the lens of Jacksonian myth-making according to which the so-called "Era of Good Feelings" is merely a preface to the "real" story of Jacksonian Democracy—an interpretation that portrays Monroe's leadership as passive and inept.

A recent American president was wont to observe, as was stated on a plaque on his desk, "You can accomplish anything in life provided you do not care who gets the credit."[124] It seems clear that this was Monroe's policy as well, or, rather, that he embraced a more extreme variant: he was able to achieve a great deal of his nationalist program only by ensuring that no one would be able to tie its implementation to him.

The best example of Monroe's imperceptible manipulation of events concerns his efforts to maintain stability during the long presidential election of 1824. Although Monroe officially remained neutral during the campaign, his choice of Adams to be his Secretary of State was tantamount to an endorsement, given the fact that all three Republican presidents had succeeded to the office from that department. "It is my situation that makes me a candidate," Adams had affirmed in 1822.[125] While the New Englander sought to minimize the significance of sectionalism in the campaign and liked to regard himself as a national candidate, Monroe had no illusions about the degree of Virginian hostility toward this second Adams.

As governor of Virginia and commander in chief of its militia during the contentious election of 1800 that brought Jefferson and the Republicans to power, Monroe knew from personal experience how close the nation had come to armed confrontation. Had the Federalists been able to maneuver a victory in the House of Representatives, Monroe had been prepared to take "drastic measures" to resist the result.[126]

The contest of 1824 bore uncomfortable similarities to 1800, with the candidates including not only a dour Adams and a states' rights southerner but also a military chieftain with Napoleonic charisma, high ambition, and a demonstrated record of resorting to unauthorized military force to accomplish his goals. Monroe exercised great caution in his dealings with Jackson, appointing him governor of Florida while delicately circumscribing his authority and hamstringing his ability to enhance his popularity. The Old General believed, perhaps not without reason, that Monroe had appointed him "to a post where the difficulties were such that he could only bring discredit on himself."[127] In any event, the posting had the effect of keeping Jackson embroiled in controversy and unable to consolidate his popular support.

At the same time, the president faced continual harassment from congressional critics (particularly partisans of Crawford), including baseless charges from John Randolph and other states' rights Republicans that Monroe wanted a third term and might even employ the military to secure it.[128] Considering the provocation, Monroe displayed considerable equanimity and ingenuity in defusing such accusations. He managed to avoid entanglement in a controversy between Virginia congressman John Floyd and Secretary of State Adams over the latter's positions as a negotiator of the Treaty of Ghent, although at the cost of his only unpleasant confrontation with Adams.[129] Monroe also appointed prominent states' rights advocate (and early Jackson supporter) Littleton Waller Tazewell, who had speculated on the propriety of Virginian secession in the event of Adams senior's reelection, to the post of commissioner of claims under the Adams-Onís treaty. Since this assignment required a close working relationship with the younger Adams, the president may have intended it to link Tazewell to Adams by personal friendship; if so, it failed miserably at this, although it did keep Tazewell in the administration fold.[130]

THE COMPETITION FOR the presidency, although by virtually all accounts devoid of ideological significance, was conducted with greater ferocity and viciousness than any since 1800. The leading candidates, Crawford and Calhoun, and their factions in and out of Congress, engaged in barely disguised bureaucratic and political warfare for the better part of three years before the election, sabotaging each others' programs and seeking to undermine each others' stature with the electorate, while both took shots at Adams, who genteelly disavowed all such politicking. The New Englander chose to rely on his accomplishments and the efforts of his "friends" on his behalf, but not with his direction—an earlier style of campaigning that looked hopelessly outdated (but which, ironically, would be precisely the strategy employed to elect Andrew Jackson in 1828).[131] The fourth candidate, Henry Clay, intended to rely on his popularity in Congress to win a closely contested vote in the House of Representatives, where it became increasingly clear the election would end up. In this poisoned atmosphere, any political program closely associated with one of the candidates, as was the nationalist plan of internal improvement and defense with Calhoun, would have come under withering attack due to the candidate's sponsorship alone.

It was not simply partisanship, however, but policy, that dictated the Crawford campaign's attack on internal improvements and on federal spending generally. Having declared himself the champion of the extreme states' rights party, Crawford adopted their position in regarding virtually any measures by the federal government not explicitly enumerated in the Constitution as deadly precedents. Moreover, Crawford's erstwhile support of a national bank and his lack of a clear position on tariffs made him suspect to strict constructionists, while his membership in the Colonization Society cast some doubt on his staunchness on slavery—considerations that, under normal circumstances, the confident Crawford would have brushed off as irrelevant.

Circumstances were anything but normal, however, and the treasury secretary was not in charge of his own campaign. Still suffering from the effects of his stroke, his political future was entirely in the hands of Martin Van Buren. To Van Buren, Crawford's appeal lay less in his Jeffersonian "orthodoxy" than in his ability to carry Georgia, Virginia, and, presumably, much of the rest of the South. The Georgian could only be sold to northern Republicans, Van Buren recognized, as the designated candidate of the party, chosen by congressional caucus, as Madison and Monroe had been. "Grimly cracking the whip of party discipline over the demoralized Republicans," a foolhardy Van Buren mistakenly believed he could bring the northern branch of the party into line by fiat.[132] Crawford's opponents, equally aware that he could only secure the nomination through a caucus, denounced the traditional practice as undemocratic and refused to participate. To Van Buren's chagrin, only sixty-six legislators—about a quarter of the House and Senate—turned up when the congressional caucus convened on February 14. As anticipated, Crawford won easily, with 62 votes; but the low turnout rendered the caucus nomination, and all the labor Van Buren had expended to secure it, worse than worthless. That this "rump caucus" was in some measure a second referendum on Missouri was made plain by the fact that among the small turnout of northerners, a disproportionate number were doughfaces. Almost half the delegates consisted of members from Virginia and New York; only six congressmen attended from New England, and of these, "two were recent converts from Federalism, and three had voted for the Missouri Compromise."[133]

Van Buren did attempt to conciliate northern Republican and particularly antislavery opinion (and to win over Pennsylvania) by securing the nomination of Crawford's distinguished Treasury Department predecessor, Albert Gallatin, for vice president—although Gallatin himself declined to attend.[134] Despite this nod to northerners, even well-drilled party regulars found it difficult to support the Georgian. Obliquely referring to rumors that Crawford had engaged in slave-trading, a Connecticut Republican congressman wrote home to a party activist: "I cannot believe, I never will believe until compelled to so do, that the people of this Country will select for their chief magistrate a man, who if he had justice done him, would be dangling between the heavens and the earth. If they select the Devil, I shall not rebel, but before this selection is made, I will do what I can, to prevent so degrading[,] so deplorable a result—Let New England keep a stiff upper lip, and all will go well enough—."[135]

Van Buren's tactics had placed a severe strain on the Crawford coalition, foreshadowing the split in the Republican party that would lead most northern states—including John Holmes's Maine—to back Adams in the coming election. But for the present, Van Buren was preoccupied with a new threat: the meteoric rise of Andrew Jackson's candidacy. Jackson, who had recently returned to the U.S. Senate, represented an immediate danger to the Crawford coalition's southern flank. Van Buren moved rapidly and recklessly to shore it up by introducing a constitutional amendment to ban most internal improvements, a bill that he probably hoped the Tennessean, who was believed to favor the administration's nationalist policies, would vote against, thereby helping to delineate the two candidates and harm Jackson's stature with the Old Republicans.[136]

Although Van Buren's constitutional amendment was decisively rejected, he had more success in his fight to scuttle a proposed treaty with Great Britain that would have defined slavery as piracy and granted each nation the right to search the other's ships for slaves. "The Radicals were in immediate opposition to the treaty," according to Remini, "fearing it would develop into a general agreement between Great Britain and the United States to destroy slavery in the South." The issue represented a serious potential embarrassment for Crawford, who had earlier derided Adams's objections to Britain's right of search as "mere declamation," and had swayed Monroe to his opinion. A year later, in 1824, the treasury secretary claimed he had never seen the treaty, which he had, in fact, fought to strengthen.[137] Crawford's Senate supporters, led by Van Buren and Holmes, succeeded in sinking the slave trade treaty under a sea of amendments, thus providing Crawford, as Rufus King observed, "a political hobbyhorse with which to ride through the South."[138]

Crawford himself was not a subtle man, and his efforts to consolidate southern political support often appeared heavy handed. But with the Georgian debilitated by poor health, Van Buren, acting as his chief national strategist, adopted a southern-oriented platform so lopsidedly proslavery as to constitute a caricature of southern interests. In addition to his fight against the slave trade convention (a measure with considerable southern support), Van Buren increasingly sought to mobilize opposition to federal support for colonization—which had the backing not only of the apostate president but also of Jefferson, Madison, and Crawford himself. If Crawford could afford, or even gain from, this apparent soft spot in his proslavery armor, Van Buren could not; rather, he viewed opposition to colonization as another opportunity to dragoon a solid southern phalanx into coalition with his Albany Regency machine. Such political opportunism, at a period when the South remained convulsed in the aftermath of the Vesey scare, generated a dangerous "whipsaw" effect: extreme states' rights southerners, such as the members of the South Carolina Association, put forward an advanced position controversial at home, only to see it embraced in full by the northern Radical leadership, always anxious to secure southern support; thus strengthened, this extreme position would now become the new standard, emboldening southern sectionalists to stake out even more extravagant terrain. Southerners came to adopt an increasingly uncompromising proslavery line that had as its most concrete effect the furtherance of the political objectives of a particular faction of northern Republicans.

6

BENEFICENCE

IF SLAVERY CEASED to command the center of national attention in the years after the Missouri settlement, this does not mean that antislavery activity ceased as well. Whatever the political or constitutional merits of Martin Van Buren's opposition to the slave trade convention, it put him increasingly at odds with the main current of national opinion. In fact, Pennsylvania senator Jonathan Roberts's hopeful assertion during the Missouri controversy that the "agitation now awakened" by the restriction movement "would be useful" in spite of its failure, and "dislike of slavery [would] gain ground," appeared to be coming true. Most significantly, the two streams of antislavery and evangelicalism, long such a potent union in Britain, seemed now to be combining in America as well. It will be recalled that evangelical Federalists such as the president of the American Bible Society, Elias Boudinot, had initiated the Missouri agitation; now that the political battle was over, evangelicals stepped forward once again to raise the banner of moral suasion. The restriction crusade had produced "a powerful and united testimony . . . against the extension of slavery," the secretary of the American Board for Foreign Missions argued in 1820, and the country had been awakened to its dangers.[1] In 1823, four of the six essays in the *Transactions* of the Andover Seminary's Society of Inquiry Concerning Missions promoted "the abolition of slavery and the elevation of the colored people," including one by Royal Washburn titled, "What is the duty of the Government, and the duty of Christians, with regard to slavery in the United States?"[2]

The year 1823 likewise saw a transformation in the nature of the colonization issue. After the exposure of the Denmark Vesey plot in Charleston, slaveholders' apprehensions cost the American Colonization Society much of its support in the Deep South, while sectional politics surrounding the pending presidential election stalemated the organization's efforts to obtain money from Congress. At the same time, prominent northerners such as Daniel Webster, Lewis Tappan, and George Blake temporarily abandoned the colonization cause.[3] After a bout of self-examination in the face of these difficulties, colonizationist leaders decided to reconstitute the organization as a self-sustaining benevolent society. Turning from a policy of private suasion of congressmen and other key individuals to the modern tactics of mass communication deployed by the Anglo-American benevolent empire, the Colonization Society helped to bring the issue of the future of blacks in America to the center of public consciousness—and with it, indirectly but inevitably, the question of slavery.

Despite its broad support from respected national figures, the colonization project appeared extremely frightening to the grassroots of Virginia slaveholders, and its promoters in Congress backed off on instructions from President Monroe's son-in-law George Hay. The elaborate efforts of its advocates to assure slaveholders that colonization would never threaten slavery, although seriously undermining northern support, remained unconvincing to many southerners—particularly since strong nationalists such as Charles Fenton Mercer, "a proponent of high tariffs and federally funded internal improvements," played such a large role in the organization.[4] Never mind that the Colonization Society's constitution eschewed interference with slavery; strict-construction southerners denounced the organization as indistinguishable from other "abolition-colonizing bible and peace societies" and unequivocally forecast that if unchecked, these would "undoubtedly push [the "general government"] to try the question of emancipation."[5] As if by some sort of Lockean association of ideas, southern conservatives believed that simply to raise the issue of colonization would inevitably open the door to schemes for gradual emancipation.

This fear soon proved justified. John Holt Rice, president of Hampden-Sydney College, admitted in an 1823 review of Colonization Society annual reports in his *Evangelical and Literary Magazine* that the "bare mention" of the society "directs, with an impulse . . . difficult to resist, towards a discussion of slavery as it exists in the United States."[6] We have already seen that South Carolina's Frederick Dalcho, in a tract often described as an early landmark of unabashed proslavery literature, desperately invoked colonization as a potential remedy for a state traumatized by fears of slave revolt, questioning whether "many Planters in South-Carolina . . . would hesitate one moment" to sell their slaves to the federal government to be colonized.[7]

The African slave trade, always the peculiar institution's most hated aspect, had few advocates, and among those few—such as the Rhode Island slaver and senator James De Wolfe, who lived in dread that Britain would annex Cuba—anxiety about the future of the profession ran high.[8] Daniel Webster, in his famous Plymouth Oration, had devoted three full pages to a "call [to] all the true sons of New England to cooperate with the laws of man, and the justice of Heaven" to "put an end to this odious and abominable trade"—a passage particularly commended by ex-president John Adams.[9] The American Colonization Society's fund-raising campaign, however mixed its motives, brought its "plea for Africa" to a wide public.[10] Purchasers of the 1824 New York edition of William Paley's *Moral and Political Philosophy*—still required reading in virtually every college in America—found a frontispiece illustrating Paley's strictures on the brutality and immorality of the slave trade that depicted two turbaned Muslims dickering over a coffle of blacks on the African coast, including a straight-haired, seminude young woman who could have served as the prototype for Hiram Powers's sculpture "The Greek Slave." The woodcut might have been intended to influence public opinion, or simply to sell copies; either way, it underscores the topicality of the subject.[11]

The depiction of Moslem slave traders is interesting for another reason: its implicit link between the cause of Africa and the Greek war of independence, at the time the most galvanizing public issue in America. This association became a commonplace of the period in literature, oratory, and even painting.[12] In 1817, the Bucktail litterateur James Kirke Paulding had dismissed "the idea of connecting feeling or sentiment with a slave" as "laughable"; to make such an assertion seven years later would be blatantly polemical and fundamentally inaccurate.[13] If some Americans excluded blacks from the revolutionary zeitgeist, others did not. Reports of the slave insurrection in Demerara occupied columns in *Niles' Register* alongside news of the Greek revolution.[14] John Randolph reputedly underscored the connection when he pointedly observed to a group of white Virginia women engaged in sewing for Greek relief, as a coffle of manacled slaves passed by, "Ladies, the Greeks are at your doors."[15]

The popularity of the Greek cause did much to rekindle Americans' memory of their own revolution, soon to enter its jubilee year. The arrival of the marquis de Lafayette in the summer of 1824 fanned this spark of patriotic nationalism into full flame. It seems highly likely that President Monroe extended his invitation to Lafayette with the conscious intention of employing the marquis's popularity and role as chief living symbol of the Revolution to promote national unity, to further Monroe's nationalist program, and to quell the sectionalism and factionalism of the presidential campaign. Demonstrably, Lafayette's visit dealt a further setback to Crawford's sectional campaign and Van Buren's effort to enforce party regularity to support it. Lafayette's arrival in America, according to Fenimore Cooper, "paralyzed all the electoral ardour" of the acrimonious campaign, and helped to ensure the nation's acceptance of John Quincy Adams, a minority candidate elected by the House under questionable circumstances—precisely the scenario that had come so close to bloodshed during his father's unsuccessful battle for reelection. The election and inauguration of the new president also would explain one of the curious features of Lafayette's visit—why it was conducted in 1824 and 1825, rather than two years later, so as to commemorate the jubilee of independence and of Lafayette's first arrival in America in 1777. The presence of "the Guest of the Nation" made unthinkable any extraconstitutional action by those unhappy with the election results, however unlikely such action might have been already. Crawford partisans chafed at the nationalist aura produced by the marquis's visit and at Congress's desire to reward him with a township, but prudently recognized, as one North Carolina Crawfordite observed, that "it would not have did [*sic*] for the Radicals to have opposed it."[16] From the point of view of the safe transition of power from Monroe to Adams, a Lafayette visit in 1826 would have been too late.

Lafayette's tour, which took him to every state in the Union, constituted a triumph not only of patriotism, but of logistics. Fortunately, the administration had a great deal of experience in such trips: it echoed Monroe's own, taken at the beginning of his first term. More work needs to be done to establish the connection, but it is probable that Monroe provided assistance in developing Lafayette's itinerary. Interpreted as political fence-mending and not simply as protocol, it is perhaps significant that Lafayette passed his first night in America under the roof of Vice President Daniel D. Tompkins, who remained, despite his incapacitation due to alcoholism, the most powerful symbol of northern Republican orthodoxy and opposition to Monroe's policies of amalgamation with Federalism.[17] Other foes of the president mollified by Lafayette's presence included former Military Affairs Committee chair William Eustis, now governor of Massachusetts, who exulted to have the hero as his guest: "I am the happiest man that ever lived."[18]

South Carolina, the heartland of southern sectionalism, had many bonds to Lafayette. General Thomas Pinckney, a vice president of the South Carolina Association, had been the Frenchman's aide-de-camp at Yorktown; in May 1825, "in the broad light of day, and in the presence of ten thousand spectators, Lafayette rapturously embraced his old comrade" in a dramatic Charleston reunion.[19] Lafayette's arrival also stirred memories of one of the most romantic episodes of southern chivalric heroism: the daring attempt of Charleston's Francis Kinloch Huger, then a medical student, to rescue the marquis from imprisonment in the Austrian fortress of Olmütz in 1794, during the French Revolution. The attempt failed, and Huger spent six months at hard labor in an Austrian prison. For the rest of his life he was known as "Olmütz" Huger, and remained a symbol of southern devotion to liberty long afterward. The reunion of Lafayette and Colonel Huger, in Boston, constituted one of the most vivid images of American unity and dedication to Revolutionary ideals, and the colonel was at the marquis's side during his visit to Charleston.[20]

Perhaps the most important date on Lafayette's itinerary was his stay in Washington, D.C., during the election of the president by the House of Representatives. On the Monday evening before the Wednesday count, Lafayette attended a gala performance in his honor at the National Theatre, with Monroe, Adams, Jackson, and Crawford in attendance.[21] It would be hard to overestimate the importance of Lafayette's presence in the nation's capital at such a moment, or of the symbolism of the presidential candidates' apparently harmonious reunion in honor of the Nation's Guest. There is no question that Lafayette himself recognized and relished his role as peacemaker in a deeply divided nation. "I have the satisfaction of thinking that my presence has effected many reconciliations between the political parties," he reflected; "men, who have not spoken to one another for more than twenty years, have made arrangements together and have invited one another to entertainments in our honor, and revive together common memories of the Revolution."[22]

By his actions and words during his fifteen-month visit, Lafayette frequently endorsed Monroe's nationalist program. In Washington, Lafayette accompanied Monroe, Adams, and James Barbour to the commencement of the Columbian College, whose charter, voted by Congress three years earlier during the Missouri controversy, had furnished the cause for one of the innumerable struggles between nationalists and strict constructionists over the federal government's proper cultural role.[23] Ever a model of consistency on the issue of federal expenditures, Nathaniel Macon discharged the "painful duty" of opposing a bill to present the general with the gift of a western township. Although Macon disapproved of public spending generally, on "principle," he was particularly sensitive to the government's use of public land for philanthropic purposes, remarking "that it would have been better to have given" the general cash from the treasury. Yet South Carolina's Robert Y. Hayne rose to defend the gift of land in ringing patriotic terms, urging that the bill be passed "with unanimity" and insisting that the "provision to be made" to Lafayette "should be worthy of the character of the nation—worthy of the American people. National character is national wealth," Hayne continued. America should always "so act as to command the respect of the world. Now, what would be thought of us in Europe, if, after all that has passed, we should fail to make a generous and liberal provision for our venerable guest?"[24]

Macon must have winced at Hayne's invocation of European opinion, so reminiscent of James Tallmadge's scornful remark during the Missouri debates about how the "'legitimates of Europe'" would laugh to find the Congress debating "the moral right of slavery."[25] The North Carolinian's testiness during the debate suggests that he was less than delighted by the marquis's visit and the effusive enthusiasm for liberty it called forth. Inevitably, as Macon well knew, Lafayette's presence focused attention on the disparity between America's Revolutionary professions of liberty and the continuing reproach of slavery. An antislavery Kentucky minister observed that the visit of Lafayette, "with the excitement it produced from Dan to Beersheba, with the dinners and toasts, and . . . talk about our struggle for liberty, and our gratitude to him for espousing our cause, &c., gave a lesson to our slaves about the worth of liberty and the way to get it, which they will not forget during the present generation."[26] A poetic address to Lafayette in the Federalist *Columbian Centinel* from "'The Slaves' in the Land of Freedom," sardonically hammered home the same point:

> What, Sir, can you fancy our feelings to be,
> When White men proclaim—'It is good to be free,—
> That violence and slaughter in Liberty's cause,
> Are sanctioned by Heaven with loudest applause,—
> That men who thus hazard their lives and their name,
> Shall shine as *Immortals* in Temples of fame?'
> How plainly they tell us the course to pursue,
> In all the applauses they lavish on you!
> The plaudits and speeches pronounced by their breath,
> Inculcate the doctrine of '*Freedom or Death*.'[27]

The latent antislavery subtext of Lafayette's visit undoubtedly aided the presidential hopes of John Quincy Adams—even though the New Englander had never taken a significant public stand against the institution or its spread. Still, as Rufus King observed, Adams had "the preference of N. England," since "after all, as between Adams and any one of the Candidates from the slave States, the mo[st] powerful argument" would be the political calculus of the slavery issue. "If what Mr. Walsh calls the Universal Yankee Nation" could come together behind Adams, particularly in New

York, King predicted, it would secure his victory; yet he felt certain that the "managers" would employ "devices" to forestall this northern union.[28]

As King had surmised, New York proved to be the crucial battleground of the election, and "managers" did indeed resort to "devices" to manipulate the result. King could not have predicted, however, that a new generation of managers, led by Thurlow Weed, would enlist on the anti-Bucktail side, and temporarily outmaneuver the Red Fox of Kinderhook and his Crawford forces by employing still more devious stratagems.[29] On top of that, the casting vote for president in the House of Representatives ultimately ended up in the hands of Stephen Van Rensselaer, the Old Patroon—brother of Solomon Van Rensselaer, the Albany postmaster and veteran of the Missouri slavery restriction battle. Although Van Rensselaer had privately assured two of his fellow lodgers at Strother's that he would vote for Crawford (thus guaranteeing Jackson's election), family and sectional obligations—as well as, one may surmise, a sense of public responsibility—ultimately outweighed the pressure of messmates and personal ties, and dictated his decisive vote for Adams.[30]

Crawford's nationwide defeat was mirrored in New York in a stunning repudiation of Van Buren's Bucktails. Already facing voter anger over the Caucus and the party's opposition to the direct election of presidential electors, the Albany Regency, rudderless with Van Buren away in Washington, committed the monumental political blunder of removing De Witt Clinton as canal commissioner. This mean-spirited move triggered an avalanche of popular support for the aging statesman that returned him to the governorship over the Bucktails' candidate by a margin of almost 17,000 votes and swept away the Bucktail majority in the House. This stunning repudiation at the polls left Van Buren, in the words of one of his enemies, looking "like a wilted cabbage." "I left Albany for Washington," Van Buren said himself, "as completely broken down a politician as my bitterest enemies could desire."[31]

The defeat of Van Buren's efforts at political manipulation "spelled the beginning of the end of northern subservience to the South in the federal executive branch," according to John Niven. "Slavery, unmentioned in the heated debates, in the public prints, in the caucuses and in the streets, was nonetheless a presence. The Missouri debates and the state constitutional convention of 1821 were still fresh in the minds of the public, if not of the legislators. A new order of politics was emerging where the North, New York—its grand canal and its great statesman, De Witt Clinton—all combined in the popular image of the state as power, as future, as prototype of progress."[32]

One key element in Van Buren's defeat missing from Niven's perceptive picture was the appeal of the Monrovian ideal of an amalgamation of parties, now nearly attained; the uprooting of "the baneful weed of party strife," with its promise of a joining together of all Americans toward the attainment of common national goals.[33] To Van Buren, this vision possessed no appeal; indeed, he found it deeply repellent. For the Red Fox, this rising spirit of "amalgamation" and nationalism on northern terms would forever be associated with his personal humiliation at the hands of a coalition of renegade Republicans and erstwhile Federalists. In his eyes, a slackening of party discipline and direction constituted the true cause of the fiasco he had suffered, not the electorate's distaste for slavery and political dictation; and he determined never to let amalgamation thwart him again.[34]

<hr />

NOTING THE "peculiar circumstances" of his election, John Quincy Adams acknowledged in his inaugural address that he entered the presidency "less possessed of [his countrymen's] confidence in advance than any of [his] predecessors." Not having won a popular majority or even a plurality, and his election by the House of Representatives darkened by vicious rumors of a "corrupt bargain" with Clay, Adams assumed his duties with even more than his habitual caution. By comparison with his predecessor's addresses, Adams appeared a strict constructionist. "My first resort will be to [the] Constitution," he declared, referring directly to the instrument a symbolic thirteen times. America's "political creed," Adams declared, is that "the General Government of the Union and the separate governments of the States are all sovereignties of limited powers, . . . uncontrollable by encroachments upon each other." Stressing the retirement of the federal debt and the importance of economy in government, Adams said nothing about the tariff, a policy Monroe had promoted; the Bank of the United States went unmentioned as well. Except for a clause about progress toward suppression of the African slave trade, an unexceptionable national desideratum, Adams did not breathe a hint of opposition to slavery, "the great and dormant issue," as his biographer Samuel Flagg Bemis called it.[35] On the contrary, a substantial portion of his address was devoted to the "inviolable duty" of maintaining the "harmony of the nation." Partisan collisions deriving from "speculative opinions" or "different views of administrative policy" were intrinsically "transitory," Adams observed, while differences "founded on geographical divisions, adverse interests of soil, climate and modes of domestic life" (a favorite southern euphemism) were "more permanent, and therefore, perhaps, more dangerous." Reconciling these differences constituted the real greatness of America's unique system of government, "at once federal and national." The sectional division mandated "a perpetual admonition to preserve alike and with equal anxiety the rights of each individual State in its own government and the rights of the whole nation in that of the Union. Whatsoever is of domestic concernment . . . belongs exclusively to the administration of the State governments. . . . To respect the rights of the State governments is the inviolable duty of that of the Union; the government of every State will feel its own obligation to respect and preserve the rights of the whole."[36]

In a passage that may have owed much to the experience of the Missouri settlement, Adams argued that personal interaction between the people's representatives in Washington played a vital role in assuaging sectional tensions. "The prejudices everywhere too commonly entertained against distant strangers are worn away, and the jealousies of jarring interests are allayed by the composition and functions of the great national councils annually assembled from all quarters of the Union at this place. . . . The harmony of the nation is promoted and the whole Union is knit together by the sentiments of mutual respect, the habits of social intercourse, and the ties of personal friendship formed between the representatives of its several parts in the performance of their service at this metropolis."[37]

On one level, Adams's observation underscored the importance of the great modern principle of representative democracy, which had offered such a signal advantage over the classical ideal of direct, participatory democracy in administering a republic over an extended territory; on another, his comment reflected the clubbish atmosphere of the Washington community, where relationships formed over mess tables and card games, in ballrooms and oyster cellars, provided the cement of alliances that transcended party and section.[38] Unfortunately, the new president himself, as Rufus King had noted, was "without friends who are knitted to him by personal attachments."[39] This would prove to be a tremendous handicap in governing the nation and combating sectionalism.

On one subject, Adams displayed no caution and appeared to anticipate little serious opposition. Internal improvement, the president prophesied, would be the legacy "from which . . . the unborn millions" of future Americans would "derive their most fervent gratitude to the founders of the Union; that in which the beneficent action of its Government will be most deeply felt and acknowledged." True, there remained "some diversity of opinion" on the constitutionality of these undertakings, patriotic doubts to which "respectful deference" was due. Yet the National Road had been undertaken with "unquestioned" authority; it had been in existence for almost two decades, and Adams honestly failed to understand how any American could object to it. "To how many thousands of our countrymen has it proved a benefit? To what single individual has it ever proved an injury?" "Repeated, liberal, and candid" legislative debates had answered all constitutional questions thus far, in Adams's view, and remaining objections would ultimately be "removed" in the same manner. In plain English, this meant the president had the votes in Congress to pass his program. "The extent and limitation of the powers of the General Government in relation to this transcendently important interest will be settled and acknowledged to the common satisfaction of all, and every speculative scruple will be solved by a practical public blessing."[40]

The commonly held impression of universal disdain for the Adams administration is a myth that was deliberately created by his Jacksonian successors. Adams received a smaller popular vote than Andrew Jackson, but after an election with the smallest voter turnout in the nation's history. Adams garnered far larger majorities in the New England states than did Jackson in the South and West, indicating a firmer core of regional support. Moreover, Adams had much greater support in the South than Jackson could muster in New England. It is natural to infer that the new president took office with more Americans supportive of or neutral to his administration than opposed to it. More important, as Joel H. Silbey has argued, presidents frequently create their own mandates after their election, regardless of margins of victory: "Successful Presidents are those who read that the fact that they won is enough to do everything they want."[41]

Southern editorial reaction to Adams's inaugural address tended to be negative, but this had more to do with the man, his parentage, and his nativity than with the specific content of his speech. Still, even within the South, Adams enjoyed a measure of support, particularly in Louisiana, many of whose citizens shared New England's views on commerce and protectionism. The Republican leaders of the Old Dominion initially adopted a stance of cautious neutrality toward the administration, and did not actively oppose the decision of James Barbour, a Virginian, to accept a cabinet post. John Hampden Pleasants, editor of the *Richmond Whig*, led the new president's backers in Virginia, while Governor H. G. Burton rallied his sympathizers in North Carolina.[42] Adams also had the support of a number of important political figures in Mississippi, where he won almost a third of the popular vote. Mississippi Adamsites included such northern transplants and protariff men as Sargent S. Prentiss, who ultimately became a Whig, and John Quitman, who evolved into a Democrat and fire-eating sectionalist. Even in South Carolina, Adams's election pleased some people who had originally backed Calhoun. If in retrospect the New Englander's hopes for southern support appear to have been doomed from the start, they did not seem so at the time.[43]

∞∞

POLITICAL DEVELOPMENTS of the president's truncated first year did not, it is true, offer much encouragement of sectional harmony. Southern distrust of the administration stemmed less from an antipathy for Adams per se than from fear of a coalition of eastern and western states under the Adams banner—a danger that seemed palpable when Henry Clay, the Colonization Society's champion, threw his support to the New Englander. Although Jackson and Adams supporters in the South had often worked together during the campaign to defeat Crawford, southern managers of all stripes—Jacksonians, Crawfordites, and Calhounites—dreaded the alliance of Adams and Clay. Such an alliance, these politicians recognized, would render the South politically irrelevant, and they turned their hands to averting it.

Shortly before the election in the House of Representatives, an anonymous letter appeared in the *Richmond Enquirer* accusing Clay of offering his electoral votes to the highest bidder between Adams and Jackson in exchange for appointment as secretary of state. The obvious intent of the letter was to force Clay to withdraw from consideration for the post, or to compromise his reputation if he accepted it.[44] A supporter of Calhoun informed Adams two days after his inauguration that if the new vice president's suggestions for cabinet appointments were not followed and the president persisted in appointing Henry Clay as secretary of state, "a determined opposition to the Administration" would be "organized from the outset," under the banner of Andrew Jackson.[45] When Adams ultimately did choose Clay, the appearance of a "corrupt bargain" between the two men genuinely shocked many observers. Additionally, the new administration unfairly but inevitably bore the brunt of widespread popular outrage over the Crawford campaign's unsuccessful manipulation of state electoral systems, providing Crawford's former managers with the opportunity to cleanse their own reputations by denouncing the new administration's corruption. The suspicion is unavoidable that many of the critics of Clay and Adams seized on manufactured evidence of unethical behavior to defend an immediate and uncompromising opposition to the administration that was not justifiable on the basis of its policies.

According to William H. Seward, who wrote a biography of Adams, "The administration of John Quincy Adams blends so intimately with that of Monroe, in which he was the chief minister, that no dividing line can be drawn between them."[46] It is entirely accurate and appropriate, then, to speak of the two administrations as constituting a "Monrovian era" between the Jeffersonian and Jacksonian periods. Monroe had been to a degree shielded from southern hostility, however, by his Virginian nativity and his unchallengeable Republican credentials. Now Adams, champion of the same policies, unprotected by these advantages and doubly exposed by his lack of skill at political infighting, felt the full weight of hostility to Monrovian nationalism descend on him.

Many contemporaries professed themselves shocked by the viciousness of anti-administration sentiment—a level of partisan passion not seen since the days of Federalist rule, and largely unprovoked. Approached at the start of the term by Vice President Calhoun about joining the opposition party, Joseph McIlvaine, the recorder of Philadelphia, objected that the new administration should be judged by its measures, of which he so far approved. Calhoun reportedly replied "that such was the manner in which it came into power that *it must be defeated at all hazards, regardless of its measures.*" McIlvaine responded "that this was very different from the principles he had learned from him (Mr. Calhoun), and it was too late for him to unlearn them and learn others. He perceived that their respective political roads now diverged, and he would therefore respectfully bid him adieu." In a similar tone to Calhoun's, the Kentucky Jacksonian Richard M. Johnson reportedly informed the editor of the *National Intelligencer* that "as for this administration [Mr. Adams's], we will turn them out as sure as there is a God in heaven. . . . By the Eternal, if they act as pure as the angels that stand at the right hand of the throne of God, we'll put them down."[47] This pure partisanship, divorced from policies or even from personalities, marked a new departure in American politics.

Neither Jackson nor the most prominent Crawfordites, including the treasury secretary himself, agreed to serve in the cabinet, although the president did secure the services of onetime Crawford supporter James Barbour to be secretary of war, perhaps his most felicitous choice.[48] Ultimately Adams assembled an administration constructed "on as broad a bottom as possible under the circumstances of personal politics that governed the day, but not broad enough to conciliate, to harmonize, and to unite the opposing factions that were now coalescing and tending to become sectional. . . . It did not appease the South, which became more and more distrustful of the Minority President as he began to speak out in Washington for strong national measures."[49] This coalescing opposition manifested itself on the first major measure of the new administration, the submission of the treaty with Colombia for suppression of the slave trade that Adams had negotiated as secretary of state—which a special session of the Senate rejected unanimously.[50] To counterbalance southern strength, however, John W. Taylor of New York won reelection to the Speakership, empowered with the president's full confidence and determined to shape committee appointments to promote his program.[51]

Provoked by this early opposition, a defiant Adams abandoned the caution he had shown in his inaugural address when drafting his first annual message. Indeed, he offered perhaps the most far-reaching scheme of national advancement ever proposed by an American president. Richard Rush, his treasury secretary, "approved the whole"; but the other members of his administration felt Adams went much too far.[52] Yet the president persevered, hardly deigning to remove a sentence. "It is not very material to me whether I should present these views in the first or the last message that I send in to the Congress. But I feel it is my indispensable duty to suggest them." Ever the Puritan fatalist, Adams disdained the breezy pragmatism of postponing politically difficult programs to a hypothetical second term. "Of the future I can never be sure," he explained. "I may not be destined to send in another message."[53]

Taking advantage of the "powerful liberalizing influence" exerted by Lafayette's visit (and perhaps personally influenced by the general himself),[54] Adams sketched out a dramatic vision of the fulfillment of America's high promise of material and social progress and the validation of its providential historical role. The number and scope of his proposals is breathtaking: a uniform bankruptcy law; a unified national militia and a "permanent naval peace establishment," including a naval academy; a national university and observatory; domestic and international scientific expeditions; an Interior Department. Yet, with the exception of a further reference to enforcement of the slave trade prohibition, Adams made only one reference to slavery: a pledge to continue to press Britain on the indemnification "for slaves carried away from the United States after the close of the late war."[55]

Perhaps the best-received section of Adams's speech was his pledge to send U.S. representatives to the Pan-American Congress called by Bolívar in 1824. "The Panama congress was, on the whole, very popular throughout the country," according to Robert V. Remini. "The destruction of Spanish power in the New World and the erection of independent republics in South America had received the cordial approbation of the citizens of the

United States. They applauded the suggestion that the free states in the Western Hemisphere should meet in Panama to discuss matters of mutual interest, and immediately contrasted this proposed congress with the hated Holy Alliance of Europe, the enemy of liberty and the protector of despots."[56]

Undoubtedly influenced by Clay's expansive pan-American republican vision, Adams suggestively described the Panama Congress as "a grain of mustard-seed." Adams perceived the congress as marking the beginning of a new era, an entering wedge toward a concord between republics that— once troublesome issues such as South America's disorder, ignorance, and the Latin penchant for Catholicism had been addressed—promised a revolution in the affairs of mankind.

Taken together with his broad array of domestic proposals, Adams's sweeping pan-American design constituted (considering the restrained emotional compass of the president's religious expression) something approaching a millennial vision. "The spirit of improvement is abroad upon the earth," Adams devoutly assured his countrymen. "While dwelling with pleasing satisfaction upon the superior excellence of our political institutions, let us not be unmindful that liberty is power; that the nation blessed with the largest portion of liberty must in proportion to its numbers be the most powerful nation upon earth, and that the tenure of power by man is, in the moral purposes of his Creator, upon condition that it shall be exercised to ends of beneficence, to improve the condition of himself and his fellow-men."[57]

Adams's first annual address thus constituted the classic document of the culture of "beneficence" that came to characterize northern antebellum evangelical society. By extrapolation, slaveholding southerners might legitimately consider their interests threatened by it. In fact, however, the address to a large degree constituted no more than a recapitulation of the program set forth in Monroe's eighth annual message, although presented in Adams's more elevated and visionary language. Moreover, as mentioned above, the message contained not a single word critical of slavery. Adams's reticence on this subject was dictated by a political imperative so basic as to have become almost second nature. His public policy toward slavery to this time had been conducted in a way utterly unexceptionable to the South, demonstrating far less public hostility to the institution than Clay's or Webster's views, or even Van Buren's.[58]

None of this mattered, however. Nor did it matter that the grand plans of improvement Adams enumerated disproportionately favored the South—with harbor improvements surveyed in South Carolina, Georgia, and Florida; roads proposed for Arkansas, Missouri, Kentucky, Mississippi, and Louisiana; and canals in Virginia and Maryland—many of them specifically intended to aid the transportation of slave-grown staples. None of these facts could obscure the larger truth grasped by cultivated southerners. Educated in the traditions of the Revolution and the Scottish commonsense philosophy, attuned to currents of outside opinion as reflected in the British reviews, and intimate with the quotidian blight of domestic slavery, the southern gentry inevitably equated any invocation of the "ends of beneficence" with a call for the end to the institution on which their way of life depended, whether Adams or any northerner cared to interpret it so or not.[59]

<hr>

IN FACT, HOWEVER, MANY Americans clearly *did* view the accession of Adams and Clay as giving a green light to projects for the "conditional termination" of slavery. By June 1825, the legislatures of eight other states had endorsed Ohio's call for emancipation and colonization of slaves, while nine states disapproved of Georgia's proposed constitutional amendment to permit states to bar blacks from their domains.[60] In the meantime, moderate southerners continued to search for national solutions to the slavery problem. The Maryland author and colonizationist (and grandson of Martha Washington) George Washington Parke Custis appealed to northerners' memories of southern aid during the Revolution, arguing that now it was the North's turn to "help save their Southern brethren from ruin. He asked them to remember the Southern warriors 'hailing the spark of freedom that northern hands had kindled, and crying out—"Go on, we are coming to support you!"'"[61] Given the intensity of some southerners' hostility toward colonization and toward any northern interference in the slavery question, Custis's sincerity in expressing such sentiments seems undeniable. John Holt Rice, although he had ceased to publish criticism of what he now termed "that subject" in his *Evangelical and Literary Magazine*, continued to encourage antislavery inquiry within the less-threatening domain of Hampden-Sydney College, where students attending the April 1824 meeting of the Literary and Philosophical Society earnestly considered the question, "What Measures Should be Adopted for the Abolition of Slavery in Virginia?"[62]

Rice's distinguished friend Thomas Jefferson had been giving thought of his own to this problem. In a letter to Jared Sparks, editor of the *North American Review*, Jefferson elaborated on an idea that he had first floated in his *Notes on Virginia*, which offered a means of implementing Ohio's plan of emancipation and colonization at a discount, by "emancipating the after-born" (in plain English, babies) and expatriating them to Haiti, whose "Chief offers to pay their passage" and to employ them, on their reaching "a proper age for deportation." The costs of the project, as Henry Meigs had suggested during the Missouri debates, could be financed by the proceeds of sales of public lands.[63]

James Madison had also proposed applying land sales to emancipation, eight months before Meigs's proposal, in a private letter to a Quaker opponent of slavery. The cost of purchasing the nation's approximately 1.5 million slaves, transporting and relocating them out of the United States, Madison estimated, would come to a staggering $600 million (the figure mentioned by Jefferson as the value of slave property). "Happily," Madison reflected, ". . . the amount of the expense is not a paramount consideration. It is the peculiar fortune, or rather a providential blessing of the U.S. to possess a resource commensurate to this great object, without taxes on the people, or even an increase of the public debt. I allude to the vacant territory the extent of which is so vast, and the vendible value of which is so well ascertained."[64] The total expense to the government of this monumental project would come to 200 million acres at $3 an acre, or 300 million at $2 per acre, "a quantity which tho' great in itself, is perhaps not a third part of the disposable territory belonging to the U.S. And to what object so good so great & so glorious," Madison effused, "could that peculiar fund of wealth be appropriated?"[65]

Rufus King, about to step down from the Senate to become minister to Britain, decided to give his colleagues the opportunity to endorse this "great & glorious" object. Among the defeated Missouri restrictionists, none were more bitter than King. He resented having been used by Van Buren, only to be discarded by him after his friendship was no longer politically useful. In order to "rally . . . the old democratic spirit ag[ains]t all other opinions" to support Crawford, King believed, Van Buren had aroused "feelings & divisions, which no one ought to desire to exist."[66] Although King had expected Van Buren to protect him from attacks in the Bucktail press, it became apparent that Van Buren had in fact directed such attacks. In particular, King was shocked by Van Buren's efforts to stage-manage New York's vote for presidential electors by what he considered corrupt and dishonorable means. "The Election of a Pope is purity, simplicity, and certainty," he wrote his son, "when compared with the system of electing a President by a caucus."[67]

King's personal sense of betrayal played a large role in his disillusionment with the Missouri Compromise and his apparent lack of interest in promoting sectional harmony and reconciliation.[68] Sick of compromise and conciliation, he composed as his swan song in the Senate a parting shot designed to puncture what he regarded as the hypocrisy of southern antislavery pretensions and the comfortable complacency of the North. On February 18, 1825, King launched his firebrand: a resolution calling for the proceeds of sales of public land, after the retirement of the federal debt, to be "inviolably applied" to the emancipation and removal from the country of slaves and free blacks.

There can be little doubt that King introduced his resolution less because he anticipated any practical benefit to come from it, than to force the issue of slavery to a head and to embarrass the South and its allies. In fact, King had long decried colonization to friends and family as a "foolish project," "doomed to failure." The only value he saw in the movement "was the attention which it drew to the desperate condition of the slave States"; and it was precisely for this purpose that he presented his proposal.[69] With his motion, King placed slaveholding senators in the position of openly opposing even the least economically and socially disruptive plan of emancipation. Furthermore, King's proposal to make the public lands pay for emancipation sharpened the choice before Congress, first posed during the Missouri debates, of whether America's vast western patrimony would be devoted to slavery or to freedom.[70] What made King's proposal a masterpiece of malice, however, was the similarity of his plan in outline to the one Jefferson had proposed in his letter to Jared Sparks—so that when southern senators exploded in paroxysms of outrage against it, as King knew they would, they in effect repudiated their revered chieftain, the living symbol of southern antislavery sentiment.

To many southern spokesmen, King's scheme appeared as yet another piece of a grand and escalating conspiracy against slavery. If historians have regarded the period as one of relative silence on the subject, a contemporary South Carolinian saw it quite differently. "There are but few numbers" of the numerous periodicals of the North and East "that have not an article on this copious topic," fumed Whitemarsh B. Seabrook; "scarcely a book whose pages are not sullied by the most distorted representations of the state of domestic servitude at the South. Whatever may be the nature of the subject; whatever the design of the publication, whether to sketch the character of the signers of the Declaration of Independence, or to instruct the youthful mind in the first rudiments of knowledge; slavery, slavery, slavery is there."[71] Georgia's "excitable Governor Troup" went further, informing his legislature that in addition to King's emancipation resolution, the Supreme Court was entertaining doctrines that would "make it quite easy for the congress, by a short decree, to divest this entire interest, without cost to themselves, of one dollar, or of one acre of public land. . . . Soon, very soon, therefore," Troup prophesied, "the United States government, discarding the mask, will openly lend itself to a combination of fanatics for the destruction of every thing valuable in the southern country. . . . I entreat you, therefore, . . . to step forth, and, having exhausted the argument, to stand by your arms."[72]

According to John Bach McMaster, the Georgia legislators, whipped up by Troup, "seemed for a time quite ready for civil war."[73] If so, their anger stemmed from the administration's interference with the state's illegal dispossession of Creek and Cherokee land, the subject that occupied two-thirds of the governor's message. It is difficult to assess, then, to what degree Troup's threats and apprehensions over slavery were in earnest, and to what degree they constituted a diversion and a smokescreen for the state's depredations against the Indians—actions highly distasteful to many Old Republicans, including Ritchie and Macon.[74] In any case, Troup's harsh proslavery rhetoric succeeded in enlisting the support of anti-emancipationist southerners and in intimidating the administration—as well as moderate Upper South southerners whom Troup feared were "loosing [sic][their] interest" in the institution.[75]

Troup's fears were well founded. The drafters of an 1827 antislavery petition from the Washington Abolition Society, while describing the "detrimental effects of slavery upon the morals of the community" as "too obvious to need illustration," argued further that the "first evil consequence" of the institution was "the prostration of industry." The petition, signed by 1,000 citizens of the District of Columbia, advocated not only the gradual emancipation of the slaves but also their eventual enfranchisement.[76] Moderate slaveholders in Tennessee, Kentucky, North Carolina, Maryland, and Virginia increasingly looked toward an end to slavery, even while confessing their own states' inability to take measures to bring this about. In large part, the morale of the planters mirrored the market for cotton and slaves. A brief spike in cotton prices in 1824 and 1825, after six years of dizzying decline, failed to buoy the market for slaves, which continued to stagnate at its lowest levels of the century; thereafter, cotton plummeted to its lowest prices ever.[77] The flow of population from southern seaboard states reached tidal proportions; even old Nathaniel Macon, the living symbol of North Carolina, wrote Charles Tait, who had recently resigned his U.S. Senate seat from Georgia to relocate to Alabama, that he would have likely joined him in moving southwest if he were younger.[78]

Virginians in particular drew an analogy between their economic pros-tration and their state's diminished political fortunes after the dismal show-ing of their favorite Crawford in the presidential election of 1824 —only the second not won by a Virginian, and the first in which no Virginian ran. "I know indeed, sir, that it is the fashion with some of our friends to mourn over what they are pleased to call the degeneracy of our State," reflected the Norfolk attorney William Maxwell in an 1826 college address that sounded at times like a funeral oration for the Ancient Dominion. Virginia's enemies "laugh among themselves," the speaker lamented, "saying, 'the sceptre is departed from Judah.'" Maxwell would not dispute the contention. "And let it depart! What did it ever give to her but the barren laurel?—with that envy and jealousy that always entwine themselves about its flowers. And let the laurel also depart—and let it bind the brow of any other who may wish to wear it—and may she wear it with as much grace and better fortune than our virgin Commonwealth—too fond of power perhaps in her day; but always using that power generously, disinterestedly, and for the benefit of every one but herself."

Although virtually referring to Virginia in the past tense, Maxwell un-convincingly foretold a vague hope for the future: "Though I have no skill to read the mystic language of the stars, I think I can see clearly that we have a better time before us than any we have left behind." A note of hyste-ria infused the speaker's wavering allegorical vision:

> And I can see the Spirit of Improvement, at this moment—there be-fore me—coming down from the skies—with the face and wings of an angel, as she is. And there, sir, I see, she moves along amongst us, gently, and gracefully, and graciously, like herself, diffusing life and happiness about her. And there she visits the cabins of the poor, and teaches them from house to house; and she gathers their little children in her arms and makes them wiser than their fathers. And now she is planting schools, and churches, as we would have them, all through the land. . . . And still she moves along, and now, at last, she touches that *all-nameless evil*—the source of so many others—and the huge impediment to all her operations, and it is gone, I know not where—across the ocean—forever!

The orator's unconcealable horror of slavery and its effects upon his state lend a Poevian quality of frenzy to what would otherwise be a banally con-ventional rhetorical figure.[79] Like Macon and his fellow southern strict con-structionists, Maxwell entertained a vision of the future in which internal improvements, in some occult or "mystic" manner, banished slavery from

America's shores; yet unlike the North Carolinian, Maxwell, who devoutly wished it, could not convince himself (nor, one suspects, his hearers) that this result would come to pass. "Is this fancy, sir, or is it fact? Does my heart deceive me?" Chivalry toward the image precludes the gaucherie of disbelief, while marking Maxwell's soothing picture as a fantasy: ". . . No, sir, I will not insult the beautiful apparition by doubting her existence. I will rather regard her very beauty as proof of her reality, of her divinity, and exult in all the delightful anticipations which she has authorized me to indulge and enjoy."[80] Plainly, these are the consolations of sentimental laudanum, not the voice of conviction.

Maxwell's friend James Mercer Garnett gave a more sober expression of Virginian malaise after a two-month tour of the state in the following year. "Virginia—poor Virginia furnishes a spectacle at present, which is enough to make the heart of her real Friends sick to the very core; the Education of her youth either neglected or perverted . . . her Agriculture nearly gone to ruin . . . ; her general politics degenerated into a scuffle. . . . I well would imply hope for better things, but hope is nearly dead, and I can see nothing in the perspective of the times calculated to renew it."[81]

More troubling still was the contrast between the prostration of the Tidewater and the marked prosperity and decorum of the North. Fifteen-year-old Edmund Ruffin Jr., writing from boarding school in New Haven to his father in Virginia, delineated a stark contrast. "I think that the people in this part of our country are enlightened and polished," Edmund wrote, finding the Yankees "all industrious and hard working, a sober and religious people." "I like their manners and customs very much indeed," he went on; "taking them in general I think they are much better than those of Virginia."[82] Indeed, it almost seemed to Edmund that even Africa was more developed that the South. The young man's headmaster, Sereno Dwight, had taken him to hear an African prince from "Tombuctoo," which young Ruffin learned was "as large as New York," with "schools and manufactures of cotton" and a higher literacy rate than Virginia.[83] The imprint of New England ideology had made deep inroads into the impressionable mind of the son of the great southern nationalist. "I wished that Virginia was as well cultivated and the manners of its inhabitants as polished as those of the inhabitants of Connecticutt [sic]," Edmund Jr. sighed. "You do not see here such very rich men or such poor ones, but all seem to have enough to support them comfortably." Backing away a bit from what he finally realized might be a touchy subject, the boy added, "I hope, my dear father, that you will not think I have been praising Connecticutt too much." While it was true, he reported (as he had no doubt often been told), that "the

Yankees sometimes cheat if they can, and they will try to get as much out of you as they can," he nonetheless felt that "Connecticutt is a much more enlightened and polished state than Virginia. Still," he assured his father, "I had rather live in Virginia than in Connecticutt." This was fortunate, for the man who was to fire the first shot against Fort Sumter hastily recalled his son back to Virginia at the end of the school year.[84]

Young Edmund Ruffin's admiration for Africa and Africans found its more mature affirmation in a remarkable essay by Alexander H. Everett, brother of Edward, a distinguished man of letters in his own right and America's minister to Spain. In *America: or A General Survey of the Political Situation of the Several Powers of the Western Continent*, Everett saluted "the example of Hayti" as providing encouragement to the "friends of humanity, in regard to the capacity of the black race for self-government and the arts and habits of civilized life." Going further, Everett presented a sweeping refutation of race prejudice and a celebration of modern "enlightened" views on the subject. "It would be difficult indeed to assign any sufficient ground for the supposition of an essential inferiority in this branch of the human family," Everett argued, "or in fact of any real inequality among the varieties of the species indicated by their differences of colour, form, or physical structure. If (which may well be doubted) such a prejudice has ever prevailed among enlightened men, it is probably rare at present, and may be expected to become continually more and more so." Rejecting the ethnocentrism of his countrymen, Everett asserted that "there are no facts . . . which authorize the conclusion that any one of the several varieties of our race is either intellectually or morally superior or inferior to the rest, and there are certainly enough that attest the contrary."[85]

Turning to the subject of Africa's current prostrate state, Everett chose to place the fact in deeper perspective, emphasizing a cyclical theory of history:

Each great division of the species has had in its turn the advantage in civilization, that is, in industry, wealth, and knowledge, and the power they confer; and during this period of conscious triumph, each has doubtless been inclined to regard itself as a favoured race, endowed by nature and Providence with an essential superiority over all the others. But on reviewing the course of history, we find this accidental difference uniformly disappearing after a while, and the sceptre of civilization passing from the hands of the supposed superior race into those of some other, before inferior, which claims in its turn, for a while, a similar distinction.

Indeed, viewed in the *longue durée*, the record of history seemed to give pride of place to African civilization. "As respects the immediate question, it would seem . . . that the blacks (whether of African or Asiatic origin) have not only a fair right to be considered as naturally equal to men of any other colour, but are even not without some plausible pretensions to a claim of superiority." While blacks had evidently been "much inferior" to whites "for several centuries," it was also true that "at more than one preceding period they have been for a length of time at the head of civilization and political power, and must be regarded as the real authors of most of the arts and sciences which give us at present the advantage over them." Continued Everett, in a vein foreshadowing the most expansive modern Afrocentrism: "While Greece and Rome were yet barbarous, we find the light of learning and improvement emanating from this, by supposition, degraded and accursed continent of Africa, out of the midst of this very woolly haired, flat nosed, thick lipped, coal black race, which some persons are tempted to station at a pretty low intermediate point between men and monkeys." Everett asserted, just as has Martin Bernal more recently,[86] that "it is to Egypt . . . that we must look as the real *antiqua mater* of the ancient and modern refinement of Europe. . . . But Egypt, as we know from Herodotus who travelled there, was peopled at that time by a black race with woolly hair. . . . It appears in fact, that the whole south of Asia and north of Africa were then possessed by a number of powerful, polished, and civilized communities of kindred origin, . . . all black." Egypt inherited its own greatness, moreover, from Ethiopia, asserted Everett; and "Ethiopia, . . . a seat of high civilization and great power, probably the fountain of the improvement of Egypt and western Asia, was inhabited by blacks." The diplomat went on to claim that Babylon, Nineveh, Phoenicia, Tyre, and Arabia were "inhabited by blacks"; although "there seems to have been some mixture of whites among them."[87]

Everett agreed with religious anti-emancipationists who argued that "Canaan, before its conquest by the Jews, [was] peopled by blacks," as scripture and other histories confirm; but he made very different use of this fact: "In these swarthy regions were first promulgated the three religious which have exercised the strongest influence on the fortunes of the world, two of which we receive as divine revelations; and, as far as human agency was concerned with it, we must look to Egypt as the original fountain of our faith. . . . This consideration alone should suffice with Christians to rescue the black race and the continent they inhabit from any suspicion of inferiority."[88]

Everett went on to demonstrate that the "high intellectual spirit that once flashed out so finely in their sunburnt climates is not yet wholly quenched," offering examples of modern African poetry, in pointed refutation to the assertion of Jefferson that "among the blacks is misery enough, God knows, but not poetry."[89] "We civilized Christians," Everett seethed, purchased persons who had been "kidnapped and reduced to slavery," from nations of which we knew nothing, speaking languages we could not understand, and dismissed them "as a degraded and stupid race of men, incapable of writing epic poems, commanding armies, enlarging the limits of science, or superintending the government of a country. It is needless to add, that this reasoning proved the stupidity and degradation of those who thought it satisfactory, and not of the Africans."[90]

In spite of his radical refutation of racial prejudice, Everett espoused a remarkably conservative policy on African Americans. "In stating these considerations in favour of what seems to be a just and humane view of this question, I would not be understood to intimate the opinion that the blacks are destined to recover, in America, the moral or political superiority over the whites which they once maintained in the old world, or even to rival them in the arts of life," he explained. "Their relative position is too unfavorable." Their best expectation, Everett insisted, would be to "show themselves capable of self-government" when they should be "thrown by circumstances into the form of independent nations."[91]

Because Everett was promoting such a view, it might be expected that he would endorse the efforts of the American Colonization Society; but such was not the case. The society's "expensive efforts," however well intentioned, "can hardly produce any important results, counteracted as they are by all the motives that ordinarily affect the human mind." The nation's free blacks, "comfortably situated," could hardly be expected to embark on a dangerous and uncertain venture to Africa. To remove the country's slave population would be "a still more doubtful question," since the slaves' natural increase far exceeded the resources of the Colonization Society to transport them.

Moreover, Everett added, it was hardly clear that the United States "ought to wish to remove from amongst us, if we could do it peaceably and easily, so large a portion of the working class. The political condition of the blacks is certainly far from being what we could wish it; but such as they are, they are nevertheless industrious and useful labourers, and the southern states would, I apprehend, suffer not a little from the loss of them." Expelling the blacks would be a comparable act of folly to Spain's expulsion of the Moors, or France's ejection of its Protestants. "Our duty, as respects the blacks," Everett argued, consists in making them "as happy as we can in their present condition, and to employ such means as may be most expedient for raising them by a slow and gradual process to a higher one." Above all, he stressed, the idea that such a change could be "effected immediately and at once" must be strictly discountenanced. To proceed otherwise, Everett warned, would engender "a morbid and mistaken sentiment in regard to the whole subject. . . . Improve the character of the blacks, and emancipation will come in due time without an effort; whereas, by a premature zeal for formal emancipation, you destroy the possibility of improvement, and thereby defeat your own object."[92]

Everett's easy confidence in an end to slavery "without an effort," his belief that racial prejudice was on the wane among "enlightened men," and his strictures against promoting "formal emancipation," all testified to his absence from the United States for the better part of fifteen years. At home, however, these issues had become so polarized that what Everett no doubt regarded as a balanced treatment of the question, at once sympathetic to the claims of humanity and to the interests of the South, and would no doubt have appeared so a decade earlier, now appeared shockingly inadequate to one side and dangerously inflammatory to the other. Further, Everett's fascinating essay probably provided a quite reliable index of the current thinking of "the legitimates of Europe" on questions of slavery and race. As such, it offered disturbing evidence to southerners on their increasing moral isolation in the Western world.

It is hardly surprising, then, that in the eyes of anti-emancipationists, northern domination appeared to wax while southern influence declined. This was most clearly visible in the new order at Washington. "The administration seems to have a pretty strong & well fixed majority in both houses of Congress," Senator Macon reported in 1826, "and nearly all the newspapers are understood to support it."[93] The *National Intelligencer*, until now a Crawford organ, entered into a collegial partnership with the new president that far outlasted his tenure and continued up until his death; numerous other papers took their lead from this preeminent national journal.[94] The astonishing coincidence of the deaths of Thomas Jefferson and John Adams on July 4 of that year, the fiftieth anniversary of American independence, lent powerful psychic support to the president's amalgamationist program of uprooting the "baneful weed of party strife," and greatly assisted his chance of reelection.[95] "I hazard little, with those who were at that day in active life, and knew the state of public feeling," wrote the politician and historian of New York Jabez D. Hammond, "in asserting, that had the question been taken between Mr. Adams and Gen. Jackson at any time during the first two years of the presidency of the former, a very large majority of the people would have declared for Mr. Adams."[96]

ADAMS'S POPULARITY, particularly in New York, dictated that Van Buren, unchallenged as the de facto leader of the Jacksonian opposition, proceed with extreme caution.[97] It is unsurprising, then, that the Bucktail press initially largely supported the Adams administration. More remarkably, the organ of Van Buren's Albany Regency, the *Argus*, offered no criticism of Adams's address or of his first annual message, in December, noting only, "It will be perceived no doubt with satisfaction that the offer of the Southern Republics, for the attendance of republics in the congress of Panama, has been accepted by our government, and that ministers will be commissioned to attend."[98] In retrospect, since the issue provided the great opening wedge of Van Buren's opposition to Adams's administration, the *Argus*'s enthusiastic support of the Panama Congress is deeply ironic.

Van Buren's opposition to Adams did not stem from constitutional scruples concerning the proper federal role in internal improvement or presidential appointment of ministers without Senate confirmation. Nor did it derive from fears of U.S. entanglement in Latin American affairs, or the dangers of tacit recognition of black government officials and diplomats, although Van Buren and his associates employed all of these arguments in their onslaught against the new administration. Rather, Adams merited Van Buren's ire because of his continuation and extension of the "Monroe heresy," the policy of party amalgamation. If southerners had to apply a loose construction to divine an antislavery intent in Adams's messages, the new president's antipathy to party—Van Buren's guiding principle—was black-letter law. "My great object will be to break up the remnant of old party distinctions and bring the whole people together," Adams had declared before his election. His inaugural address had celebrated the extirpation of "party strife."[99]

Although Van Buren sensed the potential for a successful anti-Adams coalition—indeed, he had begun discussions with potential allies in the anti-Crawford camp even before the election—the drubbing his Bucktails had taken in New York and the administration's real popularity there left him hamstrung, if not chastened. "He had alienated himself from a large segment of the electorate of New York," Remini notes, and had to "become once again a grass-roots politician" in order to recover his political base. Van Buren's defeat in 1824 had taught him the lesson that Calhoun never lost sight of: that support at home is a precondition for ventures onto the national stage.

Van Buren's ideological home, however, was Monticello. According to

Robert Remini, "In his concepts of government, the Senator followed Jefferson. There was nothing original in his thinking; its content was all secondhand, and tempered with a sense of the all-hallowed party."[100] It was to Jefferson that Van Buren had turned in the dark days of the waning Crawford campaign. On a trip to Monticello with Governor Mahlon Dickerson of New Jersey in May 1824, Van Buren had "soak[ed] up the purest form of Republicanism" with the party's founder, and received Jefferson's blessing on his ideas concerning internal improvements, states' rights, and the importance of party regularity.[101] It was there, too, as Remini explains, that Jefferson filled the Little Magician with tales of valiant opposition to Federalist tyranny in the dark days of '98, "when Mahlon Dickerson and Thomas Cooper, both victims of the Alien and Sedition Acts, walked 'arm in arm' to prison."[102]

It was a good story. It also provided an ideological and historical link between the fiery radicalism of the republican past that Cooper, the freethinking English immigrant scientist, embodied, and the militant states' rights, negrophobic, proslavery conservatism he currently championed. Whether Jefferson intended to make such a connection is not clear. In any event, the usefulness of the association was not lost on Jefferson's northern guests.

Adams's message on Panama provided Van Buren with the ideal link between strict republicanism and racial fear. Ironically, he seems to have made this connection earlier than any of his southern congressional colleagues. Shortly after Adams's speech, Van Buren met with Calhoun in the latter's Georgetown mess to determine the Jacksonians' stand on the Panama Congress. Calhoun assured the senator that the states' rights party would fight the president on the grounds that he had abused his prerogative by announcing the mission without the consent of Congress. This was the same strict-constructionist ground taken by Crawford, writing to denounce Adams from his retirement in Georgia. It was left to the New Yorker, Van Buren, to point out "the correct and most efficacious method to conduct the campaign": to play the race card.[103] American ministers would have to treat with colored delegates, including Haitians; and, as the historian Hermann von Holst long ago noted, if slaveholders "could have blotted one page out of the book of history, it can scarcely be doubted that they would have chosen the one which told the story of the successful negro revolution in Hayti."[104] In Panama, the slave trade would also undoubtedly be discussed. Perhaps most ominously, the United States might find itself implicated in Latin American efforts to liberate Cuba and Puerto Rico from Spanish rule. Southern slaveholders dreaded this outcome, since it implied the almost certain emancipation of the islands' slaves, at least in the gradual fashion endorsed by most of the Hispanic American republics. Yet much of the American public and press welcomed the prospect of colonial liberation as the natural or providential extension of American ideals.[105]

Panama indeed proved to be a hot button for the South. After Van Buren's conversation with Calhoun, anti-Adams southerners, who had been "somewhat at a loss" as to how to attack the widely popular Panama mission, "suddenly experienced the heartening effect of the New Yorker's powers of organization."[106] Within weeks, the old Republican machinery was oiled and running with an efficiency and verve not seen since the glorious struggles with Federalism—except this time the machine ran on two distinct tracks, a northern and a southern. To the North, Mahlon Dickerson of New Jersey, John Holmes of Maine, Levi Woodbury of New Hampshire, and others stressed the constitutional argument against the mission and the danger of foreign entanglements. To the South, figures as varied as Calhoun, John Randolph, John Branch, Nathaniel Macon, Littleton Tazewell, Thomas Hart Benton, George McDuffie, Robert Hayne, and James Hamilton underscored the racial issue and hinted at unnamable administration conspiracies in a way calculated to excite fear and apprehension in their constituents.[107]

Ultimately the administration won the battle over Panama, as Van Buren always assumed it would; but it proved to be a Pyrrhic victory. By the time the Senate approved the president's ministers, it was too late for them to reach Central America; thus Van Buren and his allies had the satisfaction of enforcing a kind of "pocket veto" over Bolívar's abortive congress.[108] By channeling southern mistrust of the Adams-Clay administration's intentions over slavery into concrete political action, Van Buren was able to weld diverse southern factions, which had been at each others' throats only a year earlier, into a an effective political force. At the same time, he regrouped his northern Republican allies and led them into a reinvigorated coalition with their southern counterparts.

The core members of this surprisingly effective opposition—Calhoun, Tazewell, Mahlon Dickerson, James K. Polk and John Bell of Tennessee, Powhatan Ellis of Mississippi and Gulian C. Verplanck of New York—boarded together at Mrs. Ann Peyton's boarding house at Pennsylvania Avenue and $6\frac{1}{2}$ street, known for decades as "a house of Southern resort."[109] In Norma Lois Peterson's words, "Subsequently dubbed 'Fort Jackson,' Mrs. Peyton's domicile was indeed the center of anti-Adams activity, and to the 'Fort' came visitors of like mind to seek allies and plot strategy. Not infrequently were Martin Van Buren, John Randolph, and Thomas Hart Benton closeted in the Peyton front parlor, hatching schemes and airing them to the lively group held together by a hearty dislike of John Quincy Adams."[110]

The chief spokesman for the southern line of opposition to the Panama Congress was South Carolina's Robert Y. Hayne, who used the occasion to present the South's position to foreign nations and the North alike. "Slavery in all its bearings is a question of extreme delicacy," Hayne asserted.

> The question of slavery concerns the peace and safety of our political family, and . . . we cannot allow it to be discussed. To the free States the language of the slave States must be that they will not permit it to be brought into question either by their sister States or by the Federal Government. Let me solemnly declare, once and for all, that the Southern States never will permit and never can permit any interference with their domestic concerns, and that the very day on which the unhallowed attempt shall be made by the authorities of the Federal Government we will consider ourselves as driven from the Union.[111]

On the troubling question of Haiti, Hayne was just as explicit. "With nothing connected with slavery can we consent to treat with other nations, and least of all ought we to touch the question of the independence of Hayti in connection with revolutionary governments. These governments have proclaimed the principles of liberty and equality," he thundered—as if nothing could be more antithetical to American values. "They have marched to victory under the banner of universal emancipation. You find men of color at the head of their armies, in their legislative halls, and in their executive departments." Other governments might do as they pleased, Hayne allowed, but the United States should "take the high ground" and insist that the "peace and safety of a large portion of our Union forbids us" to discuss such questions. Hayne would grant but one legitimate role to U.S. diplomacy in Latin America: "to protest against the independence of Hayti"![112]

As Hayne's expostulations against governments proclaiming "principles of liberty and equality" demonstrate, the campaign Van Buren coordinated against the Panama Congress consisted of something more important than simply exploiting racism for political advantage. Rather, the drive represented a frontal attack on the revolutionary, millenarian ideology that had been gathering steam for a decade and that implicitly threatened the legitimacy, and ultimately the existence, of slavery. Hayne's fear of the contagion of Latin American liberty found its echo not only in the speeches of Hugh Lawson White of Tennessee and John M. Berrien of Georgia, but also in those of Dickerson of New Jersey and Woodbury of New Hampshire, which stressed the shortcomings—implicitly racial—of Latin Americans, rather than the threat posed by the congress to slavery. The importance of the issue was such that the signature of Nathaniel Macon, unchallenged symbol of Old Republican purity, appeared on the unfavorable report of the Committee on Foreign Relations (although it was actually written by Tazewell, as Macon cheerfully acknowledged).[113] As before, during the Missouri controversy, the word went out to Republicans that their traditional preference for liberty must in this case defer to more important principles.[114] In the process, the Panama debate helped to defuse the enthusiasm for liberty inspired by the Greeks, by the Lafayette visit, by the whole climate of revolutionary excitement, with strictures on constitutionalism and racial propriety. The speeches against the Panama mission represented a new level of skepticism regarding the possibility of progress—new, at any rate, for Republicans, who now outpaced even old Federalists in their gloom about flawed human nature.

A subtler and ultimately more significant tone was adopted by Thomas Hart Benton, who uncompromisingly denounced treating with black delegates or with nations that had black generals or high officials, but did not adopt a philosophy of conservatism to go along with this. It is not surprising that Benton, a Missourian, should have been one of the first significant public figures to view explicit racism as fully compatible with democracy and progress; Missourians had unambiguously linked the two during the Missouri statehood controversy, while westerners in general still understood that the nation's astounding expansion had come at the price of condemning the Indians to near extinction. Benton candidly linked his opposition to the Panama mission to the fact the president's choice of John Sergeant as one of the proposed ministers, denouncing Sergeant, the floor leader of the Missouri slavery restriction effort in the House of Representatives, as an "agitator" who had sought to bar Benton's state from the Union "on the single isolated point of free negroes' rights!"[115] Benton's speech, together with the protests of South Carolina and Georgia on the enforcement of their Negro seamen acts, further spelled out the consequences of the ambiguous language of Clay's second Missouri Compromise. Increasingly, southerners weighed the rights of free blacks against the peaceful preservation of the Union—a heavy burden for free blacks' rights to bear.

Benton's speech offered the still-hazy outline of a new narrative of American destiny. Benton transformed white Americans' contempt for persons of color from a common prejudice, enshrined in custom but conceded as unjustifiable and irrational in principle, into a foundation stone of the national edifice. As elaborated in later orations, Benton put forth the doctrine that white supremacy—later paired with geographical expansion—constituted the proper and essential basis for the American republic. In so doing, he helped to crystallize the fundamental tenets of what would become the Democratic Party.[116]

The adoption of this view did not come easily to most Americans, including many southerners. Speakers on the administration side arraigned their opponents for insincerity in their principles and claimed that they only argued such a perverse case out of political expediency. One defender of the mission suggested, for instance, that the talented trial lawyer Littleton Tazewell, the author of the Committee on Foreign Relations' caustic report against the Panama mission, found more sheer professional satisfaction in supporting "error" than in vindicating "truth."[117]

In reality, however, the opposition's philosophical objection to the Panama Congress had an inescapable political logic behind it—sufficient reason for Van Buren to accept it, while his future candidate, Andrew Jackson, embraced it wholeheartedly. As president, Jackson ultimately betrayed a deep strain of pessimism regarding Latin America, to the surprise of many contemporaries. "In view of Jackson's strong republican sentiments," remarked Samuel Eliot Morison, "it was assumed that he would maintain the Monroe Doctrine and cultivate the new republics of Latin America. But he and Van Buren never invoked or even mentioned the Monroe Doctrine, regarding it apparently as an Adams shirt to be discarded; and their Latin American policy gravely offended Argentina and Mexico."[118] This marked a fundamental break with Republican tradition, including Jefferson's original high hopes, and began the familiar modern phenomenon of Latin America regarding the United States as a threat rather than an ally, and vice-versa.

Indeed, this shift constituted, in the context of the mid-1820s, nothing less than a radical rewriting of the ruling narrative that had governed American political discourse. As Holst bitterly observed,

> The American league of the people which, in opposition to the princes' league of European despots, was to be a refuge of freedom for the whole world, had indeed dissolved into mist. Instead of a formal protest against the machinations of the Holy Alliance and a spirited exhortation to enslaved nations to maintain unbroken courage in the holy struggle for freedom, the world was comforted with a sweeping, unreserved confession of faith of the slavocracy, which made the slaveholding interest the starting-point, the means and the goal of the national policy of the only free state. . . . This gave a permanent meaning to the otherwise absolutely fruitless and aimless struggle over the Panama mission.[119]

In Benton's rhetoric in particular, the lineaments of a new narrative were beginning to take shape—one that would seek to write Africans, native Americans, and even the administration of John Quincy Adams out of history. It is hard to recall, in retrospect, that Van Buren and his coalition lost virtually every major battle they fought with the administration during the first congressional session of Adams's presidency: on the Panama mission, a bill to restrict executive patronage, the Dismal Swamp Canal, and repair of the Cumberland Road. But the president had been thrown off his stride, and was incapable of organizing an equally effective response. In addition, as Remini notes, although "Clay and Adams had walked off with most of the laurels—bedraggled as they were—an opposition had been formed, along rather indefinite lines, which was ready to challenge every move the administration made."[120] Now it was Van Buren's task to convince this opposition to place Jackson at its head—a decision the New Yorker had early calculated was inevitable, but which still presented significant political, moral, and above all psychological hurdles for many of his associates.

7

DEMOCRACY

PERHAPS NO HALF DECADE in American history witnessed as many dizzying shifts in sectional political power as the years between 1827 and 1833. The period began with John Quincy Adams's National Republicans apparently firmly in control, with every expectation of northern dominance in Washington for some time to come, and with states' rights southerners beginning to "calculate the value of the Union." The year 1828 witnessed Andrew Jackson's triumph and the apparent ascendancy of state and slaveholders' rights—a perception challenged by the president's appointments and John Calhoun's fall from grace, but materially strengthened by Jackson's veto of the Maysville Road in 1830. The following year saw the Nat Turner rebellion, the establishment of Garrison's *Liberator*, and the beginning of the Virginia emancipation debates, all suggesting that slavery was yet again on the defensive. In 1832, the tide turned once again, with Thomas Dew's fierce proslavery counterblast, Jackson's decisive reelection, and South Carolina's nullification of the tariff law. Jackson's firm stand against nullification in late 1832 and 1833, combined with tariff concessions to the South, appeared to signal a new period of sectional tranquillity, with the threat to the Union laid to rest and discussions over slavery pushed to the sidelines; but the passage of the West Indian Emancipation Act in August introduced an explosive new element into the American debate that returned sectional considerations to center stage, in more bitter and divisive terms than ever before.

ANDREW JACKSON'S 1828 presidential campaign operated on two levels. Overtly, the campaign called for ending corruption and instituting reform, pointing to the "corrupt bargain," abuse of executive patronage, and use of federal spending as a political tool as examples of administration venality. Obviously, although historians have made much of these claims, the policy shifts Jackson's advocates endorsed consisted of essentially generic, almost obligatory campaign rhetoric, rooted in traditional republican ideology.[1] On a more significant level, the campaign was about the symbolism of Jackson himself.

Indeed, Jackson's first backers for the presidency sought to employ the Old General as pure symbol. In 1822, the Tennessee political faction headed by William Blount and John Overton, having been routed in the previous year's elections because of their support for banks, seized on the idea of putting up Jackson for president as a way to baffle an angry electorate and ride back into power on the Old Hero's popularity. Once Jackson's campaign had "served its local purposes," these politicians assumed, his popularity would have peaked, the implausibility of his campaign would become obvious, and it could be quietly shelved. To the Blount-Overton men's chagrin, however, Jackson slipped out from under their management and embarked on a populist campaign of opposition to all banks. Despite their best efforts, the Tennesseans could not put the Jackson genie back in the bottle—nor could anyone else.[2]

In the approach to the 1824 election, Jackson operated as a kind of political "black box." Since he was revered by Americans for his actions, and unencumbered by a history of many words (in modern politics, a "paper trail"), voters could read into him anything they wanted. His success, as his supporters recognized, would depend on his ability to avoid taking controversial stands on divisive issues. This was an early application of the technique that would work so well for the Whigs in the "log cabin and hard cider" campaign of 1840, and would become the norm in the divisive years to follow: muzzle the candidate.

What, then, constituted the Jackson message? Fundamentally, the Old Hero embodied force. As Philip Shriver Klein has noted, "Old Hickory was the one, among all the presidential aspirants, who possessed a tangible kind of power. Few could appreciate the intelligence of Adams or the ingenuity of Crawford but there was none who could not see Jackson at the head of his troops, hear the roar of his cannon, or sense the firmness of his commands. What appealed most to the mass was evident power, not abstractions."[3]

Jackson's candidacy replaced an articulated narrative with the courageousness, nationalism, and simple victory conveyed by the battle of New Orleans. As a candidate in 1828, moreover, the General inevitably evoked echoes, however strained, of George Washington. Jackson, like Washington, displayed those "virile qualities of decision, courage, and patriotism, joined to simple courtesy and stout independence" that constituted what James Fenimore Cooper called a "Doric" character.[4] The image of the Roman general Cincinnatus, the Old Soldier returning from his plow to public life, constituted a highly effective narrative in the early republic. "Uncomfortable though it was, Jackson played the role of Cincinnatus and played it well."[5] Scripture offered an even more powerful narrative framework than classical history; Jackson himself had assented in pseudo-Biblical language when pressed to run in 1822, responding, "Let the people do as it seemeth good unto them"—thus seeming to embrace providential anointment as leader at the hands of the public, in the manner of the judges of ancient Israel.[6] Jackson had merely to supply the slightest gestures, then, for the American electorate to fill in the detail of the elaborated narratives to which his schematized gestures alluded.

It is all very well to say that Jackson's actions spoke louder than words. But his actions included his campaigns in the Creek country and the Floridas as well as New Orleans; and these episodes, particularly the Florida escapades, offered the framework of a very clear message—a message of action, ironically, that had been put into words by John Quincy Adams in his inflammatory diplomatic memorandum in defense of Jackson in 1819.[7] Not only had Adams, who alone took Jackson's part in Monroe's cabinet, rescued the career of the man who would defeat him; it was Adams who first articulated the almost theological doctrine of which Old Hickory was the living embodiment: an exceptionalist American morality based on the projection of force in the service of the nation's unique destiny that might appropriately be denominated "Jacksonian Providence."[8]

Southern Republicans had more difficulty supporting Jackson than did any other element of the Jacksonian coalition, though only in rare cases did such qualms stem from any reservations about the Tennessean's status as a "gentleman." As historian James C. Curtis has suggested, Jackson had long since established his "gentlemanly credentials" to the satisfaction of most southerners.[9] Rather, the southern gentry regarded Jackson as virtually the embodiment of classical Republican fears: a military hero, impetuous and imperious, riding to power on the shoulders of the "rabble." If it was true that Jefferson had suggested that Jackson had "more of the Roman" than any other American, the resemblance to Caesar or to Catiline seemed more apt than to Cincinnatus or Cato. Moreover, many southerners recoiled from Jackson's personal vindictiveness and violence, the arbitrary and sometimes brutal incidents of his military career, and especially from the larger implications of Jacksonian Providence, which Thomas Ritchie, editor of the *Richmond Enquirer* and chief of the Richmond Junto, had denounced as "new maxims of public law, as dangerous as they are cruel, and abhorrent from the national character for moderation, clemency and justice."[10] Their involvement with slavery notwithstanding, most southern Jeffersonians held in the abstract to almost fastidious humanitarian and republican principles. Jackson's cold-bloodedness as a duelist, Indian killer, and authoritarian commanding officer offended their philanthropy; his apparent willingness to countermand orders of his civilian superiors and to entangle his country in foreign adventures served as affronts to their strict republican code; and his charismatic hold on the public affronted and alarmed their conservatism.

Initially, therefore, many distinguished southerners resisted the Jackson-headed opposition to Adams and Clay. "The Crawford party will have to stand aloof," predicted an influential North Carolina Radical in 1826; "they will not be able I fear to support this administration; and the alternative as yet presented [i.e., Jackson]—is perhaps still more objectionable."[11] Jackson's appeal to the public over the heads of their leaders particularly rankled the southern gentry. Another North Carolinian lamented that throughout his district, "Demagogues have used the name of Genl Jackson as a passport to political promotion."[12] A figure who inspired such sentiments appeared to represent the antithesis of republicanism.

Most revealing was Thomas Ritchie's continuing reluctance to endorse Jackson. No major political figure was more genuinely appalled by the scent of corruption given off by the alliance of Adams and Clay, which Ritchie considered "an effort to parcel out the empire between Pompey and Caesar." Nor was any southern leader more convinced of the threat to slavery posed by the nationalism of the Adams administration, or better able to gauge the political arithmetic that dictated Jackson as the candidate to overthrow it. Ritchie's associates in the Richmond Junto had decided as early as February 1825 that they would be willing to "take Jackson and any body now in preference to Adams." Moreover, Ritchie's long political association with the Jackson campaign's de facto manager Martin Van Buren, cemented in the Crawford campaign of 1824, should have ensured the editor's support almost as a matter of course. Yet Ritchie resisted, until Van Buren put the case for the general in irrefutable, inescapable terms.[13]

Martin Van Buren's letter to Thomas Ritchie of January 13, 1827, calling for the establishment of a coalition of the "planters of the South and the plain Republicans of the North," is justly considered "one of the most important documents in American history."[14] It is so, however, not because it launched a North-South alliance in defense of slavery, since, as Richard H.

Brown has argued, such a relationship had been in place since "the inauguration of Washington,"[15] but rather because no other document ever spelled out the terms of the relationship with such clarity and candor. "We must always have party distinctions and the old ones are the best of which the case admits," Van Buren argued.

> Political combinations between the inhabitants of the different states are unavoidable and the most natural and beneficial to the country is that between the planters of the South and the plain Republicans of the North. The country has flourished under a party thus constituted and may again. It would take longer than our lives (even if it were practicable) to create new party feelings to keep those masses together. If the old ones are suppressed, geographical divisions founded on . . . prejudices between free and slave holding states will inevitably take their place. Party attachment in former times furnished a complete antidote for sectional prejudices by producing counteracting feelings. It was not until that defense had been broken down that the clamour ag[ains]t Southern Influence and African Slavery could be made effectual in the North. Those in the South who assisted in producing the change are, I am satisfied, now deeply sensible of their error. . . . Formerly, attacks upon Southern Republicans were regarded by those of the North as assaults upon their political brethren and resented accordingly. This all powerful sympathy has been much weakened, if not, destroyed, by the amalgamating policy of Mr. Monroe. It can and ought to be revived.[16]

In effect, Van Buren called for the resuscitation of extinct party sentiment—the manufacture of artificial partisan competition—for the purpose of distracting northern Republicans from their concern with slavery. Thus Van Buren sought to employ the same tool—which I have elsewhere called the "technology of sympathy"[17]—wielded so successfully by the antislavery movement, in order to produce sentiments in the public countervailing to those elicited by the abolitionists on behalf of the slave.

This letter has proved something of an embarrassment to scholars of what Ronald Formisano calls the "neo-progressive school," who are wont to take the partisan rhetoric of the Jacksonian movement—which Van Buren here describes as an artificial creation deployed for strategic political purposes—at face value. One of the most knowledgeable historians of the period, Robert V. Remini, for example, discounts the significance of the slavery issue in Van Buren's formulation, noting that "the issue of slavery was never seriously raised" during the election of 1828, and citing a comment by the

Jacksonian editor Duff Green: "The anti slave party in the North is dying away."[18] But this simply demonstrates that the policies promoted by Van Buren, Ritchie, and Calhoun to replace "party feelings" for "geographical divisions" were working—just as Green observed in a portion of the same letter that Remini did not quote: "It has been a part of my business so far as I could to prevent the agitation of that question." As Green's biographer observes, "The editor's confidence in the imminent death of the abolitionists did not indicate a spirit of blithe indifference so much as satisfaction in a job well done."[19] In 1827, Green wrote that Jackson's election would put "the anti-slave party in the North . . . to sleep for twenty years to come." The following year he avowed his desire to "crush" antislavery sentiment and to "roll the chariot wheels of Jackson's popularity over it." To the editor of Jackson's campaign organ, then, the threat to slavery constituted one of the chief issues of the day, and Old Hickory's election represented the surest way to combat it.[20]

One is at a loss to know just what contemporary politicians would have had to write in order to convince Remini and others of his school that slavery represented a central issue, if not *the* central issue, of national politics at this time. Alternatively, one is left to wonder whether the modern chroniclers of the Democracy are not still engaged in the same project of distracting attention from the issue by means of artificial class appeals as their historical subjects—and if so, why.[21]

Although Ritchie ultimately acquiesced in Jackson's candidacy, yielding to the force of Van Buren's logic, he refused the New Yorker's request to come to Washington to edit a party newspaper. Ritchie retained his suspicion of Jackson well into his administration, confiding to Van Buren that he rarely went to bed "without apprehension that he would wake up to hear of some *coup d'état* by the General, which he would be called upon to explain or defend."[22] Other Virginians became equally reluctant supporters. One easterner wryly commented that "the western part of the state will I think settle down in favor of Jackson, the people of that part of the country not having that habitual respect for the law that prevails here will feel less repugnance to Jackson." Norma Lois Peterson observed that Jackson's supporters "encouraged the 'common man' to demand from state governments a greater share in political matters," thus alienating eastern Virginians; but they endorsed states' rights, "a useful antidote to Adams's insistence on increasing the power of the federal government, and, more particularly, the power of the president."[23] Despite serious lingering questions about Jackson's own commitment to states' rights and to Republican orthodoxy, strict Old Republicans such as Macon, Randolph, Floyd and

Tazewell all embraced the General;[24] significantly, although his followers provided the crucial margin of support, old William Crawford, retired to his home in Georgia, refused to do so until appealed to personally by Van Buren in 1827.[25]

The "persuasive selling point" for Jackson in the area east of the Blue Ridge was that he alone was capable of defeating Adams; and the press of events convinced most slaveholders that they had to defeat Adams at all costs.[26] Duff Green believed that Adams intended to "revive the party distinctions engendered in the discussions on the Missouri question" to secure reelection by "rally[ing] a Northern party against the South."[27] The most unsettling evidence for this purpose was the alliance between Adams and Henry Clay.

If the New England president felt constrained about raising the slavery issue, his secretary of state felt no such compunction. Although Clay had led the South in opposing the Tallmadge Amendment in 1819, he had opened his political career twenty-two years earlier with a blistering attack on slavery.[28] After 1825, Clay became the American Colonization Society's most powerful advocate in Washington, a fact that raised the eyebrows of Jackson supporters, who saw it as at once a bid to gain northern support and a threat in itself. For years, Clay had been the nation's chief proponent of protectionism, urging the rest of the country to throw off the political domination of antitariff southerners and avoid becoming "the slaves of slaves."[29] Unlike Calhoun and most other slaveholding southern leaders, Clay's sense of self was not wrapped up with slavery. He derisively dismissed elaborate defenses of the institution as "the whine of interest." His western orientation, his nationalism, and his progressive temperament all superseded his own involvement in the institution. Moreover, the fact that slave prices stagnated at a twenty-five-year low made slaveholders uniquely receptive to schemes for manumission, and weakened slavery's hold on the Upper South generally.[30]

More to the point, however, Clay's alliance with Adams and the bitter controversy surrounding it (which earned for him from Jackson the nickname "Judas of the West") dictated that henceforth his political fortunes lay in alliance with the North. He thus had less incentive than other national politicians to cater to southern fears and demands. Routinely Clay denounced slavery as a "foul blot," the "deepest stain on the character of our country." "Whether or not he was sincere in these protestations is an unimportant question," observed a later commentator on early antislavery. "If sincere, they are a striking proof of the state of public opinion as exemplified in this most representative man; if insincere, they are a still stronger proof of the state of public opinion as estimated by this most accomplished politician."[31]

As a moderate antislavery spokesman from the Upper South, Clay posed a particular threat to the solidarity of the slaveholding states. Paradoxically, the fact that his views "were those of an extreme racist," as his biographer Clement Eaton avowed, rendered him more dangerous to slavery than sincere equalitarian abolitionists, because of his willingness to fuse the endemic racism of much of the northern and western electorate with the moderate antislavery outlook of the "benevolent empire." Racism constituted a blunt weapon against slavery, and a dangerous one, but potentially a powerful one as well. Moreover, in the Whiggish tradition espoused by Clay, white Americans' antipathy toward blacks could be interpreted in the salutary terms of Burke's "cloth of prejudice," rather than as malevolence. If such prejudice could be linked with humanitarianism in the service of philanthropy, utilitarian Americans might suggest, so much the better.

The American Colonization Society's application to Congress for federal funding in 1827, made with Clay's support, set off alarm bells throughout the South. Although Clay disclaimed any desire to tamper with slavery and dutifully assured slaveholders that colonization aimed only at the removal of free blacks, with their own consent, anti-emancipationists refused to believe him or other colonizationists. Opposing the use of U.S. funds for the Colonization Society, Littleton Tazewell employed a curious argument. The federal government, he asserted, had no right to transport abroad any portion of the nation's population. Although the society's plans currently called only for the removal of "a portion" of the black population on a "quasi-voluntary" basis, Tazewell argued, "could not this precedent be used at some future time to force emigration of both blacks and whites, urging them by use of bounties and rewards to leave the country?" The government had no authority to "intrude within the confines of a state" to remove its inhabitants and thereby "impair" its "political strength" by depriving it of numbers—thus rendering its congressional representation subject to reduction. Moreover, Tazewell added, the framers of the Constitution "wisely abstained from bestowing upon the government they created any power over the black population of the country, whether this population was bond or free."[32]

It is hard to see how Tazewell conceived the bizarre argument that the voluntary emigration of free blacks could provide a precedent for the forced removal of "both blacks *and whites*" (or, for that matter, how the use of "bounties and rewards" could be construed as compulsion). Perhaps, as part of the constant effort of anti-emancipationists to invoke the "spirit of '98" in their cause, he meant to stir memories of forced deportations of government critics under the Alien Act.[33] Still, the real basis of Tazewell's concern is plain: that the demographic tide against the southern states would be accelerated, and their political power weakened, by the removal of members of a class of persons—blacks—who, whether bond or free, having no votes themselves, augmented the influence of the slave states by being counted for purposes of congressional representation.

By this measure, free blacks, generally regarded as a liability in the slave-holding states, were even more valuable than slaves, who counted only as three-fifths of a person. This was a canny line to take in order to enlist wa-verers in the border states against colonization, since these states—Mary-land and Delaware in particular—had high proportions of free blacks rela-tive to slaves. But for the South generally, slave representation constituted a more urgent interest, and one that appeared to be threatened by the Adams administration.

Ever since Rufus King's attack against slave state power during the Mis-souri debate, many northerners had begun to regard the three-fifths clause with a newly critical eye. Southern anger at Adams's election and lingering public resentment of the methods of choosing electors had sparked a volley of constitutional amendments to change the current system, as well as other amendments designed to limit presidential power. By focusing attention so relentlessly on the matter of Jackson's plurality of the electoral vote in the 1824 election, his supporters unintentionally raised the issue of slave representation once again. Jackson received fifty-five of his ninety-nine electoral votes from the slave states. With this nonvoting and unconsulted augmentation to the southern electorate removed, the general's electoral vote total would have been seventy-seven to Adams's eighty-three.[34] Such ruminations spawned others: the elder Adams had also been deprived of his reelection by the same means, since Thomas Jefferson, too, relied on the slave vote for the margin of his victory in 1800. Thus the two most decisive shifts in the nation's political course up to this time would likely have been decided differently had there been no "federal ratio."

Henry Clay, still smarting from the vicious personal attacks on his char-acter stemming from Adams's victory (one of which, made by John Ran-dolph, had led to a duel), realized that "his course in relation to the presi-dential election" would be "*severely* handled" during the debates on the proposed constitutional amendments, and apparently decided to take de-cisive action to squelch them. A Clay partisan privately approached North Carolina senator Willie P. Mangum and informed him that if "any reflex-ion should be cast upon their party in the debate—they had determined to propose another amendment—to-wit, that the weight 3–5 of our slaves shd. be no longer operative in that election—indeed to abolish that feature of the compromise." Mangum had no doubt that Clay was directly behind the threat: "He is the only man amongst them of *boldness* enough to go that length and touch that delicate subject. Now sir," Mangum exclaimed, "any southern man, who is capable of touching that subject in that manner, and *at a moment when there is so much known feeling upon the subject to the north* . . . is reckless of everything to gratify a bad ambition.—Indeed Clay perceives that he has but little to expect from the South—and by a movement of this kind he may effectually secure the north" (emphasis added).[35]

How is one to evaluate Mangum's assertion of "so much known feeling" in the North concerning slavery, when virtually every modern account of the politics of the period describes the slavery issue as in a dormant state at the time? Part of the answer is that current historians anachronistically discount any discussion of slavery associated with colonization as ipso facto conservative—or even proslavery—and unthreatening to the institution. Since by far the larger part of antislavery activism at this date was related to colonization, it has been ignored as a possible factor for real change. Mangum's analysis of Henry Clay's sectional political arithmetic suggests that the potential strength of antislavery needs to be taken more seriously.

The resolutions on colonization sponsored by the Ohio legislature and by Rufus King, and the southern states' hostile reaction against them, kept the question of slavery near the forefront of public consciousness throughout 1825. Seminarians at Andover Theological Seminary, coordinated by the recent graduate Leonard Bacon, fanned out across New England during the summer break to deliver Independence Day addresses on "the subject of slavery in its *political* aspect upon our country," tentatively seeking to unite "the feelings of patriotism" in their listeners with "those of the Christian."[36] In early 1826 Representative Edward Everett of Massachusetts, a close confidant of the president—who had recently offended the Georgians with a humanitarian speech on the Creeks and Cherokees—sought to reassure the South of the administration's reliability with an inflammatory speech in the House in which he assured slaveholders of his willingness to "buckle a knapsack on my back, and put a musket on my shoulder" to help them suppress a slave insurrection. With this speech, Everett not only outraged almost every shade of northern opinion but "called forth an instant and indignant rebuke from several eminent natives and champions of the South," notably including John Randolph.[37]

Among the most forceful northern responses to Everett was that of Leonard Bacon, a young New Haven Congregational minister, who argued in a Fourth of July sermon of 1826 that the responsibility to promote the abolition of slavery constituted "a duty binding on every citizen of the United States," because "the evil of slavery is a *national* evil." Bacon then laid out a set of fundamental principles relating to slavery: "1. It diminishes the national strength. 2. It diminishes the national wealth. 3. That it is a national evil is apparent from the indirect acknowledgements of the Southern people. Therefore the duty of promoting the abolition of it is the duty of every citizen." In Bacon's view, slavery constituted "an evil at war with all the principles of our national happiness, at war with the very essence of our political institutions, at war with the spirit and influence of the gospel . . . an evil threatening by its moral turpitude to bring down upon our nation from above the wrath of heaven—an evil which continually gives warning that by its own inherent influences it will ere long explode beneath us, scattering in fragments the fabric of our institutions, and sending over the wide land the fiery waves of a volcanic flood."[38]

Although unsparing in his denunciation of slavery, Bacon counseled "a spirit of liberal kindness towards those who have been born and whose opinions and feeling have been formed under the malignant influence of a system so pernicious." He urged that those who "so exaggerate the evils attendant on the operation of the system so as to implicate the body of the slaveholders in the charge of cruelty and tyranny" should be "rebuked and shamed by the nobler spirit that pervades his fellow citizens." But Bacon reserved his strongest reproof for Everett and doughfaces of his ilk, vowing that "the man who dares to stand up in Congress and, presuming on the forbearance of those who sent him, attempts to purchase popularity by defending the principle of slavery, shall find himself greeted, on his return to his constituents, with one loud burst of indignation and reproof."[39]

When he preached such sentiments from the pulpit in the 1820s, Bacon later recalled,

> the religious feeling of the country was strongly and, I may say, unanimously pronounced against the institution of slavery. . . . Certainly there was in Connecticut no party, religious or political, that dared speak for slavery as if it were a just or beneficent arrangement, or as if the institution was capable of any defense, either on grounds of natural justice or in the light of the Christian religion. . . . From the beginning of my official ministry, I spoke without reserve, from the pulpit and elsewhere, against slavery as a wrong and a curse, threatening disaster and ruin to the nation. Many years I did this without being blamed,

except as I was blamed for not going far enough. Not a dog dared to wag his tongue at me for speaking against slavery.[40]

Noteworthy in the critique of slavery in the 1820s was its close association with the ideals of the Revolution. Colonizationists found it natural to stress the parallel of the providential birth and flowering of the North American colonies with the nascent African colony of Liberia, frequently burdening the analogy with more weight than it could bear. But other factors hammered home the association. On July 4, 1827, for instance, New York's remaining slaves received their freedom under the terms of the emancipation act sponsored by Governor Daniel Tompkins in 1817. (New York City's blacks circumspectly celebrated the event with a public meeting, but held "no parade.")[41] By 1828, indeed, the Independence Day antislavery sermon had become so firmly established that a Fourth of July orator could employ it as a model for another sort of jeremiad. "*Slavery not Independence* will be my theme," promised Heman Humphreys, the president of Amherst College. "Would that there was no such discord in the jubilant sounds of the day we celebrate. But the mortifying truth is . . . that after the lapse of nearly fifty years of undisputed political freedom, the blood-freezing clank of a cruel bondage is still heard amid our loudest rejoicings. You will naturally suppose I allude to that grievous anomaly in our free constitution, which darkens all the southern horizon," the orator continued; "but I have a more brutifying and afflictive thraldom in view. . . . INTEMPERANCE."

To heighten the effect of his comparison, and, perhaps, to soften its harshness on southern ears by taking ground he considered unobjectionable to them, Humphrey drew his analogy of intemperance not with slavery per se but with the African slave trade, which he described, apparently without fear of contradiction, as a "terrible scourge of humanity, which has fallen under deep and universal reprobation." Humphrey's surprising premise was "*that the prevalent use of ardent spirits in the United States, is a worse evil at this moment, than the slave-trade ever was, in the height of its horrible prosperity*" (emphasis in original). While the orator realized that his position might "shock and stagger belief," he asserted that he could maintain it "without the least extenuation on one side, or exaggeration on the other."[42] We are not concerned here, of course, with the aptness of the orator's analogy, which, it could be argued, blurred essential moral and political distinctions and promoted ethical confusion. What is important is Humphrey's evident certitude that his audience will accept without dissent his employment of the slave trade as the ultimate yardstick of evil:

The bare mention of the slave trade, is enough to excite indignation and horror, in every breast that is not twice dead to humanity. Any thing short of these emotions, would be counted disgraceful in the last degree to an American citizen. The wretch who should be accessary [*sic*] to a foreign traffic in human flesh and sinews and torment, would be branded with eternal infamy, if not hunted as a monster from the face of civilized society. I would set the mark of Cain upon such a reprobate if I could, and so would every one that hears me.[43]

Humphrey's oration referred to the slave trade only, and not to slaveholding. For decades, the defense of slavery had rested on the essential ground that a fundamental distinction existed between the two practices. The most pro-emancipation class of slaveholders, those of the Upper South, had been thrown on the defensive during the Missouri debate by accusations that their opposition to the slave trade stemmed merely from their desire to prevent foreign competition for the domestic slave market, from which they profited. Although many proslavery southerners abjured the African slave trade and sought to stress what one later called the "vast difference between a system of civilized and a system of barbarian slavery,"[44] this distinction eluded Nathaniel Macon, who took the unpopular, but consistent view — essentially similar to the later Garrisonians'—that if "it is made piracy by the laws of the U.S. to bring a slave from Africa, what then is it, to hold one on land being descendant of an African[?]"[45] Macon's point had additional pertinence since it was by now clear that abolition of the slave trade had resulted in no decline in the number of slaves in the United States. For this and other reasons, the British antislavery movement had begun to move from abolition of the slave trade to support for emancipation. Thus the once-firm distinction between attacks on the traffic and attacks on slavery itself had started to erode.

These renewed pressures on slavery intensified southerners' sectional response. According to the historian Edwin Wilson, John Randolph warned Clay that if any amendment touching the three-fifths clause reached the floor of Congress, southern members would walk out in a body.[46] No such amendment was introduced. Shortly thereafter, however, due in part to the efforts of the Adams administration, Senator John Randolph was defeated for reelection by John Tyler, who had supported Adams in 1824 and had recently informed Secretary of War James Barbour that it made no difference to him whether the president came "from this or that side of the Tweed."[47] This replacement had more than symbolic significance to defenders of southern rights, who regarded the erratic Randolph as their leader, or at least their conscience. Earlier in the session, the House of Representatives had passed a bill to impose a 50 percent tariff on woolens, which was defeated in the Senate only by the deciding vote of Vice President Calhoun. Thus on crucial, sectionally volatile issues, the Virginia Senate seat represented the margin of victory for the administration.

Randolph's defeat, occurring on the same day that Van Buren penned his famous letter to Thomas Ritchie urging him to join the Jackson coalition, lent special urgency to the request. It also helped to focus attention on the tariff issue, which now became the critical point of contention between the North and South. This was so because Massachusetts, its woolen manufacturing industry reeling from a worldwide glut of wool and deliberate British "dumping," had now reversed its traditional mercantile opposition to tariffs and had joined Pennsylvania and the other high-tariff states in endorsing a stiff increase in duties.[48] South Carolina sectionalists such as Thomas Cooper and Robert Y. Hayne found antitariff activism more prudent than agitating the slavery question, and just as effective in arousing their state to a determination to stand up for its rights. On July 2, 1827 (perhaps pointedly not on July 4), Cooper gained lasting notoriety with his famous speech calling on Carolinians to "calculate the value of the Union," in which he denounced the tariff and refrained from mentioning slavery at all.[49]

A still more influential document, however, Robert J. Turnbull's "The Crisis," appeared in thirty-three installments under the pseudonym "Brutus" in the *Charleston Mercury* in the same summer. Consciously and ironically modeled on the *Federalist Papers*, "The Crisis" explicitly linked the tariff, federal internal improvements, the National Bank, and appropriations for the Colonization Society as alike intruding on "the '*internal order*' and government of the population of the United States, and the 'LIVES, liberties and properties' of the WHITE people of the Southern States." In Turnbull's view, the ultimate consequence of loose construction of the Constitution would be, as "the ultra fanatics and abolitionists of the North contend, that Congress can alter, whenever it pleases, the whole domestic policy of South-Carolina." The real question was not internal improvements, Turnbull asserted; nor was it ceaseless taxation; it was not even "whether we are to have our Northern brethren, as our task masters, and to make bricks for them without straw." The central question was rather "whether the institutions of our forefathers" were "to be preserved according to ancient usage, free from the rude hands of innovators and enthusiasts" and from interference by outside legislatures, or "whether, like the weak, the dependent, and the unfortunate colonists of the West Indies, we are to drag on a miserable state of political existence, constantly vibrating between our hopes and our fears, as to what a Congress may do towards us."[50]

Turnbull, an immigrant from the former British colony of East Florida, retained a close interest in the fortunes of the West Indian colonies and regarded their experience as instructive for the South. "When Mr. WILBER- FORCE first brought forward his bill for the abolition of the slave trade, he was even *more cautious* than the Colonization Society," Turnbull warned. "He took especial care not to profess that the abolition of the slave trade was but the *first* step towards . . . the emancipation of the negroes of the West Indies . . . yet we have seen that he no sooner succeeded in the ostensible object, than he was observed to come out of his concealment, and to commence an indirect attack upon the whole system of slavery." The lesson for the South was clear, and the prescription irrefutable, Turnbull asserted. Simply to admit discussion of the Colonization Society would afford Congress "an occasion, *officially* to express its opinion against slavery as an *evil*, and the profession of a desire to eradicate it from the land." To allow even this would be going too far. "It will afford us . . . not ONE atom of security, that Congress does *not intend emancipation*. This it DARES not do at THIS time. . . . Congress *must not* be permitted *to express any opinion*, that slavery (which is the fundamental policy of this State) is an EVIL."[51]

Notably, Turnbull did not deny the assertion, but rather insisted that "if there be an evil in slavery, the evil is ours." For Congress to plant the seed of doubt, however, "will have a tendency to *weaken* the attachment of our citizens to the policy, which is the LIFE BLOOD of the State, and without which, we must *cease to exist as a State*, excepting in name." We must pause a moment to examine this statement because, though Turnbull's meaning is plain, it is breathtaking in its implications: Whether or not slavery is evil, it is South Carolina's essence, without which it must "cease to exist." Slavery is not simply a question of property, a source of revenue, of political power, or even of status; it represents the ground and being of the state. Note that this is not a "proslavery" argument, which Turnbull in fact never essays, or even an argument for self-preservation, for safety against insurrections, since, "thank God," South Carolinians felt themselves "competent" to defend themselves "under any circumstances." Nor is it even a defense of freedom, since that is of secondary importance: "Make me a colonist, not of England, (for that would be going 'from the frying-pan into the fire') but, if you please, of Spain, France, or Holland, rather than compel me to be a permanent resident of South-Carolina, with a power on the part of an American Congress, to legislate, directly or indirectly, on the subject of slavery."[52] Turnbull's argument is anterior to all of these: it is an argument about ontology, about being itself. Thus any discussion of the evil of slavery, by raising doubts about the institution in the minds of slaveholders, threatened not only the institution, but the very existence of society.

Anticipating (and, it may be said, elucidating) the arguments of southern anti-emancipationists against the acceptance of antislavery petitions during the congressional debates of 1836–37, Turnbull spelled out the objection to congressional discussion of colonization: "To countenance the American Colonization Society, will be to proceed upon the principle, that slavery is a rank weed in our land. . . . It will be a declaration of WAR, and MUST be treated and resisted as such. It will be the ENTERING WEDGE, with which, at some future day, our VITAL interests are to be SPLIT asunder.—It will be the LANDING of an enemy, and a bitter enemy too, on our soil."

Indeed, the mere discussion of the question must be resisted. "There must be no discussion. Discussion will cause DEATH and DESTRUCTION to our negro property." More than this: "Discussion will be equivalent to an act of emancipation, for it will universally inspire amongst the slaves, that hope."[53]

To the argument, raised by contemporaries and historians alike, that Congress could hardly be expected to pass emancipation legislation, Turnbull replied, "It is *no consolation* to say to us, that on any petition to be presented before Congress, the votes shall be in *our favour*, even if those votes be in the proportion of *ten* to *one*." Only a "trifling" number had supported emancipation in Parliament when it was first proposed, yet now, "the West Indies are hastening, with a very quick step, towards complete ruin. . . . And so will South-Carolina be ruined, if at this day, there are twenty men in Congress, who are for emancipation, sudden or gradual, and the right of Congress to take *even a vote*, is not RESISTED as an ACT OF WAR by South-Carolina." With uncompromising clarity, Turnbull laid out the terms for continued southern participation in the federal government, and the litmus test for southern politicians: "Those who would give the Southern Agriculturalist real and substantial comfort, must assure him that a petition shall never be received, and a vote NEVER shall be taken in Congress, on any subject connected with slaves, without its being followed by an immediate dissolution of the Union, and then would be seen a CONFIDENCE abroad in our land, to which we have been entire strangers, since the unfortunate Missouri question was agitated."[54]

The contemporary impact of Turnbull's essays cannot be overestimated. "*The Crisis* was the first bugle-call to the South to rally," nullifier James Hamilton Jr. later recalled. "Its notes struck upon the public ear with a shrill, yet full volume, that aroused us from the deep trance in which we had long slumbered."[55] Thus one of the most prominent South Carolina antitariff leaders acknowledged that Turnbull's analysis of the threat to slavery first inflamed the South, not the tariff question. It should not be surprising, given the extreme sensitivity Turnbull displayed over the discussion of slavery, that southern spokesmen should be thankful for an issue other than slavery around which to organize, which, had it been successful, would have offered a precedent for protecting slavery, as well as for opposing tariffs.[56]

Turnbull's angry screed found its Virginia echo in the "Political Disquisitions" of William Branch Giles, published in the *Richmond Enquirer* in January. Giles took new ground by denouncing emancipation and colonization as "sins," although he did not elaborate on this claim.[57] In practice, Giles fell into the "necessary evil" school. "The principle of slave labour, as a matter of choice, is directly incompatible with the writer's political principles," he avowed. "As a matter of necessity," however, Giles was "disposed to make the best of the principle of slave labour," which, though "unhappily introduced, and diffused amongst us," he regarded as "a matter of necessity, not of choice." After "much reflection," Giles found an approach that offered "material alleviation to his feelings" on this "delicate subject." Observing that "the evils of this world are relative, not positive," he was able to make a favorable comparison of condition of American slaves with British laborers, discovering the evil of British working-class exploitation to be worse than that of black slavery. The Virginia slave had his labor coerced by corporal punishment. "Bad enough that for the poor slave!" The English free laborer, on the other hand, had his labor coerced "by the horrors of starvation and pauperism. Worse for the poor free labourer there!" While the English worker was subject to "all the responsibilities of the law," including taxes, tithes, and the enforcement of debts, the Virginian slave was exempt from the "responsibilities of the law, except for the commission of crimes—No tithes, no taxes to pay, no inexorable Sheriffs to take from him his last pittance."[58]

Given the considerable attention that has been paid in recent years to antebellum southern critiques of the capitalist order, it is important to note that Giles seized on the comparison of the "white slaves" of England and the black slaves of the South, explicitly and avowedly as a rationale by which "to make the best of" the unfortunate necessity of slavery in Virginia. It is also crucial that Giles is comparing evils of different magnitudes, not claiming that slavery is a "good." By enumerating the evils to which white operators were subjected and black slaves were not, however, Giles drew the lineaments of the developing "positive good" defense of slavery—

a position that, by elevating the slaves' absence of responsibilities to the status of a privilege, struck close to the heart of traditional Protestant and republican conceptions of liberty and virtue. Even viewed in Giles's rosy light, his defense of slavery is problematic. Certainly the idea that the subservience, irresponsibility, and well-fed dependency that he described as the lot of slaves could be regarded as superior to freedom, no matter what deprivations it entailed, was "directly incompatible" with Giles's staunch, Old Republican "political principles," and it cannot have been congenial for him to assert it; although by restricting the comparison of the slave to the British laborer (who, as the subject of a king, could be said to have no liberty in the first place), the Virginian avoided the more troubling implications that would have accompanied a comparison with American workers. Such an analogy was not long in coming, however, and it caused considerable difficulty when it did.[59]

At about the same time that Giles's and Turnbull's articles appeared, Martin Van Buren canvassed the South on behalf of Jackson, to take the region's pulse and offer assurances of his own and his candidate's soundness on the region's "domestic and internal policy." Somewhat to his chagrin, Van Buren discovered that he had "wasted his time and talent on people who were already committed to Jackson"—the southern political "lions" Van Buren spoke to had fully recognized that they had no alternative to Old Hickory.[60] Ironically, the crucial regions Jackson needed to win were the West and Northwest: precisely those sections that most ardently desired a higher tariff.

Consequently, in spite of the fact that he most surely had been extensively briefed during his trip on the South's deep-seated hostility to the principle of a protective tariff, Van Buren returned to Washington and set to work on legislation for a drastically augmented tariff designed to reward the West and punish the East.[61] Perhaps no bill passed to that time had been so flagrantly designed to fuel sectional animosities. In the short run, the "Tariff of Abominations," as it soon came to be called, achieved its objectives of pleasing the hemp, iron, and wool-producing states of Kentucky, Pennsylvania, Missouri, and Ohio, and all of those states ended up in the Jackson column in November—although it is possible, even likely, that they would have backed Old Hickory even without the bill. Moreover, as Van Buren expected, the southern states backed Jackson as well, having nowhere else to turn.

In the slightly longer run, however, even though it had been designed to leave the South economically unharmed, the Tariff of Abominations greatly exacerbated southerners' outrage against the federal government, because their chief objection was not to the specifics of rates and duties on particular products but to the principle of a protective tariff, and to the revenues that such a tariff would generate. This aspect of the tariff question Van Buren seems not to have fully grasped. If he did understand it, his actions must be viewed, particularly in light of the Union-shaking crisis over the tariff three years later, as shockingly irresponsible. As Remini has sternly noted, "As an example of his political astuteness [the tariff bill] was one of his most successful accomplishments. It was also one of the most dangerous issues he ever tampered with in his life."[62]

———∞———

WHILE RICHARD H. BROWN has stressed Jackson's election as a signal victory for slaveholders in their effort to maintain control over federal policy, this is incorrect. Certainly, the patrician, ex-Federalist eastern establishment did experience a drastic reduction of its influence. This loss was decisive; it led many New Englanders to a thorough alienation from the national political arena, and prepared the ground for some to embrace an almost antinomian rejection of government, as the Garrisonian abolitionists did in the late 1830s. But the South did not gain by New England's loss. In fact, Jackson's presidency undermined the traditional southern style of patrician rule and alienated that region's leadership almost as fundamentally as it did New England's.

In the months leading up to and following Jackson's victory, the southern gentry seemed disposed to see virtue in necessity. Initially attracted to him primarily because he could win, states' rights spokesmen increasingly began to regard Old Hickory as one of their own, encouraged particularly by the assurances of Van Buren, Ritchie, and Virginia's Governor John Floyd. Ironically, one of Jackson's strongest selling points among these southern leaders was his popularity in Pennsylvania, which they believed might be strong enough to overcome the state's protariff sentiment. Jackson's supporters, however, saw the matter differently. Counting implicitly on southern backing, they strove to convince Pennsylvania and the West that the general was the true "friend of Domestic Manufactures," while Adams and Clay were antitariff.[63] "The great mystery of the case to me," wrote one bemused Pennsylvania Jacksonian to another, "is that the South should support General Jackson avowedly for the purpose of preventing tariffs and internal improvements and that we should support him for a directly opposite purpose."[64]

Southern Jacksonians dutifully played their appointed part in the campaign. John Randolph of Roanoke adopted the highly uncharacteristic stance of partisan leader—albeit in his own scandalous style.[65] Ritchie's *Enquirer* denounced reports of secessionism in the Jackson ranks as administration scare tactics. Backers of the Old Hero in South Carolina rallied to "stop seditious expression" in the state, and one reported with satisfaction that at the several Fourth of July barbecues he attended "not a toast was permitted which had the least savor of disaffection toward the government." Even the fire-eating *Charleston Mercury* pledged fidelity to the Union, and competed with the pro-administration *Charleston Courier* in its censures of sectionalism.[66]

Obviously, after so much yeoman labor in the cause, states' rights southerners had reason to expect both appointments and policies to their liking from the new administration. They soon found themselves "sorrowfully . . . disappointed." Bemoaned John Floyd:

> We believed that Langdon Cheves, Littleton Waller Tazewell, John McLean of Ohio, Thomas H. Benton, James Hamilton, Jr., of South Carolina, [Robert Y.] Hayne, a senator of that State, Hugh L. White of Tennessee, and so forth and so forth, would have been called; and that Mr. Calhoun, the Vice-President, would have been consulted and allowed his due weight. . . . Instead of giving us such men, he has surrounded himself with men of narrow minds, some of them hardly gentlemen and none of them have much character and no principles, moral or political, except Ingham and Branch.[67]

Few besides dévotés of Calhoun would have lauded the "principles" of Treasury Secretary Samuel Ingham of Pennsylvania, described by a judicious historian as "morally obtuse," and Navy Secretary John Branch's chief qualification for office seemed to be his inveterate opposition to Clay; but Floyd's point, from a southern perspective, was well taken.[68] Never had an administration been so dominated by professional politicians. Never before had a president convened a cabinet without a single Virginian. Never, indeed, had the South commanded less sway.

The early months of Jackson's administration appeared trivial and sordid enough to dishearten even strong supporters. The day of the inauguration itself, with its press of office seekers, constituted "a scene from which every feeling of delicacy revolted," according to one New England Jacksonian. "The throng that pressed on the president before he was fairly in office, soliciting rewards in a manner so destitute of decency, and of respect for his character and office, is . . . among the most disgraceful reproaches to the character of our countrymen." "Before I would behold such another 4th of

March," expostulated another, "I would see the whole district of Columbia blown to heaven, with all that it contained."[69]

The most unpleasant early episode of the administration involved the marriage of John Eaton, the new war secretary, to Peggy O'Neill Timberlake, a young widow with whom Eaton was believed to have had an intimate relationship before her husband's suicide. "There is a vulgar saying of some vulgar man, I believe Swift, on such unions," wrote one Washington wag, " — about using a certain household . . . and then putting it on one's head."[70] In the young American republic, achingly conscious of propriety and anxious about social standing, the ramifications of such an incident quickly escalated to the level of an affair of state. The wives of the other cabinet ministers, led by the indomitable Floride Calhoun, ostracized Mrs. Eaton from Washington society. The president, who blamed campaign accusations of his wife Rachel's bigamy for her untimely death just days before his departure for the inauguration, responded volcanically to the Eaton charges and virtually ordered his cabinet to receive socially the woman he insisted on describing as "chaste as a virgin." When they refused, Jackson simply ceased meeting with them.[71]

Distasteful as these proceedings appeared to orthodox republicans in the South and elsewhere, they found rumblings about wholesale removals from political office still more ominous. The appointment of the highly regarded Postmaster General John McLean to the Supreme Court, and the elevation of his replacement, the pliable William T. Barry, to cabinet rank, raised apprehensions that this most powerful and widely dispersed branch of government was being converted into a political tool—apprehensions that gained substance when responsible postmasters began to be sacked and replaced with "*partizans*," newspaper editors prominent among them.[72] A similar revolution took place in the customs houses, land offices, and other sources of government patronage. It is true, as historians have noted, that Jackson's replacements amounted to only a small percentage of federal offices; what is significant, however, is that previously, officeholders, routinely among the most upstanding men of their communities, had been removed only for incompetence or corruption. Indeed, just shortly before Jackson's inauguration, Postmaster General John McLean had reaffirmed the department's pledge that no officeholders would be removed without cause.[73] The game of "to the victor belong the spoils" had not yet been taught to the American public, and thus 919 respected federal officials returned to private life in the first year of the new administration under the imputation of scandal.[74]

While it may be wrong to view Andrew Jackson's victory as an unambiguous triumph for the slaveholding South, it unquestionably represented a catastrophic setback for African and Native Americans. With the backing of Van Buren, Amos Kendall, and Francis Blair, Jackson early decided to make state control over Indians—that is, forced removal—one of the defining issues of his administration and the party it launched. In addition to its decisive racial implications, this policy at once cemented the president's popularity in Georgia and much of the West and represented a powerful nod toward southern supporters of states' rights.[75] Opposition to Jackson's Indian removal bill quickly became a rallying point for his opponents, who mobilized churches, benevolent associations, and philanthropic organizations of all types to defeat it. This impressive coalition nearly mustered the votes to kill the bill on three occasions, all of which required the deciding vote of the pro-Jackson Speaker of the House. The leader of the antiremoval campaign, Theodore Freylinghuysen of New Jersey, who chaired an informal "evangelical caucus" in the House of Representatives, sufficiently distinguished himself with his forceful oratory and impressive moral bearing to receive the nod as Clay's running mate in the election of 1832.[76] Yet it is difficult to avoid the conclusion that the great moral concern shown for the Indian during Jackson's first term represented, at least in part, the sublimation of the slavery issue into less politically and constitutionally explosive channels.

Emblematic of the changed situation regarding blacks was the renewal of the controversy over black seamen in the South and the new administration's response to it. In 1829 the Georgia legislature enacted a law subjecting ships with free blacks aboard to a forty-day quarantine. Any free black who came ashore during the quarantine period would be subject to imprisonment until the ship's departure. While superficially similar to the earlier South Carolina seamen act, the Georgia statute contained important differences. First, it applied to *all* free blacks on board, whether passengers or employees, not simply to mariners. Second, by imposing "quarantine" provisions, it shifted the thrust of the law from the domain of police regulations—which, while draconian, might theoretically be justifiable on the basis of the steps necessary to defend a slave regime—to the province of "public health," thus applying literally the idea of "contagion" from free blacks that had been employed more metaphorically by the representatives of the South Carolina Association a half-dozen years before. Compounding the irrationality of the law, it permitted those on shipboard to come ashore after the expiration of the "quarantine" period—thus making a mockery of the public safety function of the regulation. Evidently, then, this was an assault on free blacks qua blacks; a legislative effort to degrade them as a class by associating them with contamination and disease.[77]

Britain's official response had also shifted since the issue first arose in 1823. On learning of the Georgia act, the Foreign Office requested a ruling from the Board of Trade on whether the law constituted "a perversion of the laws of quarantine" and a violation of international law or the Commercial Convention of 1815. The board's solicitor ruled that the law seemed to be permissible as a police regulation under international law, and allowable under the convention's provision that the freedom of commerce it guaranteed was "subject always to the laws and statutes of the two countries respectively." Aware of the new administration's sympathy with the concerns of the slaveholding states, and unwilling to jeopardize its new, more constructive relationship with Washington over West Indian trade and other matters, the British government decided this time not to provoke a feud over the rights of its black British citizens.[78]

A few months later, however, the British minister in Washington gingerly raised with Secretary of State Van Buren the case of an imprisoned black cook in Charleston. This episode led to a ruling from the attorney general, J. M. Berrien, that South Carolina's Negro Seamen Act "was a necessary measure of internal police, not in conflict with the Constitution or in violation of the convention with Great Britain."[79] Thus the Jackson administration officially repudiated the earlier decisions of Supreme Court Justice William Johnson and Attorney General William Wirt and further undermined the legal and constitutional position of blacks.

The pressure on free blacks increased drastically in the North as well as the South after Jackson's election. In the summer of 1829, the trustees of the township of Cincinnati announced their intention to enforce the hitherto ignored "black laws" of 1804–7, requiring all blacks to register with the authorities, show their free papers, and post a $500 bond as a guarantee of good behavior, or leave the city. A Fourth of July editorial in the *Cincinnati Chronicle* insisted that "we must remove that population from our territory, while the power is still in our hands." A Cincinnatian who facetiously adopted the pen name "Wilberforce" agreed, adding: "Our constitution was framed and adopted by white people, and for their own benefit, and they of course had a right to say on what terms they would admit black emigrants." Other citizens strongly disagreed. "We are, by straining the construction of the constitution, paving the way for the destruction of our own liberties," responded one. "It is just as constitutional to proscribe a man for the size of his head, as for the color of his skin."[80] The families of some of these black "emigrants," moreover, had lived in Cincinnati for years, having located there when the town was still virtually unsettled; and there is evidence that one important motive for antiblack agitation may have been to permit the expropriation, Georgia-style, of valuable land owned by blacks.[81] In August, the controversy moved out of the newspaper columns and into the streets, as "some two or three hundred of the lowest canaille" attacked the city's blacks in a weekend-long riot, perhaps the worst incident in the republic's history of mob violence against free blacks to that time. About half of the city's blacks fled for Upper Canada, whose lieutenant governor had reputedly informed their leaders earlier, "Tell the *Republicans* on your side of the line that we Royalists do not know men by their colour. Should you come to us, you will be entitled to all the privileges of the rest of His Majesty's subjects."[82] Rather quickly thereafter, the town fathers recognized that Cincinnati had shot itself in the foot by evicting a productive and valuable population at a time when labor costs were high and the supply of workers inadequate. Despite an apologetic appeal to the emigrating blacks to return to the city, about half of those who had left—perhaps 1,200—continued on to Canada, where some of them formed the settlement of Wilberforce.[83]

The fall of 1829 witnessed other outbreaks of violence against blacks in the North, including one in Philadelphia on November 22.[84] Five days later, South Carolina's Governor Stephen D. Miller made the leap from anti-emancipationism to proslavery, declaring: "Slavery is not a national evil; on the contrary it is a national benefit. . . . Upon this subject it does not become us to speak in a whisper, betray fear, or feign philanthropy."[85] But it was an otherwise unrecorded act of cruelty against a black man in Boston's Park Street Church that may have been the spark that convinced a black used-clothes dealer named David Walker to pen one of the most powerful denunciations of America's sins against Africans ever written.

Walker's *Appeal . . . to the Coloured Citizens of the World* marked a bold departure in many ways. It was the first time that a black American had openly called for massive slave resistance in print. It was one of the earliest appeals for universal black solidarity, and as such one of the founding documents of the doctrine of black nationalism. But these insights, while important, are derived from a retrospective reading. Viewed instead from the perspective of 1829, the *Appeal* reads less like a clarion call to future revolt and "a complete rupture with abolitionist writings of the day,"[86] as the editor of a modern edition has described it, than a cry of anguish in a venerable providential antislavery idiom fast losing ground.

For decades, British antislavery writing, true to its evangelical roots, had been solidly grounded in a passionate biblical vernacular. Central to this outlook was the sense that all of history constituted a continuation of the biblical narrative, that God still acted in history, and that nations would be called to judgment for their sins just as individuals would, and that slavery constituted the nation's most malignant and injurious sin.[87] By 1830 or thereabouts, this outlook had gained the adherence of a substantial core of the British public and was soon to gain triumphant vindication with the abolition of West Indian slavery.

In America, by contrast, this evangelical antislavery imperative had always been checked—among whites—by a variety of factors: the nation's far deeper and first-hand involvement with slavery and the political entanglements and racial antipathies that this involvement generated; the roadblocks to national action erected by the federal system; and the checks on evangelical influence imposed by America's political culture. In the United States in the 1820s, the baiting of "blackcoats" remained a popular pastime, and active Christians had to tread carefully. The Jackson campaign had made hay of an expenditure of $2.50 by Clay's State Department for printing "directions for Minister's dress," asserting that "to make people pay for directions for such trash, or indeed to meddle with a Minister's coat and breeches, is contemptible, and beneath the character of a free and enlightened people."[88] If ministers were frequent targets of democratic ridicule, clerical antislavery activists exposed themselves to charges of subversion, threats of violence, and organized boycotts and loss of salary—a consequence not to be taken lightly. In a country without benefices, ministers had to pursue the "ends of beneficence" with circumspection.

What made Walker's *Appeal* uniquely bloodcurdling to slaveholders was that for the first time a black American called upon slaves to wreak the kind of providential judgment against whites that Christian abolitionists had been prophesying for more than half a century. To modern historians, the *Appeal*'s chief significance is as a militant statement of black resistance and solidarity; for many contemporaries, slaveholders in particular, it sounded a fearful warning that the events they most dreaded were hastening to fruition.

In fact, however, David Walker's *Appeal* is more important historically for what it said than for what it portended. The document should be read principally, in my view, as the most compelling radical Protestant indictment of African slavery to be penned in America. But it is not merely a denunciation of slavery; it is more precisely an essay on the threat to a global moral order posed not simply by slavery but by the persistence in, and justification of, an unprecedentedly vicious form of slavery by a civilized, Christian, and republican people.

To be sure, Walker was appalled by the conditions of slavery—moved to rage, to lamentations, nearly to despair. Yet two facts moved him still more deeply than slavery itself. One was the collaboration of some blacks themselves with slaveholders and slavecatchers, a phenomenon that pained him so profoundly that he could barely bring himself to write about it. The second fact, a significant cause of the first, was the increasing acceptance of the theory that blacks constituted a separate and inferior race, a doctrine claiming the authority of none other than Thomas Jefferson. This view, Walker asserted, "having emanated from Mr. Jefferson, a much greater philosopher the world never afforded, has in truth injured us more, and has been as great a barrier to our emancipation as any thing that has ever been advanced against us." As Walker recognized, the stature of the author of the Declaration of Independence ensured that his views would carry great weight precisely with those whites most inclined to support the Africans' cause. Blacks were caught in a vicious circle: the more they internalized whites' disdain, the further they debased themselves and their race by "servile deceit" and mean submission to "murderous lashes," the less evidence they gave of their fitness for emancipation in the eyes of their white advocates. Sorrowfully, Walker declined to condemn former abolitionist "backsliders" who could see no evidence for hope that blacks could better their condition: "Yes, how can our friends but be embarrassed, as Mr. Jefferson says, by the question, 'What further is to be done with these people?' For while they are working for our emancipation, we are, by our treachery, wickedness and deceit, working against ourselves and our children—helping ours, and the enemies of God, to keep us and our dear little children in their infernal chains of slavery!!! Indeed," Walker groaned, "our friends cannot but relapse and join themselves 'with those who are actuated by *sordid avarice* only!!!'"[89]

Under such truly desperate conditions, it appeared to Walker not only that nonviolent change had become impossible, but even that organized resistance by blacks was futile. This left divine intervention as the one remaining hope for their deliverance—and this was the hope that Walker invoked. He frankly acknowledged the apparent difficulty of relying on religion as a refuge when it was Christians who had enslaved the descendants of Africans: "Indeed, the way in which religion was and is conducted by the Europeans and their descendants, one might believe it was a plan fabricated by themselves and the *devils* to *oppress* us. But hark!" Walker continued, rejecting this temptation, "My master has taught me better than to believe it—he has taught me that his gospel as it was preached by himself and his apostles remains the same, notwithstanding Europe has tried to mingle blood and oppression with it." An expectation of God's vengeance could hardly be viewed as escapist, given Walker's interpretation of scriptural, classical, and modern history, according to which nations that perpetrated the kinds of sins of which America was guilty had all inevitably been scourged with divinely ordained pestilence, war, and destruction. Passing briefly over a litany of examples from the destruction of Egypt to the fall of Constantinople, Walker singled out the plight of the Spanish, suffering under a bloodthirsty tyranny, as an unambiguous case: "All who are permitted to see and believe these things, can easily recognize the judgments of God among the Spaniards. Though others may lay the cause of the fierceness with which they cut each other's throats, to some other circumstances, yet they who believe that God is a God of justice, will believe that SLAVERY *is the principal cause.*"[90]

Although Walker prophesies a bloody divine judgment against white Americans for their crimes, it is hard for the reader not to detect an uneasy sense that it may not come to pass, that God will permit these supremely arrogant people to go unpunished. The chasm between Americans' pronouncements and their practices is simply too wide, and their prosperity too great, in spite of their enormities. How could Jacksonian Providence and God's Providence coexist in the same universe? "I say, if God gives you peace and tranquility, and suffers you thus to go on afflicting us and our children, who have never given you the least provocation,—Would he be to us *a God of justice?*" The possibility that injustice might be allowed to go unrequited does not raise in Walker the typically modern doubt of the existence of God; rather, the entire ontological structure of the world is called into question: "I say that if these things do not occur in their proper time, it is because the world in which we live does not exist, and we are deceived with regard to its existence."[91]

Walker's calmly stated yet overwhelming proposition represents, in my view, the most concise and penetrating depiction of a profound shift in historical and religious consciousness—the erosion of the concept of Providence as the motive agency in human affairs. The *Appeal* brilliantly illuminates one of the central paradoxes of the rise of humanitarian sensibility over the late eighteenth and nineteenth centuries. Jeffersonian optimism concerning the attainability of real human liberty, in this life, provided a tremendous impetus toward the abolition of slavery and the elevation of African Americans, as Walker unhesitatingly, indeed, almost reverentially acknowledged. Yet the very fact that freedom might be attainable by human effort seemed a reproach to those who obstinately remained enslaved. Since all men are created equal, moreover, those who failed to measure up—whether in intelligence, beauty, or liberty—were themselves responsible for their own shortcomings, not society or God. Those who succeeded, by contrast, had only themselves to thank. Humility, as countless foreign visitors observed with annoyance, had ceased to be a virtue with Americans; rather, it had become a mark of servitude. "Do the whites say, I being a black man, ought to be humble, which I readily admit?" asked Walker. "I ask them, ought they not to be as humble as I? or do they think they can measure arms with Jehovah?"[92]

Even more significantly, the image of God Himself was in the process of a transformation, softening from the angry predestinarian Calvinist God of vengeance to a benevolent deity who unambiguously granted free agency to his creatures—a God, as his Unitarian apostle William Ellery Channing avowed, appropriate to the dignity of freemen in a free republic.[93]

Here again, however, the implications of the change were double edged. If one's station in life were not foreordained from eternity, then those who were oppressed and enslaved could aspire to alter their condition; they were not fated to misery by divine command. On the other hand, such a conception of God drastically reshaped the moral economy of the cosmos, placing the means of achieving justice in human hands and in effect rendering the idea of divine retribution obsolete, and placing humans on a level with God. If God granted his creatures the freedom to liberate themselves by their own efforts, He could not consistently wreak collective punishment on oppressors; this would be to deny the free agency of the oppressed. Besides, the very idea of divine judgment against a "sinful nation" had an anachronistic ring to it—and an unconstitutionally "consolidationist" ring as well. The image of a benevolent God of loving-kindness, then, while it offered comfort to the prosperous, could provide little hope of justice to the persecuted.

By June 1830, when Walker died in Boston under suspicious circumstances, his pamphlet had already become part of an accelerating wind of change that was shaking the slave system to its foundation. From this point on, even while political developments seemed to signal a grave setback to emancipation, events moved steadily and inexorably toward a national confrontation over slavery. Yet the world in which David Walker lived, a providential world of divine judgment and redemption, still seemed to slip away.

8

⨯⨯⨯

FORCE

IT IS HARDLY SURPRISING, given the background of sectional tension reviewed in the previous chapter, that the first great congressional showdown between North and South since the Missouri controversy should have originated in a debate over the disposition of the public lands of the West. In the great struggle between the sections, as both sides knew, the influence of the western people would be decisive, and their allegiance, as yet, was still unpledged.

On December 29, 1829, Connecticut senator Samuel Foot proposed an inquiry into the wisdom of suspending new land surveys, limiting sales of public lands to those currently on the market, and abolishing the position of surveyor-general—a post currently held by a protégé of Nathaniel Macon.[1] Thomas Hart Benton leapt upon Foot's proposal, denouncing it as an unwarranted attack on the West by eastern capitalists. Benton "summoned the gallant South to the rescue of the Western Dulcinea, and Senator Hayne of South Carolina was the first to play Don Quixote."[2] Daniel Webster, alarmed by this developing courtship between South and West and provoked by Hayne's reflexive allusion to the Hartford Convention, sallied forth with a blast at the slaveholding South and a pointed comparison with the free North, employing the familiar device of the contrast between the two sides of the Ohio. "The orator's purpose, of course," writes Merrill Peterson, "was to make his issue with the South rather than the West and, having vindicated New England, to carry the campaign into enemy country."[3] Whether or not he deliberately intended to provoke Hayne, a one-time nationalist, into an elaborate defense of South Carolina particularism and the doctrine of nullification, Webster placed Hayne in a position that virtually required him, given the political climate of his native state, to plunge into the deep waters of extreme states' rights dogma.

This was precisely the scenario dreaded by the Calhounite editor Duff

Green, who had warned Calhoun that his "leading men should not look to the little squad who collect at your public dinners and cry 'no tariff!'", but rather "to the nation." As Green had predicted, for Calhoun's lieutenants to engage in such fire-eating was "taking the surest way to defeat the great objects [they had] in view."[4] But Hayne did more than shout "no tariff!" He presented a full-blown exposition of the radical South Carolina dogma on slavery and abolitionism, denouncing "the spirit of false philanthropy" and the "fanatical and mistaken" enthusiasts who threatened his state and the harmony of the Union.[5] Since Robert Turnbull's *The Crisis* had taught Hayne to regard any mention of slavery in Congress as an act of war, he charged that Webster had "crossed the border, he has invaded the State of South Carolina, is making war upon her citizens, and endeavoring to overthrow her principles and institutions."[6] Stung by Webster's "*significant hint of the weakness of the slave-holding states*," Hayne mounted a trailblazing defense of the high character, philanthropy, prosperity and greatness of Southern slaveholders. Moreover, while refusing "to speculate on abstract questions of theoretical liberty," or "to inquire whether the black man . . . is of an inferior race," Hayne firmly asserted that southerners had approached the management of Africans, "a people whose physical, moral and intellectual habits and character, totally disqualified them from the enjoyment of the blessings of freedom," as "a practical question of *obligation* and *duty*." The slaveholder was the true philanthropist, Hayne asserted, not the "visionary enthusiast" of the North. Finally, he concluded his oration with a pointed attack on Daniel Webster's inconsistency on the tariff, New England's inconstancy to the Union, and the sacred southern precedent of the Virginia and Kentucky Resolves.[7] It was a great performance, but one that possessed the same flaw that Duff Green had pointed out in a recent speech of George McDuffie: "Addressed to Southern men it is conclusive. But how is it when addressed to New England?"[8]

In Webster's brilliant hands, this flaw was fatal. By simultaneously attacking Federalist threats of disunion and defending the current southern variety, Hayne had offered Webster the opportunity to occupy the moral high ground, to reclaim what Ronald P. Formisano has called the "revolutionary center" of American politics, and to leave Hayne—and his sponsor, Calhoun—entrenched in the extremist periphery.[9] In his second reply to Hayne, Webster launched into a stirring defense of American nationhood and the sacredness of the Union that fatally undercut the pretensions to patriotism of the emerging "Carolina Doctrine," and effectively crushed the ideological underpinnings of nullification. "It was really the Mammoth deliberately treading the cane break," wrote one observer.[10]

Webster's was the first and most celebrated volley in what Kenneth Stampp has described as "an explosion of Unionist rhetoric" that elaborated the case for a perpetual union.[11] Taking advantage of Hayne's nominal allegiance to the Democratic-Republican Party, Jackson's standard, Webster pointedly and wittily made reference to the Jacksonian version of "amalgamation," the fact that so many Federalists had flocked to the Jackson standard: "We all know a process, sir, by which the whole Essex Junto could, in one hour, be washed white from their ancient federalism, and come out, every one of them, an original democrat, dyed in the wool!"[12]

His sarcasm notwithstanding, Webster was in fact engaged in a similar process. Exploiting South Carolina's current flirtation with disunion, the erstwhile New England particularist was finally able to redirect debate about Massachusetts away from the embarrassing episodes of the War of 1812 and back toward the earlier glories of the Revolution, the "Sacred War": "There is her history; the world knows it by heart. The past, at least, is secure. There is Boston, and Concord, and Lexington, and Bunker Hill; they will remain forever"—while Hartford and Essex County have vanished into oblivion.[13]

With his vaunting nationalist rhetoric, Webster was not simply propounding the contested constitutional theory in which the nation's sovereignty resided in "the people," not the states; he was piecing together the elements of a new national mythology that transcended and rendered obsolete the party battles of the Federalist period. This was an astute political move, since the New England Federalism of which Webster was one of the most distinguished—or notorious—representatives clearly had no future and thus, by Webster's calculation, no usable past. As historian Thomas Brown has astutely observed, "Webster's nationalism was more than the centerpiece of his ideology; it was also a personal political stratagem" designed to help him "leave behind his early reputation as a spokesman for particularistic interests."[14] Webster had truly grasped the fact that many Americans believed that Jackson's election had saved the nation "from some dreadful danger," as he had marveled after the inauguration; he was determined to demonstrate that no such danger need be feared from him.[15]

To do so, Webster sought to cleanse himself not only of the taint of the Hartford Convention, but of the Missouri restriction campaign as well.[16] To this end, his "Second Reply to Hayne" was not merely a tour de force of nationalism, but a sweeping repudiation of northern antislavery intentions. From the time of the ratification of the Constitution, Webster asserted, northern statesmen had disavowed any intention of interfering between master and slave. A committee made up of northerners had laid to rest the Quaker petition against slavery presented to the First Congress, "and from that day to this," no northern representative had ever "maintained or contended that Congress had any authority to regulate, or interfere with, the condition of slaves in the several States." All southern claims of designs against slavery, Webster charged, constituted a "gross and enormous injustice towards the whole North"; but even such dastardly imputations would not induce him to violate his principles and to "overstep the limits of constitutional duty, or to encroach on the rights of others. The domestic slavery of the South I leave where I find it—in the hands of their own governments. It is their affair, not mine."[17]

Going far beyond his explicit renunciation of designs against slavery, Webster also repudiated the notion of an evolving, progressing nation. "I go for the Constitution as it is, and for the Union as it is," he insisted, as he reached the coda of his famous peroration. In the context of the previous decade of sectional controversy, more specifically the renewed agitation over the three-fifths clause, there could be little doubt from Webster's language that he was signaling a unilateral truce in northern assaults on southern slavery-derived constitutional advantages in exchange for a halt in southern threats of disunion. It is surprising that historians have not recognized what a momentous departure from what would become normative Whig ideology Webster undertook when he proclaimed his devotion to "the Union as it is," rather than "the Union as it ought to be."[18]

Webster's ringing assurances completely stole the thunder from Hayne's charges of northern hostility to slavery. They won over most westerners. They also convinced most historians. As much as any other factor of the antebellum period, Webster's declarations inculcated the idea that American slavery and American freedom were not incompatible: that "Liberty" and the "Union *as it is*," intertwined with slavery, could indeed be "one and inseparable." Indeed, Webster's lofty oratory provided much of the emotional if not the ideological underpinning of the Unionist strain of anti-abolitionism that would characterize the policies of both the Democratic and Whig parties throughout the lifetime of the Second Party System. As such, his speech constituted a major milestone in the national effort to change the subject permanently and render the slavery issue inert. Yet Webster signally failed to convince those southerners who recalled the passions of the Missouri debates of 1819–21. "What was said then," writes the historian of South Carolina, "the South could not forget."[19]

While Congress debated the Foot Resolution, the protariff National Republican editor Hezekiah Niles engaged in precisely the same project of appropriating the "revolutionary center" as Webster in the pages of his *Weekly Register*. On January 23, 1830—three days before Webster's "Second Reply to Hayne"—Niles argued that the doctrines of protection "are older than the *treason* of 'Hancock and Adams.' ... WASHINGTON had no doubt concerning the right of them— ... JEFFERSON, and ... HAMILTON ... advanced and supported *every* principle that we contend for, and all were cherished and nursed by *every* congress from the days of the 'giants' to the present time; and by *every* chief magistrate of this republic, including president JACKSON,—who, in his late message, has entirely recognized the *protecting* principle."[20] Thus, by solidifying his position with the crucial manufacturing constituency, Jackson gained entry into the elite company of national icons of Washington, Jefferson, and Hamilton, meriting capital letters for his whole name in the newspaper of one of his most severe policy critics. Here one can see the construction of a kind of suprapartisan, perpetual, and eternal Union of the kind so exalted by the "consensus" school of historians of the mid-twentieth-century, in relation to which slavery is but an epiphenomenon; and at the same time, the marginalization and delegitimization of southern dissent, and of the principles of classical republicanism on which, though compromised by proslavery, this criticism was grounded.

It was not immediately clear to the nation at large who had won the contest between nationalism and nullification—indeed, it would not truly be clear until the summer of 1863. In terms of public reception, Webster was the victor; the elegant periods of his "Second Reply" would soon be pronounced by schoolchildren across the nation. The more urgent question, however, was who the president thought had won. The South Carolinians received some encouragement when Jackson's close friend from Tennessee, Congressman Felix Grundy, endorsed Hayne's contention that the Union had been formed by sovereign states that retained the right of interposition against unconstitutional federal laws.[21] The question attained the level of high drama on April 13, when Jackson and Calhoun both attended a subscription dinner in honor of Jefferson's birthday that proved to be "got up to inaugurate" the "new doctrine of nullification" and "to make Mr. Jefferson its father." After an evening of "ardent" toasts in support of the Carolina Doctrine, Jackson raised his glass to deliver his own, which proved to be a six-word synopsis of Webster's six-hour speech: "Our Union: It must be preserved."[22]

This sentiment struck the states' rights radicals as a stunning rebuke. In the consternation that followed, Hayne tried to salvage some shred of comfort for the nullifiers by requesting that Jackson place the word "federal" before the word "Union." Jackson agreed; and Van Buren, ever solicitous of southern opinion, stated later that this was the wording of Jackson's original toast, the president having inadvertently left off the word "federal" when transcribing the phrase to his toast card. Unquestionably, the toast to "Our Federal Union" was much more acceptable to the great majority of his southern constituency; but there is no testimony other than Van Buren's that Jackson had originally intended to deliver the modified toast.[23]

In either case, Benton recalled later that Jackson's "brief and simple sentiment, receiving emphasis and interpretation from all the attendant circumstances, and from the feeling which had been spreading since the time of Mr. Webster's speech, was received by the public as a proclamation from the President, to announce a plot against the Union, and to summon the people to its defence."[24] This is probably an exaggeration; but it is undoubtedly true that Jackson's powerful statement, coupled with the influence of Webster's speech (of which 40,000 copies were distributed through the offices of the *National Intelligencer* alone, in addition to countless reprintings in newspapers all around the nation), all but destroyed the pretensions to patriotism of the Carolina Doctrine and radically undermined the stature and influence of Calhoun.[25]

States' rights southerners naturally strove to put their best construction on Jackson's toast and on his administration's prospects for their cause. For his part, Van Buren sought to smooth ruffled southern feathers and maintain the Jacksonian coalition intact. His own volunteer toast at the Jefferson dinner summed up his essential political principle as well as the president's did his: "Mutual forbearance and reciprocal concessions: thro[ugh] their agency the Union was established—the patriotic spirit from which they emanated will forever sustain it."[26] Although Van Buren had approved of Jackson's toast (and later, in his autobiography, virtually claimed coauthorship for it), vigorous expressions of uncompromising nationalism unnerved him, and he genuinely feared a possible split in the Jacksonian ranks that might vault Clay into power. Accordingly, Van Buren saw the need for the president to send a strong signal to the states' rights party of the administration's support for their concerns. This came in the form of the veto of the Maysville Road.

This federally funded works project, which would connect two points in Kentucky, had universal support in the state. From Van Buren's vantage point, it was the ideal target for a veto. First, it would announce an end to the era of boundless internal improvements that had marked the presidency of Adams. Second, it would be a powerful demonstration of political independence from Clay's Kentucky, the center of protariff sentiment and the state that the Jacksonians had gone the farthest to propitiate at the expense of the South. Third, because the proposed road would run entirely within a single state, its true constitutional significance would be limited, since the president could argue that it specifically had no national value, without seriously limiting his options to promote other, more truly "national" projects, or unduly alienating the supporters of such plans.

Van Buren's plan worked like a charm. Southern states' rights advocates were elated by the veto of the Maysville Road, and they correctly attributed it to the influence of the secretary of state. "The rejection of the Maysville Road Bill," toasted an Old Republican at a dinner for John Randolph of Roanoke before his departure as American minister to Russia: "—It falls upon the ear like the music of other days."[27] Ritchie's *Richmond Enquirer* celebrated the veto, as did Duff Green's *United States' Telegraph*. But as Andrew Jackson's personal and philosophical conflict with John C. Calhoun came to a head over nullification, Van Buren's prosouthern coup turned out to be a red herring.

IT BECAME CLEAR EARLY in Jackson's administration both from his pronouncements and from his appointments that he would not secure the level of protection from federal interference that states' rights southerners considered minimally necessary to preserve their interests. Jackson's endorsement of the principal of a protective tariff in his inaugural address, even though couched in almost agonizingly cautious terms, rejected the conclusions of Calhoun's anonymously penned *South Carolina Exposition*, which had pronounced such an impost as unconstitutional. Despite his veto of the Maysville Road Bill, the new president had specifically pledged his support for "internal improvement and the diffusion of knowledge," the two great goals of his predecessor; and the Old Hero had struck out still more forceful language on these subjects only on the advice of his advisers, a fact of which some in the South might have been aware.[28] In addition, Jackson continued to emphasize his commitment to extinguishing the public debt—long a shibboleth of Jeffersonian Republicanism, but now seemingly within reach, a terrifying prospect to slaveholders. Two weeks before the Jefferson Day Dinner, Duff Green described the imminent extinction of the debt as a "crisis in the history of nations." The idea that a federal budget surplus could constitute a crisis is a surprising but revealing point. Perceptive southerners recognized that money in the federal treasury would open the door to calls for new federal programs. With the retirement of the debt, the government would either have to reduce revenues, or be faced with a substantial and growing surplus, and with it, the temptation to employ it in the removal of slavery. This circumstance, Green and Calhoun agreed, placed the Republican Party "in more imminent peril than it ever was."[29]

As Jackson's vice president, Calhoun found himself in a difficult position. No man had done more to assist Jackson's passage to the White House. No other member of the administration had stronger credentials as a nationalist. Calhoun's personal conflict with the president, over the Eaton affair and Jackson's conduct in Florida, had placed him "in Coventry" with the administration, to use one of Jackson's favorite terms; yet the vice president was now generally regarded as the South's last, best hope in the federal government. Calhoun's struggle to reconcile these conflicting roles and allegiances resulted in his emerging doctrine of nullification. As the South Carolinian viewed it, it was a conservative solution: the nullification of those specific federal laws regarded as "unconstitutional" by the states would permit them to remain in the Union while protecting their essential rights. For precedent, Calhoun naturally turned to the Kentucky and Virginia Resolutions of 1798–99; but whereas those resolutions had been drawn as an extraordinary response to a perceived constitutional crisis, by implication suggesting that the bond of union itself had been threatened, Calhoun advanced his new doctrine as an orderly, nonviolent method of redress to which the states might turn as necessary, without compromising the ties of union — of the attenuated, contingent form of union presupposed by his system, at any rate.[30] This position must have been difficult for Calhoun to maintain in the face of his lieutenant George McDuffie's assertion in 1821: "If after the National judiciary have solemnly affirmed the constitutionality of a law, it is still to be resisted by the State rulers, the Constitution is literally at an end; a revolution of the government is already accomplished; and anarchy waves his horrid sceptre over the broken altars of this happy Union."[31]

The historian David Duncan Wallace has argued that "the inconsistencies of Calhoun [and] McDuffie . . . merely show that men are little concerned with the meaning of the Constitution in itself but primarily with it as a means of promoting whatever at the moment may be their vital interests."[32] Whether Wallace is accurate in his harsh assessment of Calhoun, however, it cannot be denied that, to his followers, the South Carolinian stood for more than the simple defense of slavery. It is true that in his elaborate alliances and complex negotiations with representatives of irreconcilable interests, Calhoun was playing what his contemporaries would have called a "deep game," and he was plainly in over his head. Yet to many of his supporters, he stood for something much more important than simply sectionalism or his own ambition.

Because Calhoun is a figure of such convoluted motivations and tortured principles, it is hard to recall that the original basis of his conflict with Jackson was Calhoun's refusal as secretary of war to endorse the Old General's unauthorized military action in Florida. Jackson's willingness to employ force improperly, in violation both of republican and of Christian principles, won for him the enmity of many Americans, North and South. By contrast, Calhoun as war secretary had earned a reputation as a humanitarian and philanthropist. The vice president, with his nonpartisan aura, New England education, and reputation for integrity, had represented the best alternative to this new doctrine of "Jacksonian Providence," even before he revealed to the world his opposition to Jackson's incursions as a member of Monroe's cabinet. Paradoxically, even bizarrely, Calhoun sought to be the champion of the vanishing providential world invoked by David Walker's *Appeal*. Henry Clay courted the same "high-minded" constituency, but with his contempt for Indians and his reputation for gambling, carousing, and drinking, capped by the charge of a "corrupt bargain" with Adams, Clay's was a hard sell.

Calhoun still sought to assume this mantle of a higher morality, and his claim to it constituted a large part of his influence on his southern followers, who, along with their champion, continued to believe in his national potential as a candidate. Calhoun actually indicated his willingness to accept the Anti-Masonic nomination for president in 1832.[33] The nomination ultimately went to William Wirt, the lawyer and former attorney general who had ruled the South Carolina Negro Seamen Act unconstitutional and defended the Cherokees before the Supreme Court. As late as the eve of the Nullification Crisis, then, Calhoun was still contesting the territory of beneficence. That Calhoun and the Anti-Masons should have taken each others' claims at all seriously testifies to the lingering power of Calhoun's reputation for scrupulous rectitude and disinterested patriotism, and to his desire to hold on to a national constituency. At the same time, however, it displays the disarray of Jackson's enemies.

As John Spencer Bassett long ago observed, Andrew Jackson's veto of the Maysville Road "robbed Calhoun of a popular policy and weakened him so much that his enemies dared to proceed to destroy him utterly."[34] With skill and subterfuge, Calhoun's foes among Old Hickory's entourage entrapped the vice president into a self-destructive course of action regarding his old opposition to Jackson's Seminole War activities. In February 1832, Calhoun published a lengthy pamphlet defending his actions as secretary of war and denouncing the motives of his antagonists (in particular Van Buren), under the mistaken belief that it had been shown to and approved by the president. This action resulted in a permanent breach between the two statesmen. With his extraordinary gift for self-deception, Calhoun attributed the relative moderation of Jackson's response to defensiveness and political weakness. Massively underestimating Van Buren's strength and overestimating public disaffection with the president, the South Carolinian set about building an opposition out of disillusioned southerners, disappointed office seekers, disgruntled ex-Clintonians, Crawfordites and Old Republicans, and wavering and former Jacksonians with a myopic eye to the main chance.[35] But Calhoun's identification with nullification had ended his career as a national candidate. Even the resolutely impractical Anti-Masons ultimately rejected the South Carolinian's overtures.

The collapse of Calhoun's makeshift alliance left its leader "broken and desperate" and its members either scrambling back to the Jacksonian fold, forced into exile with the National Republicans, or, particularly in the case of some southerners, as radically alienated from practical politics as blue-light Federalists had been after the Battle of New Orleans. Joseph M. White, a politician from Florida Territory, continued to urge southerners to seek salvation from Jackson with the Anti-Masons, arguing, in Virginia governor John Floyd's interpretation, that "Wirt would unite all the fanatics and discontents" behind the party's standard "and succeed at all events." Floyd rejected this appeal, insisting that he would "never sanction success by calling fanatics to aid. If liberty cannot be preserved without them, then it can not be preserved at all."[36] For his part, Floyd began to explore the possibility of extrapolitical action by the South. Few other southern leaders followed White's prescription either—although Wirt, the Anti-Masonic candidate, was himself a Virginian. Still, the flirtation of southern Old Republicans and antinomian northern Anti-Masons vividly demonstrates the disordered condition of American political culture at the end of Jackson's first term.

FLOYD HAD REASON TO FEAR fanaticism in 1831. Casting his eye across the Atlantic in the spring of that year, he had envisioned a continent on the brink of explosion:

> The Russians, Poles, French, Italians, Spain, Portugal and Germany are preparing for war. England is disturbed, the people clamor for a reform in the government. . . . The people . . . are crushed under a load of taxes, are in want of something to eat, one fifth of the whole popula-

tion of England is on the parish and some die daily throughout that kingdom of hunger. Yet strange to tell, the rich clergy and aristocracy refuse any change! Poor unfortunate avarice, which will utterly destroy them as it did the King of France, Louis XVI, in our own day.[37]

Vice President Calhoun had expressed similar apprehensions for the fate of Europe a few months earlier. "I cannot but fear, that Europe is on the eve of a great revolution," he brooded. "The sperit [sic] of the [July] revolution must spread from France to the adjacent countries, which must rouse to madness and despair the already deeply excited jealousy of the crowned heads of Europe. There is much in the wheel of time."[38]

Yet there was no reason to assume, as Calhoun and Floyd appeared to do, that the United States should be exempt from the turbulence that both recognized as a likely consequence of brutal oppression leavened with a whiff of hope. In its slaves, America possessed a class more profoundly exploited than the meanest peasants of Europe. Nor was America free from portents of unrest. In June 1831, the streets of Richmond filled with itinerant preachers, as perhaps the nation's greatest revival to date approached its high-water mark. Conservatives such as Floyd well understood the potential for violence inherent in religious enthusiasm. The great Methodist leader Francis Asbury had described the camp meeting, the central expression of the revival, as "the battle ax and weapon of war,"[39] a metaphor that Floyd would have regarded as scant exaggeration. Luckily, however, American institutions provided insurance against religious instability. "It is fortunate that the Constitution permits everybody to preach and pray as they please," Floyd remarked ominously to his diary, "else this fanaticism which has seized upon the minds of the people, or new zeal, or as they call it a 'revival of religion' *would* seek to satisfy itself by shedding the blood of their fellow citizens 'for love of the Lord they adore' as was done so often in England and most of the governments on the continent of Europe."[40]

Yet, however well designed the Constitution might be in defusing the danger of religious conflict, it was not equally supple in regulating such substantive and potentially explosive national topics as slavery. Still less were American institutions adequate to contain the fusion of antislavery and religious zeal that was now beginning to emerge in various parts of the country.

National political developments played no small role in what one might describe, in retrospect, as the radicalization of evangelicalism. Evangelical Christians had been comfortably integrated into the administration of John Quincy Adams—far too comfortably for the tastes of such anticlerical crusaders as Anne Royall and Richard M. Johnson.[41] The election of Andrew Jackson signaled the commencement of a wholesale campaign to combat the influence of evangelical "theocrats" in public life. Rudely expelled and radically excluded from the political center, evangelicals launched a counteroffensive, organizing a drive to prohibit the movement of the mails on the Sabbath. The Sabbatarian movement, together with such other drives as temperance and Anti-Masonry, represented what historian Richard R. John has called an effort to "moralize the state."[42] Given the climate of the times, it was inevitable that this effort would soon turn to the issue of slavery.

To a significant extent, the growing alliance of evangelicalism with antislavery was, like so many other American cultural trends, a British import. During the summer of 1830, after gaining strength throughout the countryside for years, the parliamentary campaign for West Indian emancipation commenced in earnest. In July, Henry Brougham electrified the British people with his fiery speech advocating immediate abolition; by the end of the year, the "desperate doctrine" had become a staple topic of newspaper comment and popular conversation throughout the United States.[43] The early 1830s represented the "nadir for antebellum blacks," as Paul Finkelman has argued; but already, before the end of the first year of the decade, the tide was beginning to turn.[44]

In early 1831, a group of evangelicals led by wealthy New York merchant and editor Lewis Tappan met in New York City to discuss moving from words against slavery to action. By June, Tappan's "Association of Gentlemen" was actively involved in planning a national antislavery association, and promoting, with the backing of an unprecedented convention of blacks in Philadelphia, a manual training school for black youth.

Meanwhile, in Boston, William Lloyd Garrison had begun publication of his strident immediatist newspaper, the *Liberator*. The impact of Garrison's paper was disproportionate to its tiny circulation, because of the prevailing custom, encouraged by postal regulations, of free exchange of newspapers between editors. Within two months of its appearance, the uncompromising language of the *Liberator* had been quoted in newspapers in Kentucky, Washington, D.C., and Camden, South Carolina.[45]

It is unknown how much news of this agitation, if any, reached the slave quarters of Southampton County, Virginia. On August 13, 1831, the moment that all slaveholders dreaded and many expected finally came. Nat Turner, the charismatic, religiously inspired son of native Africans, led an uprising of slaves that systematically murdered more than sixty white men, women, and children. As Governor John Floyd observed with breathtaking understatement, "This will be a very noted day in Virginia."[46]

It seems at least as likely that the Southampton massacre was precipitated by despair as by evanescent hope. Yet Governor Floyd could hardly be blamed for believing that Turner had been inspired by northern antislavery agitation. On the same day that he learned of the uprising, he received for the first time a copy of the *Liberator*. Reading Garrison's caustic attacks on slavery and slaveholders within hours after hearing a horrific account of the bloodbath in Southampton left Floyd with no room to doubt that the newspaper was printed "with the express intention of inciting the slaves and free negroes in this and the other States to rebellion and to murder the men, women and children of those states." Yet Floyd recognized that Garrison was probably within his rights to publish the paper. "The amount of it then is this," Floyd reasoned: "a man in our States may plot treason in one state against another without fear of punishment, whilst the suffering state has no right to resist by the provisions of the Federal Constitution. If this is not checked it must lead to a separation of these states."[47]

Shocked and demoralized, other Virginians also considered their alternatives. Jane Randolph, wife of Jefferson's grandson Thomas Jefferson Randolph, urged her husband to abandon Virginia and slavery for the free soil of Ohio.[48] Local officials repeatedly confronted Governor Floyd with two sets of demands: for arms and emancipation. Requests for rifles came not only from the vicinity of Southampton but also from every part of the state where slaves substantially outnumbered whites. As late as the end of November, officials in Norfolk, bordered by an extensive swamp that often harbored undetected fugitive slaves, anxiously pestered the governor for ever more weapons. "There are still demands for arms in the lower country," Floyd confided to his journal. "I could not have believed there was half the fear amongst the people of the lower country in respect to their slaves. Before I leave this Government," he vowed, "I will have contrived to have a law passed gradually abolishing slavery in this State."[49]

For black abolitionists, as for some of their white counterparts, the appalling event and its aftermath of bloody revenge had a somehow liberating quality, despite their horror. It was as if an impenetrable fog of deep depression had suddenly been lifted by shock treatment. Though Nat Turner and his followers had "done vastly wrong," wrote an anonymous white contributor to the *African Centinel and Journal of Liberty*, "still it is not to be wondered at. Their struggle for freedom is the same in principle as the struggle of our fathers in '76. . . . I shall for one, wish them success whenever the battle may come."[50] James Forten, the wealthy black Philadelphia sailmaker and abolitionist, believed that the Turner rebellion would aid the antislavery cause by "bringing the evils of slavery more prominently before the public." Forten explicitly linked the Southampton insurrection with the struggles for freedom in Europe and the reform movements in America: "Indeed, we live in stirring times, and every day brings news of some fresh effort for liberty, either at home or abroad—onward, onward, is indeed the watchword."[51]

Forten's optimism, shared by many, represented a dramatic shift from the pessimism and despair of the late 1820s, when the Colonization Society's disparagement of blacks represented the closest thing to a white antislavery movement, and when African Americans, as David Walker had lamented, seemed to have been alone excluded from the great march of freedom taking place in the world. Forten's white countrymen had hailed the struggles for liberty of the Greeks, South Americans, Neapolitans, Poles, Belgians, French, and even Cherokees and Creeks, while regarding the oppressed class of enslaved Africans as a case apart. After Southampton, this arbitrary conceptual segregation became much harder to maintain. "The autocrat of Russia does not more deserve the name tyrant for sending his hordes of barbarians to plant the blood-stained banner on the walls of Warsaw . . . than does the petty tyrant, who, in any quarter of the globe, is equally regardless of the acknowledged rights of man," proclaimed a Virginian legislator in support of slave emancipation. Another Virginian described the abolition movement as "a great political revolution" comparable to the "generous efforts of the Parisian patriots" of the July days.[52] Many white Americans could no longer ignore the demands of African Americans for justice—nor, perhaps more important, could whites negate blacks' role as authentic actors on the stage of history.

The immediate effect of the Nat Turner insurrection was to force the question of slavery, "which was deemed too delicate to mention before," into the forefront of public debate.[53] In every part of the state, Virginians held meetings, circulated petitions, and drew up memorials calling for legislative action. While a few of the petitions opposed emancipation in any form, these represented a distinct minority of the total, and came only from the heavily slaveholding districts of the Piedmont and Tidewater. Even these strongholds of slavery produced petitions requesting emancipation, however; and memorials from the rest of the state advocated everything from the simple removal of free blacks to Jefferson's *post-nati* emancipation plan to the call by 343 women of Augusta County for immediate and total abolition.[54]

Virginia's governor quietly took the lead in confronting the problem. In a letter to South Carolina governor James Hamilton, Floyd suggested that Virginians had been living in a fool's paradise, ignoring the activities both of northern incendiaries and of black preachers and other potential rebels at home. Laws regulating free blacks and slaves had been routinely flouted, as whites, particularly "pious" and "respectable" females, had taught blacks to read, instructed them in dangerous religious doctrines of spiritual equality, and permitted them to assemble in large groups for religious meetings. Floyd planned to call on the Virginia legislature to put a stop to this laxness and impose a "consolidation of slavery" within the state.[55]

But Floyd regarded his draconian proposals as merely provisional. Ultimately, he considered all such restrictions to be stopgap measures designed to protect the public until the institution of slavery could be removed from the state. To this end, the governor employed his influence with his younger political associates in the Assembly to push a gradual emancipation plan in the 1831–32 session. Other influential figures, notably Jefferson's grandson Thomas Jefferson Randolph, took leading roles in the effort. Both of the major Richmond papers, Thomas Ritchie's *Enquirer* and John Hampden Pleasants's *Constitutional Whig*, endorsed the proposal. In cautious but unambiguous terms, the *Enquirer* urged that a plan be "firmly and deliberately introduced, for striking at the roots of the evil . . . for reducing surely but quietly, the number of our slaves." "It is not the non-slaveholder, or the visionary Philanthropist, or the fanatic," who called for action to put an end to slavery, asserted the *Whig*, "but the mass of slave-holders themselves. It is *their* question."[56]

If the "mass of slave-holders" wished to discuss finding a solution to the "evil" of slavery, many of the smaller group of Tidewater and Piedmont slaveholders who dominated Virginia politics wanted no such thing. Throughout the fall of 1831, these conservative easterners, led by William O. Goode of Mecklenburg, managed to bottle up discussion in a special committee and restrict the scope of proposals to the removal of the state's free blacks. One episode offered a curious contrast to the slavery controversy of the first federal congress of 1790 and the antislavery petitions controversy of 1835–36, however. When Goode introduced a resolution to "relieve" the special committee from the obligation to consider a petition from a Quaker group near Richmond, the measure was resoundingly rejected by a vote of 93 to 27. This vote clearly demonstrates, if demonstration is required, what a serious mistake it would be to construe southern near-unanimity against the discussion of slavery in a federal forum as at all tantamount to solid southern support for the institution at the state level. The Virginia Assembly refused to countenance the gagging of the state's own citizens, "incendiary" Quakers included.

IN EARLY 1832, RITCHIE'S *Enquirer* grew tired of the special committee's stalling, and demanded action in a memorable, impassioned editorial. "Are we forever to suffer the greatest evil which can scourge our land, not only to remain but to increase in its domains?" the editorial demanded. Quoting from "an eloquent South Carolinian" (a strategically effective touch that, considering that state's unchallenged reputation for "orthodoxy" on slavery, lent a profound force to the words), the *Enquirer* continued:

> We may shut our eyes and avert our faces, if you please . . . but there it is, the black and gnawing evil at our doors—and meet the question we must at no distant day. God only knows what is the part of wise men to do on that momentous and appalling subject. Of this I am sure, that the difference, nothing short of frightful—between all that exists on one side of the Potomac and all on the other side, is owing to that cause alone. The disease is deep rooted—it is at the heart's core—it is consuming, and has all along been consuming our vitals, and I would laugh, if I could laugh at such a subject, of the ignorance and folly of politicians who ascribe that to an act of government which is the inevitable effect of the eternal laws of nature. What is to be done? O my God, I don't know; but something must be done![57]

With scarcely a change, this paragraph could have come from the commonplace book of an anguished young seminarian in the throes of conviction of sin. It is hardly surprising, given the ubiquity and the intensity of religious revival at the moment of the Nat Turner uprising, that evangelically inclined southerners would interpret the event as a brutal judgment and a divine warning.

The response to the *Enquirer*'s editorial demonstrated that it had touched a chord with Virginians. "Within a very few days," historian Charles Ambler reports, it "appeared in whole or in part in practically the entire press of the state."[58] Reprinted in the columns of *Niles' Register* and the *National Intelligencer*, two of the nation's most widely quoted publications, the piece soon circulated throughout the country. Virginia's emancipation debates now became the focus of a national drama. The country, and particularly the South, watched with fascination and concern as Virginia wrestled with its conscience. In the idiom of the revival, Virginia found itself on the "anxious bench."

The accepted scholarship of an earlier era asserted that the South would have been willing to relinquish slavery, gradually and peacefully, had not northern extremists espoused a strident abolitionism which impugned southern honor and endangered southern safety. Certain events would seem to lend credence to this view. It is true, for instance, that the rise of William Lloyd Garrison's influence coincided with Virginia's emancipation debates. On January 1, 1832, Garrison presided over the founding of the New England Anti-Slavery Society, whose charter represented a radical commitment to civil and political equality.[59] Six weeks later, the society opened its attack on African colonization, a stance that, presumably, made the efforts of Virginia emancipationists considerably more difficult.

Yet such an interpretation at once lends too much weight to these comparatively minor events (only fifteen individuals attended the founding meeting of the New-England Anti-Slavery Society, for example) and ignores the impact of internal Virginian developments, as well as of much larger national events not explicitly connected with slavery. As early as 1819, it will be recalled, "An American," writing in the columns of the *Richmond Enquirer*, had promoted the opinion that "no plan" of emancipation could "be devised" that would not cause "incalculable suffering," and that "all humane schemes" had "either failed, created new mischiefs, or increased the evil they were intended to relieve."[60] This outlook was not dead. On the contrary, after more than a decade of sectional tension, it had burgeoned into a substantial movement.

Now, it is true, the *Enquirer* expressed its satisfaction that, after years of silence, the "bloody massacre" in Southampton had "released the floodgates of discussion" over slavery; and the Richmond *Whig* fairly exulted "that the great mass of Virginia herself triumphs that the slavery question has been agitated," and that even "in the heaviest slave districts of the State, thousands have hailed the discussion with delight, and contemplate the distant, but ardently desired result, as the supreme good which Providence could vouchsafe to their country."[61]

Other slaveholding Virginians, however, desired no such thing. Governor Floyd detected an ominous change in the tone of the House debate over slavery late in January. By the twenty-fifth, although the House stood in recess, Floyd recorded that "the members from the South side of the James River talk of making a proposition to divide the State by the Blue Ridge Mountains sooner than part with their negroes."[62] On February 3, the easterners turned from angry words to action, spitefully voting down a bill for improvements to the western part of the state while "saying they had no interest in such improvements and in revenge for the debate on the negro subject of abolition." After the debate on the "slave question" came to an end, William Goode, the legislative leader of the eastern slaveholders, hectored Floyd, a westerner, in terms no less vitriolic and intransigent than southern sectionalists would employ against the North a generation later. Goode asserted that "the Eastern and Western [Virginian] people were not at all the same people, that they were essentially a different people, that they did not think alike, feel alike, and had no interests in common, that a separation of the State must ensue, and rather than have the subject of abolition again debated he would be glad for a separation. Both sides seem ready to separate the State if any one would propose it," Floyd reflected, adding prophetically, "I think that event from appearances highly probable."[63]

Note that Goode's Manichaean distinction between two peoples, two cultures, two irreconcilable societies, while explicitly grounded on attitudes regarding slavery, related exclusively to Virginians, and had no connection to northern antislavery agitation, indeed to anything northern at all. So great a cultural divide was not the result of historical antipathies between Cavaliers and Roundheads; it was created by nothing more than the Blue Ridge Mountains and a distinction in topography and soil. It is important to stress this point, and to bear it in mind when considering the later great national sectional crises and the historical explanations that have been offered for them.

To a significant extent, the Virginia slavery debates of 1831–32 recapitulated the political struggles of the state constitutional convention of 1829–30, in which the eastern slaveholding elite sought to maintain its disproportionate political power against a burgeoning, largely nonslaveholding trans-Appalachian population who perennially felt cheated of their fair share of state resources. Then, the issue of slavery had been muted, submerged beneath a mountain of oratory on the dangers of excessive democracy and political equality; now, it stood starkly illuminated as the basis of Southsiders' power, wealth, and influence—which they would not willingly surrender.

Just as the maintenance of southern influence within the federal congress required a disciplined and united southern front, so eastern influence within Virginia demanded as nearly solid a block of slaveholders as possible. Counting heads in January 1832, John Floyd estimated that the fate of an emancipation scheme rested on "about two votes which will depend upon the slave part of the state."[64] Under such circumstances, the pressure on individual eastern slaveholders to conform became overwhelming; the tolerance of dissent minimal; the pressure of doubt often unbearable. Those politicians and intellectuals who were willing to offer a bold defense of slavery found a ready and grateful audience. Defending slavery would "add much to my reputation," wrote John Thompson Brown, an ambitious Petersburg legislator. Although Brown himself only owned a single slave, and although, as he acknowledged, his Petersburg district was sharply divided on the question, this *arriviste* young politician recognized that a forthright stance in support of the institution would secure him the support and admiration of powerful slaveholding easterners who might be uncomfortable taking such a morally ambiguous position themselves.[65]

Significantly, Brown made no claim for slavery as a "positive good." On the contrary, he described it as an "evil,—the greatest, perhaps, that an angry Providence could inflict on a sinning people." It was an evil, however, which was "so interwoven" with the "habits and interests" of Virginians that nothing could be done to remove it.[66] On its face, this might appear to be a thoroughly indefensible and immoral argument; in fact, it represented a subtle appeal to a highly orthodox religious sentiment. The "sinning people" afflicted with the punishment of slavery were not Africans, Brown averred, but Virginians! All the dangers, moral compromises, and condemnations of a reproachful world occasioned by the bitter institution of slavery constituted chastisement justly inflicted by God for Virginia's transgressions. Thus Virginians' true obligation was to submit to its existence with Christian fortitude and resignation, to shoulder their duties to their slaves, and to eschew all efforts to root out the institution as rebellion against God and the righteousness of His judgments. In the masterful reinterpretation pioneered by Brown, self-interest was transformed into self-sacrifice; inaction became humble submission, and all of the dangers and drawbacks of slavery were converted into tests of Christian fortitude. Thus this "positive evil" defense of slavery, so contrary to common sense and so alien to modern sensibilities that it has been largely overlooked by historians, proved to be the ideal justification of the institution for a pious, God-fearing, and conscience-troubled people. This rationale, in one form or another, would rarely be absent from any later proslavery arguments and would become the most widely accepted defense of slavery in the South until the Civil War.

The claim that slavery was the cross the South must bear had appeal across the spectrum of slaveholding society. Fully compatible with the stern Calvinism of Presbyterians and hard-shell Baptists, it could be equally congenial to enthusiastic Arminianism or to the self-abnegating, sentimental Christianity that characterized the emerging "cult of domesticity." It spoke to the concerns of the philanthropist while it conformed to the most pessimistic principles of the skeptic; it could be squared with the doctrines of moral philosophy or the tenets of modern utilitarianism. Once it gained currency, indeed, the "slavery as cross" argument lent weight, even when unstated, to virtually every justification offered for the institution.

Nowhere was this clearer than in Thomas Roderick Dew's seminal "Abolition of Negro Slavery," later expanded as *Review of the Debate in the Virginia Legislature of 1831 and 1832*. Dew, a professor at William and Mary (and, like John Thompson Brown, a young and ambitious champion of Virginian interests), took each of the arguments of the emancipationists head-on in a masterpiece of rhetoric. Since he addressed such a broad spectrum of concerns, each with an argument finely honed to that particular point, Dew's essay is not noteworthy for its consistency either of theme or tone. Dew's principal target, as Alison Freehling has observed, is the colonization scheme; yet his broader aim was to refute all philanthropic objections to slaveholding. To those masters whose "conscientious scruples about the holding of slaves" might impel them to abandon Virginia for "a land where this evil does not exist," Dew replied by artfully condemning such conduct as "very unphilosophical," and "even immoral upon their own principles."

> Let us admit that slavery is an evil, and what then? why it has been entailed upon us by no fault of ours, and must we shrink from the charge which devolves upon us . . . ? No! this is not philosophy, it is not morality. . . . To the slave-holder has truly been intrusted the five talents. Let him but recollect the exhortation of the Apostle—'Masters, give unto your servants that which is just and equal; knowing that ye also have a master in Heaven'; and in the final day he shall have nothing on this score with which his conscience need be smitten, and he may expect the welcome plaudit—'Well done thou good and faithful servant, thou has been faithful over a few things, I will make thee ruler over many things; enter thou into the joy of the Lord.'[67]

Dew's tone of Christian philanthropy sounds sincere, or at least plausible and unsarcastic—in marked contrast to the open hostility of the *Richmond Enquirer*'s "American" essays or the extreme anticlericalism of Thomas Cooper. But Dew sounds equally convincing when adopting the pose of the utilitarian, the strict constructionist, the promoter of internal improvements. As William Freehling put it, later proslavery ideologues who hailed Dew's publication as "the most important book they had read" would "have to pick and choose among the professor's sentences" to construct a coherent defense of slavery out of it.[68] We should keep in mind that Dew's aim was to convince his fellow Virginians, by any and all means necessary and available—and not to convince us, the modern reader.

Dew's objectives in writing his essay were to prevent what he viewed as the likelihood of severe economic damage to Virginia by the precipitate removal of its slaves, to protect an interest in which he and his family had a substantial stake, and also, undoubtedly, to establish himself as a principal spokesman of Virginia's slaveholding classes and thereby to earn their patronage and support. As such, he naturally tried to espouse their interests as faithfully as he could. Ironically, however, Dew may have misjudged the tenor of the times. In compiling his essay, he wrote to Littleton Waller Tazewell requesting a copy of his 1828 senate report against colonization, which the Jacksonians had deployed so effectively in the campaign against Adams and Clay; Tazewell complied with the request, and his arguments formed one of the most powerful components of Dew's discourse. Yet Tazewell himself, regarding the Southampton insurrection as a lesson, had abandoned his strict states' rights stance and now favored federal assistance for emancipation and colonization; unfortunately, however, he did not inform Dew of his change of heart.[69]

In fact, despite the celebrity of Dew's bold, if ambiguous, defense of slavery, support for emancipation did not diminish precipitately in Virginia after 1832, as has generally been assumed. "The trouble with seeing Dew as [a] transitional [figure]," William Freehling notes, "is that no transition took place." Support for what Freehling calls the "conditional termination" of slavery continued unabated in Virginia, as the first bill to commit state funds to colonization on an annual basis, passed in 1833, attested.[70] Indeed, as Patricia E. P. Hickin suggests, the popular view of a dramatic Virginian about-face over slavery after 1832 probably owes more to changing attitudes about colonization in the face of radical abolitionist attacks than to any shift in the positions of Virginians themselves. "Before 1833 a colonizationist was usually considered an antislavery man; after Garrison's attack on the movement in 1832 colonizationists were considered almost proslavery. But that attitudes of the colonizationists themselves shifted at that time is dubious."[71]

If Hickin overstates the impact of the abolitionist critique, her basic point is still valid: many, perhaps most, Virginians remained committed to "conditional termination," accomplished through the emancipation and removal of slaves. Yet if colonization remained a serious option for many slaveholders, Garrison's and Dew's attacks did indeed reduce the available room to maneuver on the slavery issue and contributed to its polarization.

Of far greater immediate significance, however, was the national political situation. In January, 1832, in a breathtaking miscalculation, Vice President Calhoun arranged to cast the tie-breaking vote in the Senate to defeat Martin Van Buren's appointment as minister to Great Britain—thus transforming the politically unappealing former secretary of state into a Jacksonian martyr, assuring him of the vice presidential nomination and the nod as Jackson's anointed successor. The prospect of the Red Fox of Kinderhook in line for the White House, in place of Calhoun, was intolerable to many southerners. The following month, on March 3, Henry Clay introduced a memorial from residents of Kentucky urging federal support for colonization, a request that seemed increasingly feasible, and hence increasingly threatening to anti-emancipationists, as the extinction of the national debt and the prospect of a budget surplus grew imminent. "*The next question to be agitated, if we submit now*," warned an angry South Carolina anti-tariffite, "*will be the Colonization Act—another word for EMANCIPATION*."[72] By May, when the Jacksonians prepared to nominate Van Buren for vice president at their convention in Baltimore, many southern Republicans were ready to bolt the party; a few began making preparations to bolt the Union.

This renewed radicalism originated, naturally, with South Carolina. A year earlier, George McDuffie, Calhoun's chief lieutenant, had ratcheted up the rhetoric of nullification to a startling new level of malice, denouncing the "Union, such as the majority have made it," as "a foul monster" and deriding those Carolinians who urged caution as terrified by "mere nursery tales of raw-heads and bloody-bones." While Calhoun had been mortified by McDuffie's unauthorized outburst, privately lamenting it as in "every way imprudent," the vice president recognized that he could not repudiate it without fatally wounding his standing at home. Yet no amount of abstruse constitutional construction or tortuous political logic could disguise the fact that Calhoun's theorizing had brought him and his followers to the brink of disunion.

This position caused intense discomfort for virtually all of Calhoun's supporters outside of South Carolina. Indeed, Calhoun, in a bid to reassure his less radical followers, indicated a willingness to support Henry Clay for president over Jackson, despite the former's continuing support for colonization and internal improvements. Clay, in turn, muted his nationalism and expressed a new flexibility on such issues as the tariff, asserting that he was "ready to consent to any disposition that would rid the country from impending perils, if any disposal of myself could contribute to that most desirable result."[73]

Jackson's reelection, in any event, could not be impeded. On October 26, with the outcome of the election obvious, the South Carolina legislature approved a state convention to consider the tariff question. The convention, meeting the following month, drafted an Ordinance of Nullification declaring the tariff acts of 1828 and 1832 to be "null, void, and no law," and requiring all state officers to take an oath to uphold the ordinance.

Leading nullifiers, swayed perhaps by the soothing language emanating from congressional allies of the vice president–elect, Van Buren, and unwilling to believe that Andrew Jackson, a fellow southerner and Republican, would raise arms against a sovereign state, persuaded themselves that the president would blink, if not actually wink, at South Carolina's stance. After all, as Robert J. Turnbull reminded his listeners in a July Fourth oration, had not "twelve solemn treaties of the United States . . . besides several acts of Congress, actually [been] put aside by the State of Georgia, with as little ceremony as if they had been the edicts of the Khan of Tartary," and as little outcry from Jackson?[74]

Turnbull's analogy with Georgia was lethally flawed, since Jackson placed matters regarding Indian removal in an entirely separate category from constitutional issues, as his military career had often testified; ironically, the South Carolinians' greater consideration for Indian rights had led them to misconstrue Georgia's precedent. Rather, Jackson personalized the issue, as usual, viewing nullification simultaneously as a treasonous attack against himself and against the Union, which he believed he embodied. As Harry Watson has asserted, Jackson "reduced American politics to a simple dichotomy. . . . Citizens were for Andrew Jackson or against him."[75] The South Carolina nullifiers were against him, and he would crush them, just as he had crushed the Creeks at Horseshoe Bend.

The president's loyal lieutenants took the same view, and prepared to capitalize on Jackson's tremendous popularity to unify the nation and rid the party of its troublesome southern extremist wing once and for all. Shortly before the South Carolina Convention, Amos Kendall wrote to Van Buren to propose "a '*Union against Nullification*' of northern, middle, and western states. . . . No men who would rally around the union would be excluded from the pale of the friends to the administration." Although Van Buren's response was not recorded, Richard Latner is undoubtedly correct in thinking that Kendall's plan must have horrified him: "He must have detected in Kendall's words a hint of the old quest for Republican unanimity which, in Van Buren's opinion, had threatened to ruin the Republican party's principles and organization during the 1820s. Kendall's suggestions, therefore, jeopardized Van Buren's vision of a revitalized Jeffersonian party as well as his own political ambitions."[76]

Indeed, the nullification crisis placed Van Buren in the most difficult position he would face as a member of Jackson's administration. Although the New Yorker may have agreed in theory with the president's position, he was more sensitive to the dangers of Jackson's militant stance both because of his own interpretation of Republican doctrine and because of his intimate acquaintance with southern states' rights leaders. Most important, Van Buren recognized that if Jackson's political stature could weather an open breach with the militant South, Van Buren's—as a northerner and the principal engineer of the Tariff of Abominations—could not.[77]

The vice president–elect read the text of Jackson's nullification proclamation of December 10 with anguish and dismay. Old Hickory denounced South Carolina's course as not merely unconstitutional, but treasonous; his uncompromising defense of the Union could have been penned by a Hamiltonian Federalist—in fact, it had been drafted by the former Federalist secretary of state Edward Livingston, whom Van Buren's adviser C. C. Cambreleng derided as "the Montesquieu of the Cabinet."[78] But the sentiments were Jackson's own.

Jackson backed up his powerful words with military force, the more convincing because it was done without fanfare. He dispatched seven revenue cutters and a warship to Charleston harbor, and reinforced its forts with troops from Fortress Monroe under the command of General Winfield Scott. It was an uncanny dress rehearsal for the crisis of a generation later.

It is likely that no other contemporary political figure could have taken such a position. Old Hickory's stance was made politically feasible only because he had succeeded in convincing so many of his countrymen that his will and the welfare of the Union were identical—that Jackson and the Union were practically one and the same. The president's willingness to use force against South Carolina represented a clean break with the equivocation of recent years, and it largely defused the growing antipathy of northern Unionists to the federal government's coalition of "Southern planters and plain Republicans of the North" because it was clear that in Jackson's hands, protecting slavery did not mean endangering the Union, and defending the Union did not mean endangering slavery.

Much as the Maysville Road veto had fallen "upon the ears" of Old Republicans "like the music of other days," Jackson's message now revived the hopes of old Federalists. "The proclamation of Jackson was one of those measures which a federal saint of the old school has a right to call providential, and which a federal sinner may regard as most wonderfully opportune and happy for the Country," marveled that arch–"federal sinner" Harrison Gray Otis:

At this juncture, to see such a poser to the State rights sticklers from such a source was certainly a source of great joy and comfort to me. . . . Hundreds who [would] have dashed the cup in the face of Mr Clay or of an angel, have been compelled to hold their noses and swallow. And thousands who would have regarded the doctrines as diabolical if broached by a federalist, will now read, ponder & inwardly digest[,] and the true character of State sovereignty will come to be better understood. For my part I thank old Hicky, tho' I never conceived that such wholesome waters would come from a bitter fountain.[79]

Van Buren shuddered to see former Federalists such as Otis and Webster greeting Jackson's boldly nationalist pronouncements "with a sinister, all hail!"[80] While the president's advisers and congressional supporters drafted the Force Bill and its accompanying presidential message, Van Buren's backers in Congress frantically struggled to pass legislation to reduce the tariff and mollify South Carolina—to undo, in other words, the tariff schedule Van Buren had personally designed in 1828 to assail New England and its president. Van Buren came closer to an open breach with the president over the policy of force than over any other issue. "You will say I am on my old track again—caution—caution," he wrote Jackson anxiously.[81] For once the Old General ignored Van Buren's suggestions and imperiously demanded his support. "Why is your Legislature silent at the eventful crisis?" Jackson demanded. "Friendship with candor compels me to say to you that your friends are astonished at the silence of your Legislature and [it] gives rise to dark innuendos of your enemies that you command them, and are waiting the result of the Virginia Legislature." In response, at Van Buren's insistence (and against their wishes), the New York legislature passed a resolution on nullification—drafted by Van Buren—that offered only tepid support for the president's course and not only repudiated the doctrine of military force against a state, but also explicitly rejected the conception of the Union that Jackson had expressed in his nullification proclamation.

According to Van Buren, this maneuver was required to prevent the Jackson coalition in New York from being destroyed by the high-tariff party. But it seems as likely that Van Buren feared that Jackson would receive the state's support unmediated by Van Buren's Bucktails, drastically diminishing Little Van's influence in the state and rendering him useless to the Virginians—just as the "dark innuendos" of his enemies had hinted.

To underscore the pointed constitutional and political lesson of the nullification crisis for the president, Van Buren sent him a copy of the New York legislature's insulting resolution and informed him that he was the author.

"Without doubt," Van Buren asserted later, "General Jackson saw in the whole proceeding a realization of the apprehensions I had expressed to him . . . , and was well satisfied with the judicious way in which the difficulty had been disposed of in the New York Legislature."[82] Given Jackson's interpretation of the meaning of loyalty, this seems not altogether convincing. Still, he did not raise the issue again with his vice president.[83]

The danger of the situation, to Van Buren's ambitions if not to the Union, was genuine. On December 17, Webster had organized a mass meeting at Faneuil Hall in support of Jackson's proclamation, and had so far convinced the Massachusetts leadership to swallow their distaste for the president as to invite him, by resolution of the legislature, to visit the state. Such a development was astonishing in a state where "Old Hicky" had received barely 20 percent of the vote in the previous election. The senator was sounding the tune that Amos Kendall had earlier proposed, and that Van Buren most feared: a "Union against Nullification" transcending existing party boundaries. Webster, according to Sydney Nathans, "anticipated that nullification might produce a new alignment of men and parties. Crisis would unite the country; patriotism would supplant partisanship; former foes would see their common interest in the Union. If Jackson wanted a new era of good feelings, Webster had signaled that New England was ready to make its peace."[84] By his patriotic and conciliatory words, Webster was laying the groundwork for a new national coalition modeled on the ancient alliance of the sections during the Revolution to which he had recurred as a touchstone in his famous reply to Hayne: a coalition in which Webster's unparalleled power of language would be wedded to Jackson's decisive talent for action.

If Jackson and Webster were ready to link arms, however, Jacksonians in Congress were divided and diffident, unwilling to depart from the "principles of '98" to authorize force against a sovereign state, even at the cost of crossing their chief. Thus Webster moved to assemble a majority for the president's program from among the opponents of the president's own party. This is less surprising than it seems. The Jacksonians had always been more expendable than Jackson; the whole rationale of Van Buren's famous 1827 letter to Ritchie urging him to support the general was based on the fact that since Jackson was going to win anyway, it was essential that he do so at the head of a party controlled by the Albany-Richmond axis, rather than alone as a symbol of nationalism.[85]

The extraordinary Unionist extravaganza at Faneuil Hall demonstrated precisely what Jackson could achieve as pure symbol, unmoored from party and aligned with Webster, Otis, and company: the weak and parasitic Massachusetts Jacksonian Party under the leadership of Collector of Customs David Henshaw found itself completely marginalized when the patrician Massachusetts establishment suddenly hailed and endorsed the Old General. Henshaw's faction was then reduced to flirting with nullifiers and seeking shelter under the wings of Calhoun. Only with difficulty and embarrassment did they manage to scurry back under the Jackson standard after the eclipse of the South Carolina doctrine.[86]

This was precisely the scenario that Van Buren had long feared in New York, particularly since his enemies, the Clintonians, had, technically, the prior claim to support of Jackson. Thus Van Buren could only be relieved that he had retained control over New York politics, whatever the cost to his relationship with the president.

In the meantime, supporters of a lower tariff received support from an unlikely source: Henry Clay, the author of the "American System." Yet in fact, as Van Buren observed in retrospect, "Clay was, in the actual state of things, the only man who had it in his power to extricate" the South Carolinians. Van Buren had early realized that South Carolina and her allies would never acquiesce in a Jacksonian-sponsored tariff reduction bill such as the one offered by his New York colleague Gulian Verplanck; but, for its symbolic value, they would likely back a bill sponsored by Clay, the Father of Protectionism, himself.[87] Although the traditional historiography has portrayed Van Buren as surprised and outfoxed by the compromise on tariff reduction worked out by Clay and Calhoun, the New Yorker was in fact well apprised of the impending agreement, and exerted all of his political ability to help his supporters in Congress quietly shepherd the measure to passage, allowing Clay to claim any laurels for the compromise, and accepting criticism without complaint.[88] Van Buren considered the damage to his reputation, and even to his relations with the president, a small price to pay for averting political disaster at home. "Time and the virtue of the people will bring all right," he wrote soothingly to a top lieutenant. "More importantly, our Albany difficulties have all blown over and the stability of the party has been greatly increased by the abortive attempt to distract it."[89]

Clay's public efforts, and Van Buren's private ones, averted the possibility of civil war. The critical, last component involved voting on the tariff reduction *first*, then the Force Bill, and not vice versa, as Unionists insisted. This permitted South Carolina to save face and argue that the Force Bill was a dead letter because the state's demands had been met, which in turn freed other southerners to back the bill (or simply to abstain, as eight of them did). To militant southerners, the Force Bill constituted nothing less than a measure for total enslavement. If the bill had passed first, then any subsequent concession would have been equivalent to an indulgence granted to a slave, at the master's sufferance; by winning the concession on tariffs first, however, South Carolina could consider the federal government to have submitted to *it*, rendering the Force Bill meaningless—without "force." With most southerners simply abstaining, the bill passed by 32 to 1. Virginia's John Tyler cast the only vote against it—a vote that not only redeemed his earlier apostasy, when he leagued with the Adamsites to win John Randolph of Roanoke's congressional seat, but that likely earned him a place on the Whig presidential ticket of 1840 as the standard-bearer of the militant South.[90]

The peaceful outcome of the nullification crisis produced jubilation throughout the nation—although it was a joy tinged with danger, since each side claimed victory, interpreting the outcome in opposite ways. Van Buren worked hard to avert what from his perspective constituted the gravest threat—a new alignment of parties and sections based on an enduring Jackson-Webster entente. If the East-West alliance of Adams and Clay, the "blackleg and the puritan," had alarmed the Democrats, the prospect of a union between the Hero of New Orleans and the "Godlike" Daniel was infinitely more distressing. "Nothing lacks now to complete the love-feast but for Jackson and Webster to solemnize the coalition with a few mint-juleps," wrote Van Buren's New Hampshire ally Isaac Hill. Fortunately for the Democrats, however, the means of breaking up this ominous new coalition was readily at hand: "But never fear, my friend. This mixing of oil and water is only the temporary shake-up of Nullification. Wait till Jackson gets at the Bank again, and then the scalping knives will glisten once more."[91]

As Hill predicted, the battle over the United States Bank proved to be the rock on which the Jackson-Webster alliance shattered, although Van Buren brought himself to support the bank's destruction only with great reluctance, and ultimately at enormous cost.[92] Yet to a degree not recognized by historians, the powerful unionist coalition assembled to defeat nullification laid the groundwork for a deep structure of cooperation between Jacksonians and anti-Jacksonians[93] that transcended rancorous, even violent partisan debate over the recharter of the bank, the removal of the deposits, and other issues—indeed, that made national politics safe for such contests. Because Jackson had taken such a strong nationalist stance against nullification, going much farther than his critics (or, for that matter, his friends) ever dreamed that he would, they were ready to stand with him on issues relating to the protection of slavery, since it was now clear that Jackson would never allow such issues to threaten the Union. Henceforth, until the issue of Texas annexation renewed the controversy, the National Republicans and their successors the Whigs had every reason to support the administration in suppressing sectional controversies, and no desire to agitate slavery for its own sake. Thus the nullification controversy played an essential role in fostering the idea of a true party system, in effect sanctioning the "rise of a legitimate opposition," which Richard Hofstadter justly considered such a remarkable and uniquely American development.

Meanwhile, the Clay tariff compromise permitted South Carolina to claim a victory, and while nullification was stripped of much of its aura of virtuous republicanism in the larger South, it was not discredited in the eyes of true believers. Indeed, after the passage of the Force Bill, the South Carolina legislature promptly nullified that legislation as well—somewhat after the model of Missouri's nose-thumbing constitutional provisions of 1821. Calhoun, more prone to self-delusion than any other of our greatest statesmen, believed that he had brought both Clay and Jackson to heel (even though Benton recalled that the Carolinian had decided to accept Clay's compromise only after being informed that Jackson was preparing to have him arrested and tried for high treason).[94] Virginia's Floyd professed to believe that "South Carolina has triumphed and has saved the confederacy and the liberties of the country from the Tyrant's grasp, has saved us from a civil war. Yet we of the South know Jackson would have been defeated."[95] Thus there was some validity to Harrison Gray Otis's blunt objection to the tariff compromise: "Give alms to a beggar who wears a drawn sword in his hand and tell him if you please it is pour l'amour de Dieu, he will laugh in his sleeve and impute it to un peur de l'Epée, and he will never beg afterward without a sword. So it will be with the Cavaliers and Wrongheads of the South, who are all united against us."[96] Like the earlier compromises regarding Missouri, then, the Compromise of 1833 may have contained the seeds of its own destruction.

Still, it must have seemed, in the spring of that year, that the Union stood on firmer ground, with the slavery issue more effectively contained, than at any time since James Tallmadge introduced his portentous amendment to the Missouri statehood bill fourteen long years before. General Jackson's triumphal ride that June through the streets of Brahmin Boston, following the route where crowds had cheered Lafayette in 1824, and where, seven years before that, another Republican president, James Monroe, had received the adulation of Federalists and Republicans alike in a moving ritual of reconciliation, truly seemed to herald a new Era of Good Feelings—of a suitably restrained Bostonian variety. Josiah Quincy wittily captured the atmosphere of grudging admiration that the Old General evoked in Boston:

Mr. Daniel P. Parker, a well-known Boston merchant, had come to his window to catch a glimpse of the guest of the State, regarding him very much as he might have done some dangerous monster which was being led captive past his house. But the sight of the dignified figure of Jackson challenged a respect which the good merchant felt he must pay by proxy, if not in person. 'Do some one come here and salute the old man!' he suddenly exclaimed. And a little daughter of Mr. Parker was thrust forward to wave her handkerchief to the terrible personage whose doings had been so offensive to her elders.[97]

Seen up close, Jackson had the same effect on most Bostonians that he had had on the old Federalist Elijah Hunt Mills at the time of the general's first presidential campaign: "He is very mild and amiable in his disposition, of great benevolence, and his manners, though formed in the wilds of the West, exceedingly polished and polite."[98] Other New Englanders might have recalled Old Hickory's letter urging then-president Monroe to appoint Federalists to his administration—and forgotten that Jackson later denied writing it. Still others might have noted with new satisfaction the large number of ex-Federalists in the administration's ranks to which Webster had alluded in his exchanges with Hayne, who now looked more like pacesetters than apostates. On June 26, to the shock of many, Old Hickory appeared on the arm of Harvard president Josiah Quincy in the College Chapel to receive an honorary doctorate of laws. Indeed, these were astounding times.

WHILE ANDREW JACKSON traveled through New England, another figure whom many Americans would come to revile as a "dangerous monster" was embarking on a different pilgrimage. The day before Jackson arrived in Massachusetts, William Lloyd Garrison met with William Wilberforce, the patriarch of the British antislavery movement, at the aging philanthropist's country estate. On July 14, Garrison shared the podium of Exeter Hall with Daniel O'Connell, the great Irish reformer, where both denounced America for the sin of slavery in caustic and uncompromising terms. Within six weeks, Wilberforce was dead, with Garrison a mourner at his funeral in Westminster Abbey. A month later, the Emancipation Bill passed in Parliament, and British philanthropists turned with passion and zeal to the next stage of the struggle: the end of slavery in America.

With the abolition of West Indian slavery, the slavery issue in the United

States inevitably moved to a new and critical stage. It is hard to conceive of a single action that could have had more far-reaching effects on the slavery question in the United States than British abolition. Most accounts of the slavery question begin in 1831, with the appearance of Garrison's *Liberator*; yet the importance of that event is retrospective, a consequence of what happened in 1833. As we have seen in chapter 2, British criticism of slavery in the United States deeply afflicted many Americans, and may have led James Tallmadge to propose his amendment to the Missouri statehood bill. The attacks of the British reviewers had been neatly parried by Robert Walsh and others, however, with the countercharge of British hypocrisy. Now at last, Britain had risen to the challenge and had "torn off the manacles" of her slaves in earnest, thereby renewing the debate and redoubling the force of her objections.

Just as important, West Indian emancipation demonstrated for the first time that slavery could in fact be ended in orderly and legal fashion, without a "servile war" of retribution or the political abdication of the planters. No longer could apologists for slavery solemnly pronounce the institution a "necessary evil," unfortunate but ineradicable. At last, a modern society had eradicated it—not just any society, moreover, but Great Britain, America's chief exemplar of conservatism and moderation, the principal arbiter of bourgeois taste and opinion and the model for the aristocratic aspirations of northern and southern gentry alike. West Indian emancipation struck a body blow to the chivalric self-image of many Anglophilic southerners, while giving sanction to Anglophilic northerners to take previously unthinkable antislavery actions. The vehemence of the southern anti-abolitionist backlash, which Charles Sellers and others have dubbed the "Great Reaction," must be examined in the light of the high moral authority—and respectability—lent to antislavery by its aristocratic British credentials.[99]

Radical abolitionism, then, viewed in an international context, appeared to be not quite so "radical." British periodicals such as the *Edinburgh Review*, which had helped to launch the slavery controversy of 1819, remained staunchly abolitionist, while continuing to attract more American readers than domestic journals, including the *North American Review*. As C. Duncan Rice notes, "It was still acceptable to ape British attitudes in the world of letters, and these journals were genuine culture carriers, with a disproportionate role in forming American opinion."[100]

Why, then, with this gilt-edged British imprimatur, did immediate abolitionism not sweep New England and the "Universal Yankee Nation"? In the first place, few even in the North could yet contemplate slave emancipation without slave removal. British abolitionists, influenced by the arguments of the black American minister Nathaniel Paul and others, consternated American humanitarians by denouncing their cherished philanthropy, the American Colonization Society, as a "diabolical" sham. William Lloyd Garrison had secured the signatures of Wilberforce, Zachary Macaulay, Thomas Fowell Buxton, and most of the other major British abolitionists (the single notable exception being Thomas Clarkson) on a protest that publicly repudiated colonization as a "humbug" designed to bolster slavery.[101] Whether the charge was accurate or not for the movement as a whole, individual colonizationists understandably took umbrage at this characterization and at Garrison's extravagant and lurid denunciations, and many, including such champions of Missouri restriction as James Gordon Bennett and James Watson Webb, became implacable opponents of abolitionism on personal grounds.

The second obstacle to immediatism sprang from the revival of unionism embodied in the Jackson-Webster entente discussed above, and from the structure of the emerging two-party system that this new nationalism made practicable. After his break with Jackson over the Bank of the United States, Webster had made up his mind to run for president in 1836; consequently, he now shared with his northern Democratic opponent Martin Van Buren an overriding need to reassure potential southern voters of his "soundness" on slavery. Additionally, British abolition, and more pointedly, British involvement in the cause of antislavery in America, offered former Federalists an opportunity to display their "independence" from the influence of the mother country by denouncing British "meddling" and interference with "American institutions." In August 1835, while the English antislavery activist George Thompson lectured throughout New England, Harrison Gray Otis assembled yet another remarkable bipartisan Unionist meeting in Faneuil Hall—an event in many ways an exact replica of the anti-nullification meeting of three years earlier, except that this time the dignitaries met to condemn abolition, not nullification.

The exigencies of politics made it expedient for northern politicians to conflate the two movements as similarly un-American. Jackson's unshakeable nationalism enabled patriots to portray both abolitionism and nullification as lethal threats to the Union and all it stood for. The caustic temper and inflammatory rhetoric of the most militant abolitionists seemed almost to validate this linkage, and to make it palatable to the public at large. The proslavery editor Duff Green, who had dreaded nullification and the unyielding assertion of federal power it had provoked—which he feared would be turned against slavery—breathed a sigh of relief when more extreme views gained influence within the antislavery camp: "When it began to fall into the hands of the religious fanatics—we thought nothing of it," he later asserted. Green recognized at once that politicians would flee the antislavery standard to avoid the taint of extremism: "Confined to religious and philanthropic fanaticism, we were content to let it [antislavery] rest in obscurity."[102]

By 1833, then, both Jacksonians and anti-Jackson unionists had developed an approach to the slavery issue that was seemingly capacious and flexible enough to weather almost any storm. By no means do I wish to suggest that the political struggles of the mid-1830s over other issues were not genuine; indeed, the battle between the president and Congress over the Bank of the United States assumed an insurgent character not seen since the War of 1812—and one, moreover, that dramatically transcended sectional allegiances. Rather, the partisan peace declared over slavery permitted the combatants to wage bank warfare without quarter, since the underlying fabric of the Union would not be endangered thereby.[103] Indeed, as Van Buren had stressed to Thomas Ritchie in 1827,[104] sectional ties could only be strengthened by partisan combat because the "unit cohesion" developed by party faithful of different regions under the fire of a hard-fought national campaign would help to cement ties of sympathy and loyalty that would provide valuable insurance against the dangers of abolition and secession.

American political leaders, then, had every incentive, and took every opportunity, to suppress the slavery question. But they could not do it. Their failure was not that of a "blundering generation," blind to the dangers of extremism; rather, the issue exploded in spite of their extensive and untiring efforts. In the bipartisan campaign to stifle antislavery agitation, defenders of the Union proved willing to sacrifice many of their citizens' most cherished liberties: freedom of speech, of assembly, of the press, and the right of petition; freedom from unreasonable search and seizure; habeas corpus and trial by jury; even the *lex suprema* of nineteenth-century America, the sanctity of private property, as the homes and businesses of free blacks, abolitionists, and their "fellow travelers," were destroyed by riotous mobs with the approbation, and even the leadership, of the constituted authorities.[105] More injurious still, the foundational tenet of the Declaration of Independence that "all men are created equal" and, eventually, the biblical principle of mankind's common paternity would come under fire in the effort to save the Union by protecting slavery.

Ultimately, however, for all their lasting damage, these measures proved unavailing. Just as southern anti-Federalists, Old Republicans, and states' rights radicals had feared, the structure of the American republic under the federal Constitution proved to be incompatible with the protection of slavery. This incompatibility was probably not intentional, and possibly not inevitable. Perhaps the chartering of the first Bank of the United States or the constitutional interpretations of John Marshall may have been essential to make it so, as the Old Republicans suspected, or the massive political disequilibrium engendered by Jefferson's purchase of Louisiana, which the Federalists would never have suspected; but in any event it was so. Even if the civil liberties enshrined in the Bill of Rights and undermined by the police requirements of a slave system had been discarded; even if northerners had been willing to acquiesce peacefully in all of the coercive measures demanded of them by slaveholders (and many of them were), considerations not of conscience but of raw political power intrinsic to the federal system would have continually agitated the slavery question. Because of the disproportionate growth of the free population in the North, the South could not renounce the delicate compromises adopted to create the Union—most notably the three-fifths clause, the "federal number." The admission of each new slave state rankled all but the most diehard northern doughfaces, since policies that promoted slavery harmed northerners' interests, all questions of morality aside.[106] Each time the issue of political power was raised again, moreover, the moral challenge resurfaced as well.

Given this fact, the passage of the first Missouri Compromise inexorably tilted the balance of the Constitution in favor of freedom. It did this both substantively, and more importantly, symbolically. Substantively, of course, the Compromise placed a check on the growth of new slave states, thus limiting the growth of slaveholders' political power. While this limitation could be skirted, as the annexation of Texas would demonstrate, as long as the 36°30' boundary remained in place, it would be only a matter of time before free states outnumbered slave states and began to reshape the political calculus.

The substantive power of the Compromise was limited. As its critics had noted from the outset, it was no more than an ordinary piece of legislation, passed by a mere handful of votes and objectionable (for different reasons) to northerners and southerners alike. It was hardly to be expected that such a slender reed could sustain the weight of the Union permanently. Symbolically, however, the Compromise took on an importance, almost amounting to sacrality, second only to the Constitution itself: it came to be viewed as a pledge of faith between the sections on which the Union rested.

When the Compromise line became inconvenient, it was not so much abrogated as annihilated: first repealed by Congress and then, for good measure, nullified by the Supreme Court—even as the racialist interpretation of the second Compromise, denying those of African ancestry the possibility of citizenship, became enshrined as the supreme law of the land. For a brief moment, the entirely racialized republic held sway, and the Compromise was dead. But in fact it proved to be the case, to paraphrase Martin Van Buren, that there is such a thing as killing a law too dead.

✦

IN HIS PATHBREAKING 1965 study, *The Political Economy of Slavery*, Eugene Genovese argued "that so intense a struggle of moral values" as that conducted over slavery "implies a struggle of world views and that so intense a struggle of world views implies a struggle of worlds."[107] To the contrary, we have seen in the preceding chapters that the struggle over slavery during this period did not constitute, in contemporaries' terms, a "struggle of moral values." That may have come later; but in 1819, and to a large extent even in 1835, northerners and southerners approached the problem of slavery with a set of values that, while nowhere uniform, shared much in common across the sections.

If northerners and southerners lived in different worlds, it was the lived reality of southern life and the power of slavery as an interest that accounted for the greater part of the difference, not the ideology of slavery. Some southerners constructed a worldview to explain and accommodate the slavery-based world in which they lived, not the other way around. More significantly perhaps, some northerners, unaffected by the daily reality of slavery, exploited the South's dependence on slavery for their own political gain, and fostered the development of proslavery ideologies designed to link northern and southern "plain"—white—"republicans" within the iron bands of party fellowship and white supremacy.

In actuality, then, northerners and southerners shared the same intellectual and moral worlds, just as they shared the same nation. The contradiction of slavery was an American contradiction, not a southern peculiarity. The southern people "are just what we would be in their situation," as Abraham Lincoln wisely observed a generation later. "If slavery did not now exist amongst them, they would not introduce it. If it did now exist amongst us, we should not instantly give it up."[108] Thus the responses developed to deal with slavery were American responses, and their effects were effects on America. The "struggle of worlds" was not a struggle between North and South, but a struggle between a world in which slavery constituted an evil, an anomaly, and flaw to repair, and one in which the institution could be conceived to coexist peacefully with liberty and justice. In a sense, the conflict could be regarded as a clash between David Walker's world and Daniel Webster's.

Unfortunately, while no political compromise could save slavery, neither did the political system abolish it. Thus slavery remained a political cancer that could be eradicated only by violence. The destruction of slavery was undertaken as a measure of war. While emancipation rectified the nation's greatest constitutional anomaly, it never received the kind of sustained debate and legislative imprimatur that it did in Great Britain and elsewhere. The most potent argument offered for emancipation in 1863 would be military necessity; the moral arguments would filter in around the edges. It is true that a providential interpretation of American history and mission returned explosively for a time with the onset of the Civil War, especially through the compelling oratory of Abraham Lincoln. But this attitude, though embodied in law in the Thirteenth and Fourteenth Amendments, did not long survive the crisis; it would not be until the middle of the twentieth century that the seeds implanted in this period would begin to flower after a hard winter.

Significantly, then, the noxious arguments developed in defense of slavery during the previous thirty years were never formally refuted, only rendered obsolete by force. Indeed, with the end of the Civil War, a new word, "racism," made its debut. It was a new term formalizing an old, but newly liberated philosophy. While slavery existed, the institution itself served as the most potent refutation of the "positive good" doctrine; paradoxically, once the rebuke of slavery was removed, the elaboration of pernicious theories of race, nourished by nostalgia and honed to a hard edge by the horror of war, could grow unchecked. It remained—indeed, it still remains—for later generations to repair completely the damage done by the failure of the early American republic to live up to its own ideals with respect to slavery.

EPILOGUE : KANSAS

ON DECEMBER 22, 1853, the *Illinois State Register* offered a suggestion concerning the future of slavery in the Nebraska Territory, an issue then being considered by the U.S. Senate's Committee on the Territories: "We believe they [the people of Nebraska] may be safely left to act for themselves. . . . The territories should be admitted to exercise, as nearly as practicable, all the rights claimed by the States, and to adopt all such political regulations and institutions as their wisdom may suggest."[1]

A close observer of territorial policy might have raised an eyebrow at the pronouncement of the *Register*, which closely reflected the outlook of Illinois senator Stephen A. Douglas, chairman of the Committee on the Territories. After all, Nebraska fell entirely within the boundaries of the Louisiana Territory north of the parallel of 36°30', and hence, by the terms of the Missouri Compromise of 1820, was permanently rendered off-limits to slavery. In 1849, Douglas had described the Compromise as "canonized in the hearts of the American people, as a sacred thing, which no ruthless hand would ever be reckless enough to disturb."[2] The compromise line had received categorical reaffirmation a year later in the settlement of the Compromise of 1850, of which Douglas had been a key architect; and even the staunchest promoter of the expansion of slavery, Missouri senator David Atchison, conceded that the Compromise line, together with the Northwest Ordinance of 1787, barred the institution from Nebraska: "There is no remedy for them. We must submit to them. I am prepared to do it."[3] There seemed to be no basis, then, for regarding the status of slavery in the territory to be open to consideration.

And yet within six months, the Missouri Compromise was dead. With its repudiation, the entire discourse of accommodation that had dominated American politics for three decades was destroyed, the authority of conservative northern leaders was shredded, and the stability of established institutions was undermined. It is asserted by many historians that the repeal of the Missouri Compromise made the Civil War inevitable, and this is likely true. More than this, however, the abrogation of the Compromise itself brought "the Union as it was" to an end, and cleared the boards for a return to first principles and a rewriting of the meaning of America. In reality, then, the impact of the repeal of the Missouri Compromise was more sweeping than its passage.

It is worth reviewing the career of the Compromise in the thirty years since we left it. A controversial measure, passed by the slenderest of majorities and regarded as deeply flawed even by its supporters, the Missouri Compromise had proved surprisingly durable. It passed its first test in 1836, when southerners filibustered the admission of Michigan until Arkansas had been let in as a slave state, reprising in miniature the epic stalemate of 1820–21. The Compromise line endured the stalemate over the Wilmot Proviso and the expansion of territory acquired out of the victory over Mexico, when southern leaders demanded the extension of the 36°30' line to the Pacific (and antislavery activists opposed it). Most recently, the Compromise line had passed through the torturous political gauntlet of 1850, apparently affirmed by all who still favored the Union.

If there were those, in both the proslavery and abolitionist camps, who regarded the compromises of 1850 as a shameful submission on basic questions of principle, they shared as well a recognition that they were beaten and that the nation had embraced the outcome. Abolitionists in particular felt stricken by the general acceptance in the North of the Fugitive Slave Law, which overturned state personal liberty laws and put the federal government in the business of slave catching. Harriet Beecher Stowe lamented to a sibling about the "incredible, amazing, mournful!!" fact that "folks in general" and "Boston ministers universally, except [her brother] Edward," had counseled obedience to the unjust — and un-Christian — law.[4] The overwhelming electoral victory two years later of Franklin Pierce on a platform of unqualified support for the Compromise of 1850 seemed to put the issue beyond the reach of political review. In the words of Moorfield Storey, "Indeed, it was the darkest moment of the struggle, not because the slave power was then most aggressive, but because there was the least resistance to slavery and the conscience of the country seemed dead."[5]

Through all the travails that marked the road to its passage, the first Missouri Compromise preserved, though tarnished and qualified, the principle that freedom was national, slavery local. As Congress filled in the final blanks on the map of the United States, this was precisely the problem for proslavery men: they could see clearly the inexorable tipping of the balance toward freedom as the remaining territories entered the Union. Some slave-holders looked toward the South, to Cuba, Sonora, and Nicaragua, where filibusterers sought to conquer colonies ripe for annexation as slave states; a few, like Kentucky senator Archibald Dixon, continued to hope that the Missouri Compromise line could be overturned and new slave states set up north of it. Given the fervor of public opinion against reopening the slavery controversy, however, as well as northern sensitivity to the designs of the "slave power," no southerner could have reopened this issue with even the most minuscule chance of success. Thus it fell to a northerner to take the ominous step.

Like its passage, the abrogation of the Missouri Compromise was by no means inevitable, and depended to a significant degree on a single man. The tale of the repeal of the Missouri Compromise is ridden with self-dealing, political bullying, hypocrisy, obfuscation, and moral obtuseness—most of which can be laid at the door of Illinois senator Stephen A. Douglas. The proximate cause of Douglas's move to annul the Compromise seems to have been his desire to secure Chicago as the eastern terminus of the Pacific railroad, a goal intended both to advance the prosperity of his Illinois constituents and to enhance the value of his extensive Chicago real estate holdings, and one that he could not achieve without southern support. His larger purpose was to promote the white settlement of the West and to overcome the obstacle presented by the resident Indians.[6]

Moreover, Douglas shared with a substantial minority of his countrymen—including his party's founder, Martin Van Buren—a signal incapacity to comprehend the crucial moral dimension of the slavery issue. Beyond this, Douglas even lacked the ability to grasp, as a purely practical matter, the political salience of its importance to others.[7]

The Democratic leaders of the 1850s forgot the central lesson learned by their predecessors during the Missouri controversy: the idea of America contained a fundamental threat to slavery. Defending the institution required eternal vigilance in hedging, circumscribing, and qualifying the dangerous concepts of liberty and equality implicit in the American project. The architects of the Second Party System had erected a government of almost overwhelming stasis, designed at all costs to preserve "the Union as it is." That Union, founded on an unsteady and impracticable system of shared sovereignty between the central government and the states, increasingly lacked any guiding and overarching principle beyond the continuation of its own ever-more-attenuated existence. To his credit perhaps, Stephen A. Douglas balked at the crabbed, reactionary approach to governing that characterized the national platforms of both major parties and that had held the Union, such as it was, together. The promise of America was so great, the glory to be won and the worlds to be conquered so glittering, that it seemed inconceivable to Douglas that his undeniable genius as a politician should be bottled up in maintaining sectional gridlock and the ritual of "frowning indignantly" on those who would upset the status quo.

To evade the crushing antinomy of slavery versus freedom, Douglas sought to displace it, by means of rhetorical splendor and political sleight of hand, with the grander and more stirring theme of the West, the majestic synthesis in which, presumably, the irresolvable conflict of North and South would be dissolved. This "growing, increasing, swelling power" represented "the hope of this nation," Douglas insisted; it was "the resting place of the power that [was] not only to control, but to save, the Union."[8] The allure of Douglas's stratagem was undeniable, and remains strong, as countless succeeding political speeches, a once-dominant and still-flourishing school of historiography, and a vast deluge of popular culture, from dime novels to movie westerns to presidential photo-ops, testify. But Douglas's hope of supplanting the deadlock over slavery with the drama of the West was plainly doomed to failure. The West remained, as it had been since the nation's birth, the inevitable battleground of the slavery controversy, not the alternative to it.

Astoundingly, Douglas initially seemed to believe that he could evade the obstacle of the Missouri Compromise without anyone noticing. Into the bill for the organization of the Nebraska Territory, submitted by Iowa senator A. C. Dodge on December 14, 1853, Douglas inserted provisions to divide the territory in two, the southern half to be called Kansas, and to treat the issue of slavery in the new territories exactly as it had been with Utah and New Mexico—where the Compromise of 1850 left the question to squatter sovereignty. The operation of the Fugitive Slave Law in Kansas and Nebraska was also specifically, and superfluously, reaffirmed.

These amendments, reported on January 4, 1854, alarmed northerners while merely whetting the appetite of the South for further concessions. Six days later, a remarkable notice appeared in the administration organ, the *Washington Globe*, stating that through a "clerical error," a portion of Douglas's bill had been omitted from the official record, and that the bill should have stated that "all questions pertaining to slavery in the Territories, and in the new states to be formed therefrom" were "to be left to the people residing therein, through their appropriate representatives."[9] This language still left southerners unsatisfied, since it would leave the slavery prohibition intact during the territorial period, keeping it out in fact if not in principle. Finally, on January 18, during a carriage ride, Kentucky's proslavery Whig senator Archibald Dixon convinced Douglas to eliminate the Missouri Compromise line entirely, although the Little Giant acknowledged with understatement that doing so would "raise a hell of a storm."[10]

The storm broke immediately. If, for Douglas, the repeal of the Missouri Compromise had been a pragmatic measure designed to surmount a political impasse, for many northerners it constituted "a gross violation of a sacred pledge; . . . a criminal betrayal of precious rights." Grasping the rhetorical and the political initiative, antislavery leaders seized the opportunity to frame the terms of the debate. Ohio senator Salmon P. Chase, after persuading Douglas to delay the introduction of his Kansas-Nebraska Bill (on the pretext of requiring more time to study it), preempted Douglas's opening speech on the measure by joining with five other antislavery leaders to release to the newspapers one of the most devastating propaganda broadsides in American history.

The "Appeal of the Independent Democrats," authored by Chase and his fellow Ohio senator Joshua Giddings, was perfectly calibrated to stoke the sense of outrage ignited by the proposed abrogation of the Compromise. In language reminiscent of Cicero's *Catiline Orations* and the prophetic books of the Bible, the "Appeal" denounced the Kansas-Nebraska Bill and sought to recall America to its historical and sacred destiny as the standard-bearer of liberty. Without identifying Douglas by name, the authors arraigned the "servile demagogues" who conspired to "extinguish Freedom and establish Slavery in the States and Territories of the Pacific, and thus permanently subjugate the whole country to the yoke of a Slaveholding despotism." Like ancient Israel, the United States had a central role to play in the drama of "the regeneration of the human race." Echoing Douglas's rhetoric of the boundless West, the "Appeal" offered an equally majestic vision of the enormous Nebraska Territory, extolling its fertility and grandeur, but reframing it in biblical terms. In this formulation, the pledges of the Missouri Compromise assumed the character of a holy covenant, while the western territories symbolized the Promised Land, which could only be settled by a righteous people. Kathleen Diffley has accurately described the "Appeal of the Independent Democrats" as "couched in the . . . form of the Puritan jeremiad, which reminded Americans of the Divine mission and promise while inspiring them to keep the faith."[11] It is equally modeled after Moses's final address to the children of Israel in Deuteronomy, which rehearses the history of God's chosen people, recalling the exodus from Egypt, the covenant at Sinai, the many episodes of the Israelites' apostasy and of God's constancy. As with many sermons and broadsides from the Revolutionary period, the "Appeal of the Independent Democrats" spoke to Americans in the familiar and demanding language of their faith.

In its recounting of legislative history, however, the "Appeal," in contrast to the confusion of earlier allusions that represented the Missouri Compromise as an uncomplicated antislavery victory, presented the facts of the Missouri statehood controversy with clarity and precision. The authors correctly noted that the North gave way to permit Missouri's entry, and that the state could never have achieved admission with slavery without barring the institution from the Louisiana Purchase north of 36°30'. The careful exposition of the "Appeal" set the tone for a raft of other speeches, pamphlets, and sermons against the Kansas-Nebraska Bill, nearly all of which offered detailed reviews of the legislative drama of 1819–21. Even more telling, the ensuing months saw the republication, often without introduction or other comment, of speeches and pamphlets from the original Missouri debates. The past became the present.[12]

As the Kansas-Nebraska Bill recentered the Missouri Compromise in a new perspective (in fact, its original one), it also cast the intervening compromises in a new light as well. It made all past compromises seem obsolete at best, corrupt at worst, and transformed their northern supporters from saviors of the Union to dupes of the South. From this new vantage point, Kansas-Nebraska offered antislavery Unionists the opportunity for redemption from a series of concessions, including the two Missouri Compromises themselves, which had diluted the faith of the covenant.

Northern party leaders had endorsed the Fugitive Slave Law with some discomfort as a necessary sacrifice of their consciences (and, incidentally, of the basic rights and security of free blacks) to the higher good of the Union. Now it seemed a scoundrel's bargain. Harriet Beecher Stowe's *Uncle Tom's Cabin* (1852) had provided the text by which to interpret the statute; with the passage of the Kansas-Nebraska Bill, the countervailing gloss of Webster's Seventh of March Speech lost much of its luster. Nor were politicians the only group in need of absolution; the clergy, a stronger bulwark of the northern establishment, had gone still farther out on the limb of expediency, and much of their flock had followed them. The "Independent Democrats" extended them an invitation to redeem themselves: "We implore Christians and Christian Ministers to interpose. Their Divine Religion requires them to behold in every man a brother, and to labor for the Advancement and Regeneration of the Human Race."[13] In fact, it was Stowe who took up the call and applied her tenacity, stamina, and influence to secure the signatures of more than 3,000 ministers—over three-fourths of the total number of clergymen in New England—on a petition denouncing the Kansas-Nebraska Act and the abrogation of the Missouri Compromise.[14]

As the frigid edifice of New England politics started to crack, the authority and legitimacy of the old order rapidly succumbed to a situation it could not control. The unraveling of Edward Everett, Massachusetts's senior senator and leading conservative, is diagnostic of the trend. The inheritor of the mantle of Daniel Webster, both as orator and as servant of the New England cotton aristocracy, Everett was not only a politician but also the dominant figure in establishment New England cultural life. An ordained Unitarian clergyman, a former president of Harvard, a former governor of Massachusetts, and a founding editor of the *North American Review*, Everett had stood as Boston's acknowledged arbiter of correct opinion for more than a generation. Like Webster before him, Everett viewed the interests of the New England gentry as inextricably tied to those of the South, and conducted his politics accordingly; but unlike Webster, he lacked the outsized personality to lend his accommodationism the aura of statesmanship. Since 1826, when he had pledged his readiness to "buckle a knapsack on my back, and put a musket on my shoulder" to put down a slave insurrection, Everett had battled the reputation of being an over-willing hireling of the slave power.[15]

The Kansas-Nebraska Bill drove a wedge between the South and the New England Whig establishment, and required Everett to break with one or the other. This was agony for him. Ever the Unitarian divine, he dreaded conflict and confrontation. As the only northern Whig on the Senate Committee on the Territories, chaired by Douglas, Everett found himself the object of unwanted, even humiliating, attention. "Had a conversation with Judge Dawson of Georgia on the subject of the Nebraska Bill," Everett confided to his diary. "I told him that I apprehended it would be impossible for me to vote for it. He intimated that one great object for which it was brought forward was 'to put me to the test.'"[16] Demonstrating both his insecurity and self-importance, Everett seems to have taken the Georgia senator completely seriously.

But if Everett could not go so far as to pass the doughface litmus test of subservience to the South, he also failed, in rather emblematic fashion, to stand up for the principles of the North. On February 8, he delivered a passionless but effective speech that dismantled Douglas's claim that the measures of 1850 had superseded the Missouri Compromise. Yet three weeks later, when the Senate voted on the bill itself, Everett, exhausted and indisposed, was absent. Although there is no reason to disbelieve his assertions that he was sick, that he would have voted against the bill, and that, as he well understood, it would have passed with or without his vote, his absence from the post of duty encapsulated his failure of leadership, and by extension, the dereliction of his cotton-afflicted class. Charles Eliot Norton passed on the assessment of Everett that he overheard from an omnibus rider: "He hasn't got backbone enough to be sexton of a church."[17]

Everett had an opportunity for at least partial redemption a few weeks later, when he was chosen to submit the petition, organized by Harriet Beecher Stowe, of New England clergymen against the Kansas-Nebraska Act. Stunned, however, by the barrage of outrage that greeted him from Douglas and the act's other supporters, he appeared to apologize and backpedal, earning himself the contempt of every side. Browbeaten and battered, he resigned his seat and returned to Boston exhausted and disgraced, a living symbol of the collapse of the old order.[18]

The institution of Congress as a whole squandered much of its remaining authority and legitimacy in the squalid bullying and deal-making of the Nebraska debates. As in 1820, the debate arrayed a nearly unanimous northern public against a partially divided South—important leaders such as Thomas Hart Benton and Sam Houston, and influential newspapers in Louisville, New Orleans, Raleigh, and Washington, D.C., all opposed the bill.[19] In contrast to the Missouri question, however, it seems safe to say that few northern supporters of the Kansas-Nebraska Bill were likely to harbor any beliefs that they were secretly engaged in a selfless effort to preserve the Union. The records of debate as recorded by John Cook Rives in the *Congressional Globe* were scandalous enough in their litany of abuse, rancor, and meanness; reporters in the gallery, however, intimated that the official version had considerably cleaned up the violent, boozy tirades that passed for the legislative process on the floors of the House and Senate. The magisterial Congress of Webster, Clay, and Calhoun, though only a few short years past, now seemed like a figment of the imagination.

For his part, the president, through his catastrophic mishandling of the distribution of offices, had already angered the political professionals and discredited his administration with the public, underscoring the primacy of spoils over principle that characterized national party politics. Pierce's subservience to Douglas in the Kansas-Nebraska matter fatally undermined the president's remaining reputation as a leader, and a nation that had handed him an overwhelming mandate to govern now counted down the months until the end of his administration.

It would not be fair to blame Douglas's Kansas-Nebraska Act for the delegitimization of most of the nation's chief institutions, for, as the preceding review demonstrates, the process of internal decay was in most cases well under way long beforehand. There is no doubt, however, that the measure accelerated the process and brought the rot into the light. In this sense, then, Douglas must be viewed as a kind of anti-Clay, applying the same gifts of persuasion, risk-taking, calculation, and brilliant leadership to the work of destruction that Clay had employed in pacification.

As the vote to annul the Missouri Compromise drew near, Charles Sumner, in a speech later called "The Landmark of Freedom," adopted a Dickensian turn in describing the Kansas-Nebraska Bill as "at once the worst and the best bill on which Congress has ever acted." It was the worst bill, of course, because of the present victory it lent to slavery; but it was at the same time the best bill, "for it annuls all past compromises with slavery, and *makes all future compromises impossible*. Thus it puts freedom and slavery face to face, and bids them grapple. Who can doubt the result?" With remarkable confidence, Sumner foretold the ultimate meaning of the vote: "It opens wide the door of the future, when, at last, there will really be a North, and the slave power will be broken; when this wretched despotism will cease to dominate over our Government, no longer impressing itself upon every thing at home and abroad; when the national Government shall be divorced in every way from slavery; and, according to the true intention of our fathers, freedom shall be established by Congress everywhere, at least beyond the local limits of the States."[20]

While this dishonorable drama was coming to a close on the floor of the House, an unparalleled demonstration of the power of the proslavery order was unfolding in the streets of Boston. For most Americans, the Fugitive Slave Act had an abstract, even literary quality: they were most likely to have encountered its effects in Stowe's *Uncle Tom's Cabin*. In 1851, a group of blacks in Boston had rescued a fugitive slave with the aptly biblical name of Shadrach, an episode that had caused an uproar on the floor of Congress; but in the past three years, the law had operated in the Massachusetts capital without incident. The show of force that descended on Boston in May 1854 to enforce the rendition of Anthony Burns, a Kentucky runaway, was unlike anything seen in the city since the British occupation at the start of the American Revolution.[21]

In immediate terms, the Pierce administration's imposition of military force on the citizenry of Boston was symptomatic of the unraveling of New England's ties of allegiance to the federal government. On a more profound level, however, Boston's confrontation with federal power marked a ritual return to the origin point of the nation, the moment when it had established its existence through bloodshed.

Organizers understood the connection perfectly. A handbill posted in the city exhorted "Men of Boston! Sons of Otis, and Hancock, and the 'Brace of Adamses'!" to ensure that "Massachusetts Laws are not outraged with your consent. See to it that no Free Citizen of Massachusetts is dragged into Slavery, WITHOUT TRIAL BY JURY! '76!"[22] The whole achievement of the Revolution was compressed into the two numerals of that abbreviated date.

By a remarkable conjunction, the simultaneous unfolding of two great dramas—the struggle over the Kansas-Nebraska Bill in the House of Representatives and the occupation of Boston in preparation for the rendition of Anthony Burns—saw the attention of the nation focused precisely on the ultimate end of the first and second Missouri Compromises, the first affirming freedom as the essential national principle, the second undercutting that affirmation by excluding Africans and their descendants from its compass.

Although a few southerners still believed that slavery would never find safety within the confines of the Union, and some abolitionists continued to call for "no union with slaveholders," these positions were rapidly losing ground. Far more prevalent were the views of those Americans who saw the national union as the vehicle for their goals, and foresaw a coming struggle for the power to control the institutions of the state. At the same time, massive waves of Catholic immigration had led to an upsurge of nativist political activity that sharpened nationalist sentiment and heightened northern anger at the perceived corruption of the political status quo. As the nature of the political game shifted from maintaining the Union to a sectional struggle for control of the government, the Second Party System became obsolete and quickly crumbled.

With the system of national parties in disarray, a deeper organizing principle reasserted itself. It was the full flowering of the "secret" that John Quincy Adams said the Missouri conflict had disclosed: an alignment between the Northeast and the West into "a new party ready formed, terrible to the whole Union, but portentously terrible to the South—threatening in its progress the emancipation of all their slaves, threatening . . . that Southern domination which has swayed the Union for the last twenty years."[23] Martin Van Buren's warning to Virginia leader Thomas Ritchie proved to be as accurate in 1854 as it was in 1827: in the absence of overriding party ties, Americans would organize themselves in relation to slavery.

If the Missouri crisis can be viewed as a "flash of lightning that illuminated the realities of sectional power in the United States," as I suggested in the introduction, then the conjunction of the Kansas-Nebraska Act and the rendition of Burns must be seen as the torch that ignited a wildfire that did not merely light up the political landscape but extirpated it. The vehicle of the destruction of the old order was the creation of a coherent political force that in a short time would identify itself as the Republican Party. In its makeup, and to a large degree in its policies, the new organization could be seen as the final full flowering of the portentous alliance of West and Northeast that Adams had prophesied in 1820. In this early stage of its organization, the Republican Party was a revolutionary organization in the literal sense of the term: its supporters regarded the existing form of government as destructive of the ends of "Life, Liberty, and the pursuit of Happiness," and believed it was their right and responsibility "to alter or abolish it." In this sense, the assertions of conservative Democrats about the radicalism of the Republicans were correct: they indeed sought the overthrow of the government.

For their part, however, the incipient Republicans asserted that the advocates of the Kansas-Nebraska Act had dissolved the national compact—not simply by abrogating the Missouri Compromise itself, but by the more fundamental abrogation of the principles of liberty, equality, and the rule of law implicit in the willingness to remove the limits that the Compromise had imposed to the expansion of slavery. In the view of the "Independent Democrats," the essence of the Union was the moral standard enunciated in the Declaration of Independence and the Constitution: "The Union was formed to establish justice, and secure the blessings of liberty. When it fails to accomplish these ends it will be worthless, and when it becomes worthless it cannot long endure."[24]

The greatest danger of a revolutionary period is of chaos and anarchy. To make a legitimate claim to restoration of the true nature of the Union, Republicans had to convince the public that they stood for law and order, while the existing regime promoted chaos and disorder. The individual who proved to be the most effective advocate of this claim was also the man who best embodied the rugged values of the West: a former Illinois congressman named Abraham Lincoln. The most important long-term effect of the Kansas-Nebraska Act, indeed, may have been to prompt Lincoln's return to politics.

Lincoln's approach to the question of slavery was carefully circumscribed. Initially, in fact, he stood aloof from the new Republican organization, until convinced that it would eschew abolitionism. Although he claimed to hate slavery as much as the abolitionists, Lincoln's approach to combating it consisted, almost entirely, in restricting it to the boundaries prescribed by the Missouri Compromise. In part, this circumspection reflected Lincoln's understanding of the constitutional limits to interference with slavery; but it was also true that he was confident that to limit slavery's expansion was to condemn it to extinction. To be sure, if no other factors intervened, the process would be an agonizingly slow one; Lincoln estimated that gradual emancipation might take as much as a century to complete.[25] But it would be effective, lawful, and minimally disruptive.

Lincoln brought to the emerging Republican Party a deep commitment to the rule of law. Unlike his future rival, William Seward, he appealed to no "higher law" above positive law, much less above the Constitution; he was confident that the application of the Constitution and the laws would of its own accord effect an end to slavery—and concomitantly, to antislavery agitation. The reasons for his belief were not based on faith (although he did possess an almost mystical faith in the destiny of the United States to redeem the world); they were pragmatically calculated. Like Stephen A. Douglas, he recognized that his region of the West held the balance of power between North and South and would decide the nation's future. If the rules of the game as they currently existed could be preserved, all future western states—and their future senators—would be free, giving the anti-slavery bloc control of the Senate, as for decades it had had control of the House. Thus Lincoln felt confident that sustaining the existing laws—including the hated Fugitive Slave Law—would preserve intact the nation's founding commitment to freedom.

Passage of the Kansas-Nebraska Act, by contrast, seemed ideally de-signed to launch the territories into chaos. "Could there be a more apt invention to bring about collision and violence, on the slavery question, than this Nebraska project is?" Lincoln asked. "I do not charge, or believe, that such was intended by Congress; but if they had literally formed a ring, and placed champions within it to fight out the controversy, the fight could be no more likely to come off than it is. And if this fight should begin, is it likely to take a very peaceful, Union-saving turn? Will not the first drop of blood so shed, be the real knell of the Union?"[26] Thus Lincoln could plausibly assert that Douglas and the Democrats had precipitated the de-scent into violence and lawlessness that in fact quickly followed upon pas-sage of the Kansas-Nebraska Bill, and that served as a prelude to the cata-clysm that would soon engulf the whole nation. Lincoln's assertion—and the bloody Kansas border wars that bore out his prediction—lent credence to Republican claims to be restorers of the moral and civic order that the Democrats were destroying.

As the old order crumbled and traditional partisan and cultural alle-giances lost their sway, Americans were forced to assess their deepest val-ues and determine where to place their faith.[27] Although most Americans would likely have cited the religion of Christ as their guiding principle, this served as a label that embraced an immeasurable variety of beliefs. The "bottom line" of belief for some, as we have seen, proved to be the prosperity, comfort and sense of superiority made possible by slavery. For others, it was the principles of liberty and equality embodied in the American Union. For still others, their rock was the Union itself: they could not or would not allow themselves to consider the damage inflicted on its ultimate purpose by the compromises required for the protection of slave property.

Among those who regarded the Union as the supreme value can be ranked the chief justice of the Supreme Court, Roger Brooke Taney. Only weeks after James Tallmadge introduced his amendment to block slavery from Missouri, Taney had passionately condemned slavery as "a subject of national concern," "a blot on our national character," and a shameful contradiction of the principles of the Declaration of Independence.[28] Even as late as 1841, Taney, along with all the southern members of the Court, had joined Justice Story's opinion in the *Amistad* case that Africans, like all other persons, had a natural right to liberty and could legitimately use lethal force against Europeans to secure that right.[29] In the wake of the crises of the 1850s, however, Taney's adamant zeal to keep the Union intact through his Court—the head of the last branch of government that had retained a significant measure of legitimacy in the eyes of the public—caused his view of the Constitution to narrow and harden, and his vision of history, even concerning phenomena of which he had been a part, to blur.

The case of Dred Scott, a black Missourian who was suing for his freedom, seemed to present Taney with an opportunity to dispatch all of the most dangerous threats to the Union's survival with a single slashing stroke. In concentrated form, *Scott v. Sandford* embodied virtually all of the conflicts at issue in the two Missouri Compromises. Born a slave in Virginia in the 1790s, Scott moved with his owner to Missouri in 1830, part of the westward migration of planters and slaves from the depleted lands of the Old South. He was then sold to Dr. John Emerson, an army surgeon stationed near St. Louis. For the next twelve years, Emerson traveled with Scott to postings in Illinois, Wisconsin Territory, and Louisiana, ultimately settling in Davenport, Iowa Territory, before his death in 1843. Thus Scott had spent several years in territories explicitly designated as permanently off-limits to slavery by the first Missouri Compromise. By long-standing legal precedent, affirmed many times by Missouri's courts, he should have become free through extended residence in free territory.[30]

Initially, Scott's case was decided the same way. After a series of exasperating delays, Missouri's circuit court affirmed that his residence in the free state of Illinois had made him free, and his wife's settlement and children's birth in territory barred to slavery by the Missouri Compromise did the same for them. Between the favorable decision of the circuit court in 1850 and the hearing of his former owners' appeal two years later, however, hard-line proslavery judges won election to the state's supreme court and reversed the judgment in favor of Scott's freedom, issuing a polemical decision that was explicitly couched as a salvo in the "cultural war" against northern abolitionism.[31]

Taney had long considered the problem of free blacks to be a key weakness in the preservation of "the Union as it is." As Andrew Jackson's attorney general, addressing the challenge to federal authority laid down by South Carolina in the Negro Seamen's Acts (discussed in chapter 5 above), Taney had unhesitatingly grasped the nettle of black citizenship in a memorandum to Secretary of State Edward Livingston:

> The African race in the United States even when free, are everywhere a degraded class, and exercise no political influence. The privileges they are allowed to enjoy, are accorded to them as a matter of kindness and benevolence rather than of right. They are the only class of persons who can be held as mere property, as slaves. . . . They were never regarded as a constituent portion of the sovereignty of any state. . . . They were not looked upon as citizens by the contracting parties who formed the Constitution.[32]

This formula, echoing the formalist racialism pioneered by South Carolina's Thomas Cooper, provided the escape hatch from the paradox of slavery in a free republic: Africans and their descendants were a group apart. They were universally despised and uniquely enslaved. Why they were uniquely qualified for slavery Taney left unclear, but the fact that they were enslaved proved their uniqueness. If this was a tautology, Taney was untroubled by it.

Taney had extended this line of formalist racialism in an 1851 Supreme Court decision, *Strader v. Graham*, which had in fact been an essential precedent for the Missouri court's rejection of Dred Scott's freedom claim. In *Strader*, Taney ruled that the status of three Kentucky slaves who had been taken into Indiana and Ohio depended on Kentucky's laws, not Ohio's—a departure from precedent favoring freedom going back to the *Somerset* case of the 1770s, and in common law before that.[33] (There was thus a notable circularity to Taney's reliance on the precedent of the Missouri Supreme Court's decision in *Scott*, since it largely rested on Taney's own decision in *Strader*.)

Although early indications suggested that the Court would rest its decision on the *Strader* precedent, sending Scott back to slavery on the basis of Missouri law and sidestepping other, more divisive questions, this was not to be the case. The court first heard the case in February 1856, but held it over for reargument in the December 1856 term, after the election of James Buchanan, a prosouthern Pennsylvania Democrat. With the new president's blessing, Taney delivered an opinion intended to settle, once and for all, the national unrest over slavery—by stripping the descendants of Africans of all citizenship rights, depriving Congress of the right to regulate slavery in the territories, and in effect ruling the entire political agenda of the Republican Party unconstitutional.

Taney opened his decision, ironically (and confusingly), by ruling that "a free negro of the African race, whose ancestors were brought to this country and sold as slaves, is not a 'citizen' within the meaning of the Constitution of the United States," and thus Dred Scott had no standing before the court. If so, why did the Court proceed to rule on the case? And why, if as Taney would assert, Scott remained a slave despite his residence in free territory, did Taney focus on the status of *free* Negroes? Ultimately, free blacks posed a problem for Taney, and for proslavery unionists in general: their very existence constituted an anomaly within their understanding of the American polity. Taney could afford to be imprecise on this point, since his ruling was intended to formalize their pariah status and render irrelevant the line between slave and free. Blacks were slaves by nature—or rather, by law and custom, since Taney and the formalist school of racism he helped to pioneer rejected a priori the doctrine of natural law and erected a doctrine of racial subordination founded on custom.

What of the Constitution's guarantee that citizens of each state are "entitled to all privileges and immunities of the citizens of the several states," the clause on which the second Missouri Compromise turned? Taney simply rejected the clause: "It does not by any means follow, because [an individual] has all the rights and privileges of a citizen of a State, that he must be a citizen of the United States. He may have all of the rights and privileges of the citizen of a State, and yet not be entitled to the rights and privileges of a citizen in any other State." Many observers, most notably Don Fehrenbacher, have commented on Taney's tortured discrimination among U.S. citizenship, state citizenship, and his unique category of state-conferred citizenship that does not constitute qualification for federal citizenship.[34] It would be hard to find a more fanciful and partial example of constitutional construction in the court's history.

Yet there is a discernible logic in Taney's interpretive acrobatics. He states quite clearly the premises from which he is proceeding: that the framers were "great men" and great communicators who were incapable of hypocrisy; that the words of the Declaration of Independence and the Constitution meant precisely what the framers intended them to mean, and that no conflict existed or could exist between the founders' ideals and slavery, as these were understood at the time. Taney concedes that the sweeping language of the Declaration—that "all men are created equal"—appears "to embrace the whole human family"; and if such words were written in a similar document today, in the middle of the nineteenth century, they would be correctly so interpreted. "But it is too clear for dispute, that the enslaved African race were not intended to be included, and formed no part of the people who framed and adopted this declaration," Taney insists; "for if the language, as understood in that day, would embrace them, the conduct of the distinguished men who framed the Declaration of Independence would have been utterly and flagrantly inconsistent with the principles they asserted; and instead of the sympathy of mankind, to which they so confidently appealed, they would have deserved and received universal rebuke and reprobation." In effect, Taney is adopting, with no sense of irony, Montesquieu's sardonic defense of African slavery from *L'esprit des lois*: "It is impossible for us to suppose these creatures to be men, because, allowing them to be men, a suspicion would follow that we ourselves are not Christians."[35]

In Taney's formulation, the search for consistency between the words and deeds of the founders, like the parallel effort to parse the intractable language of the second Missouri Compromise, led inexorably to the conclusion that blacks stood outside the civil order: that their status was not properly a subject for legislation or debate. His effort to prove this thesis with historical precedents from the states was of dubious effectiveness, since it also showed that the supposedly closed question remained a point of contention. Moreover, many of his examples were misleading, incomplete, or simply spurious—as the many Americans who had lived through the episodes he cited would have been well aware.

One further step was required to transform the revolutionary principles of the founders of the American republic into shackles to sustain slavery: the doctrine that, while society might advance, constitutional interpretation could never change, and would forever be chained to a darker past. "It is not the province of the court to decide upon the justice or injustice, the policy or impolicy, of these laws. The decision of that question belonged . . . to those who formed the sovereignty and framed the Constitution. The duty of the court is, to interpret the instrument they have framed, with the best lights we can obtain on the subject, and to administer it as we find it, according to its true intent and meaning when it was adopted."[36] In this passage, Taney reveals the principle underpinning a doctrine of original intent: the will of the founders—as interpreted by those with the power to do so—outweighed justice, utility, and public policy. In Taney's ruthless jurisprudence, a declaration that affirmed "the Right of the People to alter or to abolish" a government destructive of their rights, and a constitution created "to form a more perfect Union" and to "establish Justice," were now invoked to sanction oppression and proscribe change.

Having determined, at great length and through tortuous constitutional logic, that Dred Scott, as a member of the African race, had no standing to bring suit before the court, Taney proceeded nonetheless not only to address the merits of Scott's case but to attack the constitutionality of the first Missouri Compromise. Since it had already been repealed by the Kansas-Nebraska Act, the function of this ruling seemed to apply prospectively to the larger question of whether Congress could regulate slave property at all—hence opening the door to a constitutional claim that even the free states had no power to restrict slavery. "No word can be found in the Constitution," Taney ominously asserted, "which gives Congress a greater power over slave property, or which entitles property of that kind to less protection than property of any other description."[37] It is not surprising that Republicans—whose entire platform had been adjudicated unconstitutional by the decision—actively feared a "second *Dred Scott*" that would bring slavery throughout the nation under the Fifth Amendment's protection of property.

Taney's performance in *Dred Scott*—at once sweepingly radical in its revisionist history and its striking departure from precedent, and deeply reactionary in its rejection of social change—represented a last-ditch attempt to thwart by judicial diktat the inexorable advance of the northern majority under the banner of the Republican Party. Instead, of course, it solidified it, while delegitimizing what in the eyes of antislavery northerners had been the last remaining unsullied branch of the federal government: "The decision, we need hardly say, is entitled to just as much moral weight as would be the judgment of a majority of those congregated in any Washington barroom," pronounced the *New-York Tribune*.[38]

The *Dred Scott* decision brought to culmination a profound irony at the heart of American society. Since the beginning of the nation, defenders of slavery had sought to overcome their fellow Americans' objections to the practice—and also perhaps their own—by picturing Africans as slaves by nature, as a degraded race, and as beneath the notice of "whites." Yet each new effort to dismiss the rights of blacks, by undermining the founding principle of equal rights, simply highlighted and intensified the struggle over the anomaly of American slavery. In *Dred Scott*, this trend reached its penultimate height, as the nation prepared to form battle lines over the matter of "beings of an inferior order" who "had no rights which the white man was bound to respect"; it achieved its final culmination when Americans hurled themselves into the greatest cataclysm in their history to sustain or destroy a government founded on the supposed "great truth, that the negro is not equal to the white man."[39]

A favorite aphorism of the nineteenth century was that "history is philosophy teaching by example." The four decades between the Missouri controversy and the Civil War offered an eloquent, agonizing, and exhaustive tutorial on the philosophy underlying the American republic. Did the revolutionary words of the Declaration and the Constitution truly mean what they plainly said? Could the nation survive if it interpreted the phrase "all men are created equal" to mean just that? Could it survive the attempt to restrict its meaning to a certain "race"?

Plainly, the formal end of slavery could not put an end to the complex network of ideologies, dogmas, and prejudices that had been employed to sustain it. Indeed, emancipation eliminated the most devastating argument against slavery, which had always been slavery itself; the abolition of slavery liberated the racist scaffolding of the proslavery argument to flourish uninhibited by the ugliness and cruelty of its object.[40] To a heartening degree, Americans have extricated themselves from the tangled web of racist thought; but the ubiquitous and invisible complex of sustaining ideas remains largely intact. Chief among these is the belief that one can tell the story of America, or understand its meaning, without acknowledging the fundamental contradiction of slavery that is at its center. That fact must be faced, if it is ever to cease to be true.

NOTES

Introduction

1. Alexis de Tocqueville, *Democracy in America*, ed. J. P. Mayer, trans. George Lawrence (Garden City, N.Y.: Harper and Row, 1966), 316.

2. Winthrop D. Jordan, *White over Black: American Attitudes toward the Negro, 1550-1812* (Baltimore: Penguin Books, 1969), 582.

3. Lerone Bennett Jr., *Before the Mayflower: A History of the Negro in America, 1619-1964*, rev. ed. (Baltimore: Penguin Books, 1964), 68; James Joyce, *Ulysses* (Paris: Shakespeare and Company, 1922), 20.

4. The value of slaves in the U.S. in 1820 can be estimated at $615,208,800 (given the Fourth Census's figure of 1,538,022 slaves at the low estimate of $400 average value), the equivalent of something like $3,076,044,000,000 in the year 2000.

5. Quoted in Werner Heisenberg, *Encounters with Einstein: And Other Essays on People, Places, and Particles* (Princeton, N.J.: Princeton University Press, 1983), 10.

6. See, e.g., the observation of David Brion Davis that Perry Miller's final masterpiece, *The Life of the Mind in America from the Revolution to the Civil War* (1965) contains no index entries "for 'slavery,' 'Negro,' 'slave trade,' 'abolitionists,' 'antislavery,' or any other topic referring to the central issue that divided the nation 'from the Revolution to the Civil War.' And this was in 1965! No other example could dramatize so powerfully the way that Miller's generation repressed and marginalized racial slavery in the New World." Davis, "The Importance of History," *OUPblog*, Oxford University Press, <http://blog.oup.com/oupblog/2006/04/on_the_importan.html> (May 9, 2006).

7. This is true of most modern historical treatments, though not of those by specialists such as Don Fehrenbacher and Shaw Livermore. It is also not true of older studies such as Hermann von Holst's *Constitutional and Political History of the United States* (1876), and other works written closer to the Civil War, which continued to regard slavery as fundamental to the structure of American society, and hence emphasized the importance of the Missouri controversy. Virtually the only modern work to grasp fully the significance of the episode is Richard H. Brown's lapidary article "The Missouri Crisis, Slavery, and the Politics of Jacksonianism," *South Atlantic Quarterly* 65 (Winter 1966): 55–72.

8. Thus Henry Simpson, in his *Lives of Eminent Philadelphians, Now Deceased*, published in 1859 (Philadelphia: Brotherhead), wrote that "A leading object of Mr. [William] Fry" in starting the *Philadelphia National Gazette* "was the advocacy of

the Missouri Compromise" (939). In fact Fry's paper *opposed* the Compromise and the state's admission with slavery; but the political situation was such when Simpson published his book that the defense of the Missouri Compromise had become a rallying point of opponents of slavery, and the idea of *opposing* the Compromise on antislavery grounds had become virtually unintelligible.

9. One of the first scholars to recognize this point is Alexander Saxton in Part 1, "National Republican Thesis, Jacksonian Antithesis," of his *Rise and Fall of the White Republic* (London: Verso, 1990), esp. 23–76. See also George Dangerfield, *The Era of Good Feelings* (New York: Harcourt, Brace, 1952).

10. U.S. Census Office, *Census for 1820* (Washington, D.C., 1821).

11. Dangerfield, *Era of Good Feelings*, 204.

12. Noble E. Cunningham Jr., "Nathaniel Macon and the Southern Protest against National Consolidation," *North Carolina Historical Review* 32 (July 1955): 380.

13. Robert V. Remini vehemently refutes this conclusion in *The Legacy of Andrew Jackson: Essays on Democracy, Indian Removal, and Slavery* (Baton Rouge: Louisiana State University Press, 1988), especially 83–85. His refutation is based on the fact that neither Jackson nor the architect of the Second Party System, Martin Van Buren, considered slavery either fundamentally important or inherently incompatible with American democracy—nor, following their lead, does Remini. But if Remini has correctly interpreted Jackson's and Van Buren's opinion on the subject of slavery's marginality, it does not follow that their opinion was either generally held or correct. See the letter from Martin Van Buren to Thomas Ritchie of January 13, 1827, in chapter 7 below.

14. Adam Smith, *Lectures On Jurisprudence*, ed. R. L. Meek, D. D. Raphael, and P. G. Stein, vol. 5 of *The Glasgow Edition of the Works and Correspondence of Adam Smith* (Indianapolis: Liberty Fund, 1982), 134.

Chapter One

1. Harry Ammon, *James Monroe: The Quest for National Identity* (Charlottesville: University Press of Virginia, 1990), 367–68; Noble E. Cunningham Jr., *The Presidency of James Monroe* (Lawrence: University of Kansas Press, 1996), 27–29.

2. James D. Richardson, *A Compilation of Messages and Papers of the Presidents, 1789-1902*, 10 vols. ([Washington, D.C.]: Bureau of National Literature and Art, 1903), 2:10.

3. Ibid., 6.

4. Ibid., 7.

5. Ibid.

6. Ibid., 10.

7. Cunningham, *Presidency of Monroe*, 30. See also Ammon, *Monroe*, 369.

8. Cited in Ammon, *Monroe*, 368–69.

9. Monroe Johnson, "James Monroe, Soldier," *William and Mary College Quarterly Historical Magazine*, 2d ser., 9 (April 1929): 110–17. Also see David W. Robson, *Educating Republicans: The College in the Era of the American Revolution, 1750-1800* (Westport, Conn.: Greenwood Press, 1985), 103–41.

10. Monroe acknowledged the excellence of Montesquieu in his posthumously published, rather leaden treatise on government, *The People the Sovereigns*, written between 1825 and 1831. Significantly, Monroe believed that Montesquieu was more favorable to freedom than he acknowledged in his work, writing it "in a spirit of such moderation that it could not be considered an attack on his own government." Monroe, *The People the Sovereigns* (1867; repr., with an introduction by Russell Kirk, Cumberland, Va.: James River Press, 1987), 49, 64–66.

11. Richardson, *Messages and Papers*, 2:177. Also see the speech of Henry Meigs, Jan. 26, 1820, in *Annals of Congress* (hereafter cited as *AC*), 16th Congress, 1st sess., 944.

12. Jon Kukla, *A Wilderness So Immense: The Louisiana Purchase and the Destiny of America* (New York: Knopf, 2003), 261–83, 304–5.

13. *AC*, 15th Congress, 2d sess., 854.

14. Ammon, *Monroe*, 225–47.

15. See Joseph Ellis, *American Sphinx* (New York: Knopf, 1997), esp. 271–74; and Robert E. Shalhope, "Thomas Jefferson's Republicanism and Antebellum Southern Thought," *Journal of Southern History* 42 (November 1976): 529–56.

16. Monroe married Elizabeth Kortright in New York in 1786 while a member of Congress—one of a series of marriages of southerners to New York belles, commented on at the time as strengthening the bonds of national union. Ammon, *Monroe*, 49; Robert Ernst, *Rufus King: American Federalist* (Chapel Hill: University of North Carolina Press, 1968), 66.

17. Ammon, *Monroe*, 99–107; David Waldstreicher, *In the Midst of Perpetual Fêtes: The Making of American Nationalism, 1776-1820* (Chapel Hill: University of North Carolina Press, 1997), 133–36. For a thorough discussion of Genêt's visit see Harry Ammon, *The Genêt Mission* (New York: Norton, 1973).

18. *Columbian Centinel*, July 12, 1817.

19. Noble E. Cunningham Jr., "Nathaniel Macon and the Southern Protest against National Consolidation," *North Carolina Historical Review* 32 (July 1955): 380.

20. Monroe had been in a similar position once before, when, at the start of the First Federal Congress, Virginia leaders had selected him as senator in place of Madison, who, as architect of the Constitution, was relegated to the junior role of congressman as reprimand for what they regarded as his excessive nationalism.

21. Stanislaus M. Hamilton, ed., *Writings of James Monroe*, 7 vols. (New York: G. P. Putnam's Sons, 1898–1903), 6:27.

22. Mathew Carey, *The Olive Branch, or, Faults on Both Sides, Federal and Democratic: A Serious Appeal on the Necessity of Mutual Forgiveness and Harmony*, 10th ed. (1818; repr., Freeport, N.Y.: Books for Libraries Press, 1969), 40.

23. Ralph Ketcham, *Presidents above Party: The First American Presidency, 1789-1829* (Chapel Hill: University of North Carolina Press, 1984), 127–30.

24. Monroe to George Hay, Aug. 5, 1817, "Letters of James Monroe, 1812–1817," *Bulletin of the New York Public Library* 6 (1902): 230.

25. Monroe, 8th Annual Message, December 7, 1824, Richardson, *Messages and Papers*, 2:248.

26. Hamilton, *Writings of Monroe*, 6:46.

27. Ibid., 6:2–4. Monroe explained somewhat ambiguously, a month before he offered the position to Adams, "I have thought that it would produce a bad effect, to place any one from this quarter of the Union in the dept. of State, or from the South or West. You know how much has been said to impress a belief, on the country, North and East of this, that the citizens from Virginia holding the Presidency, have made appointments to that dept., to secure the succession, from it, to the Presidency of the person who happens to be from that state."

28. Michael Wallace, "Changing Concepts of Party in the United States: New York, 1815–1828," *American Historical Review* 74 (December 1968): 453–91. See also Ketcham, *Presidents above Party*, 141–58.

29. Joseph Hobson Harrison Jr., "Martin Van Buren and His Southern Supporters," *Journal of Southern History*, 22 (November 1956): 438–58.

30. Ammon, *Monroe*, 469–72, 494–95; Cunningham, *Presidency of Monroe*, 49.

31. Rick Meigs, "Return Jonathan Meigs II," *Meigs Family History and Genealogy*, <http://www.meigs.org/rjm191.htm> (April 26, 2006); Richard John, *Spreading the News: The American Postal System from Franklin to Morse* (Cambridge, Mass.: Harvard University Press, 1995), 107.

32. William T. Utter, "Saint Tammany in Ohio: A Study in Frontier Politics," *Mississippi Valley Historical Review*, 15 (December 1928): 328–29.

33. Ammon, *Monroe*, 364.

34. "American Bible Society and the Military," Bible Resource Center, American Bible Society, February 3, 2003, <http://www.bibleresourcecenter.org/vsItemDisplay.dsp&objectID=50D3334F-812A-413A-97D632669D3FF2A3&method=display> (July 7, 2004).

35. Charles Louis de Secondat, Baron de Montesquieu, *The Spirit of the Laws* (London, 1755), bk. 15, chap. 1.

36. Douglas Egerton, *Gabriel's Rebellion: The Virginia Slave Conspiracies of 1800 and 1802* (Chapel Hill: University of North Carolina Press, 1993), 50–51; personal conversation with Daniel Preston, editor in chief, James Monroe Papers.

37. Louis Weeks III, "John Holt Rice and the American Colonization Society," *Journal of Presbyterian History* 46, no. 1 (1968): 26–41.

38. See, e.g., James Brewer Stewart, *Holy Warrior: The Abolitionists and American Slavery* (New York: Hill and Wang, 1976), 30–31.

39. This is the view portrayed by Douglas R. Egerton, "'Its Origin Is Not a Little Curious': A New Look at the American Colonization Society," *Journal of the Early Republic* 5 (1985): esp. 480.

40. Sheila Mason, "Livy and Montesquieu," in *Livy*, ed. T. A. Dorey (London: Routledge and K. Paul, 1971), 118–58.

41. Edmund Burke, *Reflections on the Revolution in France* (London, 1790), 182.

42. Charles Louis de Secondat, Baron de Montesquieu, *Persian Letters* (London, 1730), letter 122.

43. Garry Wills, *Inventing America: Jefferson's Declaration of Independence* (Garden City, N.Y.: Doubleday, 1978), 301, 302, 304, 306.

44. Saul D. Alinsky, *Rules for Radicals* (New York: Vintage, 1971), 128. Alinsky continues, "You can kill them with this, for they can no more obey their own rules than the Christian church can live up to Christianity."

45. On the rise of black political consciousness and activity, see Patrick Rael, *Black Identity and Black Protest in the Antebellum North* (Chapel Hill: University of North Carolina Press, 2002); James Brewer Stewart, "The Emergence of Racial Modernity and the Rise of the White North, 1790–1840," *Journal of the Early Republic* 18 (Summer 1998): 181–217; and John Wood Sweet, *Bodies Politic: Negotiating Race in the American North, 1730-1830* (Baltimore: Johns Hopkins University Press, 2003), esp. 243–67.

46. Scott L. Malcomson, *One Drop of Blood: The American Misadventure of Race* (New York: Farrar, Straus and Giroux, 2000), esp. 277–92.

47. This is evident from the first issue; see, e.g., "T.R.," "Observations on the Early History of the African Race," *African Repository* 1 (March 1825): 7–13.

48. For a useful recent study of this theme in Kentucky, see Harold D. Tallant, *Evil Necessity: Slavery and Political Culture in Antebellum Kentucky* (Lexington: University Press of Kentucky, 2003), esp. chaps. 1 and 2.

49. Henry Clay, *An Address Delivered to the Colonization Society of Kentucky, at Frankfort, December 17, 1829* (Frankfort, Ky., 1830), 7.

Chapter Two

1. Waller Taylor to Jedidiah Morse, January 27, 1819, Gratz Mss., case 2, box 4, Historical Society of Pennsylvania (hereafter cited as HSP), Philadelphia, Pa.

2. Wilhelmus Bogart Bryan, *A History of the National Capital: From its Foundation through the Period of the Adoption of the Organic Act*, 2 vols. (New York: Macmillan, 1916), 2:133–35.

3. Shane White, *Somewhat More Independent: The End of Slavery in New York City, 1770-1810* (Athens: University of Georgia Press, 1991), 53–54.

4. U.S. Bureau of the Census, *Third Annual Census*, 1820; W. O. Blake, *The History of Slavery and the Slave Trade, Ancient and Modern* (Columbus, Ohio: H. Miller, 1860), 498; Ray W. Irwin, *Daniel D. Tompkins: Governor of New York and Vice President of the United States* (New York: New-York Historical Society, 1968), 212.

5. William W. Story, ed., *Life and Letters of Joseph Story*, 2 vols. (Boston: Charles C. Little and James Brown, 1851), 1:335.

6. The works reviewed included *Travels in Canada and the United States, in 1816 and 1817*, by Lieutenant Francis Hall, 14th Light Dragoons, H.P. (London, 1818); *Journal of Travels in the United States of North America and in Lower Canada, performed in the Year 1817, &c. &c.*, by John Palmer (London, 1818); *A Narrative of a Journey of Five Thousand Miles through the Eastern and Western States of America . . .* by Henry Bradshaw Fearon (London, 1818); and *Travels in the Interior of America, in the Years 1809, 1810, and 1811, &c., &c.*, by John Bradbury, F.L.S. (London, 1817).

7. *Edinburgh Review* 30 (June 1818): 121; (December 1818): 146, 148.

8. *Annals of Congress* (hereafter cited as *AC*), 15th Congress, 2d sess., 1170.

9. Glover Moore, *The Missouri Controversy, 1819-1821* ([Lexington]: University of Kentucky Press, 1953), 41.

10. The term "buncombe" (or "bunkum") derives from the fatuous and pathetic remark of Representative Felix Walker of North Carolina, whose district included Buncombe County. On February 25, 1820, after an interminable session in which every imaginable change had been rung on the Missouri question, Walker pleaded to be allowed to give still one more speech, explaining that he needed to prove to his constituents (by the printed transcript of the speech) that he was doing his job. "I shall not be speaking to the House," he reputedly acknowledged, "but to Buncombe." The House rejected Walker's request "by almost a unanimous vote." The bare outline of the episode is at *AC*, 16th Congress, 2d sess., 1539.

11. Joseph Gales and William Seaton, the chroniclers of congressional proceedings, merely reported that the motion "gave rise to an interesting and pretty wide debate." *AC*, 15th Congress, 2d sess., 1166.

12. Ibid., 1177; *New-York Daily Advertiser*, February 26, 1819. Clay's outburst, indeed, fit the pattern of earlier congressional discussions of slavery, such as the 1790 Quaker petition controversy, when southern leaders such as William Loughton Smith, James Jackson, and Pierce Butler took such an extreme, preemptive proslavery stance as to rout any possible more moderate southern response, or the 1804 debate over slavery in Louisiana, in which Jackson again performed the same office. See Howard A. Ohline, "Slavery, Economics, and Congressional Politics, 1790," *Journal of Southern History* 46 (August 1980): 342–44; Gary Nash, *Race and Revolution* (Madison, Wis.: Madison House, 1990), 40–41; and Don Edward Fehrenbacher, *The Dred Scott Case: Its Significance in American Law and Politics* (New York: Oxford University Press, 1978), 95. It is interesting to speculate to what degree the comments of these figures, and of Clay, were intended to enforce southern solidarity rather than to intimidate northerners.

13. *AC*, 15th Congress, 2d sess., 1170–71.

14. Ibid., 1171–74.

15. *Census for 1820* (Washington, D.C.: Gales and Seaton, 1821).

16. Steven Deyle, "The Irony of Liberty: Origins of the Domestic Slave Trade," *Journal of the Early Republic* 12 (Spring 1992): 50–51; Ulrich B. Phillips, *American Negro Slavery* (Baton Rouge: Louisiana State University Press, 1966), 370–71.

17. Deyle, "Irony of Liberty," 51.

18. *AC*, 15th Congress, 2d sess., 1179–81.

19. See Philip F. Detweiler, "The Changing Reputation of the Declaration of Independence: The First Fifty Years," *William and Mary Quarterly*, 3d ser., 19 (October 1962): 572–73.

20. *New-York Daily Advertiser*, February 26, 1819. On the Haitian precedent, see David Brion Davis, *The Problem of Slavery in the Age of Revolution, 1770-1823* (Ithaca, N.Y.: Cornell University Press, 1975), 137–48.

21. *AC*, 15th Congress, 2d sess., 1185.

22. Ibid., 1188–90.

23. Hermann von Holst, *The Constitutional and Political History of the United States*, vol. I, *1750-1833: State Sovereignty and Slavery*, trans. John J. Lalor and Alfred B. Mason (Chicago: Callaghan, 1889), 364.

24. Examples of this tendency include William Pinkney, John Randolph, and John Floyd. The reverse is also true; for example, William Loughton Smith of South Carolina, generally recognized as the most extreme exponent of the "positive good" defense of slavery before 1800, was also a strongly pronorthern Federalist whom Rufus King regarded as his closest southern ally in the Senate and who was burned in effigy along with Fisher Ames in Charleston in 1794 (*Works of Fisher Ames*, ed. W. B. Allen, 2 vols. [Indianapolis: Liberty Classics, 1983], 2:1034). See also Robert McColley, *Slavery and Jeffersonian Virginia* (Urbana: University of Illinois Press, 1973), 126–27, and Ohline, "Slavery and Politics," 342.

25. *AC*, 15th Congress, 2d sess., 1191–93.

26. Ibid., 1193.

27. Ibid., 1201–3.

28. Ibid., 1205. Arbuthnot and Ambrister were British subjects executed in Florida by Andrew Jackson for incitement of the Indians.

29. Samuel Eliot Morison, *The Life and Letters of Harrison Gray Otis, Federalist, 1765-1848*, 2 vols. (Boston: Houghton Mifflin, 1913), 2:225–26; Moore, *Missouri Controversy*, 38–41.

30. *AC*, 15th Congress, 2d. sess., 1204–5.

31. Ibid., 1210.

32. Ibid., 1211.

33. Ibid., 1213.

34. Holst, *Constitutional and Political History*, 355. In this work the lowercasing of words that are typically capitalized is perhaps an artifact of the translators' overzealous correction of the German capitalization of common nouns.

35. *AC*, 15th Congress, 2d sess., 1214.

36. On Taylor's Arkansas amendment, see William R. Johnson, "Prelude to the Missouri Compromise: A New York Congressman's Effort to Exclude Slavery from Arkansas Territory," *New-York Historical Society Quarterly* 48 (January 1964): 31–50; and Fehrenbacher, *Dred Scott Case*, 102–6.

37. *Daily National Intelligencer*, April 19, 1819.

38. Whitman failed to note that the extension of slavery to Kentucky had also been a subject of debate. Although he maintained that he supported the restriction of slavery in Missouri, Whitman, along with Henry Baldwin of Pennsylvania, cast no vote on the Tallmadge amendment and voted against the Taylor Amendment. Philemon Beecher and John W. Campbell of Ohio and Charles Kinsey of New York voted for the restriction of slavery in Missouri but against its exclusion from Arkansas. Johnson, "Prelude to Missouri Compromise," 44–45.

39. *New-York Daily Advertiser*, February 24, 1819.

40. *AC*, 15th Congress, 2d sess., 1280.

41. Ibid., 1281–82.

42. Morison, *Otis*, 2:226.

43. Deyle, "Irony of Liberty," 46–47.

44. Quoted in Holst, *Constitutional and Political History*, 360.

45. As Holst notes, William Pinkney and Philip Barbour both conceded that the extension of slavery would result in a net increase in slaves. Ibid., 361.

46. Ibid.

47. A comment by Pennsylvania senator Henry Baldwin tends to support this claim: "When I compare the state of public opinion on this subject now [in 1820] with what it was two years ago it seems hardly possible to believe it[.] I was one of the Committee that reported the bill to admit Missouri into the Union[.] There was no opposition in the Committee or the House[.] The bill would have passed if we could have readied it and this question would never have been . . . It was not thought of by any one." Baldwin to [John] Gilmore, February 12, 1820, Society Small Collection, HSP.

48. George Dangerfield, *The Era of Good Feelings* (New York: Harcourt, Brace, 1952), 200.

49. The first 200 years of development of the paradoxical interrelationship between freedom and bondage in Virginia is brilliantly traced in Edmund S. Morgan's *American Slavery—American Freedom* (New York: Norton, 1975); see also Donald L. Robinson, *Slavery in the Structure of American Politics, 1765-1820* (New York: Harcourt Brace Jovanovich, 1971).

50. Fehrenbacher, *Dred Scott Case*, 91.

51. Harrison Gray Otis asserted in February 1820 that "none of us anticipated the magnitude and political tendency of this question last year.—Mr. [Rufus] King admits that he did not—Indeed I first told him of the debate in the house, and he treated the question as of little or no importance." Morison, *Otis*, 2:225–26.

52. *Richmond Enquirer*, February 25, 1819. Ominously, just below this editorial ran an article about the theft from the city magazine of "15 to 25 kegs of powder, 25 lbs. each," of which 3 kegs were "found in possession of a negro man slave," the rest remaining unaccounted for.

53. Harry Ammon, *James Monroe: The Quest for National Identity* (New York: McGraw-Hill, 1971), 449–50.

54. Certain qualities of style and diction suggest that one of Dwight's congressional correspondents was Rufus King.

55. *New-York Daily Advertiser*, March 29, 1819.

56. Moore, *Missouri Controversy*, 73.

57. Letter to constituents, March 4, 1819, in *Circular Letters of Congressmen to Their Constituents, 1789-1829*, vol. 3, *Fifteenth Congress–Twentieth Congress, 1817-1829*, ed. Noble E. Cunningham Jr. (Chapel Hill: University of North Carolina Press, 1978), 1074.

58. Works Project Administration of Cleveland, *Annals of Cleveland*, 10 vols. (Cleveland: Cleveland W.P.A. Project, 1938), 1:659.

59. *Niles' Weekly Register* 16 (May 8, 1819): 177. The other propositions Niles discussed included "That it is true wisdom to exalt the minds of the slaves"; "That the present emancipation of slaves in the southern states should not be extensively supported, unless efficient provision is made for separating the free negroes from those who are not"; and "That the states in which slavery is not allowed, should

offer every reasonable facility and encouragement to free people of color wishing to reside therein; and adopt some measures to lessen the prejudices and antipathies of the whites." This interesting series of articles, appearing in such an influential publication, deserves the serious attention of scholars.

60. Robert Walsh, *An Appeal from the Judgments of Great Britain Respecting the United States of America: Part First. Containing an Historical Outline of their Merits and Wrongs as Colonies; and Strictures upon the Calumnies of British Writers* (Philadelphia: Mitchell, Ames, and White, 1819).

61. Jefferson to Robert Walsh, February 6, 1820, in *The Works of Thomas Jefferson*, ed. Paul Leicester Ford, 12 vols. (New York: G. P. Putnam's Sons, 1904–5), 12:156.

62. Walsh, *Appeal*, 232. On Walsh as a proslavery ideologue, see Larry E. Tise, *Proslavery: A History of the Defense of Slavery in America, 1701-1840* (Athens: University of Georgia Press, 1987), 47–52; here, as elsewhere, Tise's assertions should be treated with caution.

63. M. Shaw to Parrott, March 12, 1819, John Fabyan Parrott Papers, box 1, folder 8, New Hampshire Historical Society (hereafter cited as NHHS), Concord, N.H.

64. Morison, *Otis*, 2:224; *New Hampshire Gazette* (Portsmouth), March 7, 1820; *Niles' Weekly Register*, vol. 16 (1819), supp., 177–79.

65. Floyd Calvin Shoemaker, *Missouri's Struggle for Statehood, 1804-1821* (Jefferson City, Mo.: Hugh Stephens Printing Co., 1916), 103–4.

66. Ibid., 105.

67. Ibid., 109.

68. Quoted in the *Richmond Enquirer*, October 8, 1819.

69. Quoted in Moore, *Missouri Controversy*, 72. Glover Moore has greatly exaggerated the role of Elias Boudinot, quintessential antiegalitarian, patrician Federalist, in agitating the Missouri question. Boudinot's efforts were truly remarkable for a man of nearly eighty; but at the time he lent his name and pen to the anti-Missouri coalition he was in the late stages of his final illness and far too weak to undertake a major role in the campaign. Presumably Boudinot's dual chairmanships of the Society of the Cincinnati and the American Bible Society made him too tempting a candidate—as aristocrat and evangelical—to reject as author of the agitation. Moore, *Missouri Controversy*, 68–73. See also George Adams Boyd, *Elias Boudinot: Patriot and Statesman, 1740-1821* (Princeton, N.J.: Princeton University Press, 1952), 289–91.

70. Quoted in Moore, *Missouri Controversy*, 27.

71. Daniel Preston, ed., *The Papers of James Monroe*, vol. 1, *A Documentary History of the Presidential Tours of James Monroe, 1817-1818-1819* (Westport, Conn.: Greenwood Press, 2003), 662–63.

72. Moore, *Missouri Controversy*, 71.

73. Walter R. Fee, *The Transition from Aristocracy to Democracy in New Jersey, 1789-1829* (Somerville, N.J.: Somerset Press, 1933), 240.

74. Moore, *Missouri Controversy*, 75.

75. Morison, *Otis*, 2:224–25.

76. *Franklin Gazette* (Philadelphia), November 22, 1819.

77. Charles R. King, ed., *The Life and Correspondence of Rufus King, Comprising His Letters, Private and Official; His Private Documents and His Speeches, Collected Papers*, 6 vols., (New York: G. P. Putnam's Sons, 1900), 6:272; Moore, *Missouri Controversy*, 74.

78. Shaw Livermore Jr., *The Twilight of Federalism: The Disintegration of the Federalist Party, 1815–1830* (Princeton, N.J.: Princeton University Press, 1962), 92–93.

79. *Richmond Enquirer*, December 3, 1819.

80. Blake, *History of Slavery*, 489–91.

81. For the lengthy, ambiguous, and ambivalent experience of Pennsylvania emancipation, see Gary B. Nash and Jean R. Soderlund, *Freedom by Degrees: Emancipation in Pennsylvania and Its Aftermath* (New York: Oxford University Press, 1991). Jan Lewis has discussed the role of Pennsylvanian James Wilson in the creation of the three-fifths clause of the Constitution in "The Three-Fifths Clause and the Origins of Sectionalism" (unpublished symposium paper, "Debates over Sectionalism," U.S. Capitol Historical Society conference, April 17, 2004).

82. King, *Correspondence*, 6:278.

83. *New Hampshire Patriot*, November 30, 1819, quoted in Moore, *Missouri Controversy*, 186.

84. Boyd, *Boudinot*, 290.

85. *Daily National Intelligencer*, November 18, 1819. The style and tenor of the essays suggests that they may have been written by William Giles, the former Virginia congressman and future governor.

86. Ibid.

87. *Daily National Intelligencer*, November 20, 1819.

88. Ibid. The references were to Bussa's Rebellion of 1816 in Barbados and, of course, the Haitian Revolution of 1794–1804. Robert Walsh's *Appeal* had made the point that abolition had not ameliorated slavery; but Walsh had reasoned that the evils of the slave trade "flowed from a source inherent in . . . slavery itself," and would last as long as the institution existed (Walsh, *Appeal*, 306). It is perhaps worth noting that Wilberforce did not "weep still more" for the white victims of the Haitian Revolution. Indeed, he wrote at the height of the French Terror: "If I thought the immediate Abolition of the Slave Trade would cause an insurrection in our islands, I should not for an instant remit my most strenuous endeavours" (John Pollock, *Wilberforce* [New York: St. Martin's Press, 1977], xiv).

89. The author of these letters appears to have been Ephraim Pentland, a lawyer and Republican politician from western Pennsylvania. The pseudonym "Phocion," earlier a popular Federalist moniker connoting brevity and conciseness, has in this context a double irony. On the one hand, Phocion was the name of an Athenian general who counseled capitulation to the Macedonians (see Plutarch, *The Age of Alexander*, trans. Ian Scott-Kilvert [Harmondsworth, U.K.: Penguin, 1973], 218–51). On the other hand, it is evocative of Phocis and the expression, "Phocensian despair," meaning desperation that terminates in victory—deriving from the unexpected triumph of the men of Phocis against a coalition of their neighbors launched

after the Phocensians defiled the sacred oracle at Delphi (William Rose Benét, *The Reader's Encyclopedia* [New York: Thomas Y. Crowell, 1948], 849). In either context, the identity of Phocion could be regarded as a peculiarly appropriate one for a northern doughface to adopt.

90. *Baltimore Federal Gazette*, quoted in the *Richmond Enquirer*, November 30, 1819.

91. Louis Clinton Hatch, *Maine: A History* (1919; repr. Somersworth, N.H.: New Hampshire Publishing Company, 1974), 161; and see Ronald F. Banks, *Maine Becomes a State: The Movement to Separate Maine from Massachusetts, 1785-1820* (Middletown, Conn.: Wesleyan University Press, 1970).

92. Hatch, *Maine*, 154.

93. *AC*, 16th Congress, 1st sess., 85.

94. Ibid., 162.

95. Banks, *Maine Becomes a State*, 185.

96. *AC*, 16th Congress, 1st sess., 831–32. In fact, Vermont was admitted on March 4, 1791, whereas Kentucky was admitted on June 1, 1792—more than a year later.

97. Ibid., 841–42.

98. Ammon, *Monroe*, 450–51.

99. *Richmond Enquirer*, October 22, 1819.

100. Lyon G. Tyler, ed., "Missouri Compromise: Letters to James Barbour, Senator of Virginia in the Congress of the United States," *William and Mary College Quarterly* 10 (July 1901): 7–8.

101. Ammon, *Monroe*, 452.

102. Catherine Allgor, *Parlor Politics: In Which the Ladies of Washington Help Build a City and a Government* (Charlottesville: University Press of Virginia, 2000), 107.

103. Moore, *Missouri Controversy*, 196–97.

104. "Editor's Correspondence," *New Hampshire Patriot*, December 28, 1819.

105. Quoted in Donald B. Cole, *Jacksonian Democracy in New Hampshire, 1800–1851* (Cambridge, Mass.: Harvard University Press, 1970), 41.

106. Clement Storer to John Fabyan Parrott, December 20, 1819; Parrott to Hon. John Taylor Gilman, January 29, 1820; Parrott to Hannah Parrott, February 21, 1820, John Fabyan Parrott Papers, box 3, folder 3. Henry Baldwin to R. Gold, Esquire, February 12, 1820; Baldwin to [John] Gilmore, February 12, 1820; John Pintard to Baldwin, March 12, 1820, Society Small Collection; Fee, *Transition from Aristocracy*, 241.

107. Banks, *Maine Becomes a State*, 185–86.

108. Hatch, *Maine*, 163–65; Banks, *Maine Becomes a State*, 188–90.

109. Hatch, *Maine*, 163–64.

110. Moore, *Missouri Controversy*, 161–62.

111. Banks, *Maine Becomes a State*, 191.

112. Ibid.

113. Daniel Cook, *Speech of Mr. Cook, of Illinois on the Restriction of Slavery in Missouri. Delivered in the House of Representatives of the United States, February 4, 1820* (n.p., [1820]), 27.

114. Tyler, "Missouri Compromise," 9.

115. *AC*, 16th Congress, 1st sess., 1113–14. Another observer who took the proposal seriously was Fanny Wright, who cited the Meigs resolution as evidence that the colonization project was "neither visionary nor impracticable." Frances Wright Darusmont, *Views of Society and Manners in America* . . . (New York: E. Bliss and E. White, 1821), 50–51.

Chapter Three

1. Michael Birkner, *Samuel L. Southard: Jeffersonian Whig* (Rutherford, N.J.: Fairleigh Dickinson University Press, 1984), 46.

2. See Robert Frazer to Jonathan Roberts, January 1, 1820, Jonathan Roberts Papers, box 3, Historical Society of Pennsylvania (hereafter cited as HSP), Philadelphia, Pa.

3. Philip Shriver Klein, *Pennsylvania Politics, 1817-1832: A Game without Rules* (Philadelphia: Historical Society of Pennsylvania, 1940), 70.

4. Harry Ammon, *James Monroe: The Quest for National Identity* (Charlottesville: University Press of Virginia, 1971), 460–61; and see William Jones to Jonathan Roberts, February 13, 1820, Roberts Papers, box 3.

5. Klein, *Pennsylvania Politics*, 111.

6. Duff Green, a prosouthern newspaper editor and business entrepreneur from Missouri, claimed much later that the Bank of the United States had played a secret but instrumental role both in the Missouri crisis itself and in its settlement. See Green, *Facts and Suggestions, Biographical, Historical, Financial and Political, Addressed to the People of the United States* (New York: Richardson, 1866), 28–29.

7. Ammon, *Monroe*, 468.

8. William Jones to Jonathan Roberts, February 13, 1820, Roberts Papers, box 3. The emphasis is Jones's.

9. Tompkins to Langdon Cheves, November 6, 1819, Conarroe Collection, vol. 4, p. 30, HSP.

10. *Franklin Gazette* (Philadelphia), November 8, 1819; *Franklin Gazette*, November 23, 1819 (reprinted from *True American*).

11. Ray W. Irwin, *Daniel D. Tompkins: Governor of New York and Vice President of the United States* (New York: New-York Historical Society, 1968), 247.

12. Ibid., 246; Charles R. King, ed., *The Life and Correspondence of Rufus King; Comprising His Letters, Private and Official, His Public Documents, and His Speeches,* 6 vols. (New York: G. P. Putnam's Sons, 1894), 6:254–55, 263–64.

13. Irwin, *Tompkins*, 250.

14. William O. Blake, *The History of Slavery and the Slave Trade, Ancient and Modern* (Columbus, Ohio: H. Miller, 1861), 487–88.

15. Judge Ambrose Spencer to Solomon Van Rensselaer, February 15, 1820, in *A Legacy of Historical Gleanings*, comp. Catharina V. R. Bonney, 2 vols. (Albany, N.Y.: J. Munsell, 1875), 1:344.

16. Ronald P. Formisano, *The Transformation of Political Culture: Massachusetts Parties, 1790s-1840s* (New York: Oxford, 1983), 63–64.

17. *Cleveland Register*, January 11, 1820.

18. *Annals of Congress* (hereafter cited as *AC*), 16th Congress, 1st sess., 115–16.

19. See chapter 8.

20. [Harrison Gray Otis,] *Letters Developing the Characters and Views of the Hartford Convention by "One of the Convention"* (Washington, 1820). For an analogous response during the abolitionist upheavals of 1833, see Theodore Dwight, *History of the Hartford Convention* (New York: N. and J. White, 1833).

21. Otis to William Sullivan, February 13, 1820, in Samuel Eliot Morison, *The Life and Letters of Harrison Gray Otis, Federalist, 1765-1848*, 2 vols. (Boston: Houghton Mifflin, 1913), 2:226.

22. Charles Gore to Rufus King, January 28, 1820, King, *Correspondence*, 6:259–61. On the same subject, see also William Tudor to Rufus King, February 12, 1820, ibid., 271–74.

23. Otis to William Sullivan, February 9, 1820, Morison, *Otis*, 2:226.

24. Glover Moore, *The Missouri Controversy, 1819-1821* ([Lexington]: University of Kentucky Press, 1953), 39n.

25. Ibid., 107.

26. Jonathan Roberts to Matthew Roberts, January 8, 1820, Roberts Papers, box 3.

27. Robert Frazer to Jonathan Roberts, January 1, 1820, ibid.

28. *AC*, 16th Congress, 1st sess., 120–27.

29. Jonathan Roberts to Matthew Roberts, January 23, 1820, Roberts Papers, box 3.

30. Jonathan Roberts to Matthew Roberts, January 27, 1820, ibid.

31. *AC*, 16th Congress, 1st sess., 335–36.

32. William Jones to Jonathan Roberts, February 3, 1820, Roberts Papers, box 3.

33. Jones to Roberts, February 13, 14, 1820, ibid.

34. Jones to Roberts, February 13, 1820, ibid.

35. Jonathan Roberts to Matthew Roberts, February 16, 1820, ibid.

36. Roberts to Matthew Roberts, February 25, 1820, ibid.

37. Roberts to Matthew Roberts, February 27, 1820, ibid.

38. Memorandum in Society Small Collection, January 19, 1820, HSP.

39. "The Late Mr. Justice Baldwin," *Pennsylvania Law Journal*, 6 (November 1846): 6; Walter Lowrie, *Memoirs of the Hon. Walter Lowrie* (New York: Baker and Taylor, 1896), 23.

40. Isaac Hill to John Parrott, January 12, 1820, John Fabyan Parrott Papers, box 1, folder 9, New Hampshire Historical Society, Concord, N.H.

41. *New Hampshire Gazette* (Portsmouth), February 23, 1820. See also Clement Storer to John F. Parrott, December 19, 1819, Parrott Papers, box 1, folder 8, and *New Hampshire Gazette*, December 21 and 28, 1819.

42. William Plumer Jr. to William Plumer, February 25, 1820, in Everett Somerville Brown, *The Missouri Compromises and Presidential Politics, 1820-1825* (St. Louis: Missouri Historical Society, 1926), 13.

43. King, *Correspondence*, 6:255–56, 265.

44. Mark L. Hill to William King, February 9, 1820, in Ammon, *Monroe*, 453.

45. Ammon, *Monroe*, 452–53.

46. Allan Nevins, ed., *The Diary of John Quincy Adams, 1794-1845; American Political, Social and Intellectual Life from Washington to Polk* (New York and London: Longmans, Green, 1929), 226.

47. Robert Ernst, *Rufus King: American Federalist* (Chapel Hill: University of North Carolina Press, 1968), 372; David Brion Davis, *Challenging the Boundaries of Slavery* (Cambridge, Mass.: Harvard University Press, 2003), 42.

48. Henry Baldwin to John Gilmore, February 12, 1820, Society Small Collection.

49. Louis Clinton Hatch, *Maine: A History* (1919; repr., Somersworth, N.H.: New Hampshire Publishing Company, 1974), 166.

50. Ibid., 166–67.

51. Shaw Livermore Jr., *The Twilight of Federalism: The Disintegration of the Federalist Party, 1815-1830* (Princeton N.J.: Princeton University Press, 1962), 71–72.

52. Van Buren to M. M. Noah, Dec. 17, 1819, in *Annual Report of the American Historical Association for the Year 1918*, vol. 2, *The Autobiography of Martin Van Buren*, ed. John C. Fitzpatrick (Washington, D.C.: U.S. Government Printing Office, 1920), 138.

53. King, *Correspondence*, 6:248.

54. See, e.g., Rufus King to J. A. King and C. King, February 20, 1820, ibid., 6:278–79.

55. Rufus King to J. A. King, March 18, 1820, ibid., 317–19.

56. Van Buren to King, March 23, 1820, ibid., 322.

57. J. A. King to Daniel D. Tompkins, March 27, 1820, ibid., 322–23.

58. Ibid., 323.

59. R. King to J. A. King, April 14, 1820, ibid., 326–28.

60. See Livermore, *Twilight of Federalism*, 89–91; Donald F. Cole, *Jacksonian Democracy in New Hampshire, 1800-1851* (Cambridge, Mass.: Harvard University Press, 1970), 41–42; and George Dangerfield, *The Era of Good Feelings* (New York: Harcourt, Brace, 1952), 225.

61. Dangerfield, *Era of Good Feelings*, 221.

62. Irwin, *Tompkins*, 255.

63. Adams, *Diary*, 224–25.

64. *Philadelphia Aurora*, October 28, 1820.

65. Adams, *Diary*, 224.

66. Livermore, *Twilight of Federalism*, 90–91.

67. William Tudor to Rufus King, February 12, 1820, King, *Correspondence*, 6:274.

68. Ferris Pell to Solomon Van Rensselaer, December 1, 1820, Bonney, *Legacy*, 1:358–59.

69. Clinton to Solomon Van Rensselaer, March 17, March 27, November 18, 1820, ibid., 1:349, 352, 354. Also see Solomon Nadler, "The Green Bag: James Monroe and the Fall of De Witt Clinton," *New-York Historical Society Quarterly* 59 (July 1975): 203–25.

70. John F. Parrott to Hannah Parrott, February 21, 1820, Parrott Papers, box 3, folder 3.

71. Henry W. Edwards to William Bristol, February 11, 1820, Bristol Family Papers, Manuscripts and Archives, Yale University Library, New Haven, Conn.

72. Abner Lacock to James Monroe, January 30, 1820, James Monroe Papers, Box 10, Library of Congress.

73. Lyon G. Tyler, ed., "Missouri Compromise: Letters to James Barbour, Senator of Virginia in the Congress of the United States," *William and Mary College Quarterly* 10 (1902): 15, 11.

74. Ibid., 17.

75. James Monroe, undated memorandum (February 1820), Monroe Papers, box 10.

76. Tyler, "Missouri Compromise," 17.

77. Ibid., 15.

78. Charles Francis Adams, ed., *Memoirs of John Quincy Adams, Comprising Portions of his Diary from 1795 to 1848*, 12 vols. (Philadelphia: J. B. Lippincott, 1874), 4:525–26. Glyndon Van Deusen flatly labels Clay's threat a "bluff," noting that "two weeks before his alarming prophecy to Adams he wrote to John J. Crittenden that he felt the struggle would end in some middle-of-the-road solution." Van Deusen, *Henry Clay* (Boston: Little, Brown, 1937), 139.

79. Ibid., 229.

80. Brown, *Missouri Compromises*, 14; Adams, *Memoirs*, 5:13.

81. Brown, *Missouri Compromises*, 14.

82. John Tyler to Henry Curtis, Washington, Feb. 5, 1820, in Robert Seager, *And Tyler Too: A Biography of John and Julia Gardiner Tyler* (1963; repr., Norwalk, Conn.: Easton Press, 1989), 69.

83. Jefferson to Hugh Nelson, February 7, 1820, in *The Writings of Thomas Jefferson*, ed. Paul Leicester Ford, 12 vols. (New York: G. P. Putnam's Sons, 1905), 12:157.

84. Jefferson to W. Short, April 3, 1820, ibid., 158.

85. Moore, *Missouri*, 92.

86. Eleazar Lord to Mathew Carey, February 27, 1820, Edward Carey Gardiner Collection, box 1, HSP. The strongest Northern support for the admission of Missouri without a restriction on slavery came from Baldwin—who, as a Supreme Court justice, would later cast the sole vote against freeing the captives of the *Amistad*.

87. Moore, *Missouri*, 89.

88. *AC*, 16th Congress, 1st sess., 1566–69.

89. Ibid., 1572–73.

90. Ibid., 467–69.

91. Ibid., 1578–83.

92. Ibid., 1583–86.

93. Ibid., 1587–88. Given the later controversy over Congress's power to bar slavery from the territories, the strong southern vote for the Thomas Amendment prohibiting slavery north of 36°30' is deeply significant. It received all but one of Maryland's nine votes, the sole votes of Alabama and Mississippi, seven out of nine

votes from Kentucky, half of North Carolina's twelve votes, four of Tennessee's six, five of South Carolina's nine, and four (including those of John Floyd, Charles Mercer, and Hugh Nelson) of Virginia's twenty-two.

94. King, *Correspondence*, 6:289.

95. Morison, *Otis*, 2:233n.

96. Moore, *Missouri*, 104; quoted from *Pittsburgh Statesman*, April 26, 1820.

97. On "doughface," see Theodore Dwight Weld, *American Slavery As It Is: The Testimony of a Thousand Voices* (New York, 1839), 114.

98. James Tallmadge to John W. Taylor, March 2, 1820; John W. Taylor to his wife, March 3, 1820, John W. Taylor Papers, New-York Historical Society, New York, N.Y.

99. See Rufus King to J. A. and Charles King, March 5, 1820, King, *Correspondence*, 6:291.

100. Floyd Calvin Shoemaker, *Missouri's Struggle for Statehood, 1804–1821* (Jefferson City, Mo.: Hugh Stephens, 1916), 114.

101. *New Hampshire Gazette*, March 7, 1820.

102. Moore, *Missouri*, 201 (and see illustration facing p. 196).

103. Henry Meigs to Josiah Meigs, October 15, 1820, Henry Meigs Papers, New-York Historical Society.

104. Moore, *Missouri*, 214–15; *Who Was Who in America, Historical Volume, 1607–1896* (Chicago: Marquis, 1963), 505; Henry W. Edwards to William Bristol, December 25, 1822, Edwards Papers.

105. Thomas Hart Benton, *Thirty Years' View; or, A History of the Working of the American Government for Thirty Years, from 1820–1850*, 2 vols. (New York: Appleton, 1854), 1:130; Moore, *Missouri*, 104–5.

106. *Philadelphia Aurora*, June 6, 1820, quoted in Moore, *Missouri*, 222; John A. Munroe, *Louis McLane: Federalist and Jacksonian* (New Brunswick, N.J.: Rutgers University Press, 1973), 109.

107. Munroe, *McLane*, 111.

108. Moore, *Missouri*, 213–17; U.S. Congress, *Biographical Directory of the United States Congress, 1774–1989* (Washington, D.C.: U.S. Government Printing Office, 1989), 753, 1489, 1884, 1945.

109. Irwin, *Tompkins*, 250.

110. Jonathan Roberts to Matthew Roberts, February 18, 1820, Roberts Papers, box 3.

111. Jonathan Roberts to Matthew Roberts, April 24, 1820, ibid.

112. Ossian Lang, *History of Freemasonry in the State of New York* (New York: Grand Lodge of New York, 1922), 96, quoted in Irwin, *Tompkins*, 304.

113. Irwin, *Tompkins*, 304.

114. See Ernst, *Rufus King*, 375–81; Jabez D. Hammond, *The History of the Political Parties of the State of New York*, 3 vols. (Syracuse, 1852), 2:76.

115. Van Deusen, *Henry Clay*, 32; correspondence in Meigs Papers.

116. Dorothy Ann Lipson, *Freemasonry in Federalist Connecticut* (Princeton, N.J.: Princeton University Press, 1977); Randolph Roth, *The Democratic Dilemma:*

Religion, Reform and the Social Order in the Connecticut River Valley of Vermont, 1791-1850 (Cambridge: Cambridge University Press, 1987).

117. Klein, *Pennsylvania Politics*, 14–16.

118. Few historical topics are more beset with pitfalls than the study of the influence of the Freemasons and other secret orders; indeed, it could justly be termed the La Brea Tar Pits of historical investigation. Nevertheless, it seems evident that the complex question of connections between the politics of the lodges and the nation during the Missouri crisis merits serious research.

119. Charles M. Wiltse, *John C. Calhoun: Nationalist, 1782-1828* (Indianapolis: Bobbs-Merrill, 1944), 217–19; John P. Kennedy, *Memoirs of the Life of William Wirt, Attorney-General of the United States*, 2 vols. (Philadelphia: Blanchard and Lea, 1852), 2:104.

120. Robert L. Meriwether et al., eds., *The Papers of John C. Calhoun*, 28 vols. (Columbia: University of South Carolina Press, 1959–2003), 5:412–14.

121. Ford, *Writings of Jefferson*, 12:158–60.

122. See David Eltis, *Economic Growth and the Ending of the Transatlantic Slave Trade* (New York: Oxford University Press, 1987), 146–48; and Franklin W. Knight, *Slave Society in Cuba during the Nineteenth Century* (Madison: University of Wisconsin Press, 1970), 50–56. I am indebted to Professor David Brion Davis for calling to my attention the significance of Jefferson's remarks concerning sugar. Ford, *Writings of Jefferson*, 12:160–61.

123. Ibid., 190. Lafayette was not convinced, replying: "Are you sure, my dear friend, that extending the principle of slavery to the new raised states is a method to facilitate the means of getting rid of it? I would have thought that by spreading the prejudices, habits, and calculations of planters over a larger surface you rather increase the difficulties of final liberation." Lafayette to Jefferson, July 1, 1821, and June 1, 1822, in *The Letters of Lafayette and Jefferson*, ed. Gilbert Chinard (Baltimore: Johns Hopkins Press, 1929), 205–9.

124. Ford, *Writings of Jefferson*, 12:185–88.

125. See the selection from Warden's translation and the editor's notes in Louis Ruchames, ed. and intr., *Racial Thought in America*, vol. 1, *From the Puritans to Abraham Lincoln: A Documentary History* (Amherst: University of Massachusetts Press, 1969), 245–55.

126. Ford, *Writings of Jefferson*, 12:179–80.

127. Ibid., 170.

128. Ibid., 165. For a discussion of Jefferson's letters on the Missouri question, see Stuart Leiberger, "Thomas Jefferson and the Missouri Crisis: An Alternative Interpretation," *Journal of the Early Republic* 17 (1997): 121–30.

129. See, e.g., Charles G. Haines to Solomon Van Rensselaer, November 20, 1820, Bonney, *Legacy*, 1:354.

130. David Brion Davis, *The Problem of Slavery in the Age of Revolution* (New York: Oxford University Press, 1975), 342.

131. "Mr Quincy . . . was opposed to the [restriction] movement here from the beginning, and for this exquisite reason; he feared the strength of these Western

States; that some day or other, they would overrun the country, and drive us all into the sea! and therefore he wished they might have slaves to weaken them! this opinion I suppose grows out of some confusion of totally different eras & events in his mind." William Tudor to Rufus King, February 12, 1820, King, *Correspondence*, 6:274; *Niles' Weekly Register*, vol. 16 (1819), supp., 179.

132. *AC*, 15th Congress, 2d sess., 1193.

133. Thus opposition to internal improvements and other federal activity became the cornerstone of Andrew Jackson's domestic policy, as orchestrated by Martin Van Buren. See John Niven, *Martin Van Buren: The Romantic Age of American Politics* (New York: Oxford University Press, 1983), 260–62; Richard C. McCormick, "The Jacksonian Strategy," *Journal of the Early Republic*, 10 (Spring 1990): 1–17; and Richard R. Ellis, *The Union at Risk: Jacksonian Democracy, States' Rights, and the Nullification Crisis* (New York: Oxford University Press, 1987), 22–40.

134. *Niles' Weekly Register*, vol. 16 (1819), supp., 179.

135. Ford, *Writings of Jefferson*, 12:158–60.

136. Moore, *Missouri*, 104; Ammon, *Monroe*, 455. On the antislavery content of southern, as well as northern, academic curricula, see Robert P. Forbes, "Slavery and the Evangelical Enlightenment," in *Religion and the Antebellum Debate over Slavery*, ed. Mitchell Snay and John R. McKivigan (University of Georgia Press, 1999), 84–93.

137. Moore, *Missouri*, 134–35.

138. Shoemaker, *Missouri's Struggle*, 100n.

139. Brown, *Missouri Compromises*, 17, 19.

140. Ibid., 19.

141. The conflict between the conceptions of slavery of upstart Missouri settlers and of established Old South planters appears to be a classic example of Pierre van den Berghe's distinction between a "Herrenvolk democracy," in which being free—and being white—constituted the principal source of status, and a paternalistic regime in which class rather than race served as the main badge of privilege. See Pierre L. van den Berghe, *Race and Racism: A Comparative Perspective* (New York: Wiley, 1967), 28–29.

142. See Moore, *Missouri*, 309.

143. Ibid., 309–10.

144. Tyler, "Missouri Compromise," 20.

145. Elizabeth Arnett Fields, "African American Soldiers before the Civil War," in *A Historic Context for the African-American Military Experience*, ed. Stephen D. Smith and James Z. Zeidler (Champaign, Ill.: Construction Engineering Research Laboratories, 1998), <http://www.denix.osd.mil/denix/Public/ES-Programs/Conservation/Legacy/AAME/aame1.html> (July 11, 2004); Harold D. Langley, "The Negro in the Navy and Merchant Service, 1789–1860," *Journal of Negro History* 52 (October 1967): 273–86.

146. State of North Carolina, *Journal of the Convention, Called by the Freemen of North-Carolina, to Amend the Constitution of the State, Which Assembled in the City of Raleigh, on the 4th of June, 1835, and Continued in Session until the 11th Day of July Thereafter* (Raleigh, 1835), 13, 21–25, 74–75; Brown, *Missouri Compromises*, 19.

147. On this subject, see Kenneth L. Karst, *Belonging to America: Equal Citizenship and the Constitution* (New Haven, Conn.: Yale University Press, 1989), esp. 43–54.

148. *AC*, 16th Congress, 2d sess., 1028, 1078–80; George D. Prentice, *Biography of Henry Clay* (Hartford: Hanmer and Phelps, 1831), 205.

149. *AC*, 16th Congress, 2d sess., 1097–98.

150. Ibid., 1116–17.

151. Ibid., 1120.

152. Ibid., 1129–34.

153. Ibid., 1134–36.

154. Ibid., 1135–37.

155. Ibid., 1141–43.

156. Brown, *Missouri Compromises*, 36–38; see also *AC*, 16th Congress, 2d sess., 1147–66.

157. Robert McColley, *Slavery and Jeffersonian Virginia* (Urbana: University of Illinois Press, 1973), 178–79; Kirk, *Randolph*, 134; Charles H. Ambler, *The Life and Diary of John Floyd: Governor of Virginia, an Apostle of Secession, and the Father of the Oregon Country* (Richmond: Richmond Press, 1918), 173.

158. Moore, *Missouri*, 288. For the persistent failure of Southern extremists to persuade most Southerners to identify the cause of slavery with the cause of the South, see William W. Freehling, *The Road to Disunion: Secessionists at Bay, 1776–1854* (New York: Oxford University Press, 1990).

159. *AC*, 16th Congress, 2d sess., 1196–98.

160. Clay later suggested that he did not know how his committee members would vote before their appointment (Moore, *Missouri*, 155–56). Such a claim must be taken as highly disingenuous. Clay placed on his committee those whose votes he knew he had, along with those he knew he *must* have (as well as several he knew he could not get). Although it may be literally true that he did not know how each member would vote, the impression that anything was left to chance in the committee's formation is wholly erroneous.

161. *U.S. Statutes at Large* (Boston: Charles C. Little and Thomas Brown, 1846), 3:645.

162. Ammon, *Monroe*, 460, 656n; Thomas J. Rogers to John C. Calhoun, March 11, 1821, Meriwether et al., *Papers of Calhoun*, 5:672–73.

163. *Philadelphia National Gazette*, March 1, 1821.

164. *Repertory* (Massachusetts), quoted in *Exeter (N.H.) Northern Republican*, March 12, 1821. Significantly, the paper had changed its name from the *Exeter Watchman and Agricultural Repository* to the *Northern Republican* just five weeks earlier.

165. *Northern Republican*, March 12, 1821.

166. Thus Thomas Hart Benton wrote in 1854: "The resistance made to the admission of the State on account of the clause in relation to free people of color, was only a mask to the real cause of opposition, and has since shown to be so by the facility with which many States, then voting in a body against the admission of Missouri on that account, now exclude the whole class of the free colored emigrant

population from their borders, and without question, by statute, or by constitutional amendment." *Thirty Years' View*, 1:10.

167. *Philadelphia National Gazette*, March 1, 1821.

Chapter Four

1. Horace Greeley, *Recollections of a Busy Life* (New York: J. B. Ford, 1868), 284.

2. Everett Somerville Brown, ed., *The Missouri Compromises and Presidential Politics, 1820–1825, from the Letters of William Plumer, Junior, Representative from New Hampshire* (St. Louis: Missouri Historical Society, 1926), 38.

3. *Annals of Congress*, 16th Congress, 2d sess., 1294–95.

4. Paul Leicester Ford, ed., *The Writings of Thomas Jefferson*, 12 vols. (New York: G. P. Putnam's Sons, 1905), 12:205–6.

5. See Shaw Livermore Jr., *The Twilight of Federalism: The Disintegration of the Federalist Party, 1815–1830* (Princeton, N.J.: Princeton University Press, 1962), 95–97.

6. "Letters on the Eastern States," *North American Review* 11 (July 1820): 74–75.

7. Roger S. Baldwin to Ebenezer Baldwin, February 23, 1821, Baldwin Family Papers, box 13, folder 168, Manuscripts and Archives, Yale University Library, New Haven, Conn.

8. E. S. Brown, *Missouri Compromises*, 38.

9. Roger S. Baldwin to Emily Perkins, May 8, 1820, Baldwin Papers, box 13, folder 166.

10. A good account of the convention is in John Niven, *Martin Van Buren: The Romantic Age of American Politics* (New York: Oxford University Press, 1983), 93–101.

11. Ray W. Irwin, *Daniel D. Tompkins: Governor of New York and Vice President of the United States* (New York: New-York Historical Society, 1968), 276–77.

12. Thomas J. Rogers to John C. Calhoun, March 11, 1821, in *The Papers of John C. Calhoun*, ed. W. Edwin Hemphill et al., 28 vols. (Columbia: University of South Carolina Press, 1959–2001), 5:672–73.

13. Samuel Moore to T[homas] J. Rogers, March 19, 1821, Dreer Collection, alphabetical series, Historical Society of Pennsylvania, Philadelphia, Pa.

14. Charles Francis Adams, ed., *Memoirs of John Quincy Adams, Comprising Portions of His Diary from 1795 to 1848*, 12 vols. (Philadelphia: J. B. Lippincott, 1874), 5:248.

15. Ibid., 431.

16. Ibid., 433–34.

17. *Annual Report of the American Historical Association for the Year 1918*, vol. 2, *The Autobiography of Martin Van Buren*, ed. John C. Fitzpatrick (Washington, D.C.: U.S. Government Printing Office, 1920), 574.

18. It should be noted that Taylor's political sin was his refusal to back Tompkins and the state Bucktail ticket, and not, as John Niven believed, his support for Clin-

ton, which was lukewarm at best, indeed, no stronger than Rufus King's. Niven, *Van Buren*, 104, and Adams, *Memoirs*, 5:438.

19. Jabez D. Hammond, *History of Political Parties of the State of New-York, from the Ratification of the Federal Constitution to December, 1840*, 3 vols., 4th ed. (Cooperstown, N.Y.: H. and E. Phinney, 1846), 2:260.

20. Niven, *Van Buren*, 105.

21. Adams, *Memoirs*, 5:437.

22. Niven, *Van Buren*, 107.

23. John A. Munroe, *Louis McLane, Federalist and Jacksonian* (New Brunswick, N.J.: Rutgers University Press, 1973), 120–23.

24. Niven, *Van Buren*, 107.

25. Adams, *Memoirs*, 5:435.

26. Richard H. Brown, "The Missouri Crisis, Slavery, and the Politics of Jacksonianism," *South Atlantic Quarterly* 65 (1966): 63.

27. Van Buren had established similar links to the editors of the *Lexington Reporter*, the *Charleston Patriot*, and other southern papers before 1820; there is little evidence, beyond the fact of Virginia's greater political importance in national affairs, and the tradition of cooperation between Virginia and New York, that Van Buren envisioned a special or exclusive relationship with the Junto at this early stage. See the *Albany Register*, November 12, 1819, and the *Richmond Enquirer*, November 19, 1819.

28. William W. Freehling, *The Road to Disunion: Secessionists at Bay, 1776–1854* (New York: Oxford University Press, 1990), 132; David Brion Davis, "The Perils of Doing History by Ahistorical Abstraction," in *The Antislavery Debate: Capitalism and Abolitionism as a Problem in Historical Interpretation*, ed. Thomas Bender (Berkeley: University of California Press, 1992), 294–96.

29. Scholars such as John Niven, Robert Remini, and Sean Wilentz are thus correct to assert that Van Buren's goal was to bolster the Republican Party, not the South, and certainly not slavery per se; what they fail to acknowledge, however, is that as a practical matter, the strength of the party was built on the foundation of southern unity in the defense of slavery.

30. Fitzpatrick, *Autobiography of Van Buren*, 99–100; also see William M. Holland, *The Life and Political Opinions of Martin Van Buren, Vice President of the United States* (Hartford, Conn.: Belknap and Hamersley, 1835), 144–47.

31. Adams, *Memoirs*, 5:452.

32. Harry Ammon, *James Monroe: The Quest for National Identity* (Charlottesville: University Press of Virginia, 1990), 498, 499.

33. Ibid., 499; Adams, *Memoirs*, 5:452, 474, 523–24. Adams told Calhoun "I told you so" enough times on this subject alone to try the South Carolinian's patience, or anyone's.

34. Catharina V. R. Bonney, comp., *A Legacy of Historical Gleanings*, 2 vols. (Albany: J. Munsell, 1875), 1:369. As James S. Young explained, the three presidents after Jefferson had replaced his intimate political dinners with "large receptions for congressmen . . . invited in alphabetical segments according to the first letter of their last names." James Stirling Young, *The Washington Community* (New

York: Columbia University Press, 1966), 170. In fact, even though Young associated the practice with weak presidential leadership, Andrew Jackson perpetuated it. In 1835, Harriet Martineau attended a presidential dinner at which, with the exception of her party, all of the guests consisted of congressmen whose last names "began with J, K, or L." Harriet Martineau, *Retrospect of Western Travel*, 3 vols. (London: Saunders and Otley, 1838), 1:111–13.

35. Bonney, *Legacy*, 1:369. I am indebted to Professor Richard John for the information concerning Van Rensselaer's support from delegations other than New York's.

36. Ibid., 367.

37. Meigs may also have supported Van Rensselaer for another reason, connected to his influence on the Military Affairs Committee. Meigs's father, Return J. Meigs Sr., was for years (as noted in chapter 1) the Cherokee Indian agent in Ohio. The power of the Indian agents was greatly diminished by the Senate's elimination of federally funded Indian trading posts, a measure sponsored by Thomas Hart Benton with the assistance of Van Buren (Ammon, *Monroe*, 500). This could have had an influence on the Ohio, Kentucky, and Tennessee delegations, which Van Rensselaer felt he could command.

38. Bonney, *Legacy*, 1:349–65.

39. Adams, *Memoirs*, 5:479.

40. Bonney, *Legacy*, 1:373.

41. Ibid., 388–90.

42. Adams, *Memoirs*, 5:480–82. Curiously, Chancellor Lansing disappeared in 1829 after leaving his hotel in New York City to post a letter.

43. Bonney, *Legacy*, 1:389.

44. See the *Journal of the Assembly of the State of New-York*, 44th sess. (Albany: J. Buel, 1820), 114–21, 131–45; see also Bonney, *Legacy*, 1:349, 352, 354, 357–59. Monroe's skillful and successful intervention in New York State politics is thoroughly documented in Solomon Nadler, "The Green Bag: James Monroe and the Fall of De Witt Clinton," *New-York Historical Society Quarterly* 59 (July 1975): 203–25.

45. I am aware that this interpretation of Van Rensselaer's appointment goes against the traditional view. For a variety of alternative accounts, see Leonard White, *The Jeffersonians: A Study in Administrative History* (New York: Macmillan, 1959), 323–35; Ammon, *Monroe*, 496–97; and Livermore, *Twilight of Federalism*, 106–10. The most complete account of the affair, and one that partially sustains my reading, is in Niven, *Van Buren*, 111–16.

46. Adams, *Memoirs*, 5:515–16. The fact that Dearborn had been the senior officer in command of the defense of New York City during the War of 1812, at the time that then governor Daniel Tompkins made the unauthorized expenditures for which he was currently under investigation, may also have been a factor in Monroe's choice.

47. Niven, *Van Buren*, 115–16.

48. Ammon, *Monroe*, 496.

49. Bonney, *Legacy*, 1:365.

50. Ammon, *Monroe*, 508. For an able discussion of Monroe's antiparty phi-

losophy of leadership, see Ralph Louis Ketcham, *Presidents above Party: the First American Presidency, 1789-1829* (Chapel Hill: University of North Carolina Press, 1984), 124–30.

51. Martin Van Buren, *Inquiry into the Origin and Course of Political Parties in the United States* (1867; repr., New York: Augustus M. Kelley, 1967), 3.

52. This fact is vividly demonstrated in Van Buren's assertion, in June 1860, that the country would be "fortunate" to have as president Bedford Brown, a Democratic North Carolina senator distinguished only for his stalwart devotion to the party and to Van Buren. Houston Jones, "Bedford Brown: State Rights Unionist," *North Carolina Historical Review*, 32 (July 1955): 321. One hesitates to imagine the course of American history had Van Buren's favorite been chosen president in 1860.

53. Van Buren, *Inquiry*, 1–3.

54. Robert V. Remini, *Martin Van Buren and the Making of the Democratic Party* (New York: Columbia University Press, 1959), 35. Remini is surprisingly uncritical of what John Quincy Adams described as "the principle . . . that the President, by faithfully performing his duty as Chief Magistrate of the nation, has violated his allegiance to the party which brought him into power, and that therefore a successor to him must be chosen who will violate his duty to the whole nation, by exclusively favoring his own party" (Adams, *Memoirs*, 6:62–3).

55. "There seems to be a propensity in free governments, which will always find or make subjects, on which human opinions and passions may be thrown into conflict. The most, perhaps, that can be counted on, and that will be sufficient, is, that the occasions for such party contests . . . will either be so slight or so transient, as not to threaten any permanent or dangerous consequences to the character and prosperity of the Republic." Madison to Monroe, May 18, 1822, quoted in Ammon, *Monroe*, 508.

56. Niven, *Van Buren*, 26. It may be objected that Van Buren's 1848 presidential campaign on the Free-Soil ticket (after he was ignominiously dropped as the Democrats' standard-bearer during the previous contest) proves the exception to this rule; except that its effect—as the unrivaled political tactician surely knew—was to guarantee the loss of a proslavery northern Democrat (Lewis Cass) and the election of a slaveholding southern Whig (Zachary Taylor).

57. Fitzpatrick, *Autobiography of Van Buren*, 133.

58. E. S. Brown, *Missouri Compromises*, 47.

59. Niven, *Van Buren*, 140.

60. Hammond, *Political History*, 2:128.

61. William J. Cooper has compellingly demonstrated this fact for the period after the election of Andrew Jackson (*The South and the Politics of Slavery, 1828-1856* [Baton Rouge: Louisiana State University Press, 1978]), but the seeds of the phenomenon were planted in the early 1820s, as Richard H. Brown makes clear. See R. H. Brown, "The Missouri Crisis," esp. 68–71.

62. Fitzpatrick, *Autobiography of Van Buren*, 132–33.

63. Alvin Kass, *Politics in New York State, 1800-1830* (Syracuse, N.Y.: Syracuse University Press, 1965), esp. 170, 174–75.

64. Niven, *Van Buren*, 98–99.

65. Vincent Harding, *There Is a River: The Black Struggle for Freedom in America* (New York: Vintage Books, 1983), 75.

Chapter Five

1. George Dangerfield, *The Era of Good Feelings* (New York: Harcourt, Brace, 1952), 243.

2. Lee Benson, *The Concept of Jacksonian Democracy: New York as a Test Case* (New York: Atheneum, 1964), 86.

3. Charles Francis Adams, ed., *Memoirs of John Quincy Adams, Comprising Portions from His Diary from 1795 to 1848*, 12 vols. (Philadelphia: J. B. Lippincott, 1875), 6:197.

4. "The whole history of the land question showed that where partisan advantage or sectional tradeoffs did not intervene, every Atlantic state could be counted on to oppose cheaper lands. And this was just as true in Virginia and South Carolina as it was in Massachusetts." Daniel Feller, *The Public Lands in Jacksonian Politics, 1812–1837* (Madison, Wis.: Madison House, 1984), 123.

5. Thomas Jefferson to Jared Sparks, February 4, 1824, in Paul Leicester Ford, ed., *The Writings of Thomas Jefferson*, 12 vols. (New York: G. P. Putnam's Sons, 1905), 12:336–37; Madison to Robert J. Evans, June 15, 1819, quoted in Louis Ruchames, ed., *Racial Thought in America*, vol. 1, *From the Puritans to Abraham Lincoln: A Documentary History* (Amherst: University of Massachusetts Press, 1969), 183–88; see also chapter 6 below.

6. See Leonard D. White, *The Jeffersonians: A Study in Administrative History, 1801–1829* (New York: Macmillan, 1959), 260–64; Merrill D. Peterson, *The Great Triumvirate: Webster, Clay, and Calhoun* (New York: Oxford University Press, 1987), 88–90; and Frank Bourgin, *The Great Challenge: The Myth of Laissez-Faire in the Early Republic* (New York: George Braziller, 1989), 154–64.

7. See, for example, Calhoun to Samuel L. Southard, "Confidential," August 16, 1825, in *The Papers of John C. Calhoun*, ed. Robert L. Meriwether et al., 28 vols. (Columbia: University of South Carolina Press, 1959–2003), 10:38–39.

8. Speech of John C. Calhoun, Feb. 4, 1817, ibid., 1:401.

9. Ibid., 5:638; 8:118, 292.

10. George P. Fisher, ed., *Life of Benjamin Silliman, M.D., LL.D.*, 2 vols. (New York: Charles Scribner, 1866), 1:309. The Cape Cod Canal was not actually completed until 1914. On the question of internal improvement in the Monroe administration, as well as the larger theme of intersectional cooperation for "making the government an instrument for public improvement," see also Bourgin, *Great Challenge*, esp. 155–75; and Peterson, *Triumvirate*, 68–88. For further substantiation of this view, as well as the elaboration of the theory that Jacksonianism represented a revolt from the consensus of Republicanism, the "antithesis" to National Republicanism's "thesis," see Alexander Saxton, *The Rise and Fall of the White Republic* (London: Verso, 1990), 23–51.

11. Speech of John C. Calhoun, Feb. 4, 1817, Meriwether and Hemphill, *Papers of Calhoun*, 1:403.

12. William W. Freehling, ed., *The Nullification Era: A Documentary Record* (New York: Harper Torchbooks, 1967), ix.

13. William W. Freehling, *Prelude to Civil War: The Nullification Controversy in South Carolina, 1816-1836* (New York: Harper and Row, 1968), 145–46.

14. David Brion Davis, *The Emancipation Moment*, 22d Annual Fortenbaugh Memorial Lecture (Gettysburg, Pa.: Gettysburg College, 1983), 19. The prototypical model of emancipation, as Michael Walzer has documented in his brilliant study *Exodus and Revolution* (New York: Basic Books, 1979), is the exodus from Egypt— a story deeply familiar to biblically minded southern whites, but rarely discussed by them.

15. Quoted in Julius S. Scott III, "The Common Wind: Currents of Afro-American Communication in the Era of the Haitian Revolution" (Ph.D. diss., Duke University, 1986), 233.

16. Freehling, *Prelude*, 52.

17. Ibid., 53.

18. Charles R. King, ed., *The Life and Correspondence of Rufus King, Comprising His Letters, Private and Official; His Private Documents and His Speeches, Collected Papers*, 6 vols. (New York: G. P. Putnam's Sons, 1900), 6:275.

19. Linn Banks to James Barbour, 20 February 1820, in "Missouri Compromise: Letters to James Barbour, Senator of Virginia in the Congress of the United States," ed. Lyon G. Tyler, *William and Mary College Quarterly*, 10 (July 1901): 21. John Lofton, in his study on the Denmark Vesey plot, misreads Banks's statement to mean that King's language would "sound the tocsin of freedom." What was important to Banks, and to Vesey, was that King's speech implied that the North fundamentally opposed slavery and would not come to its defense. Lofton, *Denmark Vesey's Revolt: The Slave Plot That Lit a Fuse to Fort Sumter* (1964; repr., Kent, Ohio: Kent State University Press, 1983), 129–30.

20. Whether Vesey's revolt constituted a genuine conspiracy or was manipulated by members of the Charleston slaveholder elite to consolidate their position remains an open question. For an extensive discussion of the matter, see "Forum: The Making of a Slave Conspiracy," parts 1 and 2, *William and Mary Quarterly* 58 (October 2001): 913–976 and 59 (June 2002): 135–202.

21. Ira Berlin, *Slaves without Masters: The Free Negro in the Antebellum South* (New York: New Press, 1974), appendix 1, 397, 399.

22. Freehling, *Nullification Era*, 11.

23. William W. Freehling, *The Road to Disunion: Secessionists at Bay, 1776-1854* (New York: Oxford University Press, 1990), 98.

24. William R. Taylor, *Cavalier and Yankee: The Old South and American National Character* (New York: G. Braziller, 1961), esp. 227–59; Larry E. Tise, *Proslavery: A History of the Defense of Slavery in America, 1701-1840* (Athens: University of Georgia Press, 1987), 139–47.

25. Thomas Cooper, "Coloured Marriages," *Charleston Courier*, September 15, 1823; "Brutus" [Robert J. Turnbull], *The Crisis; or, Essays on the Usurpations of the Federal Government* (Charleston: A. E. Miller, 1827), 163, 165.

26. Freehling, *Nullification Era*, ix; Freehling, *Prelude*, 65–74. See also David

Brion Davis, *The Slave Power Conspiracy and the Paranoid Style* (Baton Rouge: Louisiana State University Press, 1969), 32–41.

27. William W. Freehling, *The Reintegration of American History: Slavery and the Civil War* (New York: Oxford University Press, 1994), 138–57.

28. Leonard Woolsey Bacon, *Anti-slavery before Garrison: An Address before the Connecticut Society of the Order of the Founders and Patriots of America, New Haven, September 19, 1902* (New Haven, Conn.: Tuttle, Morehouse and Taylor, 1903), 36.

29. See, e.g., Isaac Holmes, *An Account of the United States of America, Derived from Actual Observation, during a Residence of Four Years in That Republic: Including Original Communications* (London: Caxton Press, [1823]), 11–13, 27; and Adam Hodgson, *Remarks during a Journey through North America in the Years 1819, 1820, and 1821*, 2 vols. (London, 1823), 1:18, 24–27, 56–58. British immediatism may also have been influenced by the failure of Council of Verona to deal effectively with the slave trade; see David Brion Davis, *The Problem of Slavery in the Age of Revolution* (Ithaca, N.C.: Cornell University Press, 1975), 72. For the rise of southern Anglophobia, see Kenneth S. Greenberg, *Masters and Statesmen: The Political Culture of American Slavery* (Baltimore: Johns Hopkins University Press, 1985), 108–12; I strongly dissent from Greenberg's facile analogy of Anglophobia and "New Anglophobia" during "America's two experiences with nation-creation" in 1776 and 1861. Far more notable than the continuity of the "spirit of '76" is its virtual absence in southern sectionalist rhetoric during most of the antebellum period, in favor of invocation of the much more conservative "spirit of '98."

30. Noting the almost complete lack of public agitation against restriction in the South, Glover Moore suggests that "it was a tribute to the self-confidence of the Southerners that they did not deem it necessary to hold meetings in Missouri's behalf. They took it for granted that their section was united, that no artificial stimulation of public opinion was necessary, and that the Southern congressional delegation could be counted upon to vote against the Missouri restriction until the end of time" (*The Missouri Controversy, 1819–1821* [(Lexington): University of Kentucky Press, 1953], 219). It would be hard to find a better example of a preconceived notion ruling contradictory evidence out of court.

31. See chapter 8 below.

32. Eugene D. Genovese, *"Slavery Ordained of God": The Southern Slaveholders' View of Biblical History and Modern Politics*, 24th Annual Fortenbaugh Memorial Lecture (Gettysburg: Gettysburg College, 1983), 7.

33. Freehling, *Road to Disunion*, 150; Freehling, *Prelude*, 82n.

34. [Edwin C. Holland], *A Refutation of the Calumnies Circulated against the Southern and Western States, Respecting the Institution and Existence of Slavery among Them* . . . (Charleston: A. E. Miller, 1822), 41–42. Although Holland's pamphlet is often described as an early proslavery tract, it devotes seven pages to discussing the iniquity of the slave trade, concluding with the statement: "If, then, we are unhappily afflicted with an evil, the curse of which is felt by every enlightened man in the Slave-holding States, it should be a matter of sympathy, rather than rebuke . . ." (22).

35. Richard Furman, *Exposition of the Views of the Baptists Relative to the Co-*

loured Population of the United States in a Communication to the Governor of South Carolina (Charleston, 1823), reprinted in James A. Rogers, *Richard Furman: Life and Legacy* ([Macon, Ga.]: Mercer University Press, 1985), 280, 275.

36. Ibid., 284.

37. See, e.g., Thornton Stringfellow, "A Brief Examination of Scripture Testimony on the Institution of Slavery," in *The Ideology of Slavery: Proslavery Thought in the Antebellum South, 1830-1860*, ed. Drew Gilpin Faust (Baton Rouge: Louisiana State University Press, 1981), 140.

38. [Frederick Dalcho], *Practical Considerations Founded on the Scriptures, Relative to the Slave Population of South-Carolina* (Charleston: A. E. Miller, 1823), 9–17.

39. See, e.g., C.-F. Volney, *Voyage en Syrie et en Egypte* (Paris, 1787); and Alexander Hill Everett, *America, a General Survey* (London, 1827), discussed in chapter 6 below.

40. [Dalcho], *Practical Considerations*, 4–5.

41. Ibid., 6.

42. C. Vann Woodward, ed., *Mary Chesnut's Civil War* (New Haven, Conn.: Yale University Press, 1981), 241.

43. Norman K. Risjord, *The Old Republicans: Southern Conservatism in the Age of Jefferson* (New York: Columbia University Press, 1967), 164–69 (quote at 165).

44. Article I, Section 8, grants to Congress the power "to lay and collect taxes, duties, imposts and excises, to pay the debts and provide for the common defense and general welfare of the United States; but all duties, imposts and excises shall be uniform throughout the United States." The second clause of the paragraph provided the necessary constitutional target for opponents of the tariff.

45. Risjord, *Old Republicans*, 166, 164. Randolph's formulation uncannily foreshadowed the essential element of the Jacksonian coalition of a dozen years later.

46. Ibid., 176.

47. John Taylor, *Tyranny Unmasked* (Washington, D.C.: Davis and Force, 1822), 4.

48. R. Kent Newmyer, "John Marshall and the Southern Constitutional Tradition," in *An Uncertain Tradition: Constitutionalism and the History of the South*, ed. Kermit L. Hall and James W. Ely Jr. (Athens, Georgia: University of Georgia Press, 1989), 115.

49. Thomas Cooper and David J. McCord, eds., *The Statutes at Large of South Carolina*, 10 vols. (Columbia, S.C., 1838–41), 7:461–62; Alan F. January, "The South Carolina Association: An Agency for Race Control in Antebellum Charleston," *South Carolina Historical Magazine* 78, no. 3 (July 1977): 195.

50. Philip M. Hamer, "Great Britain, the United States, and the Negro Seamen Acts, 1822–1848," *Journal of Southern History* 1 (May 1935): 3–28.

51. On this subject, see Julius S. Scott, III, "The Common Wind: Currents of Afro-American Communication in the Era of the Haitian Revolution" (Ph.D. diss., University of Michigan, 1986); and Greenberg, *Masters and Statesmen*, 112.

52. Lofton, *Denmark Vesey's Revolt*, 125, 137, 19–25.

53. Hamer, "Negro Seamen Acts," esp. 3–12; Lofton, *Denmark Vesey's Revolt*,

120–23, 197–210; Freehling, *Prelude to Civil War*, 111–16; [Dalcho], *Practical Considerations*, 33n. The danger of "infection" by American principles was ironically underscored in the weeks immediately following the disclosure of the Denmark Vesey plot when officials of the Swedish West Indian colony of St. Bartholomew's refused to receive the *American* consul "because during the French Revolution a consul from France had been admitted there, and had proved very troublesome by his turbulence." Adams, *Memoirs*, 6:32.

54. Philip Hamer, whose 1936 article is the foundation for secondary research on the subject, does note the oddness of a public law being defended by a private organization ("Negro Seamen Acts," 5).

55. Donald J. Morgan, *Justice William Johnson, the First Dissenter: The Career and Constitutional Philosophy of a Jeffersonian Judge* (Columbia: University of South Carolina Press, 1954), 50, 168–180. Also see Oliver Schroeder Jr., "The Life and Judicial Work of Justice William Johnson, Part II," *University of Pennsylvania Law Review* 95 (May 1947): 344–86.

56. Hamer, "Negro Seamen Acts," 4–5; *Niles' Weekly Register* 25 (Sept. 6, 1823): 13. It is unfortunate that these crucial discussions took place during a period of two months when Adams made no entries in his diary. See Adams, *Memoirs*, 6:129.

57. Alan F. January, "The South Carolina Association: An Agency for Race Control in Antebellum Charleston," *South Carolina Historical Magazine* 78, no. 5 (July 1977): 195.

58. *Niles' Weekly Register* 25 (Sept. 6, 1823): 13.

59. Ibid.

60. Ibid.; Schroeder, "Justice William Johnson," 363.

61. January, "South Carolina Association," 193.

62. Ibid., 192–93. It should be noted that the South's restrictive laws concerning blacks were apparently rarely enforced to the letter, and that such enforcement, when it occurred, often took place in the context of competing political factions within the white elite.

63. Ibid., 195.

64. Hamer, "Negro Seamen Acts," 7.

65. Ibid., 5.

66. Benjamin Faneuil Hunt was a native of Boston who had migrated to Charleston some time before 1812 and became a well-regarded criminal lawyer. Isaac E. Holmes, an 1815 Yale graduate, achieved some success for a literary piece he wrote while a student consisting of idealized vignettes of genteel, aristocratic life in Charleston and England. Samuel Eliot Morison, *The Life and Letters of Harrison Gray Otis, Federalist, 1765-1848*, 2 vols. (Boston: Houghton Mifflin, 1913), 2:276n; *Biographical Directory of the United States Congress, 1774-1989* (Washington, D.C.: U.S. Government Printing Office, 1989), 1205.

67. Morgan, *Justice William Johnson*, 193–94.

68. *Niles' Weekly Register* 25 (Sept. 6, 1823): 15.

69. Ibid., 16.

70. Ibid.

71. Ibid., 12–15; Hamer, "Negro Seamen Acts," 9.

72. *Niles' Weekly Register* 25 (Sept. 6, 1823): 15–16. Judge Johnson's authorization of Elkison to take his case to the state courts represented in itself a small victory of sorts, since Holmes and Hunt had argued that, because South Carolina law declared blacks to be prima facie slaves, Elkison had no standing to move for a writ *de homine replegiando*, the writ of Ravishment of Ward being instead the appropriate forum to determine the question of freedom of a person of color. Johnson exposed the sophistry of this argument by noting that the "act operates only as to freemen, . . . so that a whole crew of slaves entering this port would be free from its provisions" (16).

73. Morgan, *Justice William Johnson*, 163; January, "South Carolina Association," 196.

74. Morgan, *Justice William Johnson*, 164.

75. Robert M. Cover, "The Supreme Court 1982 Term: Foreword: *Nomos* and Narrative," *Harvard Law Review* 97, no. 4 (1983): 4.

76. Thomas Cooper, "The Right of Free Discussion," 4, 17; appended to Cooper, *Lectures on the Elements of Political Economy*, 2d ed. (Columbia, S.C.: M'Morris and Wilson, 1831).

77. Dumas Malone, *The Public Life of Thomas Cooper, 1783–1839* (New Haven, Conn.: Yale University Press, 1926), 299; *Niles' Weekly Register* 25 (November 15, 1823): 175. It has been suggested—in jest, one hopes—that Crawford's actual incapacity to discharge the office of the presidency represented the surest test of his "soundness" in the minds of the strictest strict constructionists.

78. "Letters of Thomas Cooper to Mahlon Dickerson," *American Historical Review* 6 (1899): 728–29. For a discussion of the antidemocratic tendencies of Van Buren's political strategy of 1824, see Alvin Kass, *Politics in New York State, 1800–1830* (Syracuse, N.Y.: Syracuse University Press, 1965), 90–91.

79. It is true, as Eugene D. Genovese has reminded us in his discussion of the philosophy of George Fitzhugh, that certain southern ideologists developed proslavery arguments that did not require racism as a condition or justification of slavery (cf. "The Logical Outcome of the Slaveholders' Philosophy: An Exposition, Interpretation and Critique of the Social Thought of George Fitzhugh of Port Royal, Virginia," in Genovese, *The World the Slaveholders Made: Two Essays in Interpretation* [New York: Vintage Books, 1971], 118–244). However, since the proslavery ideology espoused by Fitzhugh rejected progress, democracy, and liberalism and made no effort to square itself with traditional American values, it falls in a different category from that with which I am most concerned. Fitzhugh's defense of slavery is much more sweeping than those of more "mainstream" slavery apologists—and thus, in a sense, much less dangerous. Genovese discusses this point in more detail in *"Slavery Ordained of God"*.

80. This is not precisely the problem with Tise's *Proslavery*, the most important work on the subject to date. Rather, the difficulty with Tise's approach is that he endows "ideologies" with a peculiarly Platonic independent existence and a perplexing concreteness. Thus "proslavery ideology" remains an unchangeable domain of concepts and ideas, accessible to partisans in every age irrespective of changed social, political, or economic conditions; and expressions of a distaste for slavery

by individuals of the early republic denominated by Tise as "proslavery" can be explained by the irresistible force of "revolutionary ideology" for their time.

81. See E. Merton Coulter, *John Jacobus Flournoy* (Athens: University of Georgia Press, 1942). Flournoy considered blacks to be evil and demonic, and wanted them removed from the nation altogether.

82. Henry Steele Commager, ed., *Documents of American History*, 6th ed. (New York: Appleton-Century-Crofts, 1958), 179, 184.

83. The *Richmond Enquirer* had described the Kentucky and Virginia resolves as "the law and the prophets" concerning the bank question (October 22, 1819).

84. The connection was particularly congenial to Thomas Cooper, one of the victims of the Sedition Act, who notably championed the "principles of '98," free speech, and virulent denunciations of abolitionists and blacks during this period.

85. The southern argument had appeal for anti-Adams Federalists as well, however. See in this context, e.g., "A Citizen of Massachusetts," *Remarks on State Rights* (Boston: Richardson and Land, 1824), a Crawfordite view of the tariff and other states' rights controversies of the period, which opportunistically reviewed the case for payment of the Massachusetts militia claims—a major Federalist desideratum—in the sympathetic light of the current southern states' rights position.

86. See, e.g., Thomas Ritchie's letter to Littleton Waller Tazewell, in Norma Lois Peterson, *Littleton Waller Tazewell* (Charlottesville: University Press of Virginia, 1983), 63. On the rhetorical uses of the "spirit of '98" during the nullification period, see Merrill D. Peterson, *The Jefferson Image in the American Mind* (New York: Oxford University Press, 1960), 53–66.

87. Noble E. Cunningham Jr., "Nathaniel Macon and the Southern Protest against National Consolidation," *North Carolina Historical Review* 32, no. 3 (July 1955): 379–80. It will be seen, however, that the developing "positive good" defense of slavery sought to argue that slavery was effective, indeed essential, in promoting precisely these ends. It should be borne in mind when reading these arguments that the Constitution itself dictated the terms of such debates.

88. Ibid., 380.

89. Ibid.

90. See A. R. Newsome, ed., "Letters of Romulus Saunders to Bartlett Yancy, 1821–1828," *North Carolina Historical Review* 8 (October 1931): 446–47, 449.

91. Speech in the House of Representatives, January 31, 1824, *Annals of Congress*, 18th Cong., 1st sess., 1 (1823–24): 138.

92. See, e.g., Forrest G. Hill, *Roads, Rails, and Waterways: The Army Engineers and Early Transportation* (Norman: University of Oklahoma Press, 1957).

93. Samuel C. Williams, ed., "Journal of Events (1825–1873) of David Anderson Deaderick," *East Tennessee Historical Society's Publications* 8 (1936): 130–31.

94. Calhoun to Charles Fisher, Washington, December 10, 1824, in "Correspondence of John C. Calhoun, George McDuffie and Charles Fisher, Relating to the Presidential Campaign of 1824," ed. A. R. Newsome, *North Carolina Historical Review* 7 (1930): 484.

95. Newsome, "Letters of Saunders to Yancy," 441–42. As late as November 1823, at a celebration for the Chesapeake and Ohio Canal, a representative of Crawford

from Virginia proclaimed his candidate in a toast "the friend of internal improvement; prevented by indisposition from attending the marriage festival of the Ohio and Potomac." *Niles' Weekly Register* 25 (November 15, 1823): 175.

96. Charles Henry Ambler, *Sectionalism in Virginia from 1776 to 1861* (Chicago: University of Chicago Press, 1910), 187.

97. Peterson, *Tazewell*, 116–17.

98. Thomas Cooper explicitly made this point in 1824: "When Mr. Jefferson proposed to abolish the internal taxes, it was not on account of the burthen of taxation from which the people would be thus relieved, but to take away the executive influence over a host of dependents, in the pay and under the control of that department." Cooper, *Consolidation: An Account of Parties in the United States, from the Convention of 1787, to the Present Period*, 2d ed. (Columbia, S.C.: Times and Gazette, 1830), 20.

99. Richard Hofstadter, *The American Political Tradition and the Men Who Made It* (New York: Knopf, 1948), 78; Freehling, *Road to Disunion*; Freehling, *The Reintegration of American History* (New York: Oxford University Press, 1994), 138–57.

100. See Robert H. Gudmestad, *A Troublesome Commerce: The Transformation of the Interstate Slave Trade* (Baton Rouge: Louisiana State University Press, 2003), 102–6.

101. John C. Fitzpatrick, ed., *Annual Report of the American Historical Association for the Year 1918*, vol. 2, *The Autobiography of Martin Van Buren* (Washington, D.C.: U.S. Government Printing Office, 1920), 310–11.

102. See William W. Freehling, "Spoilsmen and Interests in the Thought and Career of John C. Calhoun," *Journal of American History* 52 (June 1965): 25–42.

103. "Report of a Committee of the Convention, to whom was referred an Act to provide for calling a Convention of the People of South Carolina," *State Papers on Nullification . . . Collected and Published by Order of the General Court of Massachusetts* (Boston: Dutton and Wentworth, 1834), 5.

104. Hamer, "Negro Seamen Acts," 7–9.

105. Schroeder, "Justice William Johnson," 365 n. 312.

106. Ibid., 366.

107. *Niles' Weekly Register* 25 (September 20, 1823): 47; Hamer, "Negro Seamen Acts," 7.

108. Hamer, "Negro Seamen Acts," 7.

109. See the insightful comments of Margaret L. Coit in *John C. Calhoun: American Portrait* (Boston: Houghton Mifflin, 1950), 300.

110. Freehling, *Road to Disunion*, 254.

111. For example, the *Richmond Enquirer* printed an influential letter on January 28, 1823, stressing Adams's "friendliness to the 'principles of '98'"—already a code word for protectiveness of slaveholders' interests. Risjord, *Old Republicans*, 256. Also see Adams, *Memoirs*, 6:284–85.

112. Herman Vandenberg Ames, *State Documents on Federal Relations: The States and the United States* (Philadelphia: Department of History of the University of Pennsylvania, 1906), 203–4.

113. Thomas Cooper, *Consolidation: An Account of Parties in the United States, from the Convention of 1787 to the Present Period* (Columbia, S.C.: Black and Sweeney, 1824), 26.

114. Ibid., 4. See also Malone, *Thomas Cooper*, 294–300. Cooper's repeated denunciations of "federalism," and his use of "federal" as an epithet, is in marked contrast to how John Taylor expresses himself in *New Views of the Constitution of the United States* (Washington, D.C.: Way and Gideon, 1823). Taylor approvingly employs the term in its accurate sense of preserving the sovereignty of the states, as opposed to the "national" form of government preferred by those politicians who came to be designated "Federalists." Naturally, this linguistic precision was much too subtle to be of any practical use in a slashing political campaign, as Cooper recognized when he abandoned it.

115. Cooper, *Consolidation*, 5; [George McDuffie], *National and States Rights, Considered by "One of the People," in Reply to the "Trio"* (Charleston, 1821), 15–18, cited in Freehling, *Nullification Era*, 5–7.

116. Hamer, "Negro Seamen Acts," 11.

117. Ibid.; Ames, *State Documents*, 205–6.

118. Ibid., 207.

119. Ibid., 208.

120. Ammon, *Monroe*, 500.

121. Ibid., 512. Compare the terse language of Madison's internal improvements bill veto (March 3, 1817; James D. Richardson, ed., *A Compilation of Messages and Papers of the Presidents, 1789-1902*, 10 vols. [(Washington, D.C.): Bureau of National Literature and Art, 1903], 2:569–70) with the wistful tone of Monroe's veto message of the Cumberland Road tolls bill and the expansive survey of future roads, forts and canals projected in his Eighth Annual Message, wherein all constitutional scruples have been forgotten (December 7, 1824; ibid., 817–33). Monroe felt more confident to take such a stand after receiving an informal opinion from the Supreme Court (drafted by William Johnson) assuring him that, on the precedent of the Bank of the United States, the Court interpreted the Constitution to authorize sweeping measures in this area. Schroeder, "Justice William Johnson," 362. For an excellent discussion of Monroe's attitude toward internal improvements, see Charles Sellers, *The Market Revolution: Jacksonian America, 1815-1846* (New York: Oxford University Press, 1991), 80–83.

122. Cunningham, "Nathaniel Macon," 377–78.

123. James Sterling Young, *The Washington Community, 1800-1828* (New York: Columbia University Press, 1966), 210.

124. A plaque with this motto, attributed to Harry S. Truman, adorned the desk of Ronald Reagan.

125. Adams to Louisa Adams, June 29, 1822, quoted in Alexander Saxton, *The Rise and Fall of the White Republic: Class Politics and Mass Culture in Nineteenth-Century America* (London: Verso, 1990), 41.

126. Ammon, *Monroe*, 193

127. Ibid., 504; Sellers, *Market Revolution*, 179.

128. According to a Connecticut congressman, Randolph's "constituents . . .

found fault with him for his silence" during the previous session," and he felt pressure to "open his mouth" in his characteristic inflammatory way. Edwards to William Bristol, 21 December 1823, Bristol Family Papers, MS #101, box 2, folder 31, Manuscripts and Archives, Yale University Library, New Haven, Conn.

129. Ammon, *Monroe*, 505–7; Adams, *Memoirs*, 5:497–526.

130. Peterson, *Tazewell*, 13, 96–97.

131. For an intriguing look at the role of Adams's wife, Louisa, in her husband's election, see Catherine Allgor, *Parlor Politics: In Which the Ladies of Washington Help Build a City and a Government* (Charlottesville: University Press of Virginia, 2002), 147–89.

132. Sellers, *Market Revolution*, 193.

133. Shaw Livermore Jr., *The Twilight of Federalism: The Disintegration of the Federalist Party, 1815-1830* (Princeton, N.J.: Princeton University Press, 1962), 143.

134. Chase C. Mooney, *William H. Crawford: 1772-1834* (Lexington: University Press of Kentucky, 1974), 257; Dangerfield, *Era of Good Feelings*, 310–11.

135. Henry W. Edwards to William Bristol, December 25, 1822, Bristol Family Papers, box 2, folder 31. The early date proves that Edwards referred to Crawford and not Jackson, who was not yet regarded as a candidate. The charge that Crawford had engaged in the slave trade emanated from his Georgia enemy, Governor John Clark, and may have been inspired by Andrew Jackson. To my knowledge, no convincing evidence has been offered to support it. See Mooney, *Crawford*, 225.

136. Robert V. Remini, *Martin Van Buren and the Making of the Democratic Party* (New York: Columbia University Press, 1959), 52, 45.

137. Chase C. Mooney suggests that Crawford's physical debilities, rather than his political liabilities, may have been responsible for his forgetfulness. Mooney, *Crawford*, 191–92.

138. Remini, *Van Buren and the Democratic Party*, 53.

Chapter Six

1. Leonard Woolsey Bacon, *Anti-slavery before Garrison: An Address before the Connecticut Society of the Order of the Founders and Patriots of America, New Haven, September 19, 1902* (New Haven, Conn.: Tuttle, Morehouse and Taylor, 1903), 12.

2. Ibid., 13. In the 1850s, the seminary would become the chief northern stronghold of the biblical defense of slavery.

3. P. J. Staudenraus, *The African Colonization Movement, 1816-1865* (New York: Columbia University Press, 1961), 76.

4. Douglas R. Egerton, "'Its Origins Are Not a Little Curious': A New Look at the American Colonization Society," *Journal of the Early Republic* 5 (Winter 1985): 476–77, 480.

5. Noble E. Cunningham Jr., "Nathaniel Macon and the Southern Protest against National Consolidation," *North Carolina Historical Review* 32, no. 3 (July 1955): 380.

6. Louis Weeks III, "John Holt Rice and the American Colonization Society",

Journal of Presbyterian History 46, no. 1 (1968): 29. I am grateful to Dr. Weeks for calling my attention to this essay.

7. See chapter 5 above.

8. Charles Francis Adams, ed., *Memoirs of John Quincy Adams, Comprising Portions of His Diary from 1795 to 1848*, 12 vols. (Philadelphia: J. B. Lippincott, 1874–77), 5:489.

9. *The Writings and Speeches of Daniel Webster*, 18 vols. (Boston: Little, Brown, 1903), 1:221; John Adams to Daniel Webster, December 23, 1821, in *Private Correspondence of Daniel Webster*, ed. Fletcher Webster, 2 vols. (Boston: Little, Brown, 1857), 1:318.

10. Staudenraus, *African Colonization Movement*, 78–79.

11. *The Works of William Paley, D.D. Complete in Five Volumes. To which is Prefixed a Life of the Author*, vol. 2, *Moral and Political Philosophy* (New York: S. King, 1824), frontispiece. On Paley's views of slavery, see Robert P. Forbes, "Slavery and the Evangelical Enlightenment," in *Religion and the Antebellum Debate over Slavery*, ed. John R. McKivigan and Mitchell Snay (Athens: University of Georgia Press, 1998), 84–85.

12. See, for example, Hugh Honour's discussion of Géricault in *The Image of the Black in Western Art*, vol. 4, *From the American Revolution to World War I*, part 1, *Slaves and Liberators* (Cambridge, Mass.: Harvard University Press, 1989), 125–26.

13. James K. Paulding, *Letters from the South* (New York: James Eastburn, 1817), 127–28.

14. See *Niles' Weekly Register* 25 (September 27, 1823): 59; (October 11, 1823): 83–84; (January 10, 1824): 295; 26 (July 3, 1824): 286–87.

15. Quoted by Ernestine Rose at the Seventh National Women's Eights Convention, New York City, 1856, cited in Jean Fagan Yellin, *Women and Sisters: The Antislavery Feminists in American Culture* (New Haven, Conn.: Yale University Press, 1989), 100.

16. A. R. Newsome, ed., "Letters of Romulus M. Saunders to Bartlett Yancy, 1821–1828," *North Carolina Historical Review* 8 (1931): 451. North Carolina's ultra–states' rights senator Nathaniel Macon was one of a small minority to oppose the grant of $200,000 and a township to Lafayette, which he did on constitutional grounds.

17. Jane Bacon MacIntire, *Lafayette, the Guest of the Nation: The Tracing of the Route of Lafayette's Tour of the United States in 1824–25* (Newton, Mass.: Anthony J. Simone Press, 1967), 6. It is also significant that James Tallmadge, then lieutenant governor of New York, delivered a speech at the reception in Lafayette's honor on July 4, 1825. For insightful discussions of Lafayette's tour, see Anne C. Loveland, *Emblem of Liberty: The Image of Lafayette in the American Mind* (Baton Rouge: Louisiana State University Press, 1971); and Fred Somkin, *Unquiet Eagle: Memory and Desire in the Idea of American Freedom* (Ithaca, N.Y.: Cornell University Press, 1967).

18. MacIntire, *Lafayette*, 34.

19. Rev. Charles Cotesworth Pinckney, *Life of General Thomas Pinckney* (Boston: Houghton, Mifflin, 1895), 228.

20. Josiah Quincy, *Figures of the Past* (Boston: Little, Brown, 1926), 96–97, 101–7; *Niles' Weekly Register* 28 (March 26, 1825): 49. Huger's memory was still alive in South Carolina in 1861; see *Mary Chesnut's Civil War*, ed. C. Vann Woodward (New Haven, Conn.: Yale University Press, 1981), 54.

21. See the description in Adams, *Memoirs*, 6:500.

22. Loveland, *Emblem*, 76.

23. Elmer Louis Keyser, *Bricks without Straw: The Evolution of George Washington University* (New York: Appleton-Century-Crofts, 1970), 30–32, 51–54; G. David Anderson, "Traditions: Lafayette at First Commencement," *Arts and Sciences* (newsletter for alumni of Columbian College and the Graduate School of Arts and Sciences, George Washington University), vol. 4 (Fall 1989): [2].

24. *Niles' Weekly Register* 27 (January 8, 1825): 300.

25. See chapter 2 above.

26. Loveland, *Emblem*, 68.

27. Ibid., 69–70.

28. Rufus King, *The Life and Correspondence of Rufus King Comprising His Letters, Private and Official; His Private Documents and His Speeches, Collected Papers*, ed. Charles R. King. 6 vols. (New York: G. P. Putnam's Sons, 1900), 6:500–501.

29. John Niven, *Martin Van Buren: The Romantic Age of American Politics* (New York: Oxford University Press, 1983), 153–55; George Dangerfield, *The Era of Good Feelings* (New York: Harcourt, Brace, 1952), 332–35.

30. Most of the standard treatments of this election follow Van Buren's account in chastising Van Rensselaer's weak-mindedness in voting for Adams—tellingly indicated by his taking the sight of an Adams ballot beneath his feet as a "providential" sign to support the New Englander (see, e.g., *Annual Report of the American Historical Association for the year 1918*, vol. 2, *The Autobiography of Martin Van Buren*, ed. John C. Fitzpatrick [Washington, D.C.: U.S. Government Printing Office, 1920], 152, the source of the story). None of the accounts based on Van Buren's report consider that Adams had the strong support of Van Rensselaer's political and family connections, not to mention a large majority of New Yorkers. For the patroon to have voted for Crawford would have been to ignore the wishes of the voters of his state, thus violating what Thomas Hart Benton called the "*demos krateo* principle," just as flagrantly as those representatives of Louisiana, Kentucky, and Missouri whose support for Adams in the House election of 1825 Benton, and many historians, so roundly condemned.

31. Robert V. Remini, *Martin Van Buren and the Making of the Democratic Party* (New York: Columbia University Press, 1959), 81; Niven, *Van Buren*, 155.

32. Niven, *Van Buren*, 155.

33. Adams, "Inaugural Address," in *Inaugural Addresses of the Presidents of the United States from George Washington 1789 to George Bush 1989* (Washington, D.C.: U.S. Government Printing Office, 1989), 56.

34. Fitzpatrick, *Autobiography of Van Buren*, 122–27.

35. Adams, "Inaugural Address," 56; Samuel Flagg Bemis, *John Quincy Adams and the Union* (New York: Knopf, 1956), 25. During the campaign, "on the restlessly sleeping issue of slavery [Adams had] declined to comment publicly or pri-

vately, notwithstanding the importunities of friends North and South that he make a statement for or against it. He would not even answer their letters" (ibid., 26–27).

36. Adams, "Inaugural Address," 57.

37. Ibid., 57–58.

38. See James Sterling Young, *The Washington Community, 1800-1828* (New York: Columbia University Press, 1966), 93–108; also Paul A. Rahe, *Republics Ancient and Modern* (Chapel Hill: University of North Carolina Press, 1992), 586–614.

39. King, *Correspondence*, 6:500.

40. Adams, "Inaugural Address," 59.

41. Quoted in David E. Rosenbaum, "The 1992 Campaign: Looking Ahead; Clinton Could Claim a Mandate, but It Might Be Hard to Define," *New York Times*, November 1, 1992.

42. Norman K. Risjord, *The Old Republicans: Southern Conservatism in the Age of Jefferson* (New York: Columbia University Press, 1967), 256–57; Bemis, *Adams and the Union*, 23. "In many places throughout the South a favorite ticket was Adams and Jackson, or, in the language of one of the newspapers—

John Quincy Adams,
Who can write,
And Andrew Jackson,
Who can fight."

John Bach McMaster, *A History of the People of the United States, from the Revolution to the Civil War*, 7 vols. (New York: D. Appleton, 1900), 5:68. Jackson was Adams's personal first choice for a running mate; his second choice was Nathaniel Macon. Adams, *Memoirs*, 6:360.

43. See, e.g., the circular letters from members of Congress to their constituents reprinted in *Niles' Weekly Register* 28 (May 28, 1825): 203–7.

44. The alleged author of the letter was George Kremer, an uneducated and somewhat pathetic congressman from Pennsylvania. Evidence pointed to Kremer's manipulation by John Eaton, one of Jackson's strongest supporters. The affair can be followed in *Niles' Register*.

45. Adams, *Memoirs*, 6:506–7.

46. William H. Seward, *The Life and Public Services of John Quincy Adams* (Auburn, N.Y.: Derby, Miller, 1849), 374.

47. Nathan Sargent, *Public Men and Events from the Commencement of Mr. Monroe's Administration, in 1817, to the Close of Mr. Fillmore's Administration, in 1853*, 2 vols. (Philadelphia: J. B. Lippincott, 1875), 1:108.

48. Barbour's hand may perhaps be detected in Adams's strong rhetorical commitment to states' rights in his inaugural address.

49. Bemis, *Adams and the Union*, 58–60.

50. Ibid., 65. Remini describes the Senate debates over the treaty as "tortuous arguments over . . . suppressing piracy in the West Indies," which "wasted valuable time without accomplishing anything." *Van Buren and the Democratic Party*, 93.

51. Bemis, *Adams and the Union*, 72–73. Bemis describes Adams's suggestion to

Taylor that he "arrange the [committee] members so that justice may be done as far as practicable to the Administration" as one of the president's "rare manifestations of practical political sense" (73).

52. Adams, *Memoirs*, 7:58.

53. Ibid., 63.

54. Mary W. M. Hargreaves, *The Presidency of John Quincy Adams* (Lawrence: University Press of Kansas, 1985), 114.

55. James D. Richardson, ed., *A Compilation of the Messages and Papers of the Presidents*, 10 vols. (New York: Bureau of National Literature, 1897), 2:869.

56. Remini, *Van Buren and the Democratic Party*, 106.

57. Richardson, *Messages and Papers*, 2:882.

58. An example of Adams's sensitivity to southern concerns may be found in his stern warnings to Mexico, Colombia, and the European powers that "if the Republicans of South America invaded Cuba, stirred up a slave insurrection, and armed the negroes, the United States would interfere" (McMaster, *History*, 5:439). On the subject of Van Buren's "soundness" on slavery, it is amusing to observe the exertions of his recent biographers to "defend" him from charges by political opponents of possessing latent antislavery views (prior to 1848) or of secretly harboring sympathy for African Americans. It appears that the efforts of Remini, Cole, Cortissoz, et al. have definitively exonerated the Red Fox from such unjust imputations.

59. "Did President John Quincy Adams mean that a Great Magnificent Government endowed with Power as well as Liberty for national internal improvement both physical and moral would one day become so powerful as to upset the sectional balance and perhaps redeem the coin of freedom by abolishing human slavery?" Bemis, *Adams and the Union*, 70.

60. Herman Vandenberg Ames, *State Documents on Federal Relations: The States and the United States* (Philadelphia: Department of History of the University of Pennsylvania, 1906), 203, 205.

61. Staudenraus, *African Colonization*, 119.

62. Charles William Dabney, *Universal Education in the South*, 2 vols. (Chapel Hill: University of North Carolina Press, 1936), 1:68.

63. Letter to Jared Sparks, February 4, 1824, in *The Writings of Thomas Jefferson*, ed. Paul Leicester Ford, 12 vols. (New York: G. P. Putnam's Sons, 1905), 12:336–37.

64. Madison to Robert J. Evans, June 15, 1819, quoted in *Racial Thought in America, Volume I: From the Puritans to Abraham Lincoln*, ed. Louis Ruchames (Amherst: University of Massachusetts Press, 1969), 285.

65. Ibid., 286.

66. King, *Correspondence*, 6:504.

67. King to C. King, December 21, 1823, ibid., 541. King's observation related to the Machiavellian maneuverings of the election of Leo XII on September 28, 1823. See "The Election of a Pope," *Niles' Weekly Register* 25 (October 11, 1823): 91.

68. Since King was a principal backer of the Missouri restriction measure, historians have taken his disgust with the terms of the Compromise as typical of restrictionists. But since King was also the principal political *victim* of the arrangement,

his conviction that it represented a victory for slaveholders should be treated with caution.

69. King, *Correspondence*, 6:457, 610.

70. This was a key concern of James Madison; see Ruchames, *Racial Thought*, 286. As George Dangerfield points out, "the nightmare of the 1820s" was "the mingling of chattel slavery with the pioneering West. It was this abomination, not the greater abomination of slavery itself, which shattered and tainted the political arrangements of the Missouri Compromise." The status of the West remained a crucial issue until the Civil War, precisely because it represented the future and destiny of the United States. Dangerfield, *The Era of Good Feelings*, 202.

71. Whitemarsh B. Seabrook, *A Concise View of the Critical Situation and Future Prospects of the Slave-holding States, in Relation to Their Colored Population* (Charleston, 1825), quoted in Bacon, *Anti-slavery before Garrison*, 15. An unsystematic review of elementary school readers, books of elocution and declamation, and so forth, of the period bears out Seabrook's assertion, since few of those published before 1835 fail to include pointed selections from Cowper, Wilberforce, or other antislavery authors. A content analysis of these readers, examined for change over time, would be a highly valuable undertaking.

72. *Niles' Weekly Register* 28 (June 11, 1825): 240.

73. McMaster, *History*, 5:205.

74. See, e.g., Macon to Bartlett Yancey, January 29, 1826, in *The Congressional Career of Nathaniel Macon*, ed. Edwin Mood Wilson, James Sprunt Historical Monographs, no. 2 (Chapel Hill: University of North Carolina Publications, 1900), 81.

75. *Niles' Weekly Register* 28 (July 2, 1825): 277.

76. Constance McLaughlin Green, *The Secret City: A History of Race Relations in the Nation's Capital* (Princeton, N.J.: Princeton University Press, 1967), 31–32.

77. As Robert W. Fogel explains in *Without Consent or Contract: The Rise and Fall of American Slavery* (New York: Norton, 1989), 63, the recovery of cotton prices was offset by a simultaneous decline in tobacco. Also see in the two-volume supplement to Fogel's book, edited with Stanley Engerman, *Markets and Production: Technical Papers*, 1:37, table 3:3; Ulrich B. Phillips, *American Negro Slavery* (Baton Rouge: Louisiana State University Press, 1966), 372 and graph facing 371; and Alfred Glaze Smith Jr., *Economic Readjustment of an Old Cotton State, South Carolina, 1820–1860* (Columbia: University of South Carolina Press, 1958), 3–18.

78. Nathaniel Macon to Charles Tait, January 9, 1825, in "Letters of Nathaniel Macon to Judge Charles Tait," ed. W. K. Boyd, *Historical Papers of the Trinity College Historical Society*, ser. 8 (Durham: Trinity College, 1908–9), 4.

79. There is a remarkable similarity between Maxwell's "Spirit of Improvement" and the allegorical figure of "American Progress" in George A. Crofutt's 1874 chromolithograph of the westward course of American empire. Ron Takaki describes the image as "a beautiful white woman, floating through the air. . . . Pure and innocent, she symbolizes the advance of civilization: In her right hand, she carries a book, emblem of education and knowledge, and holds in her left hand telegraph wires which she is stringing across the plains. Behind her, in a clear, lighted sky, are cities, facto-

ries, steamboats, and railroad trains." A family of half-naked Indians retreats westward before her into the shadows. Ronald T. Takaki, *Iron Cages: Race and Culture in 19th-Century America* (Seattle: University of Washington Press, 1979), 171–73 (the chromolithograph is reproduced on p. 172; a high-quality reproduction can be found on the Library of Congress website at <http://memory.loc.gov/service/pnp/ppmsca/09800/09855v.jpg>). The threat posed by "improvement" to "backward" slaveholding society is underscored by a comment of Mary Chesnut in 1861: "If we are not *improved* from the face of the earth, as the Yankees clear away the Indians . . ." Woodward, *Mary Chesnut's Civil War*, 254.

80. A[lfred] J. Morrison, ed., *Six Addresses on the State of Letters and Science in Virginia Delivered Chiefly before the Literary and Philosophical Society at Hampden-Sidney College and the Institute of Education of Hampden-Sidney College, 1824–1835* (Roanoke, Va.: Stone Printing and Manufacturing Co., 1917), 18–20.

81. Robert P. Sutton, "Nostalgia, Pessimism, and Malaise: The Doomed Aristocrat in Late-Jeffersonian Virginia," *Virginia Magazine of History and Biography* 76 (January 1968): 42. In his essay, though it is studded with noteworthy quotations, Sutton fails to grasp the background or the content of Virginia's malaise.

82. Mrs. Kirkland Ruffin, ed., "School-Boy Letters of Edmund Ruffin, Jr., 1828–1829," *North Carolina Historical Review* 10, no. 4 (October 1933): 318.

83. Ibid., 295. On the remarkable story of Prince Abd al-Rahman Ibrahima Ibn Sori, see Terry Alford, *Prince among Slaves* (1977; repr., New York: Oxford University Press, 1986).

84. Ruffin, "School-Boy Letters," 318, 326. See also Avery Craven, *Edmund Ruffin, Southerner: A Study in Secession* (1932; repr., Hamden, Conn.: Archon Books, 1964), 22–23, 28.

85. [Alexander H. Everett], *America: Or a General Survey of the Political Situation of the Several Powers of the Western Continent, with Conjectures on their Future Prospects* (1827; repr., London: John Murray, 1828), 204.

86. Martin Bernal, *Black Athena: The Afroasiatic Roots of Classical Civilization* (New Brunswick, N.J.: Rutgers University Press, 1987).

87. [Everett], *America*, 204–7.

88. Ibid., 207–8.

89. Ibid., 211; Thomas Jefferson, *Notes on the State of Virginia*, ed. William Peden (Chapel Hill: University of North Carolina Press, 1955), 140.

90. [Everett], *America*, 212–13.

91. Ibid., 213.

92. Ibid., 214–16.

93. Wilson, *Congressional Career of Nathaniel Macon*, 85. Macon's House colleague from North Carolina, Willie P. Mangum, confirmed this opinion: "The present Congress will be [pro-]administration—'The powers that be' have been gaining strength I should imagine." Mangum to Bartlett Yancey, January 15, 1826, ibid., 109.

94. Ibid., 93–94.

95. Ibid., 90; Merrill D. Peterson, *The Jefferson Image in the American Mind* (New York: Oxford University Press, 1960), 3–8; [Everett], *America*, 298–322. Jefferson's death cut short a marked southward shift in his political thought.

96. Jabez D. Hammond, *The History of Political Parties in the State of New-York, from the Ratification of the Federal Constitution to December, 1840*, 3 vols., 4th ed. (Cooperstown: H. and E. Phinney, 1846), 2:253–54. See Mangum to Bartlett Yancey, January 15, 1826: "Judging from what I can learn here, I presume that Mr. Adams will be reelected easily" (Wilson, *Congressional Career of Nathaniel Macon*, 109).

97. Robert V. Remini, "Martin Van Buren and the Tariff of Abominations," *American Historical Review* 63, no. 4 (July 1958): 903.

98. Remini, *Van Buren and the Democratic Party*, 101.

99. Adams, *Memoirs*, 6:474; Richardson, *Messages and Papers*, 2:862.

100. Remini, *Van Buren and the Democratic Party*, 61.

101. Fitzpatrick, *Autobiography of Van Buren*, 182, quoted in Remini, *Van Buren and the Democratic Party*, 60. On the southern trip of Van Buren and Dickerson, see also Adams, *Memoirs*, 6:365–66.

102. Remini, *Van Buren and the Democratic Party*, 61.

103. Ibid., 106; Norma Lois Peterson, *Littleton Waller Tazewell* (Charlottesville: University Press of Virginia, 1983), 126.

104. Hermann von Holst, *Constitutional and Political History of the United States*, 8 vols. (Chicago: Callaghan, 1889), 1:424.

105. Ibid., 424–32.

106. Remini, *Van Buren and the Democratic Party*, 106.

107. The effectiveness of this strategy may be seen in the Maryland legislature's response to proposed resolutions of support for the Panama mission. Although the committee to which the resolutions were charged avowed "the most entire confidence in the fidelity, ability, and patriotism of the administration," they noted ominously that Congress possessed "avenues of information . . . to which this body has not access," and therefore the committee requested "to be discharged from the further consideration of the subject." *Niles' Weekly Register* 29 (February 4, 1826): 365, (February 18, 1826): 402–3. See also Thomas Hart Benton, *Thirty Years' View; or, A History of the Working of the American Government for Thirty Years, from 1820 to 1850*, 2 vols. (New York: D. Appleton, 1854), 1:65–70; Dangerfield, *Era of Good Feeling*, 356–59; Remini, *Van Buren and the Democratic Party*, 105–9; Peterson, *Tazewell*, 126–27. Among northerners, only James Buchanan openly espoused the slaveholders' cause—commencing, it would seem, his long and successful effort to atone for his opposition to the expansion of slavery in 1819.

108. Dangerfield, *Era of Good Feelings*, 360–65. One commissioner, Richard C. Anderson of Kentucky, died on the way to Panama; John Sergeant, the other, chose not to set out at all.

109. William J. Grayson, *Witness to Sorrow: The Antebellum Autobiography of William J. Grayson*, ed. Richard J. Calhoun (Columbia: University of South Carolina Press, 1990), 122.

110. Peterson, *Tazewell*, 115.

111. McMaster, *History of the American People*, 5:445–46.

112. Ibid., 446.

113. Benton, *Thirty Years' View*, 1:118.

114. In this context, Van Buren's remarkable audacity in invoking Washington's

Farewell Address, America's foundational text against the "spirit of party," in his speech against the Panama mission, is noteworthy.

115. Benton, *Thirty Years' View*, 1:449.

116. Cf. Alexander Saxton, *The Rise and Fall of the White Republic: Class, Politics and Mass Culture in Nineteenth-Century America* (London: Verso, 1990), 127–61.

117. Peterson, *Tazewell*, 93.

118. Samuel Eliot Morison, *The Oxford History of the American People* (New York: Oxford University Press, 1965), 441.

119. Holst, *Constitutional History*, 1:433.

120. Remini, *Van Buren and the Democratic Party*, 117.

Chapter Seven

1. See, e.g., Stanley Elkins and Eric McKitrick, *The Federalist Era* (New York: Oxford University Press, 1993), 4–25; Lance Banning, *The Jeffersonian Persuasion: Evolution of a Party Ideology* (Ithaca, N.Y.: Cornell University Press, 1978), 42–90; and Michael D. Goldhaber, "The Tragedy of Classical Republicanism: Duff Green and the *United States' Telegraph*, 1826–1837" (senior essay, Harvard University, 1990).

2. Charles Sellers, *The Market Revolution: Jacksonian America, 1817-1846* (New York: Oxford University Press, 1991), 172–73.

3. Philip Shriver Klein, *Pennsylvania Politics, 1817-1832: A Game without Rules* (Philadelphia: Historical Society of Pennsylvania, 1940), 120.

4. Marvin Meyers, *The Jacksonian Persuasion: Politics and Belief* (Stanford, Calif.: Stanford University Press, 1957), 71, 73, 98.

5. James C. Curtis, *Andrew Jackson and the Search for Vindication* (Boston: Little, Brown, 1976), 89. See Garry Wills, *Cincinnatus: George Washington and the Enlightenment* (Garden City, N.Y.: Doubleday, 1984), for a brilliant treatment of the power of this theme.

6. Sellers, *Market Revolution*, 181.

7. See *Memoirs of General Andrew Jackson, Together with the Letter of Mr. Secretary Adams, in Vindication of the Execution of Arbuthnot and Ambrister, and the other Public Acts of Gen. Jackson, in Florida* (New York, 1824).

8. Still essential for understanding John Quincy Adams's view of American expansion is Albert K. Weinberg, *Manifest Destiny: A Study of Nationalist Expansionism in American History* (1935; repr., Chicago: Quadrangle Books, 1963). Also useful is Walter LaFeber, ed., *John Quincy Adams and the American Continental Empire* (Chicago: University of Chicago Press, 1965), esp. 14–15.

9. Curtis, *Andrew Jackson*, 16.

10. *Richmond Enquirer*, January 5, 1819.

11. Willie P. Mangum to Bartlett Yancey, January 15, 1826, in *The Congressional Career of Nathaniel Macon*, ed. Edwin Mood Wilson, James Sprunt Historical Monographs, no. 2 (Chapel Hill: University of North Carolina Publications, 1900), 107. See also the *Norfolk and Portsmouth Herald*, February 4, 1825: "The great majority of Mr. Crawford's friends in Virginia are so decidedly opposed to Jackson,

that under no circumstances whatever could they be induced to favor his election; put Mr. Crawford out of the question to the people of Virginia, J. Q. Adams would be President without a doubt." Quoted in Norman K. Risjord, *The Old Republicans: Southern Conservatism in the Age of Jefferson* (New York: Columbia University Press, 1967), 256.

12. James Graham to William A. Graham, August 27, 1825, in *The Papers of William Alexander Graham*, ed. J. G. de Roulhac Hamilton, 3 vols. (Raleigh: State Department of Archives and History, 1957), 1:147.

13. Charles Henry Ambler, *Thomas Ritchie: A Study in Virginia Politics* (Richmond: Bell Book and Stationery Co., 1913), 99. Ritchie did not formally endorse Jackson until April 27, 1827.

14. Robert V. Remini, ed., *The Age of Jackson* (Columbia, S.C.: University of South Carolina Press, 1972), 197.

15. Richard H. Brown, "The Missouri Crisis, Slavery, and the Politics of Jacksonianism," *South Atlantic Quarterly* 65 (1966): 55.

16. Remini, *Age of Jackson*, 6.

17. Robert P. Forbes, "Slavery and the Meaning of America, 1819–1833" (Ph.D. diss., Yale University, 1994), 100.

18. Robert V. Remini, *The Legacy of Andrew Jackson: Essays on Democracy, Indian Removal, and Slavery* (Baton Rouge: Louisiana State University Press, 1988), 86.

19. Goldhaber, "Tragedy of Classical Republicanism," 31. Throughout his career as an editor, Green sought to combat what he called an "anti-slavery conspiracy" spawned "as far back as 1817" by John Quincy Adams, and designed to restore the "federal party" to power. See Green, *Facts and Suggestions, Biographical, Historical, Financial and Political, Addressed to the People of the United States* (New York: Richardson, 1866), 30–33.

20. Green to William Snowden, November 16, 1827; Green to Worden Pope, January 4, 1828, Duff Green Papers, Library of Congress, Washington, D.C.

21. The most logical explanation is that the link between the urban North and the once–"Solid South" remains the cornerstone of the current Democratic Party's hopes of national electoral success, as the election of Bill Clinton, along with every other recent Democratic victory, demonstrates. The modern historiography of the period, launched by Arthur Schlesinger Jr.'s *Age of Jackson*, remarkably replicates the old Bancroftian tradition of active participation by historians in the political affairs of the Democratic Party. Thus many politically engaged historians remain committed, even unconsciously, to perpetuating Van Buren's more-than-150-year-old political agenda. For a pertinent recent illustration, see Peter B. Kovler, ed., *Democrats and the American Idea: A Bicentennial Appraisal* (Washington, D.C.: Center for National Policy Press, 1992), a collection of essays on the enduring heritage of the Democratic Party by historians and party activists timed to commemorate the 200th anniversary of the founding of the party by Thomas Jefferson. For a recent treatment of Van Buren's Ritchie letter sympathetic to Van Buren's aims, by a contributor to the Kovler volume, see Sean Wilentz, *The Rise of American Democracy: Jefferson to Lincoln* (New York: Norton, 2005), 295–97.

22. Martin Van Buren, *Inquiry into the Origin and Course of Political Parties in the United States* (New York: Hurd and Houghton, 1867), 322.

23. Norma Lois Peterson, *Littleton Waller Tazewell* (Charlottesville: University Press of Virginia, 1983), 134, 135.

24. Before his candidacy, although his views on specific policies were virtually unknown, Jackson had a reputation as a nationalist on economic questions and of being conciliatory toward Federalism. In an episode that later proved an embarrassment, Jackson denied having written a letter to Monroe urging him to appoint Federalists as well as Republicans to positions in his administration—only to be contradicted by both Pennsylvania senators, staunch Republicans, to whom the president had read the letter. See Walter Lowrie, *Memoirs of the Hon. Walter Lowrie* (New York: Baker and Taylor, 1894), 23–24.

25. Robert V. Remini, "Martin Van Buren and the Tariff of Abominations," *American Historical Review* 63, no. 4 (July 1958): 903–4.

26. Peterson, *Tazewell*, 135.

27. Goldhaber, "Tragedy of Classical Republicanism," 29.

28. E. L. Magoon, *Living Orators in America* (New York: Baker and Scribner, 1849), 119.

29. Merrill D. Peterson, *The Great Triumvirate: Webster, Clay, and Calhoun* (New York: Oxford University Press, 1987), 75.

30. Clement Eaton, *Henry Clay and the Art of American Politics* (Boston: Little, Brown, 1957), 118. Clay's fifty to sixty slaves made him a large slaveholder by Kentucky standards, but did not compare to the great slave plantations of the Deep South and Southwest. See ibid., 119–22. William Henry Smith, in his study of Cincinnati antislavery editor Charles Hammond, supplies evidence suggesting that some supporters in the campaign of 1824 regarded Clay as a genuine antislavery candidate—albeit a discreet one. Smith, *Charles Hammond and His Relations to Henry Clay and John Quincy Adams; or, Constitutional Limitations and the Contest for Freedom of Speech and the Press* (Chicago: Chicago Historical Society, 1885), 32–37.

31. Leonard Woolsey Bacon, *Anti-slavery before Garrison* (New Haven, Conn.: Tuttle, Morehouse and Taylor, 1903), 17.

32. N. L. Peterson, *Tazewell*, 153.

33. Duff Green's *United States' Telegraph* had similarly "characterized minor new restrictions on foreigners in the navy as the equivalent of the Alien Act." Goldhaber, "Tragedy of Classical Republicanism," 25.

34. This figure is derived in the following manner. The total number of slaves in the United States, according to 1820 census figures, was 1,538,125. Three-fifths of this figure gives a "federal number" of 911,400 for purposes of electoral representation. The average size of a congressional district in 1824 was approximately 41,000 persons; thus slaves accounted for approximately 22 additional congressional seats, and electoral votes. Adams actually received 84 electoral votes; but by applying the same rule to him, his total would have declined to 83 as a result of subtracting the slave representation (the equivalent of 41,051 "federal votes") from the 6 electoral votes he received from slave states (3 from Maryland, 2 from Louisiana, and

1 from Delaware). See William H. Seward, *Life and Public Services of John Quincy Adams* (Auburn, N.Y.: Derby, Miller, 1849), 149–50; and Calvin Colton, *The Life and Times of Henry Clay*, 2 vols. (New York: A. S. Barnes, 1846), 1:290–93. For analysis of the impact of slave representation on the election of 1800, see William W. Freehling, *The Road to Disunion: Secessionists at Bay, 1776-1854* (New York: Oxford University Press, 1990), 147; on the broader question, see Arthur F. Simpson, "The Political Significance of Slave Representation, 1787–1821," *Journal of Southern History* 71 (1941): 315–42.

35. Willie P. Mangum to Bartlett Yancey, January 15, 1826, Wilson, *Congressional Career of Nathaniel Macon*, 109–10.

36. Bacon, *Anti-slavery before Garrison*, 24–25.

37. Paul Revere Frothingham, *Edward Everett, Orator and Statesman* (Boston: Houghton Mifflin, 1925), 105–7; Horace Greeley, *Recollections of a Busy Life* (New York: J. B. Ford, 1868), 281; Bacon, *Anti-slavery before Garrison*, 26–28. Bacon notes that William Lloyd Garrison, then a newspaper editor in Newburyport, printed Everett's speech in his paper without criticism. Ibid., 28.

38. Bacon, *Anti-slavery before Garrison*, 29–31. It is perhaps worth noting in passing that such attitudes were insufficient to save Bacon from being listed as an influential proslavery clergyman in Larry A. Tise's *Proslavery: A History of the Defense of Slavery in America, 1701-1840* (Athens: University of Georgia Press, 1987), 34.

39. Bacon, *Anti-slavery before Garrison*, 29–31.

40. Ibid., 32–33.

41. *New York Freedom's Journal*, July 6, 1827.

42. Heman Humphrey, *Parallel between Intemperance and the Slave Trade: An Address Delivered at Amherst College, July 4, 1828* (Amherst, Mass.: J. S. and C. Adams, 1828), 4–6.

43. Ibid., 7.

44. James Johnson Pettigrew, *Report of the Minority of the Special Committee of Seven, to Whom Was Referred So Much of His Late Excellency's Message No. 1, as Relates to Slavery and the Slave Trade* (Columbia, S.C.: Carolina Times, 1857), 35, quoted in Clyde N. Wilson, *Carolina Cavalier: The Life and Mind of James Johnson Pettigrew* (Athens: University of Georgia Press, 1990), 102; see also C. Vann Woodward, ed., *Mary Chesnut's Civil War* (New Haven, Conn.: Yale University Press, 1981), 357.

45. Wilson, *Congressional Career of Nathaniel Macon*, 77.

46. Ibid., 114.

47. Risjord, *Old Republicans*, 268. Tyler's willingness to work with the Adamsites marked him as potentially "unsound" among Old Republicans, and undoubtedly contributed to his later states' rights extremism—a familiar pattern displayed by George McDuffie, John C. Calhoun, and countless fire-eaters of 1860.

48. John Bach McMaster, *A History of the People of the United States, from the Revolution to the Civil War*, 7 vols. (New York: D. Appleton, 1900), 5:240–42.

49. *Niles' Register* 33 (September 8, 1827): 28–32.

50. "Brutus" [Robert J. Turnbull], *The Crisis; or, Essays on the Usurpations of the Federal Government* (Charleston: A. E. Miller, 1827), 18, 67.

51. Ibid., 128–30.

52. Kenneth S. Greenberg has ingeniously, but in my view erroneously, recast the southern proslavery argument as an antislavery argument—an argument, that is, against the enslavement of Southern whites (*Masters and Statesmen: The Political Culture of American Slavery* [Baltimore: Johns Hopkins University Press, 1985]). Turnbull's pamphlet and its reception demonstrate that slavery took priority over freedom, at least for South Carolinians.

53. "Brutus," *Crisis*, 130, 148, 131.

54. Ibid., 132–33.

55. William W. Freehling, ed., *The Nullification Era: a Documentary Record* (New York: Harper Torchbooks, 1967), 26.

56. Thus Michael Goldhaber: "In the back of their minds, [southerners] knew that the same loose interpretation of the Constitution that made possible high tariffs could pave the way for emancipation by law. 'Had the South united in opposition to the tariff,' [Duff] Green later mused, 'the slave question would have been put to rest forever.' Nullification was, at least partially, a method to thwart the abolitionists without directly rebutting them." Goldhaber, "Tragedy of Classical Republicanism," 71.

57. William Giles, "Political Disquisitions. No. I," *Richmond Enquirer*, January 6, 1827.

58. Ibid.

59. Ibid. For an insightful discussion of the complications surrounding rhetorical comparisons of southern and northern "slaves," see David R. Roediger, *The Wages of Whiteness* (London: Verso, 1991), 43–92, and Jonathan A. Glickstein, *Concepts of Free Labor in Antebellum America* (New Haven, Conn.: Yale University Press, 1991), 149–70.

60. Remini, "Van Buren and the Tariff of Abominations," 904.

61. Ibid., 904–6; F. W. Taussig, *The Tariff History of the United States* (1888; repr., New York: G. P. Putnam's Sons, 1931), 89–98.

62. Remini, "Van Buren and the Tariff of Abominations," 917.

63. *United States' Telegraph* 1, no. 5 (April 12, 1828): 92–93.

64. Edward Pessen, *Jacksonian America: Society, Personality and Politics*, rev. ed. (Urbana: University of Illinois Press, 1985), 166.

65. Russell Kirk, *John Randolph of Roanoke: A Study in American Politics* (1954; repr., Indianapolis: Liberty Press, [1978]), 506–33.

66. Chauncey Samuel Boucher, *The Nullification Controversy in South Carolina* (Chicago: University of Chicago Press, 1916), 16–32.

67. Charles H. Ambler, *The Life and Diary of John Floyd: Governor of Virginia, an Apostle of Secession, and the Father of the Oregon Country* (Richmond: Richmond Press, 1918), 123–24. Floyd later described Jackson's cabinet even more harshly as "blackguards, not gentlemen, men without knowledge, learning, or morals, as violent and vindictive as Jackson himself." Ibid., 147.

68. Philip Shriver Klein, *Pennsylvania Politics, 1817-1832: A Game without Rules* (Philadelphia: Historical Society of Pennsylvania, 1940), 126–27.

69. [Henry Orne], *The Letters of Columbus; Originally Published in the Boston Bulletin: To Which Are Added Two Letters of Col. Orne to Gen. Duff Green* (Boston: Putnam and Hunt, 1829), 80–81.

70. John Niven, *Martin Van Buren: The Romantic Age of American Politics* (New York: Oxford University Press, 1983), 224.

71. Pessen, *Jacksonian America*, 288. This remark of the general's might be classed with his statement to James A. Hamilton, son of Alexander Hamilton, "*Colonel, your Father was not in favor of the Bank of the United States.*" Robert V. Remini, *Andrew Jackson and the Bank War* (New York: Norton, 1967), 49. On the Timberlake affair, see Catherine Allgor, *Parlor Politics: In Which the Ladies of Washington Help Build a City and a Government* (Charlottesville: University of Virginia Press, 2002), 190–210.

72. *Niles' Register* 36 (July 11, 1829): 313–15.

73. Richard R. John, *Spreading the News* (Cambridge, Mass.: Harvard University Press, 1995), 213–16.

74. Pessen, *Jacksonian America*, 315; John Spencer Bassett, *The Life of Andrew Jackson* (1911; repr., [Hamden, Conn.]: Archon Books, 1967), 446–57.

75. On the centrality of Jackson's Indian policy, see Richard B. Latner, *The Presidency of Andrew Jackson: White House Politics, 1829-1837* (Athens: University of Georgia Press, 1979), 86–98; for its popularity among southern states' rights supporters, see ibid., 92.

76. Ibid., 91–93; Robert J. Eells, *Forgotten Saint: The Life of Theodore Frelinghuysen; A Case Study of Christian Leadership* (Lanham, Md.: University Press of America, 1987), 20–24.

77. Philip M. Hamer, "Great Britain, the United States, and the Negro Seamen Acts, 1822–1848," *Journal of Southern History* 1 (1935): 12–13.

78. Ibid., 13.

79. Ibid., 14–15.

80. Richard C. Wade, *The Urban Frontier: Pioneer Life in Early Pittsburgh, Cincinnati, Lexington, Louisville, and St. Louis* (Chicago: University of Chicago Press, 1964), 225–26.

81. An example is a mechanic named Watson, who at one time had "owned all of the cornfields that now form the business block in the heart of Cincinnati, bounded by 3d, Elm, 4th and Race Streets." Wendell Phillips Dabney, *Cincinnati's Colored Citizens: Historical, Sociological and Biographical* (Cincinnati: Dabney Publishing Company, 1926), 231. For the rise in property values in and near Cincinnati, see Morris Birkbeck, *Notes on a Journey in America, from the Coast of Virginia to the Territory of Ilinois* (London, 1818), 81–83.

82. Ebenezer Davies, *American Scenes and Christian Slavery: A Recent Tour of Four Thousand Miles in the United States* (London: J. Snow, 1849), 128. In actuality, the Canadians' response to uprooted American blacks was decidedly chilly. See Jason Silverman, *Unwelcome Guests: Canada West's Response to American Fugitive Slaves, 1800-1865* (Milwood, N.Y.: Associated Faculty Press, 1985). See also Robin

W. Winks, *The Blacks in Canada: A History* (Montreal: McGill-Queen's University Press, 1971), 155–56.

83. Winks, *Blacks in Canada*, 156; Austin Steward, *Twenty-two Years a Slave, and Forty Years a Freeman* (Rochester: W. Alling, 1857), 173–84. See also Nikki M. Taylor, *Frontiers of Freedom: Cincinnati's Black Community, 1802-1868* (Athens: Ohio University Press, 2005), 50–79.

84. Leonard P. Curry, *The Free Black in Urban America, 1800-1850: The Shadow of the Dream* (Chicago: University of Chicago Press, 1981), 104. This riot was "the first significant anti-Negro outbreak in Philadelphia," according to Curry.

85. William W. Freehling, *Prelude to Civil War: The Nullification Controversy in South Carolina, 1816-1836* (New York: Harper and Row, 1968), 81.

86. William Loren Katz, introduction to David Walker, *Walker's Appeal in Four Articles*, and Henry Highland Garnet, *An Address to the Slaves of the United States of America* (New York: Arno Press, 1969), ii. A more compelling discussion, but one with which I take issue on several points, is found in Lawrence J. Friedman, *Inventors of the Promised Land* (New York: Knopf, 1975), appendix B, "David Walker's *Appeal* Reconsidered," 315–23.

87. This subject is discussed in detail in chapter 3 above.

88. *United States' Telegraph* 1, no. 9 (May 7, 1828): 144. The *Telegraph* did not feel the need to inform its readers that the appropriation doubtless pertained to diplomatic ministers' dress, not to clerical dress.

89. *Walker's Appeal . . . to the Coloured Citizens of the World, but in Particular, and Very Expressly, to Those of the United States of America . . .* , 3d ed. (Boston, 1830), in Herbert Aptheker, *One Continual Cry: David Walker's Appeal to the Colored Citizens of the World* (New York: Humanities Press, 1965), 90–91.

90. Ibid., 66–67.

91. Ibid., 68, 83. Compare Walker's statement with British abolitionist Granville Sharp's 1797 discussion of Psalm 11:3, "If the foundations be destroyed, what can the righteous do?": "[The psalmist] did not mean *the natural foundations of the earth*, but *foundations* of much more importance to mankind, *the foundations of law and righteousness*; on which, indeed, depend the very existence even of *the natural foundations of the earth*." Sharp, *Serious Reflections on the Slave Trade and Slavery. Wrote in March, 1797* (London, 1805), 7–9.

92. Walker, *Appeal*, 144.

93. "We cannot bow before a being, however great and powerful, who governs tyrannically." William Ellery Channing, *Selected Writings*, ed. David Robinson (New York: Paulist Press, 1985), 87.

Chapter Eight

1. This was the same Foot, though chastened, who had voted with the South for the first Missouri Compromise in 1820 and had been denied renomination to the House of Representatives. On this incident, see Thomas Hart Benton, *Thirty Years' View; or, A History of the Working of the American Government for Thirty Years, from 1820 to 1850*, 2 vols. (New York: D. Appleton, 1854), 1:130–43; Merrill D.

Peterson, *The Great Triumvirate: Webster, Clay, and Calhoun* (New York: Oxford University Press, 1987), 170–83; and Samuel Eliot Morison, *The Oxford History of the American People* (New York: Oxford University Press, 1965), 434–35.

2. Morison, *Oxford History*, 434.

3. Peterson, *Great Triumvirate*, 173.

4. Michael D. Goldhaber, "The Tragedy of Classical Republicanism: Duff Green and the *United States' Telegraph*, 1826–1837" (unpublished senior essay, Harvard University, 1990), 47, 48.

5. Herman Belz, ed., *The Webster-Hayne Debate on the Nature of the Union: Selected Documents* (Indianapolis: Liberty Fund, 2000), 48–49.

6. Ibid., 55.

7. Ibid., 44–45, 49, 53–55, 76–79.

8. Goldhaber, "Tragedy of Classical Republicanism," 48.

9. Ronald P. Formisano, *The Transformation of Political Culture: Massachusetts Parties, 1790s–1840s* (New York: Oxford University Press, 1983), 57–83.

10. Nicholas P. Trist to James Madison, February 6, 1830, cited in Peterson, *Great Triumvirate*, 175.

11. Kenneth M. Stampp, "The Concept of a Perpetual Union," in *The Imperiled Union: Essays on the Background of the Civil War* (New York: Oxford University Press, 1980), 30.

12. Belz, *Webster-Hayne Debate*, 118.

13. Ibid., 122; see Formisano, *Transformation of Political Culture*, 57.

14. Thomas Brown, *Politics and Statesmanship: Essays on the American Whig Party* (New York: Columbia University Press, 1985), 65. Daniel Walker Howe, in his superb *The Political Culture of the American Whigs* (Chicago: University of Chicago Press, 1979), thus draws too neat a distinction between the typical Democratic rejection of the past and the Whig appeal to history—failing to acknowledge the degree to which Whigs (or, in this case, proto-Whigs) fashioned their own version of history to abet their rhetorical and political purposes. (Howe's claim also downplays the importance of the Democratic historical imagination as employed, for example, in the romances and stories of James Fenimore Cooper and Nathaniel Hawthorne.) See Howe, chap. 4, "The Whig Interpretation of History," esp. 69–84.

15. Robert V. Remini, *The Election of Andrew Jackson* (Philadelphia: J. B. Lippincott, 1963), 202.

16. In meeting this objective Webster proved remarkably successful, as few of his biographers mention his Missouri efforts at all.

17. Belz, *Webster-Hayne Debate*, 76–77.

18. Ibid., 91. On the Whig commitment to an evolving, improving union, and its contrast to the Democratic view, see, e.g., Major Wilson, *Space, Time, and Freedom: The Quest for Nationality and the Irrepressible Conflict* (Westport, Conn.: Greenwood Press, 1974), 3–21, and Howe, *American Whigs*, 72–74.

19. David Duncan Wallace, *South Carolina: A Short History, 1520–1948* (1951; repr., Columbia, S.C.: University of South Carolina Press, 1961), 383.

20. *Niles' Weekly Register* 37 (January 23, 1830): 353–54.

21. Maurice G. Baxter, *One and Inseparable: Daniel Webster and the Union* (Cambridge, Mass.: Belknap Press of Harvard University Press, 1984), 187.

22. Benton, *Thirty Years' View*, 1:148.

23. John Spencer Bassett, *The Life of Andrew Jackson* (1911; repr., [Hamden, Conn.]: Archon Books, 1967), 555; *Annual Report of the American Historical Association for the Year 1918*, vol. 2, *The Autobiography of Martin Van Buren*, ed. John C. Fitzpatrick (Washington, D.C.: U.S. Government Printing Office, 1920), 413–16. It is astonishing, and to me inexplicable, how many historians not only place unquestioning confidence in Van Buren's account, but even transcribe Jackson's original toast as "Our Federal Union." Examples include Samuel Rhea Gammon, *The Presidential Campaign of 1832* (Baltimore: Johns Hopkins University Press, 1922), 138; Edward Boykin, *Congress and the Civil War* (New York: McBride, 1955), 96; John William Ward, *Andrew Jackson: Symbol for an Age* (New York: Oxford University Press, 1962), 86; and even *Bartlett's Familiar Quotations*, 14th ed. (Boston: Little, Brown, 1968), 503.

24. Benton, *Thirty Years' View*, 1:148.

25. Baxter, *One and Inseparable*, 188.

26. John Niven, *Martin Van Buren: The Romantic Age of American Politics* (New York: Oxford University Press, 1983), 257.

27. Bassett, *Life of Jackson*, 489. The phrase is often mistakenly attributed to Randolph himself, but it is unlikely that that keen-eyed detector of cant would have offered a ringing endorsement of such an archetypal example of Van Buren "noncommittalism" as the Maysville veto. It is also likely that the high-strung Virginian's dispatch to Russia, an astonishing appointment, which, as Van Buren frankly admitted, exposed the sickly Virginian to an unfavorable climate and undoubtedly shortened his life, was designed to forestall any possible "Randolphian *escapade*" against the administration. Fitzpatrick, *Autobiography of Van Buren*, 418–23. Why Randolph accepted the post is another mystery; although it seems likely that the consummate American admirer of aristocracy could not resist an invitation to the court of an authentic emperor.

28. James D. Richardson, ed., *A Compilation of Messages and Papers of the Presidents, 1789–1902* (Washington, D.C.: Bureau of National Literature and Art, 1903), 2:437; Bassett, *Life of Jackson*, 429–30.

29. Goldhaber, "Tragedy of Classical Republicanism," 40.

30. John C. Calhoun, "Rough Draft of What Is Called the South Carolina Exposition," November 25, 1828[?], in *The Papers of John C. Calhoun*, ed. Robert O. Meriwether et al., 28 vols.(Columbia, S.C.: University of South Carolina Press, 1959–2003), 10:444–532; Hermann E. von Holst, *John C. Calhoun* (1899; repr., New York: Chelsea House, 1980), 75–102; Lacy K. Ford Jr., "Inventing the Concurrent Majority: Madison, Calhoun, and the Problem of Majoritarianism in American Political Thought," *Journal of Southern History* 60, no. 1 (February 1994): 45–55.

31. Wallace, *South Carolina*, 387.

32. Ibid., 388.

33. Charles H. Ambler, *The Life and Diary of John Floyd: Governor of Virginia,*

an Apostle of Secession, and the Father of the Oregon Country (Richmond: Richmond Press, 1918), 163; Calhoun to Christopher Van Deventer, August 4, 1831, in *Annual Report of the American Historical Association for the Year 1899*, vol. 2, *Calhoun Correspondence*, ed. J. Franklin Jameson (Washington, D.C.: U.S. Government Printing Office, 1900), 296.

34. Bassett, *Life of Jackson*, 496.

35. Ibid., 517–19; Ambler, *Floyd* , 126–29. On the flirtation of Massachusetts Jacksonians with Calhoun, see John Barton Derby, *Political Reminiscences, Including a Sketch of the Origin and History of the "Statesman Party" of Boston* (Boston: Homer and Palmer, 1835), 100–119.

36. Ambler, *Floyd*, 168–69.

37. Ibid., 138.

38. Jameson, *Calhoun Correspondence*, 274.

39. Francis Asbury to "My dear wrestling Jacob [Gruber]", September 1, 1811, quoted in John B. Boles, "Tension in a Slave Society: The Trial of the Reverend Jacob Gruber," *Southern Studies* 18 (Summer 1979): 179.

40. Ambler, *Floyd*, 145–46.

41. See Alice S. Maxwell and Marion B. Dunlevy, *Virago! The Story of Anne Newport Royall (1769-1854)* (Jefferson, N.C.: McFarland, 1985), 78–80.

42. Richard R. John Jr., "Taking Sabbatarianism Seriously: The Postal System, the Sabbath, and the Transformation of American Political Culture," *Journal of the Early Republic* 19 (Winter 1990): 517–67; also see Donald L. Robinson, *Slavery in the Structure of American Politics, 1765-1820* (New York: Harcourt Brace Jovanovich, 1971), 77.

43. Gilbert Hobbs Barnes, *The Antislavery Impulse, 1830-1844* (New York: Harcourt, Brace and World, 1964), 31–32.

44. Paul Finkelman, "Prelude to the Fourteenth Amendment," *Rutgers Law Journal* 17 (1986): 420–21.

45. [Wendell Phillips Garrison and Francis Jackson Garrison], *William Lloyd Garrison, 1805-1879: The Story of His Life Told by His Children*, 4 vols. (New York: Century, 1885), 1:234–35.

46. Ambler, *Floyd*, 155.

47. Ibid., 161.

48. Alison Goodyear Freehling, *Drift toward Disunion: The Virginia Slavery Debates of 1831-1832* (Baton Rouge: Louisiana State University Press, 1982), 6.

49. Ambler, *Floyd*, 170.

50. Theodore M. Whitfield, *Slavery Agitation in Virginia, 1829-1832* (Baltimore: Johns Hopkins Press, 1930), 61–62.

51. Philip S. Foner and Ronald L. Lewis, eds., *The Black Worker: A Documentary History from Colonial Times to the Present*, 8 vols. (Philadelphia: Temple University Press, 1978–84), 2:392.

52. Charles H. Ambler, *Sectionalism in Virginia from 1776 to 1861* (Chicago: University of Chicago Press, 1910), 197, 198.

53. *Richmond Constitutional Whig*, November 17, 1831, in A. G. Freehling, *Drift toward Disunion*, 85.

54. A. G. Freehling, *Drift toward Disunion*, 86–87; Ambler, *Sectionalism in Virginia*, 188–89.

55. A. G. Freehling, *Drift toward Disunion*, 84–86.

56. Ibid., 86.

57. *Richmond Enquirer*, January 7, 1832, quoted in Ambler, *Sectionalism in Virginia*, 190–91.

58. Ambler, *Sectionalism in Virginia*, 191.

59. [Garrison and Garrison], *William Lloyd Garrison*, 1:279.

60. *Richmond Enquirer*, November 23, 1819. See chapter 2 above, text at n. 85.

61. Quoted in Harriet Martineau, *Society in America*, 3 vols. (London: Saunder and Otley, 1837), 2:127.

62. Ambler, *Floyd*, 174–75.

63. Ibid., 177.

64. Ibid., 175.

65. A. G. Freehling, *Drift toward Dissolution*, 151–53, 162.

66. Ibid., 127.

67. Thomas Roderick Dew, "Abolition of Negro Slavery," in *The Ideology of Slavery: Proslavery Thought in the Antebellum South, 1830–1860*, ed. Drew Gilpin Faust (Baton Rouge: Louisiana State University Press, 1981), 62–63.

68. William W. Freehling, *The Road to Disunion: Secessionists at Bay, 1776-1854* (New York: Oxford University Press, 1991), 193.

69. Norma Lois Peterson, *Littleton Waller Tazewell* (Charlottesville: University Press of Virginia, 1983), 197.

70. W. W. Freehling, *Road to Disunion*, 193–94.

71. Patricia Elizabeth Prickett Hickin, "Antislavery in Virginia, 1831–1861" (Ph.D. diss., University of Michigan, 1969), 7.

72. Quoted in "A Citizen of Pennsylvania" [Mathew Carey], *The Dissolution of the Union. A Sober Address to All Those Who Have Any Interest in the Welfare, the Power, the Glory, or the Happiness of the United States* (Philadelphia: J. Bioren, 1832), 4.

73. Calvin Colton, ed., *The Private Correspondence of Henry Clay* (New York: A. S. Barnes, 1855), 331–33. John Floyd approached Clay in March 1832 with a plan for Calhoun to run in the South, intended to deny Jackson an electoral majority and force the decision into the House of Representatives, where Clay's election would be likely. After this plan was abandoned, Calhoun and his allies attempted to place states' rights Virginian Philip Barbour on the ticket with Clay.

74. Robert J. Turnbull, *An Oration Delivered in the City of Charleston before the State Rights & Free Trade Party, . . . on the 4th of July, 1832, Being the 50th Anniversary of American Independence* (Charleston: A. E. Miller, 1832), 20.

75. Richard B. Latner, *The Presidency of Andrew Jackson: White House Politics, 1829-1837* (Athens: University of Georgia Press, 1979), 86–98; Harry L. Watson, *Jacksonian Politics and Community Conflict: The Emergence of the Second American Party System in Cumberland County, North Carolina* (Baton Rouge: Louisiana State University Press, 1981), 2.

76. Latner, *Presidency of Andrew Jackson*, 155.

77. Ibid., 152–53.

78. Niven, *Van Buren*, 322.

79. Samuel Eliot Morison, *The Life and Letters of Harrison Gray Otis, Federalist, 1765–1848*, 2 vols. (Boston: Houghton Mifflin, 1913), 2:292–93.

80. Fitzpatrick, *Autobiography of Van Buren*, 547.

81. Latner, *Presidency of Andrew Jackson*, 153.

82. Niven, *Van Buren*, 321–25; Fitzpatrick, *Autobiography of Van Buren*, 553.

83. In 1839, however, Jackson wrote a letter to Van Buren's long-time ally Isaac Hill in New Hampshire, rejoicing that "the anathemas of the virtuous people have consigned [the] traitors to the democratic cause, to that doom that awaits all traitors," and urging Hill to spearhead a national convention to support James K. Polk, not Van Buren, for the Democratic presidential nomination. None of Van Buren's or Jackson's biographers appear to be aware of this letter. Jackson to Isaac Hill, October 31, 1839, Isaac Hill Papers, folder 5, New Hampshire Historical Society, Concord, N.H.

84. Sydney Nathans, *Daniel Webster and Jacksonian Democracy* (Baltimore: Johns Hopkins University Press, 1973), 52.

85. See chapter 7 above.

86. Derby, *Political Reminiscences*, 112–17.

87. Fitzpatrick, *Autobiography of Van Buren*, 553.

88. William Hoffman, "The Friends of Martin Van Buren and the Nullification Crisis" (unpublished paper, Society of Historians of the Early American Republic, University of North Carolina, Chapel Hill, July 1993). Hoffman does not suggest that Van Buren personally influenced Clay to undertake the tariff compromise, but it does not seem unlikely, and nothing in Van Buren's autobiography precludes such an interpretation. I am grateful to Professor Hoffman for making a copy of his paper available to me.

89. Van Buren to Silas Wright, February 23, 1833, Niven, *Van Buren*, 329.

90. See Oliver Perry Chitwood, *John Tyler, Champion of the Old South* (New York: Appleton-Century, 1939), 115–22. For Tyler's speech opposing the Force Bill, see *Register of Congress*, 22d Congress, 2d sess., 360–77.

91. Baxter, *One and Inseparable*, 222.

92. Niven, *Van Buren*, 330–31.

93. I have largely refrained in this account from employing the party designation "National Republicans," because even though it had some contemporary currency it implies a degree of party cohesion absent both in the reality and the ideology of the loosely constituted anti-Jackson coalition. Indeed, it is the persistence of a powerful ideal of nonpartisanship that made seeming shifts like Webster's and Clay's not only accepted but even lauded by the public at large. Martin Van Buren's vigorous defense of parties remained the exception, not the rule, until well into the 1830s or even later. See Formisano, *Transformation of Political Culture*, 93–106, and Richard Hofstadter, *The Idea of a Party System: The Rise of Legitimate Opposition in the United States, 1780–1840* (Berkeley: University of California Press, 1969), especially his insightful discussion of Martin Van Buren, 212–52.

94. Benton, *Thirty Years' View*, 1:343.

95. Ambler, *Floyd*, 212.

96. Morison, *Otis*, 2:293.

97. Josiah Quincy, *Figures of the Past* (Boston: Little, Brown, 1926), 305. Quincy's is the most appealing account of Jackson's visit to Massachusetts.

98. Arthur Schlesinger Jr., *The Age of Jackson* (Boston: Little, Brown, 1946), 38n.

99. Charles Grier Sellers, "The Travail of Slavery," in *The Southerner as American*, ed. Charles Grier Sellers (Chapel Hill: University of North Carolina Press, 1960), 51. This important essay deserves careful rereading.

100. C. Duncan Rice, *The Scots Abolitionists, 1833–1861* (Baton Rouge: Louisiana State University Press, 1981), 10.

101. [Garrison and Garrison], *William Lloyd Garrison*, 1:360–80.

102. Goldhaber, "Tragedy of Classical Republicanism," 76, 70.

103. Daniel Webster and Pennsylvania's Horace Binney (both of whom had been prominent opponents of Missouri slavery) joined South Carolina's William Campbell Preston on the dais at a "monster panic meeting" in Baltimore on the bank question on a Sunday—where a "reverend minister of the Gospel, in excuse of such a gathering on the Sabbath, said that in revolutionary times there were no Sabbaths." Benton, *Thirty Year's View*, 1:422.

104. See chapter 6 above.

105. See Russell B. Nye, *Fettered Freedom: Civil Liberties and the Slavery Controversy, 1830–1860* (East Lansing, Mich.: Michican State University Press, 1949); Clement Eaton, *The Freedom-of-Thought Struggle in the Old South* (Durham, N.C.: Duke University Press, 1964); Leonard Richards, *"Gentlemen of Property and Standing": Anti-Abolition Mobs in Jacksonian America* (New York: Oxford University Press, 1970); Howard Alexander Morrison, "Gentlemen of Proper Understanding: A Closer Look at Utica's Anti-Abolitionist Mob," *New York History* 62 (January 1981): 61–82; and Robert Pierce Forbes, "Setting the Imps to Work: Anti-abolitionism and the Election of 1836" (unpublished paper, 1989).

106. See "Brutus" [Robert J. Turnbull], *The Crisis; or, Essays on the Usurpations of the Federal Government* (Charleston: A. E. Miller, 1827), 116–17, for a penetrating exposition of this view.

107. Eugene D. Genovese, *The Political Economy of Slavery: Studies in the Economy and Society of the Slave South* (1965; repr., Middletown, Conn.: Wesleyan University Press, 1989), 7.

108. "Speech on the Kansas-Nebraska Act, Peoria, Illinois, October 16, 1854," in Abraham Lincoln, *Selected Writings and Speeches* ([New York]: Vintage Books/ Library of America, 1992), 94.

Epilogue

1. *Illinois State Register*, December 22, 1853, as quoted in Allen Johnson, *Stephen A. Douglas: A Study in American Politics* (New York: Macmillan, 1908), 228–29.

2. Speech before the Illinois Legislature, October 23, 1849, cited in Johnson, *Stephen A. Douglas*, 235.

3. Cited in Allan Nevins, *The Ordeal of the Union*, vol. 2, *A House Dividing, 1852–1857* (New York: Scribner, 1947), 90.

4. Harriet Beecher Stowe, letter to sibling, December 1850, in *Life and Letters of Harriet Beecher Stowe*, ed. Annie Fields (Boston: Houghton, Mifflin, 1897), 130–31.

5. Moorfield Storey, *Charles Sumner* (Boston: Houghton, Mifflin, 1900), 101.

6. James C. Malin, *The Nebraska Question, 1852–1854* (Lawrence, Kans.: n.p., 1953), 9, 17–18.

7. For a philosophical, sympathetic, but ultimately devastating analysis of Douglas's thought concerning slavery, see Harry V. Jaffa, *Crisis of the House Divided: An Interpretation of the Issues in the Lincoln-Douglas Debates* (Garden City, N.Y.: Doubleday, 1959), 42–180. An important investigation, building on Jaffa's study, is John Burt, "What We Can't Agree to Disagree About: Lincoln's Peoria Speech of 1854" (1999), at <http://people.brandeis.edu/~burt/peoriachapter.pdf> (accessed October 6, 2006).

8. Quoted in Malin, *Nebraska Question*, 10–11.

9. David M. Potter, *The Impending Crisis, 1848–1861* (New York: Harper and Row, 1976), 159.

10. Ibid.

11. Kathleen Diffley, "'Erecting Anew the Standard of Freedom': Salmon P. Chase's 'Appeal of the Independent Democrats' and the Rise of the Republican Party," *Quarterly Journal of Speech* 74 (1988): 402.

12. See, e.g., [William Darlington], *Desultory Remarks on the Question of Extending Slavery into Missouri as Enunciated during the First Session of the Sixteenth Congress, by the Representative from Chester County, State of Pennsylvania* (West Chester, Pa.: L. Marshall, 1856), and James Madison's anxious parable on slavery, inspired by the Missouri controversy, *Jonathan Bull and Mary Bull* (Washington, D.C., 1856). The speech by James Tallmadge that sparked the controversy had been published shortly before the passage of the Compromise of 1850 (*Speech of the Hon. James Tallmadge, of Dutchess County, New York, in the House of Representatives of the United States, on Slavery* [Boston: Ticknor, 1849]).

13. "Appeal of the Independent Democrats," *New York Times*, January 24, 1854.

14. Albert J. Von Frank, *The Trials of Anthony Burns: Freedom and Slavery in Emerson's Boston* (Cambridge, Mass.: Harvard University Press, 1999), 13–15.

15. See chapter 7 above, text at n. 37.

16. Paul Revere Frothingham, *Edward Everett, Orator and Statesman* (Boston: Houghton Mifflin, 1925), 345.

17. Ibid., 354. Such a judgment of Everett is not entirely fair, since as president of Harvard, he had shown vanishingly rare courage and principle in that position when he responded to opponents to the possible enrollment of the college's first black student: "The admission to Harvard College depends upon examinations: and if this boy passes the examinations, he will be admitted; and if the white students choose to withdraw, all the income of the College will be devoted to his education." Ibid., 299.

18. Ibid., 356–57.

19. In addition, of the nine sitting northern state legislatures, five passed resolutions protesting the Kansas-Nebraska Bill, three were noncommittal, and only one, Illinois, endorsed it. Of the nine southern legislatures in session, only Georgia endorsed the bill. See Andrew Wallace Crandall, *The Early History of the Republican Party* (Boston: Gorham Press, 1930), 20.

20. *Congressional Globe*, 33d Congress, 1st sess., appendix, 785.

21. On the Shadrach incident, see Gary L. Collison, *Shadrach Minkins: From Fugitive Slave to Citizen* (Cambridge, Mass.: Harvard University Press, 1997); for Burns, see Von Frank, *Trials of Anthony Burns*.

22. Von Frank, *Trials of Anthony Burns*, 11.

23. Charles Francis Adams, ed., *Memoirs of John Quincy Adams, Comprising Portions of His Diary from 1795 to 1848*, 12 vols. (Philadelphia: J. B. Lippincott, 1874–77), 4:529.

24. "Appeal of the Independent Democrats," *New York Times*, January 24, 1854.

25. Fourth Debate with Stephen A. Douglas, Charleston, Illinois, September 18, 1858, in *The Collected Works of Abraham Lincoln*, ed. Roy P. Basler, 18 vols. (New Brunswick, N.J.: Rutgers University Press, 1953–90), 3:181.

26. Basler, *Works of Lincoln*, 2:80.

27. I use the term in Paul Tillich's sense of a subject of ultimate concern. In Tillich's view, no one is without faith, since everyone possesses, whether consciously or not, such an ultimate allegiance. See, e.g., his *Dynamics of Faith* (New York: Harper and Row, 1957).

28. *Trial of the Rev. Jacob Gruber, Minister in the Methodist Episcopal Church, at the March Term, 1819, in the Frederick County Court, for a Misdemeanor* (Fredericktown, Md.: David Martin, 1819), 42–43. Taney served as the attorney for the antislavery minister, who had been charged with sedition for preaching an antislavery sermon to a crowd that included slaves.

29. *The Amistad*, 40 U.S. 518 (1841).

30. Don E. Fehrenbacher, *The Dred Scott Case: Its Significance in American Law and Politics* (New York: Oxford University Press, 1978), 253–65.

31. Ibid., 257, 262–65.

32. Ibid., 70.

33. The actual legal impact of the *Somerset* ruling was much more restricted than popular opinion recognized; however, Taney's opinion ignored both this exaggerated estimate and the more limited actual impact of the 1772 decision. The most thorough study of the incident is Steven M. Wise, *Though the Heavens May Fall: The Landmark Trial That Led to the End of Human Slavery* (Cambridge, Mass.: Da Capo Press, 2005).

34. Fehrenbacher, *Dred Scott*, 342–47.

35. Charles de Secondat, Baron de Montesquieu, *L'esprit des lois* (Paris, 1748), 15:5.

36. *Scott v. Sandford*, 60 U.S. 405 (1857).

37. Ibid., 452.

38. *New-York Tribune*, March 7, 1857.

39. Alexander H. Stephens (vice president of the Confederate States of America),

"Cornerstone Speech," March 21, 1861, as recorded in the *Savannah Republican* and reprinted in Henry Cleveland, *Alexander H. Stephens, in Public and Private: With Letters and Speeches, before, during, and since the War* (Philadelphia: National Publishing Co., 1866), 721.

40. A superb study of this phenomenon is John David Smith, *An Old Creed for the New South: Proslavery Ideology and Historiography, 1865-1918* (Westport, Conn.: Greenwood Press, 1985).

ACKNOWLEDGMENTS

This book had its genesis in two courses I took as an undergraduate at the George Washington University. The first assignment in Jim Horton's "Jacksonian America" was an analysis of the Tallmadge Amendment. In Bob Kenney's seminar in British history, I researched the roots of British abolitionism. In one way or another, I have been pursuing the intersection of these two threads ever since, and this book is a significant chapter in that story.

The two streams of transatlantic slavery come together most fruitfully in the brilliant works of David Brion Davis, and an insightful friend suggested that I apply to study with him at Yale. I began this book with his guidance, and his wisdom, insight, unmatched scholarship, and unflagging support as teacher, adviser, and colleague at the Gilder Lehrman Center for the Study of Slavery, Resistance, and Abolition have been truly extraordinary. I owe my greatest intellectual and professional debts to him.

This study of the Missouri Compromise and its ramifications has been a long time in coming, and I am grateful to my friends, family, and colleagues who stood by me through the entire process. Many people who provided facts and suggestions that improved this work are cited in the notes; I wish to thank them collectively here. Several people deserve special recognition. Dan Howe and Doron Ben-Atar pushed me to finish, and I am grateful for their inspiration and nagging. Jim Stewart and Lois Horton, both in person and in print, have contributed greatly to my understanding of the racial dynamics of the early republic, and have helped me in so many ways. Bill Freehling, Eric Foner, Ron Formisano, and Bert Wyatt-Brown have given unstintingly of their time and expertise, and Sy Drescher has been generous and encouraging with his advice.

The late Robert Wiebe, whom I met on a plane, requested to see the manuscript and (less than a week later) offered the most trenchant, concise, and useful advice I received on developing it into a genuine book. Iver Bernstein and Ira Berlin, the readers for the University of North Carolina Press, gave me important insights that strengthened my argument. John Reda provided a thoughtful reading of the first section of the book and offered valuable suggestions and criticisms. Mike Fitzgerald and Art Scherr served as sounding boards for my revisionist theories about James Monroe and shared their significant work on our most underrated president. Dan Preston, editor of the James Monroe Papers at Mary Washington College, many times lent his comprehensive expertise and tracked down several critical Monroe letters. Rick Meigs and Paul and Dottie Ridenour offered valuable information about the Meigs family, and Dottie kindly provided editorial advice. Barrie Bracken has been a constant source of encouragement and insights.

I have greatly benefited from the expertise of Alphonse Vinh, formerly of Yale's Sterling Memorial Library and now of National Public Radio; Richard Szary, Judy Schiff, and the staff of Yale University Library's Department of Manuscripts and Archives; Ms. Elizabeth Hamlin-Morin, manuscripts curator at the New Hampshire Historical Society; Beatrice McLaughlin of the Pennsylvania Historical Society; Phil Lapsansky of the Library Company of Philadelphia; and the staffs of the Boston Public Library; the American Antiquarian Society in Worcester, Massachusetts; the New-York Historical Society in New York City; the Filson Historical Society in Louisville, Kentucky; and the Southern Historical Collection and the North Carolina Collection at the University of North Carolina at Chapel Hill.

I am also grateful for the patience and expertise of my two faithful editors at UNC Press, Lew Bateman (now of Cambridge University Press) and Chuck Grench, and I thank my copyeditor Paul Betz and the rest of the Press staff for their assistance.

Finally, I owe the greatest debt to my family. My late mother and my father, Grace and Crosby Forbes, were unflaggingly supportive in ways too numerous to mention. My in-laws, Marilyn and Ed Foodim, have been like a second set of parents. Rachel and David have spent their entire lives under the shadow of this book, and Joanne has put up with it for most of our marriage. I am sure they are as glad as I am that it is finally done.

INDEX

American Colonization Society: and Thompson, 26; and Clay, 28, 31, 216, 217; and Monroe, 28, 50, 55; contradictions of, 31; and campaign against slave trade, 34; establishment of, 34; and Dalcho, 151; and Crawford, 176; as benevolent society, 180; and slavery issue, 180; fund-raising campaign of, 181; and Alexander H. Everett, 201; federal funding request, 217, 223, 224–25; disparagement of blacks, 251; attacks on, 269

American democracy: and racism, 1, 207; relevancy of slavery to, 49, 294 (n. 13); as representative democracy, 187

American destiny, 207, 212

American master narrative: and slavery as epiphenomenon, 2; and meaning of Missouri Compromise, 3; and Democratic Party, 4, 209; and progress of white race, 11; reconsideration of, 13

American republicanism: second Missouri Compromise as undermining of, 10; slavery as contradiction of, 11, 27, 145, 146, 164, 270–71, 272, 273, 276, 291; and Tallmadge Amendment debate, 38–39; and white supremacy, 207–8; and Jackson, 211, 213; and southern Jeffersonians, 213

American System, 9, 264

Ammon, Harry, 51, 63–64, 135, 173

Anderson, Richard Clough, 46–47, 332 (n. 108)

Andover Theological Seminary, 179, 219, 325 (n. 2)

Anti-Masonic Party, 102, 246, 247, 249

Antislavery arguments: and Compromise line, 3–4; and abstract ideals, 5, 6; and liberty as national ideal, 6; and morality, 39, 42, 44, 45, 48, 54, 84, 107, 179, 196, 202, 249, 271; and Tallmadge Amendment debate, 41–42; of Federalist Party, 49, 54–55; and pragmatists, 69; and evangelicals, 82, 179, 233–34, 249, 301 (n. 69); and Missouri constitution, 110; and termination plans, 141; and effect of Missouri Compromise, 147–48; and biblical defense, 150, 233–34, 270, 278–79; and free blacks, 155; and Christianity, 179, 201, 234, 235, 279; and African colonization, 219; slavery as national issue, 220; and Revolutionary ideals, 221; and British support, 268; and repeal of Missouri Compromise, 278; and defense of Missouri Compromise, 294 (n. 8)

Argentina, 208

Arkansas, 10, 45–46, 125, 193, 275

Asbury, Francis, 248

Atchison, David, 274

Austin, Stephen F., 26

Bacon, Leonard, 219–21, 336 (n. 38)

Baldwin, Henry, 66, 82, 84, 96, 117, 154, 299 (n. 38), 300 (n. 47), 307 (n. 86)

Baldwin, Roger S., 123

Bank of the United States: and Jackson, 12, 270; public support for, 23; and Roane, 51, 64; and Biddle, 71; and Missouri Compromise, 71, 124, 304 (n. 6); constitutionality of, 142; and Republican Party, 153; and Adams, 186; and southern sectionalism, 223; and Van Buren, 265; and Webster, 269, 345 (n. 103)

Banks, Linn, 109, 317 (n. 19)

Barbados, 302 (n. 88)

Barbour, James: and Missouri's statehood linked to Maine, 64–65, 66, 67–68, 83; and Missouri Compromise negotiations, 78, 80, 92–94, 96–97, 109, 139; as nationalist southerner, 143; and Lafayette, 183; as secretary of war, 188, 190, 328 (n. 48); and Tyler, 222

Barbour, Philip P., 40–41, 46–47, 113, 127–30, 300 (n. 45)
Bassett, James Spencer, 246
Bateman, Ephraim, 51–52
Beecher, Philemon, 299 (n. 38)
Bell, John, 205
Bemis, Samuel Flagg, 186, 328–29 (n. 51)
Benton, Thomas Hart, 8, 108, 205–9, 238, 243, 266, 281, 311–12 (n. 116), 314 (n. 37), 327 (n. 30)
Berrien, John M., 206, 232
Biddle, Nicholas, 71, 118, 123
Black Americans: pariah status of, 8, 288; embrace of constitutional liberty, 30; and Declaration of Independence, 39; presumptive inferiority of, 40, 114, 150, 163, 200–201, 235, 239, 290–91, 322 (n. 81); Alexander H. Everett on, 201–2; white Americans' prejudice against, 217; and Jackson, 231; violence against, 233; as abolitionists, 250–51. See also Citizenship, black; Free blacks
Black codes, 146, 155–62
Bloomfield, Joseph, 66, 99
Bolívar, Simon, 11, 191, 205
Bonus Bill (1816), 23, 24, 143
Boudinot, Elias, 54–55, 58, 179, 301 (n. 69)
Branch, John, 205, 229
Britain: condemnations of American slavery, 34–35, 44, 52, 148, 267, 268; American condemnations of slavery of, 35, 36, 52, 59, 172–73, 268; and Negro Seaman Acts, 157, 159, 160, 172–73, 232; southern alliance with, 170; and right of search for slaves, 177–78; and evangelicalism and antislavery, 179, 233–34, 249; and emancipation, 222, 267, 268, 273; working class of, 226, 227
Brown, John Thompson, 256, 257
Brown, Richard H., 128, 213–14, 228, 293 (n. 7)

Buchanan, James, 56, 288, 332 (n. 107)
Bucktails (New York political faction): and Van Buren, 24, 25, 86, 87, 123, 133, 137, 138, 139, 185, 262; and Tallmadge Amendment, 50, 72; and Clinton, 91, 185; and Solomon Van Rensselaer, 130, 131, 133; and John Quincy Adams, 203
Burke, Edmund, 29, 217
Burns, Anthony, 282–84

Calhoun, Floride, 230
Calhoun, John C.: and West, 19; and Bonus Bill, 23, 24, 143; and transportation network, 23, 25; as secretary of war, 24–25, 142, 246–47; and Samuel Southard, 70; and Roberts, 77; on threats to Union, 94, 103; and sectional harmony, 102–3; and War of 1812, 111; and Rogers, 123; and John W. Taylor, 126, 130; and Van Buren, 127, 137, 204, 215, 246, 247, 258–59; and Philip Barbour, 129, 130; and election of 1824, 130, 175–76; and Solomon Van Rensselaer, 131, 133; and People's Party, 139; and internal improvements, 142–43, 166, 168, 176; constitutional interpretation of, 143, 149; and southern alliance with Britain, 170; and Thomas Cooper, 171; and McIlvaine, 190; and Panama Congress, 205; and political party system, 215; and slavery, 216; and tariffs, 223; and Hayne, 239; and Jackson, 244, 245–47; and nullification, 245, 247, 259, 266; on Europe, 248; and Clay, 259, 264, 266, 343 (n. 73)
Cambreleng, C. C., 261
Canada, and free blacks, 233, 338 (n. 82)
Canning, Stratford, 157, 158, 159
Cape Cod canal, 143, 316 (n. 10)
Case, Walter, 97, 100

44, 270; value of Union transcending, 129, 270; and French Revolution, 145; and Kansas-Nebraska Act, 284

"Era of Good Feelings," 4, 8, 21, 23, 39, 73, 174, 266

Erie Canal, 142

Eustis, William, 121, 130, 131

Evangelicals and evangelicalism: and Monroe, 23, 26–27; and antislavery arguments, 82, 179, 233–34, 249, 301 (n. 69); and culture of beneficence, 192; radicalization of, 248–49

Everett, Alexander H., 199–202

Everett, Edward, 199, 219, 220, 280–81, 336 (n. 37), 346 (n. 17)

Family Party, 70, 123

Federal government: role of, 6–7, 15, 19, 20, 22, 68, 152–53; and tariff revenues, 12, 167, 168; sovereignty of Congress over territories, 37, 40–43, 52, 53, 307 (n. 93); and African colonization, 50, 217, 259; and public land revenues, 142, 171, 194, 195; and proslavery arguments, 152–53, 156, 160, 162, 164, 165–66; and slavery as national problem, 171; and surplus, 244–45, 259

Federalist conspiracy, charges of: and Second Party System, 8; and Monroe, 10; development of, 75–76; and Republican Party, 75, 84–85, 90; and Rufus King, 75, 77, 79, 81, 83; and Roberts, 77, 79, 81; and slavery restriction, 83, 84; and Bucktails, 87; and Van Buren, 88; and Jefferson, 95

Federalist Party: collapse of, 7, 14; opposition to War of 1812, 7, 20, 56; revival of, 8, 76, 90; and western territories, 18–19; and Monroe, 21, 22–23; and British view of slavery, 35; antislavery arguments of, 49, 54–55; and slavery restriction, 54, 55–56, 62,

72, 73–74, 75, 84, 122; and first Missouri Compromise, 99, 100; tactic to divide states, 105; Jefferson on, 121–22; apathy in, 122–23; and Solomon Van Rensselaer, 132, 135; and Rufus King's credibility, 135; and extension of slavery into Missouri, 148; and states' rights, 162; and internal improvements, 171–72; and Jacksonian Party, 240; and Jackson, 267, 335 (n. 24)

Fehrenbacher, Don E., 49, 288, 293 (n. 7)

Fifth Amendment, 290

Fitzhugh, George, 321 (n. 79)

Florida, 104, 193, 212, 245, 246, 299 (n. 28)

Flournoy, John J., 163, 322 (n. 81)

Floyd, John, 115–17, 175, 215, 228–29, 247–52, 254–55, 266, 299 (n. 24), 337 (n. 67), 343 (n. 73)

Foot, Samuel, 100, 238, 241, 339 (n. 1)

Formisano, Ronald P., 214, 239

Forten, James, 250–51

Fourteenth Amendment, 273

Free blacks: Missouri's barring of, 10, 108, 110, 113–15, 170; Indian removal as template for treatment of, 12; and American Colonization Society, 29, 217; and War of 1812, 111; rights of, 112, 207, 231–33, 279; South Carolina's barring of, 145, 155–61, 168–69, 172, 232; and antislavery arguments, 155; population of, 218, 271; Georgia's barring of, 231–32; and Canada, 233, 338 (n. 82); and Taney, 287, 288; Niles on, 300–301 (n. 59). See also Black Americans; Citizenship, black

Freedom: meaning of, 2; slavery as contradiction of, 10, 11, 275–76, 282; and American master narrative, 11; Montesquieu on, 18; black Americans' embracing principles of, 30; value of Union transcending, 129,

207, 208; as dangerous idea, 156,
160, 162, 320 (n. 53); slavery's com-
patibility with, 241; and first Mis-
souri Compromise, 271, 283; slavery
as priority over, 337 (n. 52). *See also*
Liberty
Freehling, Alison, 257
Freehling, William, 143, 147, 151, 167–
68, 257, 258
Freemasonry, 101, 102, 309 (n. 118)
French Revolution, 27, 145, 320 (n. 53)
Fugitive Slave Act, 13, 58, 112, 152,
275, 279, 282, 285
Fuller, Timothy, 38–39
Furman, Richard, 149–50

Gaillard, John, 115–16
Gales, Joseph, 36, 298 (n. 11)
Gallatin, Albert, 105, 177
Garnett, James Mercer, 198
Garrison, William Lloyd, 28, 31, 42,
139, 164, 210, 228, 249–50, 254, 258,
267–69, 336 (n. 37)
Genêt, Citizen, 20
Genovese, Eugene, 149, 272, 321 (n. 79)
Georgia, 170, 173, 192, 193, 195–96, 231
Giles, William Branch, 226–27, 302
(n. 85)
God's Providence, 2, 11, 236–37
Goldhaber, Michael, 337 (n. 56)
Goode, William O., 252, 254–55
Greek war of independence, 181, 207
Greeley, Horace, 121, 123, 141
Green, Duff, 215, 238–39, 244–45,
269–70, 304 (n. 6), 334 (n. 19), 335
(n. 33), 337 (n. 56)
Greenberg, Kenneth S., 318 (n. 29),
337 (n. 52)

Haiti, 142, 156, 194, 199, 204, 206
Haitian Revolution, 27, 39, 61, 144,
145, 155, 204, 302 (n. 88)
Hamilton, Alexander, 22, 171–72, 242
Hamilton, James, Jr., 157, 159, 205,
225–26, 251

Hamilton, James A., 137, 338 (n. 71)
Hammond, Jabez D., 126, 138, 202
Hartford Convention, 51, 73, 74, 121,
163, 238, 240
Hay, George, 64, 65, 93, 180
Hayne, Robert Y., 74, 100, 162–63, 169,
183–84, 205–6, 223, 238–42, 263,
267
Hickin, Patricia E. P., 258
Hill, Isaac, 58, 65–66, 82, 265, 344
(n. 83)
Hill, Mark L., 62, 66–67, 82, 83, 134
Historicism, 1–2
Hoar, Samuel, 112
Hoffman, William, 344 (n. 88)
Hofstadter, Richard, 167, 266
Holland, Edwin C., 149, 318 (n. 34)
Holmes, Isaac E., 159, 320 (n. 66), 321
(n. 72)
Holmes, John, 61–62, 66–67, 83–85,
96, 103–4, 107, 134, 177, 205
Holst, Hermann von, 41, 45, 204, 208,
293 (n. 7), 300 (n. 45)
Honor, national, of America, 34–35, 36,
56, 66
Hopkinson, Joseph, 55, 81
Horsey, Outerbridge, 97
Howe, Daniel Walker, 340 (n. 14)
Humphreys, Heman, 221–22
Hunt, Benjamin Faneuil, 159–60, 320
(n. 66), 321 (n. 72)

Illinois, 36, 37, 49, 148
Immigration, 283
Indiana, 37, 116, 148
Indian removal, 12, 231, 260. *See also*
Native Americans
Internal improvements: and Jackson,
12, 168, 243–44, 246, 261, 310
(n. 133); and southern sectionalism, 12, 142, 173, 223; and Monroe,
16, 18, 21, 23, 24, 64, 142–43, 316
(n. 10); transportation network,
16, 18, 23, 24, 25, 142, 165, 166;
and Republican Party, 21, 153;

and Supreme Court, 50; and John
Quincy Adams, 142, 187–88, 192–93,
243, 329 (n. 59); and Calhoun,
142–43, 166, 168, 176; and John
Randolph, 165–66, 244, 341 (n. 27);
and states' rights, 165–67; and Crawford, 166, 176, 322–23 (n. 95); and
Virginia, 167, 197–98; and Federalist
Party, 171–72; and Maxwell, 197–98,
330 (n. 79)

Jackson, Andrew: on slavery, 11, 294
(n. 13); and internal improvements,
12, 168, 244, 246, 261, 310 (n. 133);
and Van Buren, 12, 209, 213, 216,
223, 227, 228, 242–43, 262–63, 310
(n. 133), 341 (n. 23), 344 (n. 83);
and Webster, 12, 263, 265, 269;
and American Colonization Society,
28; and Battle of New Orleans, 111,
211; and sectional harmony, 129;
as economic nationalist, 166, 335
(n. 24); and Thomas Cooper, 171; as
strong president, 174; and Monroe,
175, 267; and election of 1828, 176,
210–16, 228; and election of 1824,
177, 188, 211, 218; and Lafayette,
183; and Panama Congress, 208;
and states' rights, 210, 215, 228, 229,
231, 243–44; and Florida, 212, 245,
246, 299 (n. 28); and Clay, 213, 216,
234, 243; cabinet of, 229–30, 337
(n. 67); and political patronage, 230;
and preservation of Union, 242, 341
(n. 23); and Calhoun, 244, 245–47;
and public debt, 244; and evangelicalism, 249; reelection of, 259–60;
policy of force, 261–62, 264–65, 266;
presidential tour, 266–67; and congressional dinners, 314 (n. 34)
Jacksonian Party: and America's
master narrative, 4; and creation of
Second Party System, 8; and proslavery arguments, 149; and Benton,
208; and Van Buren, 213–15, 223,

243, 259, 263, 264, 265, 283; and
Hayne, 240; and anti-Jackson coalition, 265–66, 270, 344 (n. 93)
Jacksonian Providence, 11, 212, 236,
246
Jefferson, Thomas: image of slavery, 3;
and Monroe, 17, 18, 19, 95, 104; and
Madison, 21; and African colonization, 29–30, 178, 193–94, 195; and
blacks' capacities, 29–30, 201, 235;
on slavery, 34–35, 38, 48, 49, 104,
105; and Britain's criticism of American slavery, 52; and John Holmes,
103–4; on Missouri Compromise,
103, 104–5, 107; on sugar, 104, 309
(n. 122); and Federalist Party, 121–
22; and Van Buren, 128, 136, 204;
on public lands, 142; and William
Johnson, 161–62; response to Alien
and Sedition Acts, 164; death of,
202, 331 (n. 95); on Jackson, 212;
and slave representation, 218; and
protectionism, 242
Johnson, Richard M., 89, 190, 249
Johnson, William, 143, 157, 159–62,
169, 232, 321 (n. 72)
Jones, William, 71, 78–79
Judiciary Act of 1789, 161

Kansas, 277
Kansas-Nebraska Act of 1854, 5, 278,
279–85, 290, 347 (n. 19)
Kendall, Amos, 231, 260, 263
Kentucky, 62, 193, 227, 299 (n. 38),
303 (n. 96)
Key, Francis Scott, 28, 33–34
King, John, 85, 86, 87–88
King, Rufus: on Pennsylvania, 7; and
African colonization, 28; and Missouri Compromise negotiations, 51,
55, 56–57, 96–97, 218; and Gore, 74;
and charges of Federalist conspiracy,
75, 77, 79, 81, 83; and Roberts, 77,
79; on slavery, 83–84, 85, 145, 317
(n. 19); and John Quincy Adams,

84, 184–85, 187; and Van Buren,
85–86, 87, 88, 133, 135, 139, 194;
and Daniel D. Tompkins, 86–87, 88,
101, 126; and Hay, 93; and Compromise line, 98; and Missouri's statehood, 118; and Missouri Compromise
results, 125, 195, 329–30 (n. 68);
emancipation resolution of, 195–96,
219; and William Loughton Smith,
299 (n. 24); and Theodore Dwight,
300 (n. 54); and Otis, 300 (n. 51)
King, William, 51, 61, 62, 66, 67,
82–83, 84, 85, 96, 134
Kinsey, Charles, 97, 99
Klein, Philip S., 70–71, 102, 211

Lafayette, Marie-Joseph-Paul-Yves-
Roch-Gilbert du Motier de, 11, 104–
5, 181–85, 191, 207, 266, 309 (n. 123)
Lansing, John, Jr., 133, 314 (n. 42)
Lewis, Jan, 302 (n. 81)
Liberty: post-Revolutionary fervor for,
4, 145; as national ideal, 6; threat
to, of northeastern "monocrats," 7;
southern reaction against, shown by
opposition to Panama Congress, 11,
207; slavery as threat to, 27, 76, 184;
black Americans' embrace of, 30; and
French Revolution, 145; and states'
rights, 164; and Jeffersonian opti-
mism, 236; and Kansas-Nebraska
Act, 284. See also Freedom
Lincoln, Abraham, 3, 8, 13, 272, 273,
284–85
Lipson, Dorothy Ann, 102
Livermore, Arthur, 42, 43, 44, 46, 107,
115
Livermore, Shaw, 90, 293 (n. 7)
Livingston, Edward, 261, 287
Louisiana, 188, 193
Louisiana Purchase, 18, 271
Louisiana Territory, 5, 10, 80, 92, 97,
279
Lowndes, William, 92, 94, 143
Lowrie, Walter, 81–82, 118

Macon, Nathaniel: and federal government, 7, 153, 166, 183; and strict
construction, 164–65, 174, 197; and
brittleness of slave system, 168; and
general welfare clause, 172; and
Lafayette, 183, 184, 326 (n. 16);
desire to relocate, 196; and Adams,
202; and Panama Congress, 205,
207; and Jackson, 215; slavery compared to slave trade, 222
Madison, James: Monroe compared
to, 6, 17, 19; Federalist principles of,
15; as Jefferson's successor, 21; veto
of Bonus Bill, 23; on Navy Department, 26; Van Buren on, 136; and
public lands, 142; and Virginia and
Kentucky Resolves, 164; and African
colonization, 178; and emancipation,
194; and party contests, 315 (n. 55)
Maine: statehood linked with Missouri,
10, 62–68, 70, 73, 76, 79, 80, 83, 92,
93; state constitution of, 61, 76; and
antirestrictionist coalition, 82–83
Mangum, Willie P., 218–19
Marshall, John, 17, 50, 64, 81, 93–94,
157, 271
Maryland, 38, 193, 218, 332 (n. 107)
Masons. See Freemasonry
Massachusetts, 56–57, 61, 62, 73, 223,
282–83
Maxwell, William, 197–98, 330
(n. 79)
Maysville Road, 210, 243–44, 246,
261
McCulloch v. Maryland (1819), 3, 6, 25,
50, 64
McDuffie, George, 144, 172, 205, 239,
245, 259
McLane, Louis, 100, 127, 128, 129
Meigs, Henry, 26, 68, 91, 95, 99, 100,
102, 142, 194
Meigs, Josiah, 26, 95
Meigs, Return J., 25, 55, 314 (n. 37)
Meigs, Return J., II, 25–26, 131, 133,
314 (n. 37)

Mercer, Charles Fenton, 47, 139, 180

Mexico, 208, 275

Michigan, 275

Miller, Perry, 293 (n. 6)

Mississippi, 188, 193

Missouri: constitution of, 8, 10, 43, 108, 110, 113–15, 170; Maine's statehood linked with, 10, 62–68, 70, 73, 76, 79, 80, 83, 92, 93; failure of bill for statehood, 47; slavery debate in, 53–54; proslavery violence in, 54, 108; bargaining over, 58–59; statehood contested, 109, 110, 115–18; and John Quincy Adams, 193; and tariffs, 227

Missouri Compromise: and meaning of slavery, 2, 5; as epiphenomenon, 3; repeal of, 3, 5, 13, 271, 274–78, 284, 290; and slavery debate, 3, 4, 5, 6, 145, 147, 148, 149, 293 (n. 7); and sectional power, 5, 283; Monroe's role in, 6, 10, 63–71, 83, 89–95, 118, 125, 131, 139, 141, 147; and Jeffersonian alliance fighting Federalism, 7; as genesis of Second Party System, 8; and Denmark Vesey rebellion, 11; Calhoun as supporter of, 70; constitutional issues of, 82; debate on, 92; role of Freemasonry in, 102, 309 (n. 118); legacy of, 120, 271, 275; and sectionalism, 122, 140, 241; and public opinion, 185. See also Tallmadge Amendment

Missouri Compromise, first (1820): and line of demarcation, 3, 5, 12–13, 46, 47, 96, 97, 106, 107, 271–72, 274, 275, 276, 279; limits on diffusion of slavery, 8; as unconstitutional, 8, 119, 271, 290; and Roberts, 75; negotiations on, 91–98; passage of, 98; reaction to, 98–100; and freedom, 271, 283; concessions of, 279

Missouri Compromise, second (1821): and black citizenship, 8, 119, 272, 283, 311–12 (n. 166); Clay's role in,

10, 112–13, 115, 118, 119, 125, 207; reaction to, 118–19, 311–12 (n. 166); concessions of, 279

Monroe, Elizabeth Kortright, 295 (n. 16)

Monroe, James: role in Missouri Compromise negotiations, 6, 10, 63–71, 83, 89–95, 118, 125, 131, 139, 141, 147; policy on African colonization, 9, 28–29, 32, 50, 95; and slavery, 9, 10, 15, 16, 27–28, 69, 125, 169–70, 172; first inaugural address, 14–17, 23, 27; and Constitution, 17, 23, 65, 133–34, 173; education of, 17; and Jefferson, 17, 18, 19, 95, 104; and western territories, 18; political philosophy of, 19, 21–23, 27, 135; presidential tours, 20–22, 26, 55, 182; and Madison, 21, 23, 295 (n. 20); cabinet selections, 23–27, 296 (n. 27); and Roberts, 78; and Venezuela, 89; policy on sectionalism, 125; and John W. Taylor, 125–26; and Solomon Van Rensselaer, 130, 131–32; and Lafayette, 181, 182, 183; on Montesquieu, 295 (n. 10)

Monroe Doctrine, 208

Monrovian nationalism: ambitious goals of, 9; America distinguished from South, 10; Van Buren's efforts against, 10–11, 186; and Compromise line, 12–13; and federal power, 15, 19, 21, 50; and national defense, 16, 20; slavery as obstacle to, 16, 141; and John Quincy Adams, 24, 141–42, 190, 191; and postal system, 25–26; and evangelical philanthropic organizations, 26–27; and abolition of slavery, 27; and Calhoun, 130; and Radical wing of Congress, 130; hostility toward, 144; and internal improvements, 173–74, 324 (n. 121); Monroe's lack of credit for, 174; and Lafayette, 181, 182, 183

Montesquieu, Baron de (Charles-Louis

73–75, 139, 261–62, 266, 269, 300 (n. 51)

27, 65, 190; and internal improvements, 21, 153; and British view of
slavery, 35; and federal power, 50;
and Tallmadge Amendment, 50, 53;
and proslavery arguments, 61, 166;
and Maine's statehood, 67; historical
narratives of, 69; Missouri statehood
with slavery, 69, 70; and Federalist conspiracy charges, 75, 84–85,
90; and first Missouri Compromise,
99; and unpopularity of doughface
stance, 123; northern/southern
linkage in, 128–29, 213–14; and Van
Buren, 128–29, 176–77, 204, 313
(n. 29); and strict construction, 153;
and states' rights, 162, 163; and Virginia and Kentucky Resolves, 164;
and John Quincy Adams, 188; and
Panama Congress, 207; and Jackson,
215–16; and public debt, 244
Rice, C. Duncan, 268
Rice, John Holt, 180, 193
Risjord, Norman K., 153
Ritchie, Thomas: and Tallmadge
Amendment, 50–51; and Bank of
the United States, 64; and slavery
restriction, 85; and Marshall, 93–94;
and Van Buren, 128, 213–15, 223,
263, 270, 283; and strict construc-
tion, 153–54; and Native Americans,
196; and Jacksonian Providence,
212; and Jackson, 228, 229, 244,
263; and emancipation, 252, 253
Rives, John Cook, 281
Rives, William, 153–54
Roane, Spencer, 7, 21, 51, 64, 108
Roberts, Jonathan, 71, 75–81, 96, 101
Rodney, Caesar A., 100, 127, 128, 129
Rogers, Thomas J., 118, 123–24
Roth, Randolph, 102
Ruffin, Edmund, Jr., 198–99
Ruffin, Edmund, Sr., 198–99

Sabbatarian movement, 249
St. Bartholomew, 320 (n. 53)

St. Domingue, 144
Schlesinger, Arthur, Jr., 334 (n. 21)
Schlesinger, Arthur, Sr., 109
Scott, John, 43, 108
Scottish common-sense philosophy, 27,
48–49, 193
Scottish Enlightenment tradition, 27, 39
Seabrook, Whitemarsh B., 146, 195,
330 (n. 71)
Seaton, William, 36, 298 (n. 11)
Second Bank of the United States, 25,
50, 153, 164
Second Party System, 8, 12, 241, 276,
283, 294 (n. 13)
Sectionalism, northern: and Maine's
statehood tied to Missouri, 10,
67–68, 79; and slavery restriction,
49–50, 56–57, 58, 65, 69, 72, 78,
90, 98; and Tallmadge Amendment,
51–52, 53, 70; and Roberts, 77; and
first Missouri Compromise, 99, 106;
and Calhoun, 102–3; and Clinton
supporters, 106; and free blacks'
rights, 112; rise of, 122; and political party system, 138; and internal
improvements, 143; and three-fifths
clause, 218; and repeal of Missouri
Compromise, 278
Sectionalism, southern: and Tallmadge
Amendment, 7, 39, 45, 63–64; and
resistance to slavery, 9; and internal
improvements, 12, 142, 173, 223; and
tariffs, 12, 61, 96, 122, 143, 144, 153,
167, 171, 223, 227–28; of Revolutionary-era southerners, 19; and Declaration of Independence, 39; and representation in Congress, 45, 218; and
opposition to slave trade, 47–48; and
antirestrictionist coalition, 61, 63–65;
and federal power, 68; and Maine's
statehood tied to Missouri, 68; and
threats of disunion, 94, 97, 159, 160,
163, 240, 241; and first Missouri
Compromise, 98; and Calhoun, 103;
and political party system, 138, 315

INDEX
364

CPSIA information can be obtained
at www.ICGtesting.com
Printed in the USA
LVHW032100060821
694637LV00009B/1523

9 780807 861837